BATTLEGROUND

WOMEN, GENDER, AND SEXUALITY

BATTLEGROUND

WOMEN, GENDER, AND SEXUALITY

VOLUME 1 (A–L)

Edited by Amy Lind and Stephanie Brzuzy

GREENWOOD PRESS
Westport, Connecticut • London

Library of Congress Cataloging-in-Publication Data

Battleground : women, gender and sexuality / edited by Amy Lind and Stephanie Brzuzy.
p. cm.
Includes bibliographical references and index.
ISBN 978-0-313-34037-6 (set : alk. paper) — ISBN 978-0-313-34038-3 (vol. 1 : alk. paper) — ISBN 978-0-313-34039-0 (vol. 2 : alk. paper)
1. Women—Social conditions—Encyclopedias. 2. Feminism—Encyclopedias. 3. Women's studies—Encyclopedias. I. Lind, Amy. II. Brzuzy, Stephanie. III. Title: Women and gender.
HQ1115.B38 2008
305.403—dcs22 2007029582

British Library Cataloguing in Publication Data is available.

Library of Congress Catalog Card Number: 2007029582
ISBN-13: 978-0-313-34037-6 (set)
978-0-313-34038-3 (vol. 1)
978-0-313-34039-0 (vol. 2)

First published in 2008

Greenwood Press, 88 Post Road West, Westport, CT 06881
An imprint of Greenwood Publishing Group, Inc.
www.greenwood.com

Printed in the United States of America

The paper used in this book complies with the Permanent Paper Standard issued by the National Information Standards Organization (Z39.48-1984).

10 9 8 7 6 5 4 3 2 1

CONTENTS

GUIDE TO RELATED TOPICS

PREFACE

"Your Body Is a Battleground," reads one of contemporary artist Barbara Kruger's most famous pieces of work. A black and white photograph of a woman's face, banded with bold red stripes of text, conveys the image of a stereotypical woman: a white, middle class housewife who has possibly achieved the "American dream." In the photographed silkscreen, half of the woman's face is white on black; the other half is black on white, juxtaposing an internal division that presumably lies within her, as well as in the external framing of her identity. The image is labeled with flashing white words on a bold, red background, causing the viewer to associate the woman's face with an advertisement or media glitz and challenging the viewer to reconsider notions of identity, power, and sexuality, as well as stereotypes about women's roles and identities in contemporary U.S. society. Ultimately, Kruger's art is a provocative call to consider how women's lives are central to—and indeed provide a battleground for—broader political, economic, legal, and cultural struggles in Western society.

How women's bodies become battlegrounds—symbolically and materially, through political and economic processes, policies, laws, educational and religious institutions, and cultural ideologies—is at the heart of this two-volume set. *Battleground: Women, Gender, and Sexuality* is among the first references to address and unpack the ways in which gender and sexuality intersect in societal understandings of women's (and men's) lives, with particular implications for how women are expected to perform their roles as workers, mothers, wives, daughters, and citizens. The 97 entries in this set reflect the now large and diverse field of women's studies, with its many strands of thought pertaining to the nature of gender, women's rights, and perceived gender and sexual inequalities in the United States and globally.

During the latter half of the twentieth century and entering the new millennium, gender identity and sexual identity, particularly as they relate to the foundation of the modern family, have been two of the most controversial themes publicly debated. From gender equity at work to women's ability to play professional sports, serve in political office, or join the military; women's reproductive decisions, including abortion, birth control and family planning; changing perceptions of female sexuality and gay, lesbian, bisexual and transgender identities; and the rights of women and sexual minorities in various realms of public and private life, this set aims to tackle these controversial themes as they have emerged in popular culture, policy and legal arenas, and in Western understandings of family and nation.

Battleground: Women, Gender, and Sexuality is designed to give the reader an accessible reference to the most controversial issues and debates pertaining to women's lives, gender, and sexuality. The incorporation of entries covering all three areas makes this work unique and brings a new contribution to the field of reference works that focus on women in a more general sense. Our goal for this project is to bring together academics from multiple fields who focus on a broad range of historical, cultural, economic, and political issues that inform current societal understandings of the most controversial topics. To begin our process, we solicited experts in various fields who gave us their opinions on the topics that should be included. From their input and our own work, we developed the list of topics included in these two volumes. They include the following general topics: body politics; families and parenting; feminisms; gender equity and sexual rights; gender identities and expressions; global political economy; media, visual arts, and communication; politics and social movements; religion and society; sexual identities and practices; social stratification; violence against women; and women's health and reproductive practices. Within each of these areas, a range of entries are included that shed light on some of the most important ideas and debates concerning women's lives and the lives of lesbian, gay, bisexual, and transgender people.

The entries range in length depending on the theme, and each entry provides readers with further references to take them deeper into the subjects.

Body Politics refers both to the symbolic realm of how women's bodies are understood and known in modern scientific and cultural discourse, and how various groups of women, from young girls to aging women, experience their bodies in modern Western society. Entries cover topics such as the influence of Barbie on female senses of self, beauty pageants and the beauty industry, experiences of disability, and body modification, including plastic surgery, Botox, tattooing, and piercing.

Under the theme of *Families and Parenting*, authors ask important and sometimes unsettling questions such as "who pays for the kids?" and whether daycare or stay-at-home parenting is better for the children; political debates on "family values"; and the recent policy and educational emphases on fatherhood and marriage initiatives.

Undoubtedly, *feminism* has been one of the most important and influential movements in the twentieth century. Do we now live in a "postfeminist" era?

Is feminism dead or is it thriving? With the institutionalization of its successes, including the establishment of Women's History Month and Women's Studies courses, and the numerous achievements women have made professionally, is feminism still relevant to our lives and, if so, how? More fundamentally, at this point in history what is feminism and how have scholars and women's rights advocates framed their political struggles in terms of feminism? These are some of the questions posed in these entries.

Gender Equity and Sexual Rights are at the heart of political struggles over the perceived "rights" of both women and sexual minorities. Although gains have been made, pay differentials between men and women for equal work remain, women represent less than 20 percent of all federally elected senators and representatives, women are devalued as professional athletes, and women are still for the most part locked out of the highest levels of most major professional endeavors, including corporate CEOs, engineers, surgeons, and architects. Feminist scholars have theorized, documented, and advocated for changes, but advancements are slow and results have been mixed. Several entries are focused on the issue of gender equity for these reasons. Why are women less represented in the public realm? Are they naturally inclined to remain at home and perform traditional gender roles in childrearing and household management? Or, are broader structural inequalities preventing them from accessing these public places of power? Do men and women think differently about these issues? These are some of the questions addressed in entries that address, among others, affirmative action, Title IX and women's sports, comparable worth, and the Equal Rights Amendment.

Even more recent is the struggle for sexual rights in U.S. law and policy. Should lesbians and gays have the right to marry? Should they be allowed to serve in the military? Do they deserve equal status under the law, just as racial minorities, or should they be treated as a different type of group? Observers continue to debate these issues as more and more lesbians and gays continue to "come out of the closet" in the United States.

What is gender? Is it a result of biology or socialization? Are we "born that way" or do we choose how to express ourselves? What role do our families and societies play in shaping our gender identities and roles as we go through life? Themes that fall under *Gender Identities and Expressions* get at the heart of these issues as they shape contemporary debates on femininities and masculinities, gender socialization, nature versus nurture, and non-normative forms of gender identity and expression; that is, forms that fall outside the realm of traditional, binary gender roles—male and female—that we are socialized to understand as inclusive of everyone's experience. In fact, as many transgendered, intersex (formerly known as hermaphrodite), and "third gender" people have pointed out, gender is potentially experienced in a much broader way than traditional scientific and psychological theories of identity might claim. Several entries address the question, "What is gender and how is it experienced?" from this perspective of rethinking this foundational concept in Western society. Topics such as sex reassignment surgery and the psychological classification of gender identity disorder are also discussed.

In the area of *Global Political Economy,* broad structural processes are addressed as they shape and influence women's lives. From the modern commercialization of the mail-order bride industry to explosive debates on immigration, militarized prostitution, terrorism and national security, globalization, and imperialism, these entries present a provocative set of ideas about how contemporary scholars and members of society think about the position of the United States in the global arena and the effects of broad institutional patterns and forms of power relations on various sectors of women.

One cannot discuss women's lives without addressing the role of media and communication in shaping how we think, feel, dress, and act in the world. Today, women are successful movie stars in Hollywood and increasingly we see strong, rather than merely docile, images of women in film, television, music, and advertising. As the authors of entries in the thematic area of *Media, Visual Arts, and Communication* point out, however, there is much to be done to change stereotypes of women, including racialized undertones, which differentially affect Latinas/Chicanas, African American, Native American, and Asian American women as they are represented visually, lyrically, and through speech and language in the media. What do images of women in MySpace tell us about how young women experience their bodies and identities? Are women themselves contributing to their own stereotypical images, and does this matter? To what extent is sexism still a factor in media production and art, and to what extent does women's participation in media production change the tone of the images? Why are images of women, rather than men, more commonly seen in television and magazine advertisements? These questions continue to challenge societal thinking about media images of women as they are increasingly commercialized.

Women have long participated in various forms of political activism and have fought for changes in their countries, both on the Right and Left of the political spectrum, despite long-held stereotypes that women's roles are "in the home" rather than in politics. In the thematic area of *Politics and Social Movements,* authors ask: How have political parties and movements recruited women for their causes? What catalyzes women to action, including those socialized to perform traditional gender roles, to leave the comfort of their homes and participate in national politics or resistance movements? Why do some women support right-wing ideologies while others believe in leftist-oriented revolutionary change, sometimes sacrificing their lives for the cause of their country or struggle? Finally, how do women respond to their calling as national citizens? In a post-9/11 era, these questions are particularly relevant to contemporary debates on the "War on Terrorism," national security and citizenship, the struggle for environmental justice, and the growing lesbian, gay, bisexual, and transgender (LGBT) movement. In the latter case, LGBT people are often viewed as threats to the family and the nation: Authors ask, why are those who are not heterosexual labeled deviant or as potentially threatening as terrorists? What are the cultural lenses through which modern forms of sexuality and gender are understood in the context of heightened anxieties about war and terrorism? These issues invoke deep feelings on all sides of the ideological spectrum.

Religion plays an important role in how we perceive our identities and in the fate of the nation. Religious discourse and institutions often set the tone for how individuals define what they view as their most important values, ethics, and morals. Under the theme of *Religion and Society,* women's roles in religious institutions are discussed, including movements to increase the leadership roles of women in traditional, male-dominated monotheistic religions. In addition, the effects of fundamentalism on women and why women choose to define themselves as part of fundamentalist movements are addressed, including controversial practices engaged in by self-defined fundamentalist communities. In the U.S. context, polygamy, a practice often associated with specific Mormon fundamentalist sects, has been debated with regard to whether this practice should be allowed on the basis of religious freedom or whether it should be criminalized, due in part to abusive sexual patterns. These questions, as well as how religion shapes our ideas about gender and sexuality, are addressed in these entries.

In the realm of *Sexual Identities and Practices,* perhaps the most controversial questions concern the origin and meaning of sexual identity. What causes homosexuality or heterosexuality? Is there a "gay gene" that determines sexual identity at birth, or can people change their sexual identity according to their social context? Where does bisexuality fall in the realm of sexual expression? Alfred Kinsey, one of the first scientists to develop a systematic study of human sexuality among both women and men, was perhaps ahead of his time. Although historically, scientific and cultural discourses have long treated homosexuality as either a criminal act or a disease, in the 1950s Kinsey discovered that more people who self-define as heterosexual actually partake in same-sex sexual practices than was previously thought, thereby shaking the foundations of America's mainstream views on "appropriate" sexual behavior and causing a revolution in how we think about identity versus actual behaviors. His national study on female sexuality also opened doors for later generations of scholars and advocates to rethink female sexuality from a place of empowerment rather than submission or passivity. As a result, women's traditional gender roles were challenged as they came to be seen as possessing their own desires rather than merely reacting passively to the desires of men. Here, too, claims about gender and sexuality converge and overlap in contemporary discussions of sexual behavior, including ongoing heated debates about whether sexual behaviors should be regulated by law or left to the decisions of individuals. Entries in this thematic area include discussions of the Kinsey scale of sexual behavior, female sexuality and dysfunction, sadomasochism and sexual deviance, heterosexism and homophobia, homosexual reparative therapy, and contemporary usages of the term *queer* and the emergent field of queer studies.

Social Stratification in U.S. society has been addressed on various levels, including in terms of how gender and sexuality intersect with other aspects of identity such as race, ethnicity, class, and religion. In this thematic area, authors discuss a range of issues pertaining to how specific groups of women, such as poor and working class women and women of color, are positioned in our socially stratified society. In particular, they discuss how gender, race, and class intersect in the lives of women and influence societal perceptions and policies concerning work, poverty, crime, and America's controversial welfare reforms.

Violence against Women is an issue that has intrigued scholars for a long time. Why are females more likely than males to be subjected to particular forms of violence within their families and households? Why are women or girls the most likely target of sexual assault? Should we understand these forms of violence as cultural patterns that would be best addressed through public policy, or as random or private acts that need no police or government intervention?

Finally, authors in these volumes address a broad range of issues pertaining to *Women's Health and Reproductive Practices.* How are women's reproductive practices, including birth control, breastfeeding, and childbirth options, regulated through laws and policies? Should the state have the right to decide when life begins or should women, who are the ones to become pregnant, be able to decide for themselves if they wish to birth a child? In relation to this question, should fetuses have the same rights under the law as pregnant women? Why has breastfeeding, which has been practiced by women across the globe for centuries, come to be seen as "obscene" by some politicians who have sponsored bills to make breastfeeding illegal in certain public places? To what extent have medical and scientific views on women's health, including their reproductive health as well as their physical and mental health, influenced women's own views on their symptoms and illnesses? How have women's rights advocates challenged models that they claim are biased toward men's anatomies and experiences, including in the cases of cancer and HIV/AIDS?

As we move through the twenty-first century, women's bodies will surely continue to be a battleground for contemporary struggles concerning science, health and medicine, policy, law, and popular culture. As long as women are viewed as central to the family and the family is viewed as an essential foundation of society, we will witness and partake in complex yet, we hope, fruitful debates about the meaning and making of gender and sexuality as they shape women's and men's lives. We invite you to explore these passionate topics and to develop your own ideas, as you will likely be transformed by reading about the diverse range of feelings and opinions expressed in these pages.

We have also included a general bibliography of the works that we feel give an overall idea of the topics currently being explored in the fields of gender, feminist, and sexuality studies today. Readers will be well equipped to continue their explorations from these reference points.

We believe we have captured the essence of issues facing us as we move forward in this early part of the new millennium and the consolidation of the information age. We are pleased with the outcome of this project and hope you will find it useful. We are grateful to the editors at Greenwood Press for supporting our original intent of these volumes to include a diverse examination of issues pertaining to women, gender, and sexuality. We want to thank all contributors for their knowledge, expertise, and commitment to bringing often complex debates to the new reader. Without their enormous and collective good will, we would still be in the visionary phase of this project. We specifically want to thank Kevin Downing, our acquisitions editor, who listened and guided us to the completion of this work. We are thankful for the support of our academic institutions, the University of Cincinnati and Xavier University. Most of all, we want to thank the students we have had the privilege to mentor over the years. Their constant questioning is a source of inspiration. We hope this set will provide a space for many more learners to begin their quest for knowledge and discover the joy in asking questions.

A

ABORTION

Acquiring and maintaining women's right to obtain an abortion is probably considered one of the most controversial issues of the century. "Pro-choice" advocates argue that a woman is not truly free without the right to control her own body and reproductive choices. "Pro-life" advocates have developed a platform in defense of fetal rights and argue that abortion is a crime, often defending the state's ability to regulate and criminalize it. Additional controversy concerns the question of when life itself begins, based on religious and cultural arguments about human development.

BACKGROUND

The regulation of reproductive practices has been long disputed on the basis of individual versus state's rights, who has the right to control women's reproductive lives and decisions, and when life itself begins. Various forms of societal and governmental regulation have inevitably shaped the condition and character of women's lives; indeed, the United States was founded on laws that regulate the realm of reproduction (Rowland 2004).

When it comes to reproductive rights, which refers to all areas of sexual reproduction, abortion has dominated the discourse. Historically, abortion has been both criminalized and made legal, opposed and supported, stigmatized and respected as a woman's choice. The debate has centered predominantly on the moral and ethical dilemma of whether or not a woman *should* be free to have an abortion and, if so, under what conditions.

Abortion is defined as the termination of a human pregnancy through premature expulsion of a fertilized egg or fetus from the uterus resulting in termination. This process may occur through natural spontaneous miscarriage, or it may be induced. If termination occurs before the 20th week of gestation, it is considered nonviable or unable to survive outside the womb. It is the inducing of an abortion that has created controversy around a woman's right to choose. Although the necessity of abortion has decreased as a result of the widespread use of birth control in Western cultures, the procedure is still used for a variety of personal, economic, and medical reasons. These include whether the health or life of the mother is at risk; whether the fetus is at risk of serious disease, deformity, or dysfunction; or whether the mother believes she or a couple believe they are unable to raise a child. Sometimes pregnancy occurs by accident, as a result of failed contraception or as the result of a forced sexual encounter, and women subsequently choose to have an abortion.

HISTORY OF ABORTION

Historical evidence indicates that induced abortions have taken place since antiquity. Abortions have been regulated and administered sporadically throughout history and cross-culturally. Pregnancies have been and continue to be terminated through various techniques including the use of abortifacient herbs, turpentine, forced falls or impalements, sharp tools, and the application of abdominal pressure, in addition to the common modern medical procedures.

In the United States, until the nineteenth century abortion was considered a private family matter, and in general it was not commonplace for governments to intrude. Early common law inherited from England focused on "quickening," when the fetus begins to move on its own and is felt by the mother, as a way to differentiate when an abortion was no longer permissible. Beginning in 1803, however, both the federal government and individual states started to pass laws that made abortion a crime. By the end of the nineteenth century, nearly every state had made performing or attempting to perform an abortion punishable "by fines and imprisonment" (Hull et al. 2004). In their book, *The Abortion Rights Controversy in America,* N.E.H. Hull, Williamjames Hoffer, and Peter Charles Hoffer argue that the imposed government restrictions were a result of the combination of two "powerful [and contradictory] currents of thinking about domestic life and women's role in society": On one hand, liberal individualistic philosophy stressed privacy within the family and influenced the notion that reproductive decisions should be a woman's decision. On the other hand, traditional views held that women's roles were set in stone as mother and wife. These views were challenged when abortion rates started to rise as a result of changing demographic patterns and cultural gender ideologies, which resulted in the increased belief in a woman's reproductive choice (Hull et al. 2004). In the early nineteenth century, first wave feminists were among the most visible supporters of women's reproductive rights. Advocates such as Margaret Sanger, a strong proponent of birth control, recognized that women would never gain full equality until they could make decisions regarding their own bodies. She once stated, "No woman can call herself free until she can choose consciously whether she will or will not be a mother" (Sanger 1920, 94).

As late as the 1960s, female reproduction was considered public property in the United States and the state had a say in "a woman's decision regarding reproduction" (Rowland 2004, 5). Abortion, along with various forms of birth control, was closely regulated by the government. In the well-publicized 1972 case, the United States Supreme Court acknowledged for the first time that a woman's freedom and equal participation in society were dependent on her ability to control her own reproduction, thereby granting women personal privacy regarding the choices they make about their bodies. The court stated, "[i]f the right to privacy means anything, it is the right of the individual, married or single, to be free from unwarranted governmental intrusions into matters so fundamentally affecting a person as the decision whether to bear or beget a child" (Baer 2002, 197). This court decision influenced the 1973 decision made in *Roe v. Wade* that set the stage for contemporary struggles concerning abortion.

ABORTION LEGISLATION TIMELINE

1803: English Parliament (Lord Ellenborough's Act) passes criminalizing attempts to induce abortion after quickening.

1821: Connecticut passes first statute that forbids using poison to induce miscarriages.

1825–80: All 50 states pass statutes punishing anyone who performs or attempts to perform an abortion.

1873: Comstock Law passes, prohibiting "obscene" materials from being distributed through the mail, including contraceptives, abortificients.

1959: The American Institute of Law drafts a model state abortion law to make legal abortions accessible.

1961: California state legislature introduces an abortion reform law based on the American Law Institute model.

1965: *Griswold v. Connecticut* Supreme Court decision strikes down Connecticut state law that prohibits giving married people information on contraception because it violated the "right to marital privacy."

1967–70: Colorado is first state to loosen its abortion laws followed by Arkansas, Delaware, Florida, Georgia, Kansas, Maryland, Mississippi, New Mexico, Oregon, South Carolina, and Virginia.

1968: President Lyndon Johnson's Committee on The Status of Women releases a report calling for a repeal of all abortion laws.

1969: Senator Robert Packwood of Oregon introduces legislation to legalize abortion in Washington D.C.; no action is taken.

1970: The Family Planning Services and Population Research Act is passed by Congress to fund family planning services that exclude abortions.

1972: *Eisenstadt v. Baird* Supreme Court decision establishes the right of unmarried people to use contraceptives.

1973: *Roe v. Wade* Supreme Court decision strikes down state laws that criminalize abortion.

1976–77: Senator Harry Hyde of Illinois sponsors the Hyde Amendment, which passes; allows states to prohibit the use of Medicaid funding for abortions.

1989: *Webster v. Reproductive Health Services* reinforces the state's right to prevent all publicly funded facilities from providing or assisting with abortion services.

1992: *Planned Parenthood v. Casey* upholds the state's right to restrict abortion through parental notifications, mandatory counseling, waiting periods, and limitations on public funds.

1994: Freedom of Access to Clinic Entrances (FACE) Act is passed by Congress to forbid the use of force or obstruction to prevent someone from providing or receiving reproductive health services.

2000: FDA approves mifepristone (RU-486), a drug approved in France in 1988 that, when administered during the first trimester in conjunction with prostaglandin, induces abortion. This drug must be administered and supervised by a doctor.

2003: President George W. Bush signs the Congressional Partial Birth Abortion Ban Act, prohibiting D&X (intact dilation and extraction) and second trimester abortions, even among women whose health is in danger.

2007: Supreme Court upholds the Partial Birth Abortion Ban Act of 2003.

1970s–1990s: *ROE V. WADE*

The Supreme Court ruled on January 22, 1973 that the right to privacy inherent in the Constitution includes a woman's right to choose to have an abortion. Although the Constitution doesn't specifically reference a right to privacy, over the years the Supreme Court's decisions (as noted in the 1972 decision) have secured the right to privacy as a fundamental human right protected by both the Ninth Amendment and the Due Process Clause of the Fourteenth Amendment of the Constitution. The Court's decision in *Roe v. Wade* overturned all state and federal laws that outlawed or restricted abortions within the first trimester before the fetus was able to survive outside the womb. The court left it up to the states to set limitations on abortions sought after the first trimester. *Roe v. Wade* was both part of the increase in the Court's attempts to strike down discriminatory civil laws that were unconstitutional and an effort to prevent reproductive choices from being limited (Baer 2002, 11).

Before *Roe v. Wade,* during the period of abortion criminalization, if a woman were to become pregnant, whether married or unmarried, and she was not emotionally, socially, or economically prepared to have a baby, her options were limited. Illegal abortion was often sought and the costs of such services were extremely high, not to mention the increased health risks associated with them. "Back-alley" abortions, a term used to refer to unsafe illegal abortions either self-induced or performed at high risk, often for high fees and sometimes by untrained providers, were common during this period, which is one issue that pro-choice advocates, those who supported the legalization of abortion, made clear in their lobbying efforts and protests. Pro-choice advocates pointed out that throughout history and across cultures, when abortions have been deemed illegal, women still seek them out. Furthermore, women who seek out illegal abortions experience higher rates of botched procedures and associated high infection and mortality rates (Rubin 1994, 66–67). Often back-alley abortions result in serious complications or the death of the mother. The societal dilemma is whether to make reliable physicians and midwives available to perform the procedures so that women are not forced to find alternative second-rate practitioners who risk women's lives. Between 1960 and 1973, if a woman wanted to have a legal abortion, she could travel to only a handful of places that had reintroduced laws allowing abortions, including Cuba (1965), the United Kingdom (1968), and Canada (1969), and, within the United States, California (1967), Colorado (1967), and New York (1970). If a woman couldn't afford to go to any of those places, her options were limited. Underground abortion services became popular during this period, including the JANE Collective in Chicago, which was started in the late 1960s as a way to provide safe abortions to women in need. This Collective provided approximately 12,000 abortions until it closed in 1973 (Kaplan 1995).

PRO-CHOICE VERSUS PRO-LIFE: THE CONTEMPORARY ABORTION CONTROVERSY

Long before *Roe v. Wade* was decided, abortion opponents and supporters held strong views on whether the practice was ethical and whether the state should in regulate it. These groups have come to be defined largely as either pro-choice advocates, who tend to emphasize women's individual choice in their reproductive decisions, or pro-life advocates, who tend to emphasize that life begins before birth and support the criminalization of abortion.

Pro-Choice

Pro-choice is the viewpoint that women should have control of their reproductive decisions. Individuals and groups who support this position are considered part of the pro-choice movement. Each year, pro-choice advocates celebrate the *Roe v. Wade* decision. Many pro-life advocates argue that, "pro-choice equals pro-abortion," but in reality this is not the view that most who believe in woman's right to choose embrace. A pro-choice advocate doesn't advocate for abortion, and some even personally oppose abortion; rather, they believe it is a woman's right to have an abortion, even if they wouldn't make the same decision for themselves; that women should have access to safe and legal abortions; that a woman should never be forced to have a child against her will because all children should be wanted children; that legal abortions prevent women from having to undergo drastic measures to have illegal back-alley abortions; and that it is not the role of government to regulate this practice—what they view as regulating women's bodies.

Pro-Life

On the opposite side of the debate, pro-life advocates argue that because life begins at conception, abortion is the equivalent of murder. Some compare abortion with wartime casualties. Pro-life advocates believe that the state should regulate abortion and even criminalize it to prevent the procedure from being performed. Each year, pro-life advocates mourn the decision in *Roe v. Wade.* They also believe that abortion providers are assisting with murder and should be punished as such. Since the 1990s, pro-life legal strategies have included, first and foremost, an emphasis on "fetal rights." These advocates believe that human life begins at conception and that the fertilized egg should have the same legal and moral rights as a person. Many pro-life advocates believe that the life of the fetus takes precedence over the mother's life. Pro-life advocates often promote narrow sex education methods, such as abstinence-only, and argue that supporting birth control methods and legal abortions will lead to higher incidents of sexual promiscuity and a breakdown of family values. The pro-life movement's ultimate goal is to ban abortion in all circumstances. Radical pro-life activists have protested abortion clinics, including taunting female clients and clinic professionals, and some pro-life groups have been criminally charged with committing arson and even murdering staff members in clinics where abortions are performed.

America's religious roots have played a key role in the status of abortion in U.S. laws. Groups often connected to what is now referred to as the Religious Right have remained a steady social force, historically opposing all forms of birth control and abortion (Martin 1996; Kintz and Lesage 1998). These groups are often made up of officials of the Catholic Church and other Christian sects who have sought out political leadership roles to outlaw abortion and to prevent family planning programs and contraceptive initiatives using literal interpretations of religious texts as justification for their platforms. Pro-life groups often align themselves with the Religious Right, maintaining a conservative approach to reproductive rights that has been increasingly visible in global political arenas as well, including at the United Nations (Butler 2006).

CONTEMPORARY ABORTION LAW

Since the 1970s, pro-life advocates have worked to dismantle *Roe v. Wade* incrementally by pushing for legal reform at the state level and by challenging the legitimacy of the ruling at the federal level. As of 2007, 15 states still have laws banning abortion throughout pregnancy; enforcement of these laws, however, is prevented by *Roe v. Wade.* Nevertheless, many laws have been passed that limit the contexts within which women have access to legal abortion.

In 2003, Congress passed the Federal Partial Birth Abortion Act, which outlaws the dilation and extraction method (otherwise known as "D&X") and all second trimester abortions, even when a woman's health is in danger. Congress had ignored an earlier court ruling in 2000 that stated a ban on abortion was unconstitutional and that all restrictions on abortions must include the protection of the woman's health. On April 18, 2007, the U.S. Supreme Court upheld the constitutionality of this act.

This decision was a moral and ethical victory for proponents of the act who argue that the D&X procedure is never medically necessary. For opponents, the decision was viewed as a political assault on women's lives; they pointed out that D&X is rarely performed and is usually done in extreme instances when a woman's life is in danger or when the fetus is malformed and has no chance of survival. The Court's decision stood for many as a monumental sign of the shift in the U.S. Supreme Court's rulings and the weakening of the protection held by the 1973 decision in *Roe v. Wade.*

ADDITIONAL POLICIES AND LAWS: ABSTINENCE-ONLY AND INFORMED CONSENT

According to the Sexuality Information & Education Council of the United States (SIECUS), beginning with the Reagan Administration in 1981, the pro-life movement began pushing for the increased federal funding of abstinence-only programming in the United States and was largely successful. Abstinence-only programming refers to education programs designed for preteens and young adults that promote the practice of refraining from sexual intercourse. Much of the programming focuses on preventing sexual activity before marriage to prevent out-of-wedlock childbearing. SIECUS reports that money is allocated through three primary funding streams: The Adolescent Family Life Act (AFLA), Title V Welfare Reform Act, and the federal Community Based Abstinence Education Program.

Many pro-choice advocates believe that the pro-life position on sex education and abstinence-only increases the need for women to seek abortions. Opponents of abstinence-only programming believe that although these programs can be helpful for some, they are exclusionary in that they do not consider all factors that shape a person's sexual behavior. Furthermore, they argue, abstinence-only programs do not provide alternative options for those who decide that abstinence is not suitable for them. For example, a person who receives abstinence-only education and who subsequently decides not to abstain may not be equipped with proper contraceptive techniques, thereby putting him/herself at risk for creating an unwanted pregnancy or contracting a sexually transmitted disease. Many agree that a healthy compromise would be for programs to cover the full range of education on sexual reproduction and sexual activity and offer abstinence-only information for those who choose that lifestyle.

Informed consent is another strategy supported by pro-life advocates to prevent women and especially legal minors from having access to abortion. Many states have passed informed consent bills, also known as "right to know" or "mandatory delay" bills. These bills require that any clinics that perform abortions must give information about the development of the fetus to those seeking abortions. These bills also seek to require disclosure of all risks associated with abortion and alternatives while imposing a daylong wait before the procedure. Furthermore, in some cases women under age 19 may not seek abortion services without prior consent from their parents or legal guardians. Many pro-choice advocates oppose legislation requiring informed consent, arguing that such tactics are intended to make it more difficult to obtain an abortion. Some claim an increased harassment of female clients seeking information about abortions, particularly in contexts where medical providers are themselves pro-life.

CONCLUSION

Abortion is one of the most debated issues today in U.S. society. On both sides of the debate, observers hold strong feelings about women's roles in making reproductive decisions, the state's role in regulating the realm of reproduction, when life begins, and whether fetuses should have legal rights. Thus far, fetal rights legislation pits mothers against their own fetuses, often criminalizing women in the process. For example, well-publicized cases of women who have used illegal drugs while pregnant have been charged with child abuse or, in cases where the fetus died, murder. This appears to be a growing legal trend in the 2000s, although many still continue to support the view that the state should not intervene in regulating reproductive decisions, and that regardless of religious and cultural views regarding when conception begins, states should not prioritize one form of life over another. What is perhaps most certain is that these debates will continue to shake the political and moral foundations of U.S. society, for the issue of abortion touches on several interconnected and deeply controversial debates about privacy and the law, family planning, parenting, and the question of when life begins.

See also Birth Control; Fetal Rights; Population Policy.

Further Reading: Baer, Judith A., *Women in American Law: The Struggle Toward Equality from the New Deal to the Present,* 3rd ed. (New York: Holmes and Meier, 2002); Butler, Jennifer S., *Born Again: The Christian Right Globalized* (Ann Arbor: University of Michigan Press, 2006); Colker, Ruth, *Abortion and Dialogue: Pro-Choice, Pro-Life, and American Law* (Bloomington: Indiana University Press, 1992); Costa, Marie, *Abortion: A Reference Handbook: Contemporary World Issues* (Santa Barbara, CA: ABC-CLIO, 1996); Garfield, Jay L., and Patricia Hennessey, *Abortion, Moral and Legal Perspectives* (Amherst: University of Massachusetts Press, 1984); Gorney, Cynthia, *Articles of Faith: A Frontline History of the Abortion Wars* (New York: Simon and Schuster, 2000); Hull, N.E.H., Williamjames Hoffer, and Peter Charles Hoffer, *The Abortion Rights Controversy in America: A Legal Reader* (Chapel Hill: University of North Carolina Press, 2004); Kaplan, Laura, *The Story of Jane: The Legendary Underground Feminist Abortion Service* (Chicago: University of Chicago Press, 1995); Kintz, Linda, and Julia Lesage, eds., *Culture, Media, and the Religious Right* (Minneapolis: University of Minnesota Press, 1998); Martin, William, *With God on Our Side: The Rise of the Religious Right in America* (New York: Broadway Books, 1996); Pojman, Louis J., and Francis J. Beckwith, *Abortion Controversy: 25 Years After Roe v. Wade: A Reader,* 2nd ed. (Belmont, CA: Wadsworth Publishing, 1998); Raymond, Tatalovich, and Byron W. Daynes, *Moral Controversies in American Politics: Cases in Social Regulatory Policy* (Armonk, NY: ME Sharpe, Inc., 1998); Rowland, Debran, *The Boundaries of Her Body: The Troubling History of Women's Rights in America* (Naperville, IL: Sphinx Publishing, 2004); Rubin, Eva R., ed., *The Abortion Controversy: A Documentary History* (Westport, CT: Greenwood Press, 1994); Sanger, Margaret, *Woman and the New Race* (New York: Brentano's Press, 1920);

Solinger, Rickie, *Abortion Wars: A Half Century of Struggle, 1950–2000* (Berkeley: University of California Press, 1998).

Jeni Jenkins

AFFIRMATIVE ACTION

Affirmative action refers to public policies and initiatives that have been implemented to increase the representation of groups that have been excluded both historically and currently from employment, education, and other opportunities, based on their race, color, religion, sex, or national origin. Affirmative action policies have been the source of intense controversy, with claims that these policies are inherently racist or sexist and do not significantly help their intended beneficiaries.

DEFINING AFFIRMATIVE ACTION

In 1965, President Lyndon Johnson used the concept of affirmative action in Executive Order No. 11246, requiring federal contractors to "take affirmative action to ensure that applicants are employed, and that employees are treated during employment, without regard to their race, creed, color, or national origin." In 1967, President Johnson expanded the Executive Order to include affirmative action requirements to benefit women. Affirmative action addresses governmental and social injustices against groups that have been discriminated against, most typically because of race, ethnicity, and gender, and seeks to increase the representation of these underrepresented groups in fields of study and work.

President Johnson was not the first president to develop affirmative action mandates. In 1941, President Franklin D. Roosevelt issued Executive Order No. 8802, barring discriminatory hiring policies in defense industries that held federal contracts and created the Committee on Fair Employment Practices to investigate complaints and to address valid grievances. President Roosevelt's signing of this order was a culmination of work by black civil rights leader, A. Philip Randolph, founder of the Brotherhood of Sleeping Car Porters.

In 1948, President Harry S. Truman's Executive Orders 9980 and 9981 outlawed discrimination in federal employment and the military, respectively. In 1961, President John F. Kennedy established the President's Committee on Equal Employment Opportunity (in government-funded employment) with Executive Order 10925 and called on federal contractors to overcome discrimination.

HISTORICAL BACKGROUND

Current debates on gender- and race-based affirmative action are rooted in the historical legacy of racial and gender inequalities in the United States. In the 1960s, the second wave feminist movement adopted the strategies of the civil rights movement to apply the concept of affirmative action to the realm of gender.

Lack of representation of racial and ethnic minority groups in America did not emerge in the twentieth century; rather, it stems from discrimination that is evident with the nation's founding. The American Constitution is based on ideals of justice and equality, yet the majority of African Americans were enslaved and exploited. Many scholars have pointed out that U.S. history is built on preferential treatment, with different laws being applied to blacks and whites during slavery, during the Jim Crow period, into the twentieth century, and, arguably, continuing today. Similar experiences of discrimination were typical for Native Americans, Latino Americans, Asian Americans, and women.

Affirmative action is built on the premise that meritocracy does not adequately address the continuing underrepresentation of minority groups. Both past and present discriminatory practices limit access to educational and employment opportunities and consequently to opportunities to gain merit. When minority group members are actively sought or preferred, it is arguably because affirmative action is necessary to compensate for advantages that groups such as males and whites have derived from racism and sexism. Thus past discrimination will be sufficiently countered that such affirmative action strategies will no longer be necessary. American affirmative action policies have primarily addressed race and gender inequalities, and women have benefited as much as racial and ethnic minorities from these policies.

The controversy over affirmative action continues to rage for several reasons. First, Americans hold conflicting ideals, which become more complex when ideas of race relations are included. These conflicting ideals include the value placed on equality; yet white supremacy is rampant. America has been built on the exploitation and exclusion of minority groups, and social and economic discrimination against many of these groups continue to characterize race relations. Second,

AFFIRMATIVE ACTION AND UNIVERSITY ADMISSIONS

Opponents of affirmative action have been most successful at dismantling legislation in university admissions. In October 1997, two white students, Jennifer Gratz and Patrick Hammacher, filed a lawsuit alleging that the University of Michigan gave preferential treatment to minority students in their undergraduate admissions process. Later in 2001, Barbara Grutter, a white student who was denied admission to the University of Michigan Law School, filed her own lawsuit alleging that because other African American applicants were accepted despite their lower tests scores, she was legally discriminated against. Both cases were brought to the U.S. Supreme Court in 2003, where the Court voted in a split ruling to uphold the University of Michigan Law School's admissions standards but to strike down the university's undergraduate admissions standards on the basis that it violated equal protection provisions of the Constitution. A similar legal process occurred in California, home to one of the largest public university systems in the nation, where race-based admissions standards are no longer allowed, and broader initiatives such as the Florida Civil Rights Initiative (2000+) have been introduced that aim to end governmental preferences toward minority groups in all realms of public policy and law.

many Americans believe that although prejudice and discrimination continue to exist, they are no longer defining social realities for most minorities.

ARGUMENTS AGAINST AFFIRMATIVE ACTION

Americans embrace the value of individual determinism. A prevailing argument against affirmative action is the charge that it subsumes individual opportunity, with merit as the basis of reward, to group entitlement. That is, it is patently unjust to select individuals on the basis of any other characteristic than merit, as we are all equal citizens. Thus critics of affirmative action call for a colorblind and gender-neutral society. This argument fuels the charge that affirmative action is reverse racial or gender discrimination. Critics argue that affirmative action is a violation of equal protection under the Fourteenth Amendment and violates individual rights. Furthering this criticism is the argument that affirmative action penalizes individuals who cannot be held accountable for past and present group actions. One individual is not responsible for slavery, which happened centuries ago, neither is he or she responsible for current discriminatory practices. Conversely, affirmative action unfairly rewards individuals for the exploitation of their ancestors centuries ago.

An ensuing argument against affirmative action is that it demeans its intended beneficiaries, members of minority groups, and promotes the perception among both minorities and nonminorities that, unlike the racial majority and model minorities, underrepresented minorities are not capable enough to be considered on their own merits and cannot attain success without preferential treatment. Furthering this contention is the idea that beneficiaries of affirmative action are not as qualified as their white and/or male counterparts. Because they are not rewarded based on their individual merit or ability, then the best positions are not reserved for those most qualified. As such, affirmative action practices undermine quality and lower standards of excellence in the labor force and educational system.

Another argument is that affirmative action is appropriate when it helps minorities who are socially and economically disadvantaged, and not middle and upper class minority members who have achieved success. The argument is that affirmative action can no longer fulfill its original objective of raising minorities out of poverty, as many minorities have already achieved middle-class status. Cases are frequently cited of middle-class minorities who receive better employment and college acceptance than comparable whites because of affirmative action. According to this point of view, affirmative action should be used to alleviate poverty among the lower classes, and not among specific racial or ethnic groups. Although not denying the experience of past discrimination, critics also argue that discrimination based on race, ethnicity, and gender are no longer salient in the labor force and on university campuses, minimizing the need for affirmative action.

ARGUMENTS SUPPORTING AFFIRMATIVE ACTION

Supporters of affirmative action argue that America has not been built on individual merit, colorblindness, and gender equality, and accordingly, that centuries of social inequalities and denied opportunities cannot be resolved by merit and colorblind or gender-neutral policies. The role of past and current institutional discrimination of minorities cannot be minimized. Although many racial and ethnic minorities and women have experienced, and continue to experience, socioeconomic mobility, employment and wage disparities remain entrenched between whites and minorities, and poverty and other means of social disenfranchisement are disproportionately evident among minorities. Affirmative action supporters assert that critics are trying to shift the blame onto minority group members who have been discriminated against, as justification for eliminating affirmative action policies.

Proponents of affirmative action also argue that eliminating affirmative action would widen social and economic gaps between whites and underrepresented minorities. The "good old boy's network," in which the power wielders in organizations select, promote, and mentor similar others within their organizations, is used to exemplify the argument that American institutions are not truly meritorious, and instead are exclusionary and bar from entry individuals not connected to these networks. Furthering this argument, supporters of affirmative action argue that it benefits all of society by diversifying the labor force with qualified workers from all backgrounds. Supporters also point out that tremendous gains have been made by racial and ethnic minorities and women in the labor force and in education, in large part as a result of affirmative action measures; however, discrimination is still evident in the labor force and education systems.

THE LEGALITY OF AFFIRMATIVE ACTION

Early civil rights programs were adopted that helped African Americans and other racial and ethnic minorities gain enfranchisement in the United States. The Thirteenth Amendment to the Constitution made slavery illegal, the Fourteenth Amendment guaranteed equal protection under the law, and the Fifteenth Amendment forbade racial discrimination in access to voting.

In 1964, the Civil Rights Act was passed. Title II of the Act entitled all persons to the full and equal enjoyment of public accommodations, without discrimination or segregation on the basis of race, color, religion, or national origin. Title VII of the Act made it illegal for an employer to discriminate in hiring, firing, promotions, and other employment practices on the basis of race and sex. The Voting Rights Acts of 1965 stipulates in Section 11 that "no person acting under color of law shall fail or refuse to permit any person to vote who is entitled to vote under any provision of this Act or is otherwise qualified to vote, or willfully fail or refuse to tabulate, count, and report such person's vote."

Title IX of the Education Amendments of 1972 prohibited sex discrimination in any educational activity or program at any educational facility that is a recipient of federal funds. Title IX is largely known for bringing further equality to women in sports. During this same period, women's rights advocates were fighting for the passage of the Equal Rights Amendment (ERA). This amendment would have provided full protection for women in all realms of U.S. law and policy. It was never passed, and the United States remains one of the only countries in the world without federal civil rights legislation of this kind.

In the 1970s and 1980s, and continuing to the present, affirmative action had become a divisive issue for the American public, particularly in regard to race. The growing perception that affirmative action may be reverse discrimination was exemplified by the *Regents of the University of California v. Bakke* (1978) case. Allan Bakke, a white male, had been rejected twice by the University of California, Davis, Medical School, although minority applicants had been admitted who were less qualified than he was. The medical school had separate admissions policies for standard applicants and for minority and economically disadvantaged students and had reserved 16 of 100 places for minority students. Bakke argued that judging him on the basis of his race was a violation of the Equal Protection Clause of the Fourteenth Amendment. In this case, the Supreme Court outlawed inflexible quota systems in affirmative action programs, which had unfairly discriminated against Bakke, who was white. The legality of affirmative action, however, was also upheld by the Supreme Court. This landmark Supreme Court case ruled that affirmative action was unfair if it resulted in reverse discrimination, and limited affirmative action to ensure that providing greater opportunities for minorities did not come at the expense of the rights of the majority.

In the *City of Richmond v. J. A. Croson Co.* (1989), local affirmative action programs were challenged. The city of Richmond, Virginia, had adopted a business program that required contractors awarded city construction contracts to subcontract at least 30 percent of each contract to one or more minority business enterprises. The Supreme Court ruled that a general assertion of past discrimination cannot justify the use of an unyielding racial quota and upheld the strict scrutiny standard that "strict scrutiny must be applied to all governmental racial classifications."

In *Adarand Constructors, Inc. v. Peña* (1995), petitioner Adarand Constructors, Inc., sued federal officials with the claim that the race-based presumptions used in subcontractor compensation clauses were violations of the Fifth Amendment's Due Process Clause, which guaranteed equal protection under the law. Again, the Supreme Court determined that "all racial classifications, imposed by whatever federal, state, or local governmental actor, must be analyzed by a reviewing court under strict scrutiny." Although Justice Scalia agreed with the application of strict scrutiny of racial classifications, he argued that, "government can never have a compelling interest in discriminating on the basis of race in order to make up for past racial discrimination in the opposite direction. Under the Constitution there can be no such thing as either a creditor or a debtor race. We are just one race in the eyes of government."

In 1997, Proposition 209 (California Civil Rights Initiative) was passed in California. The proposition states that: "The state shall not discriminate against, or grant preferential treatment to, any individual or group on the basis of race, sex, color, ethnicity, or national origin in the operation of public employment, public education, or public contracting." This restatement of the Civil Rights Act effectively bans affirmative action programs in California. Implementation of the proposition had been delayed by a court ruling, which was subsequently overturned.

GLOBAL AFFIRMATIVE ACTION POLICIES

Although affirmative action is generally defined as measures designed to increase the representation of underrepresented groups, countries differ significantly in their scope and implementation of affirmative action policies. In general, gender-based affirmative action policies have been much more successful in countries other than the United States. In many European and Latin American countries, for example, national governments have adopted legislation affirming female political quotas and gender-based affirmative action agendas in the areas of employment, health care, and housing, among others. Whereas the Equal Rights Amendment was never passed in the United States, many other countries have in fact passed similar types of federal legislation.

Affirmative action policies on the basis of race, ethnicity, or caste have also been implemented in several other countries. In India, for example, policies have been introduced to address wide disparities in the caste system, which bears similarity to the American racial stratification system. Low castes in India's caste system historically have experienced extreme discrimination and deprivation that remains persistent, despite the constitutional dismantling of the caste system. India's affirmative action policy is called the reservation system, which is based on quotas that reserve places for the underprivileged groups to be represented in government jobs and educational institutions. This system was adopted in Article 15 of the Indian Constitution in 1950.

South Africa explicitly mandates a system of preference for disadvantaged minorities, largely in response to the history of severe racial segregation in that country. In South Africa, black people (Africans, Coloreds, and Indians), who constitute the overwhelming numerical majority, have been grossly disadvantaged compared to whites. Affirmative action policies in South Africa were outlined in the 1998 Employment Equity Act and guaranteed in the South African Constitution. The law mandates the implementation of affirmative action policies by employers to ensure representation and equity in the workforce of both people of color and women, with explicit numerical goals and timetables. Significantly, the policy rejects traditional definitions of merit by stating that a person may not be discriminated against because of a lack of relevant experience as long as the person has the capacity to gain the experience and to do the job.

In contrast, the European Union has espoused race-blind policies. The European Union member states have adopted two directives that attempt to apply principles of equality without regard to race or ethnicity, and to ensure that everyone living in the European Union is legally protected against discrimination. The first directive, Council Directive 2000/43/EC, prohibits discrimination on the basis of race and ethnicity and addresses racism and xenophobia in member states. The second directive, Council Directive 2000/78/EC, addresses equality in employment and occupation. All of these examples point to the difficulty of addressing racial and gender inequalities at the level of policy and law.

CONCLUSION

How the affirmative action controversy will evolve is uncertain, with supporters and opponents polarized on opposite ends, and no compromises seemingly likely. What is certain is severe and mounting legal opposition to affirmative action, for example, as reflected in the University of Michigan court cases and the Florida Civil Rights Initiative (2000) to end governmental discrimination and preferences. Political and popular backlash against affirmative action is also on the rise. Regardless of the future of affirmative action both globally and in the United States, race relations are becoming more tenuous as we experience growing social and economic distress. Likewise, there has been a strong backlash against feminism and a growing perception by white men that white women are no longer disadvantaged, despite clear socioeconomic evidence to the contrary. Some Americans oppose affirmative action, based on the allegation that it results in reverse discrimination, primarily against white males. Others continue to believe in its importance as a step toward racial and gender equality in the nation.

See also Equal Rights Amendment; Race and Racism: Social Stratification in the United States; Title IX and Women's Sports.

Further Reading: Blanchard, Fletcher A., and Faye J. Crosby, *Affirmative Action in Perspective* (New York: Springer-Verlag, 1989); Department of Labour, Republic of South Africa, Employment Equity Act, No. 55 of 1998, available at: http://www.labour.gov.za; Deshpande, Ashwini, "Affirmative Action in India and the United States," Equity and Development, World Development Report, 2006; Dimitrova, Antoaneta, and Mark Rhinard, *The Power of Norms in the Transposition of EU Directives.* European Integration online Papers (EIoP) 9, no. 16 (2005), available at: http://eiop.or.at/eiop/texte/2005-016a.htm; Eisaguirre, Lynne, *Affirmative Action: A Reference Handbook* (Santa Barbara, CA: Contemporary World Issues, 1999); Fobanjong, John, *Understanding the Backlash against Affirmative Action* (Huntington, NY: Nova Science Publishers, Inc, 2001); Sabbagh, Daniel, "Affirmative Action Policies: An International Perspective," United Nations Development Programme (New York: Human Development Report Office, 2004); Skrentny, John D., *The Ironies of Affirmative Action: Politics, Culture, and Justice in America* (Chicago: The University of Chicago Press, 1996); U.S. Department of Labor, "Executive Order 8802: Fair Employment Practice in Defense Industries." Poster on E.O. 8802, with FDR's signature (1941), available at: http://www.dol.gov/oasam/programs/history/fair_employment.htm; U.S. Department of Labor, Employment Standards Administration, Office of Federal Contract Compliance Programs, *Executive Order 11246—Equal Employment Opportunity,* September 24, 1965; U.S. Department of Labor, Office of the Assistant Secretary for Administration and Management, *History at the Department of Labor: Departmental Timeline*; Weiss, Robert J., *We Want Jobs: A History of Affirmative Action* (New York: Garland Publishing, Inc., 1997); Yates, Steven, *Civil Wrongs: What Went Wrong with Affirmative Action?* (San Francisco: Institute for Contemporary Studies, 1994).

Danielle Smith

AGING

Popular culture provides an indication of the contested, conflicted, and multiple messages that women in the United States receive about aging. American women growing older do so in a youth-oriented culture historically hostile to women in midlife, as well as to women who have achieved the maturity of their fifties, sixties, seventies, and beyond.

BACKGROUND

From the slogan that "growing old is not for sissies" to the Red Hat Society's bodacious motto "when I am an old woman I shall wear purple," to ubiquitous advertising campaigns featuring antiaging serums, creams, and surgeries, to the menopause joke that "it's not a hot flash: it's a power surge," women are given conflicted messages about what it means to grow older. During the twentieth century, however, women as a group generally lived longer than men, raising interesting questions about whether women are physically better equipped to achieve longevity than men, as well as how gendered differences in lifestyles, including differences in men's and women's work, men's and women's capacity for building social networks, and men's and women's receipt of support in marriage, contribute to gendered differences in longevity. Both men and women are living longer in the twenty-first century, and as members of the baby boom cohorts enter midlife and old age, they are working to redefine what those phases of life look like, for both women and men.

FEMINIST ANALYSIS

A conventional feminist analysis of the status of women and aging centers on several foundational principles in classic critiques of patriarchy. Historian Gerda Lerner (1993), for example, describes five major assumptions about gender in a

---

SISTER MADONNA BUDER: THE IRONMAN NUN

Anyone who questions whether women in their seventies could be competitive in endurance sports should meet Sister Madonna Buder. Buder started running at age 49; at 51, she bought her first 10-speed bicycle and began participating in triathlons. She now holds Iron-distance age group records in Canada for athletes ages 60–64, 65–69, and 70 plus, and has finished the Ironman World Championship race (a 2.4-mile swim, 112-mile bike ride, and a marathon run) more than 20 times. A recent article on the womenssportsfoundation.org Web site (Schuyler and Boman 2007) profiling "masters" or senior athletes describes the dearth of opportunities for girls and women in sports before Title IX: "Before Title IX, there was the completely unfair stereotype of girls not being able to play sports," says Neena Chaudhry, senior counsel at the National Women's Law Center in Washington, D.C. "And if they played sports, the conventional wisdom was that they were damaging their reproductive organs." Every year women break new barriers in sporting competitions around the world.

---

patriarchal society: women and men are different biologically and in their social roles; men are "naturally" superior to women and therefore should be dominant to their weaker counterparts; men are more rational and more geared to public life while women are more nurturing and sustain the functions of daily life; men have the right to control the reproductive functions and sexuality of women; and only men hold the divine ability to mediate between the human species and God (Lerner cited in Ruth 1990).

In the context of these assumptions, which are supported by a wide range of economic, social, cultural, and legal practices, women's value in society, as determined by men, grows less and less as we age. If women's primary functions in a patriarchal society are to provide men with sexual pleasure, children, and the domestic and social labor that allow men to participate in the public, political, productive, and intellectual worlds, as women age and their bodies, sexuality, and reproductive capacities change, their status in society decreases. Ironically and obviously, the inverse is often true for men, who are correctly seen as more powerful and desirable as they age, as a result of having accumulated both wealth and experience—often with the support of the women in their lives (Richardson 1988) and as a function of their exploitation of women's work in the economic and domestic sphere.

THE CHALLENGES OF AGING FOR WOMEN IN THE UNITED STATES

In the United States women face multiple challenges as they age. These difficulties range from cultural displacement to health concerns and health care inequality, from workplace discrimination to high rates of poverty, and from the burden of caring for elderly parents to the burdens of the extended parenting of adult children. As women age, in both rural and nonrural environments, the greater their risk of falling into poverty. In the United States, 10 percent of urban women ages 65–74, along with 11.3 percent of rural women, were in poverty in 2003; among women ages 75–84, poverty rates remain the same for urban women, but rise to 15.0 percent for women living in rural areas; among women ages 85 and older, rates of poverty are 16.8 and 16.9 percent for urban and rural women, respectively. Rates of poverty are higher among widowed women than married women. Rates of women in poverty in old age are greater than those of men, in part because more women survive to older ages, and in part because of the economic inequality and gender expectations women face across the life course. According to the USDA Economic Research Service (USDA 2005), "economic status in later life is a cumulative product of earnings, savings and spending, and participation in pension, health insurance, and public assistance plans. Many older women today have spent all or most of their lives in non-paid traditional household labor roles and thus have limited paid work experience. Those who worked in the formal labor market often had breaks in their paid labor histories due to having and raising children."

In a capitalist society, access to financial resources determines access to a wide range of other resources, goods, and services, including medical care,

THE RED HAT SOCIETY

One group of women taking a whimsical approach to redefining images of older women is the Red Hat Society, a network of small social groups of women 50 and older that meets for fun and support. Sue Ellen Cooper, after reading the poem "Warning" by Jenny Joseph, which describes an older woman who wears a red hat and purple clothing, felt an immediate connection to the author, as she had in the past bought a red fedora at a thrift shop and wore it. After that she bought several friends red hats and gave them copies of the poem. One day they realized they were becoming a social group of sorts and decided to go out for tea in their red hats and purple dresses. Since then there have been three large conventions and chapters have begun in numerous cities.

Adapted from the homepage of the Red Hat Society: http://www.redhatsociety.com/info/howitstarted.html

transportation, and the basic necessities of food and shelter. Because of historical patterns of inequality in the workplace and traditional patterns of women's access to resources being determined by their relationships with men, older women have less access to resources accumulated over a lifetime of paid work than do men, as well as less access to the labor market in their older years. As a result, women's overall well-being in their older years is seriously compromised. For women who are lesbian, nonwhite, never married, and economically or educationally disadvantaged, as well as women in more traditionally patriarchal societies, this trend is often even more pronounced.

Dominant cultural patterns influenced by a capitalist economy also contribute to women's challenges at advanced ages. The "nuclear family" model dictates that heterosexual couples live with their children until the children are grown; grandparents and other extended family members are not expected to live with their relatives, and so many older people do not have the benefit of sharing resources with family members. Conversely, because of family mobility tied to economic opportunities, many children are deprived of the benefit of relationships with their grandparents, who do not live with them and may not live within easy visiting distance.

ALTERNATIVE VISIONS OF AGING FOR WOMEN IN THE UNITED STATES

Despite the grim economic realities facing women as they age, demographic and cultural shifts are creating alternative visions of positive aging for women. As members of the baby boom generation enter middle and older ages, they are redefining both the expectations and the possibilities for women. Many of these women participated in the second wave of the feminist movement and consider themselves lifelong feminists. As these women enter middle and older age, they bring with them a critical perspective on cultural assumptions and pressures on women in these phases of life. For example, second wave feminists have frequently interrogated social expectations of women regarding sexuality, childbirth, and parenting, and their questions around traditional expectations in these areas now extend to how maturity affects sexuality and reproduction. More women are extending their childbearing into their forties, including women who are waiting until midlife to have their first children. Many refuse to accept the idea that sexuality ends at menopause; indeed, they argue that sex for heterosexual women gets better after worries about unwanted pregnancy end.

Many women of the baby boom and earlier generations are discovering athletics as a way of restoring or maintaining their health and fitness, as "masters" sports events around the country indicate. This development is especially heartening, given that women currently in their forties and older were not often socialized in environments that supported girls' and women's development of athletic talent. Deprived of opportunities to participate in well-supported team sports in high school and college, many women are nonetheless discovering the joys of physical fitness in midlife and later. Of interest, many women who begin their sports careers in midlife become successful competitive athletes, particularly in the area of endurance sports, lending some support to the theory that women's bodies are especially well designed for long-distance and endurance events.

Second-generation feminist women have also turned their attention to the issue of women's health and women's access to health care during midlife and later. The authors of a classic feminist text on women's health from the early years of the second wave of the feminist movement, *Our Bodies, Ourselves,* have, in recent years, extended their analysis to women's health issues in maturity. In *Ourselves, Growing Older* (Doress-Worters and Laskin Siegal 1994) and *Our Bodies, Ourselves: Menopause* (Boston Women's Health Book Collective 2006), members of the Boston Women's Health Book Collective take on the challenge of advocating for a view of menopause as a natural developmental event in women's lives, as an alternative to a dominant view that the end of menstruation at midlife is a pathological sign of the beginning of physical decline in women, a definition historically related to patriarchal views of women's value as being tied to reproduction. They also address the complex financial and social issues related to women's health care in old age, including social security, the stresses of multiple-generation caregiving that often situates midlife women between duties toward their own ailing parents and their children, and women's vulnerability to

AGING IS NOT A MEDICAL CONDITION

Just as the path-breaking 1970s text *Our Bodies, Ourselves* offered generations of women new, accurate, and affirming information about their bodies, health, and sexuality, Paula B. Doress-Worters and Diana Laskin Siegal's *Ourselves, Growing Older* (1994) took on the issue of women and aging from a feminist perspective. *Ourselves, Growing Older* addresses the historically classic defining rite of passage from the childbearing years to menopause, but also takes up reform of the medical care system, housing issues, HIV/AIDS, cosmetic surgery, and breast cancer, all of which affect women's health. The text, designed for women 40 and over, emphasizes the "positive potential of the second half of life" based on both empirical research and the personal narratives of women from diverse walks of life.

the chronic disorders related to lifestyles in modern industrialized capitalist societies: diabetes, hypertension, and heart disease.

CONCLUSION

Although economic inequality between the sexes remains constant in the United States, women of the baby boom cohorts have enjoyed greater access to educational and economic opportunities than women in previous generations. Many of this cohort have entered and will retire from formerly male-dominated professions in far greater proportions than previous generations. Many women of this generation, aware, and critical, of the economic risks of femininity and of marriage have established legal structures to protect their financial assets either within or independent of marriage. As a result, greater numbers of women in middle and old age can be expected to have greater access to financial and cultural resources in their later years. Likewise, although women remain seriously underrepresented in politics, and women's interests are therefore not often served in public policy, more women than ever have been elected to political office in the United States in recent decades, and their impact on public policy may benefit women over time in areas related to health, healthcare, economics, the labor force, and aging. As the baby boom cohort of women continues to move through life stages with a feminist critique of dominant expectations toward women, its members are likely to continue to redefine what it means to be female at any given age and to advocate for changes that improve the possibilities and the quality of life for themselves and coming generations.

See also Beauty Industry; Medicine and Medicalization: Views on Women's Bodies.

Further Reading: Boston Women's Health Book Collective, *Our Bodies Ourselves: Menopause* (Boston: Touchstone Publishing, 2006); Clasanti, Toni M., *Age Matters: Realigning Feminist Thinking* (New York: Routledge, 2006); Connell, Robert W., *Masculinities: Knowledge, Power, and Social Change* (Berkeley: University of California Press, 2005); Coyle, Jeanne M., ed., *Handbook on Women and Aging* (New York: Praeger, 2001); Cruickshank, Margaret, *Learning to Be Old: Gender, Culture, and Aging* (Lanham, MD: Rowman and Littlefield, 2002); Doress-Worters, Paula B., and Diana Laskin Siegal, *Ourselves, Growing Older* (Boston: Touchstone, 1994); Kimmel, Michael, *Manhood in America: A Cultural History* (New York: Oxford University Press, 2005); Lamb, Sarah, *White Saris and Sweet Mangoes: Aging, Gender, and Body in North India* (Berkeley: University of California Press, 2000); Lerner, Gerda, *The Creation of Feminist Consciousness: From the Middle Ages to Eighteen-Seventy* (New York: Oxford University Press, 1993; cited in Ruth, Sheila, *Issues in Feminism: An Introduction to Feminism* [New York: Mayfield, 1990]); MacDonald, Barbara, and Cynthia Rich, *Look Me in the Eye: Old Women, Ageing, and Ageism* (Midway, FL: Spinsters Ink Books, 2001); Matthaei, Teresa, *Race, Gender, and Work: A Multicultural Economic History of Women in the United States*, rev. ed. (Boston: South End Press, 1996); Morganroth, Margaret, *Aged by Culture* (Chicago: University of Chicago Press, 2004); Red Hat Society, "How It Started," 2007, available at: http://www.redhatsociety.com/info/howitstarted.html; Richardson, Laurel, *Dynamics of Sex and Gender* (New York: HarperCollins, 1988); Rogers, Carolyn, "Older Women and

Poverty in Rural America," in *Amber Waves: The Economics of Food, Farming, and Natural Resources, Rural America.* USDA, September 2005, available at: http://www.ers.usda.gov/AmberWaves/September05/Findings/OlderWomen.htm; Schuyler, Nina, and Steve Boman, "Maidens of Mettle," 2007, available at: womenssportsfoundation.org; United States Department of Agriculture (USDA), Economic Record Service, "Low Earnings But Steady Job Growth in Low-Employment Countries," (USDA, 2007).

Amber Ault

B

BARBIE AND THE FEMININE IDEAL OF BEAUTY

The Barbie doll is one of the most popular, and indeed, one of the most widely discussed toys of the twentieth and twenty-first centuries. Its curvaceous figure and often overtly sexualized look have raised important questions in the study of female representation and has often sparked controversy as to the message this doll sends to the vast population of (primarily) young girls that play with her.

BACKGROUND

The Barbie doll was the brainchild of Ruth Handler, who, along with her husband Elliot Handler and business associate Howard "Matt" Matson, co-founded the Mattel Corporation in 1945. Inspired with the idea to create a doll like Barbie from seeing her daughter, Barbara, playing make-believe and dress-up with paper dolls, she realized that there was a gap in the toy market. Baby dolls such as Tiny Tears and Betsy Wetsy were marketed to young girls for the purpose of playing with and trying on domestic roles and mothering, and paper dolls allowed little girls to experiment with fashion and style, but what the market lacked, in Handler's opinion, was a three-dimensional young adult doll that little girls could explore their dreams through. Shortly after she had the idea, but before the doll's design had been concretized, she came across the Lilli doll, a three-dimensional version of a popular postwar cartoon character who first appeared in the West German tabloid, *Das Bild Zeitung,* in 1952, while traveling in Germany in the late 1950s. A German doll standing 11-and-a-half inches tall,

SOME LITTLE KNOWN FACTS ABOUT BARBIE FROM THE MATTEL CO.

According to Mattel, the Barbie doll's full name is Barbara Millicent Roberts, and her birth date is March 9, 1959. She is from Willows, Wisconsin, and she is a graduate of Willows High School. At last tally, Barbie has had more than 80 careers since her debut in 1959. Starting out as a teenage fashion model, the doll's occupations have varied vastly, from a paleontologist to an Olympic swimmer, from a three-time presidential candidate (1992, 2000, and 2004) to a medic sergeant enlisted in Desert Storm. The Barbie doll has also represented more than 45 nationalities. Statistics show that two Barbie dolls are sold every second of every day in any one of the 150 nations the doll is marketed in, making Barbie the #1 girls brand in the toy industry.

and sporting a platinum ponytail, recognized now as a signature Barbie hairstyle, Lilli was Barbie's little-known predecessor. Handler purchased three of the dolls and brought them back to the United States as a model for her "Barbie" doll. In 1959 "Barbie" was officially introduced for the first time to the market at-large at the Toy Fair in New York City, along with 22 stylish new outfits, and was an instant success. The Mattel Co. sold more than 300,000 Barbie dolls during the first year on the market, quickly propelling Mattel to the forefront of the toy industry.

One of the features of the Barbie doll that has remained a top selling point over the years is her unique ability to play any role her creators design for her and, by extension, her ability to transform into just about any role a child's imagination desires for her. The Mattel Co. has taken full advantage of this doll's malleability and has profited from placing her in the guises of a multitude of nationalities, and accessorizing her for a plethora of careers over the years, ranging from an army foot soldier, to a WNBA player, to an Eskimo. Perhaps most remarkable, however, save a very slight increase in waist size and the acquisition of a belly button in the late 1990s, Barbie has managed to keep the same figure over an almost 50-year lifespan.

BARBIE AS A POSITIVE SOURCE OF INSPIRATION FOR THE IMAGINATIONS OF YOUNG GIRLS

From the vast population of young girls that own Barbie dolls (statistics show that the majority of girls who own the doll own more than one, the average being eight), to the overwhelming amounts of adults that purchase the doll for their children, or, as is often the case, for themselves as collectors, it seems that those who see Barbie as a positive and beneficial toy for the imaginations of young children are in the majority. Writers and researchers who have studied Barbie and the imaginative play that children engage in with the doll, particularly M. G. Lord (2004), author of *Forever Barbie: The Unauthorized Biography of a Real Doll,* have highlighted that play with Barbie dolls allows little girls to place themselves in a primarily female-centered universe where all imaginable possibilities are open to them. Lenore Wright (2003), author of *The Wonder of Barbie: Popular Culture and the Making of Female Identity,* concurs with this idea, and underscores what she feels are the important distinctions between the often discussed image of the Barbie doll in contrast to images of women on television and in advertisements. In her opinion, despite the Barbie doll's stereotypical and idealistic feminine appearance, children's imaginative play with the doll is not defined by its appearance but open to the widest range of possibilities stemming from the mind of the child. Thus in her words, "In the fictive world created by Barbie participants, imaginative, identity-informing possibilities emerge that can serve to empower the participant in unexpected ways" (Wright 2003, 2). Authors that seek to highlight the positive aspects of play with this doll tend to downplay the importance of Barbie's physical appearance, and the feminine beauty ideal she has come to represent. For example, researchers such as Lord, LaFerle, and Schank offer their own personal experience with Barbie as evidence that the doll did not negatively affect their relationships to their own physical appearance or self-perception. Schank reveals, "Like LaFerle and Lord, I have never had feelings of inadequacy because of Barbie (LaFerle 1997, 19; Lord 2004, 66–69). Barbie was always a toy" (Schank 2000, 3).

CRITIQUES OF BARBIE

The main distinction between those who feel the Barbie doll has a decidedly positive, or conversely, negative effect on a young girl's psychological growth and development is whether or one aligns herself or himself with the position that toys (and Barbie dolls, in particular) stipulate rules for identity formation, or whether they simply act as vehicles for the exploration of the child's own identity. The feminist critique of the Barbie doll arises from the position that children, during imaginative play or "make-believe," project themselves onto the toy and attempt to identify with it. Thus through the process of self-identification that the child engages in while playing with the Barbie doll, the doll has a profound effect on the young girl's identity formation and self-perception. As Ann Ducille succinctly states, "More than simple instruments of pleasure and amusement, toys and games play crucial roles in helping children determine what is valuable in and around them. Dolls in particular invite children to replicate them, to imagine themselves in their dolls' images. What does it mean, then, when little girls are given dolls to play with that in no way resemble them?" (Ducille 1994, 48). The unlikely chance of having a physical appearance similar to the Barbie doll was actually proven in a study conducted by researchers at University of South Australia and the University of New South Wales, UK, titled "Ken and Barbie at Life Size I," published in 1996. Using their skills in anthropometry, the study of human body measurement for use in anthropological classification and comparison, and allometry, the study of the change in proportion of various parts of an organism as a consequence of growth, they scaled Barbie and Ken dolls to adult, life-size proportions, and compared their measurements to the actual proportions of several representative adult groups of predominantly Anglo-Australian males and females. Their studies showed that the probability of a woman having a body shape like Barbie's is less than 1 in 100,000. Interestingly enough, Ken's body shape proved more realistic; the probability that an Anglo-Australian man would have such body proportions was calculated at about 1 in 50.

Simply put, the feminist critique of the Barbie doll is grounded in the notion that dolls such as Barbie reinstill the oppressions of patriarchy and the detrimental aspects of capitalism in the most dangerous manner in the guise of child's play. Feminist perspectives on beauty call attention to the high value that Western, patriarchal society places on attractiveness in women. Particularly in North American culture, the message to young girls and women that beauty is a central feature of women's identity and worth is consistently reinscribed through the ever-present media. Feminists argue that the conflation of beauty and being results in many women relating to their physical selves as objects in constant need of monitoring and maintenance, and moreover fosters the social control of women (Travis and Meginnis-Payne 2001).

According to feminist perspectives, Barbie is an example of the conflation of beauty with identity *par excellence.* As stated previously, the only feature of the Barbie doll that has remained overwhelmingly stable over the almost half-century of her existence is her figure. Her physicality and the ideal of feminine beauty she has come to represent are what make Barbie recognizable, and perhaps even appealing to the hundreds of thousands of people who purchase the doll every day. In Ducille's words, "Regardless of what color dyes the dolls are dipped in or what costumes they are adorned with, the image they present is of the same mythically thin, long-legged, luxuriously haired, buxom beauty" (Ducille 1994, 50). The propagation of such an unattainable beauty ideal, manifested in the Barbie doll, starts young girls very early on an often lifelong (and ultimately futile) struggle to personally attain that standard of physical "perfection."

BARBIE SYNDROME

Barbie syndrome is a term used to loosely describe the desire of some females to have a physical appearance and lifestyle characteristic of the Barbie doll. Although the syndrome is mostly associated with preteens and adolescents, women of any age can be afflicted with the disorder, which is characterized by striving for an unattainable body type, more specifically that of the classic and contemporary doll whose real life measurements have been said to be somewhere around 39–18–33. Cindy Jackson is perhaps the most famous person afflicted with so-called Barbie syndrome, as her attempts to (according to many, successfully) transform herself into a human Barbie doll have brought her celebrity status. After eye lifts, nose jobs, cheek implants, lip enhancement, cosmetic dentistry, a chin reduction, a reshaped jaw, facelifts, breast implants (and removal of breast implants), dermabrasion, chemical peels, fat transfers, liposuction, filler injections, laser treatment, and much more, she feels satisfied with her appearance as the closest human simulation of the Barbie doll. (See www.cindyjackson.com)

In a proactive effort to combat the narrowly defined, normative standards of beauty propagated by Western culture, Ophira Edut founded a Web site in 1998 titled *AdiosBarbie.com: A Body Image Site for Every Body.* Promoting body love and self-acceptance "through thick AND thin," this site aims at providing a space for women of all cultures, shapes, and sizes to explore all issues related to the body, speak out against impossible beauty standards (represented in Barbie's "plastic perfection," in Ophira's words), and ultimately encourage people to develop their own understanding of beauty and power, rooted in their own experience.

OTHER CONTROVERSIES: BARBIE IN GLOBAL PERSPECTIVE

Since her first appearance as a white teenage fashion model in 1959, the Barbie doll has been manufactured in more than 45 different nationalities and marketed in more than 150 nations, although not all reactions to Barbie's attempts at multicultural integration have been positive. For example, in response to the Mattel Co.'s Barbie *Dolls of the World Series,* first launched in 1980, which offers the Barbie doll in a range of nationalities and cultural attire spanning the globe from Nigerian Barbie to Malaysian Barbie, charges have been leveled that reduce Mattel's attempts to include vastly varying cultures in their "Barbie-world" to little more than a thinly veiled commodification of racial and cultural difference. A comparison of the classic Caucasian, blonde-haired, blue-eyed doll to any one of her multiethnic counterparts reveals that the appearance of cultural or racial difference is achieved through the dye used to color the doll's body, occasionally a slight modification of facial features (such as slightly slanted eyes for the Asian models of Barbie, or a slightly wider nose and thicker lips in her African versions), and a dramatic change in costume reflecting the Mattel Co.'s understanding of the particular country's "traditional" dress. No modifications are made to the doll's body shape and size, or general facial structure. Critics such as Ann Ducille have argued that Mattel's approach to racial and cultural difference through the Barbie *Dolls of the World* series trivializes the particulars of diversity to produce, conversely, an overgeneralized sense of sameness across cultures. In her words, Mattel's commodification of multiculturalism is "an easy and immensely profitable way off the hook of Euro-centrism" (Ducille 1994, 52) that provides the consumer with little more than the shallow appearance of cultural diversity. The issue raised here, specifically how racial and cultural difference can be accounted for in a mass-produced doll without resorting to stereotypes, is indeed an important question that does not succumb to any quick or easy solutions.

The propagation of the Western, Anglo-Saxon beauty ideal that Barbie represents, even in the guise of various nationalities, has also come under intense scrutiny from the governments of some of the non-Western nations that the doll is sold in. The Malaysian Consumers Association of Penang started the trend in 1995, when they called for a nationwide ban on Barbie, citing an alarming increase in anorexia nervosa and plastic surgery since the doll's introduction to the Malaysian market. Officials were quoted as saying that the doll promotes a Western ideal of beauty that does not include dark skin or hair, physical features characteristic of the Malaysian people. In 2002, Iranian police confiscated Barbie dolls from toy store shelves, calling the doll a Trojan horse sneaking in Western influences and un-Islamic sensibilities that corrupt the minds of young girls. Similarly, in 2002, Russia's president Vladimir Putin was quoted as saying the Barbie doll's "outrageous curves are corrupting the minds of children," and Barbie was included on a list of toys compiled by the Russian Ministry of Education that face a ban in Russia because of their supposed inability to promote "wholesome" values. A year later, religious police in Saudi Arabia followed suit, banning the sale of Barbie dolls in the country; and a warning stating, "Jewish Barbie dolls, with their revealing clothing and shameful postures, accessories and tools are a symbol of decadence to the perverted West," was posted on the official Web site of the Saudi Arabian Committee for the Propagation of Virtue and Prevention of Vice (Associated Press 2003).

CONCLUSION

The Barbie doll is one of the most popular children's toys and equally one of the most complex cultural icons of the twentieth and twenty-first centuries. The power and pervasiveness of this small plastic figure are reflected in the often deeply contradictory meanings assigned to the doll, as well as in the reactions it stirs in far-reaching areas of the world. Many researchers and theorists who have worked closely with the multiple meanings attached to the Barbie doll throughout her history have concluded that Barbie is nothing more than a plastic child's toy, devoid of any "sexist or occult" meanings (Schank 2000; also see Wright 2003; Ducille 1994; and LaFerle 1997 for similar conclusions). Therefore they see the Barbie doll as something like a container that holds the meanings that a society places on it, or a prism that reflects the general societal concerns involving women, or the complex issues of female representation, of any given culture or era. Although that is a valid and compelling point, the mass production and global distribution of the female figure that the Barbie doll represents do hold a message, within its form, of what the society that is responsible for manufacturing it understands as *female*. That, in itself, deserves its fair share of critical attention and analysis.

See also Beauty Industry; Beauty Pageants; Gender Socialization; Media Images of Women: Advertising; Self-Injury and Body Image.

Further Reading: Associated Press, "Iran enforces Barbie Ban," *The Sydney Morning Herald* (Sydney, Australia), May 23, 2002, available at: http://www.smh.com.au/articles/2002/05/22/1021882068091.html, accessed October 30, 2006; Associated Press, "Saudi Police Outlaw Barbie," *The Sydney Morning Herald* (Sydney, Australia), September 10, 2003, available at: http://www.smh.com.au/articles/2003/09/10/1062902076884.html, accessed October 30, 2006; BillyBoy, *Barbie: Her Life and Times* (New York: Three Rivers Press, 1992); Dittmar, Helga, Suzanne Ive, and Emma Halliwell, "Does Barbie Make Girls Want to Be Thin? The Effect of Experimental Exposure to Images of Dolls on the Body Image of 5- to 8-Year-Old Girls," *Journal of Developmental Psychology* 42, no. 2 (2006): 283–292; Ducille, Ann, "Dyes and Dolls: Multicultural Barbie and the Merchandising of Difference," *Differences: A Journal of Feminist Cultural Studies* 6, no. 1 (1994): 46–67; Edut, Ophira, Ihsan Muhammad, Pia Guerrero, and Annie Tomlin, eds., *AdiosBarbie.com: A Body Image Site for Every Body,* available at: http://www.adiosbarbie.com, accessed October 26, 2006; Grassel,

Kathleen, "Barbie Around the World: Healthy Human Growth," *New Renaissance* 8, no. 4, issue 27 (1999), available at: http://www.ru.org/barbie.htm; INTERNET, accessed October 24, 2006; Kuther, Tara L., and Erin McDonald, "Early Adolescents' Experiences With, and Views of, Barbie," *Adolescence* 39, no. 153 (2004): 77–82; LaFerle, Cynthia G., "Barbie: Her Figure Isn't Everything," *Christian Science Monitor* 19, no. 6 (1997), available at: http://www.csmonitor.com/1997/1212/121297.opin.opin.1.html, accessed October 30, 2006; Lord, M. G., *Forever Barbie: The Unauthorized Biography of a Real Doll* (New York: Walker and Co., 2004); Norton, Ken I., Timothy S. Olds, Scott Olive, and Steven Dank, "Ken and Barbie at Life Size," *Sex Roles: A Journal of Research* 34, nos. 3/4 (1996): 287–294; Schank, Kristen, "Quite a Little Woman," *Fresh Writing: University of Notre Dame*, 2000, available at: http://www.nd.edu/~frswrite/mcpartlin/2000/Schank.shtml, accessed October 24, 2006; Travis, Cheryl Brown, and Kayce L. Meginnis-Payne, "Beauty Politics and Patriarchy: The Impact on Women's Lives," *Encyclopedia of Women and Gender*, vol. 1 (San Diego: Academic Press, 2001); Unknown Author, "Barbie is Banned from Russia; without Love, *The London Guardian* (London, England), November 24, 2002, available at: http://observer.guardian.co.uk/international/story/0,6903,846403,00.html, accessed October 30, 2006; Wright, Lenore, "The Wonder of Barbie: Popular Culture and the Making of Female Identity," *Essays in Philosophy: A Biannual Journal* 4, no. 1 (2003), available at: http://www.humboldt.edu/~essays/wright.html, accessed October 24, 2006.

Kathryn Gentzke

BEAUTY INDUSTRY

The beauty industry is a multibillion-dollar enterprise in the United States, generating profit, critics argue, by unnecessarily reinforcing and intensifying women's continued obsession with appearance at the cost of other endeavors or personal health. Defenders of the industry claim that such preoccupation with appearance is naturally female and evolutionarily necessary.

BACKGROUND

Current debates surrounding the beauty industry's impact on women ask the question, what is the function of beauty? If the function of beauty is to realize the goal of reproduction via the attraction of a mate, then the beauty industry does not harm women. Rather, it fulfills a demand required by our nature as human beings. On the other hand, the feminist perspective places the effects of the beauty industry on women in the larger picture of women's historical emancipation. It asks the question, how has the beauty industry helped or hurt women? Feminists argue that beauty is not a mechanism of nature so much as a political and economic tool to maintain a gender hierarchy of male superiority and female subjugation.

SUPPORTERS OF THE BEAUTY INDUSTRY

In *Survival of the Prettiest*, Nancy Etcoff (1999) argues that the beauty industry is a natural extension of the biological criteria for successful femaleness.

The beauty industry does not create or exacerbate a social phenomenon marked by women's obsession with appearance; instead, it is merely the evolution of a universal female preoccupation with appearance that is both ahistorical and necessary for the perpetuation of the human species. We find beautiful those bodies that appear fertile. As a result, both females and males attempt to appear fertile and healthy to attract mates. Supporters of the beauty industry describe beauty as a marker of genetic superiority; its commercialization is a logical outgrowth of a natural value.

Etcoff contrasts beauty with fashion, which she asserts is a status marker that indicates one's level of access to resources. If an individual is not beautiful, fashion can be exploited to make up for this lack. If an individual is fashionable, then the individual has the expendable income required to change his or her wardrobe as fashion commands. Thus beauty is an indicator of fertility and fashion is an indicator of economic status. Both are criteria for mate selection.

Many, however, critique arguments like Etcoff's because they fail to account for the beauty industry's disproportionate emphasis on women. Etcoff maintains, without substantiation, that men value beauty in their mates more than women do; this is simply our nature. She fails to consider, however, that in nature, it is often the males who must flaunt their beauty to attract females. She gives no explanation for this reversal in human mating practices.

CRITICS OF THE BEAUTY INDUSTRY

The feminist argument, as presented by Naomi Wolf, asserts that the beauty industry maintains the second-class status of women by reinforcing biological explanations for beauty. Wolf finds that theories like Etcoff's perpetuate a "beauty myth" whose principal effect is the continued oppression of women. Rather than viewing beauty as biologically valuable, the concept of beauty—and especially its commercialization—functions to create an additional obstacle to women's empowerment.

Wolf finds that both political and economic gains are made through a beauty industry that targets women. First, Wolf argues that as women gain agency and access to power and resources, they are simultaneously and not coincidentally increasingly burdened with arbitrary and unrelated expectations of physical beauty. This, she suggests, is a last-ditch attempt by patriarchal institutions to distract women from the ultimate goal of uninhibited self-determination. As such goals are slowly met, she speculates, social definitions of beauty will predictably become less attainable. Wolf asserts that the beauty myth became especially powerful as Western women began achieving more social equality. The myth engendered competition between women, which undermines women's progress and hinders the project of true equality. She states, "The stronger women were becoming politically, the heavier the ideals of beauty would bear down upon them, mostly in order to distract their energy and undermine their progress" (Wolf 1991, 3). Second, she echoes Betty Friedan's argument that the industry benefits from unattainable standards of beauty because it creates a psychological deficiency that must be compensated for with various products or fashions. Women are deemed below the beauty standard and then made to feel guilty so that they purchase beauty products. In this way, the industry creates both the need to buy products and supplies the products themselves. Third, as feminist scholars are quick to point out, biological excuses for the beauty industry are inherently heteronormative, operating under unexamined assumptions of universal heterosexuality that do not account for the experience of same-sex desire.

The beauty myth asserts the following: Individuals are attracted to other individuals that they find beautiful. Attraction unites people for the purpose of procreation. Thus nonprocreative sex, as well as beauty detached from sex, is unaccounted for.

CONCLUSION

Although the beauty industry's implication in the continued objectification and subjugation of women is contested, the existence and growth of the industry are undeniable. Whether the industry is comprised of innocent commercial endeavors that are merely filling the contemporary manifestation of the natural imperative of female beauty, or instead is itself implicated in the construction of a socially and politically driven beauty imperative with no biological justification continues to be debated.

See also Barbie and the Feminine Ideal of Beauty; Beauty Pageants; Eating Disorders; Media Images of Women: Advertising.

Further Reading: Black, Paula, *The Beauty Industry: Gender, Culture, Pleasure* (New York: Routledge, 2004); Chapkis, Wendy, *Beauty Secrets: Women and the Politics of Appearance* (Boston: South End Press, 1986); Etcoff, Nancy, *Survival of the Prettiest: The Science of Beauty* (New York: Random House, 1999); Freidan, Betty, *The Feminine Mystique* (New York: W. W. Norton and Co., 1963); Gimlin, Debra, *Body Work: Beauty and Self-Image in American Culture* (Berkeley: University of California Press, 2002); Jeffreys, Sheila, *Beauty and Misogyny: Harmful Cultural Practices in the West* (New York: Routledge, 2005); *Killing Us Softly 3*, DVD, directed by Sut Jhally (Media Education Foundation, 1999); Maine, Margo, *Body Wars: Making Peace with Women's Bodies* (Carlsbad, CA: Gurze Books, 2000); Peiss, Kathy, *Hope in a Jar: The Making of America's Beauty Culture* (New York: Metropolitan Books, 1998); Wolf, Naomi, *The Beauty Myth: How Images of Beauty Are Used Against Women* (New York: HarperCollins, 1991); Zeglin Brand, Peg, *Beauty Matters* (Bloomington: Indiana University Press, 1990).

Lisa Nicolosi and Sarvani Prasad

BEAUTY PAGEANTS

Since the start of beauty competitions in this country more than 150 years ago, their value and effects in our society have been intensely debated. As the world's leading source of scholarships to young women, beauty pageant supporters advocate that the women who compete are role models for young women around the world and that pageants provide these women with extraordinary opportunities. Critics of beauty pageants have condemned these events as oppressive, as competitors are judged primarily on their appearance and adherence to dominant America's ideal image of beauty. Regardless of how people feel about beauty pageants, there is no denying that they have become a cultural institution in this country.

BACKGROUND

Beauty competitions have existed in many cultures throughout history. In Greek mythology, there is a legendary competition between the Goddesses Hera, Aphrodite, and Athena to determine who is the most beautiful. The outcome of this competition is said to have resulted in the start of the infamous Trojan War. Contemporary American beauty pageants trace their roots to newspaper man, P. T. Barnum, who held beauty contests for women beginning in 1854 through photographs that were published in newspapers. In 1880, Barnum's concept was expanded, and one of the first bathing beauty pageants was held as part of a summer festival in a resort in Delaware. Over time, bathing beauty pageants and pageants of other various sorts were held in many locales. The most illustrious of these pageants was held in 1921 in Atlantic City in an attempt to attract business to the resorts and boardwalk following the usual labor-day decline. Women from across the country were invited to participate in a competition for bathing beauties, and it was determined that the winner would be crowned Miss America (Savage 1998). Only eight women actually entered the contest and 16-year-old Margaret Gorman, from Washington, D.C., was crowned the winner and draped in an American flag. Miss America's symbolic fate as both ideal beauty and patriot was sealed at her inception.

By 1923, more than 70 women competed in what was now called the National Beauty Tournament in Atlantic City. Two main rules for the pageant developed after this event: contestants must not be married and they must reside in the locale they represent. These rules were enacted after it was discovered that Miss Alaska, Helmar Leiderman, was not only married, but also a resident of New York City (Pageant Center 2007).

The tournament continued on and off throughout the 1920s and early 1930s. It was temporarily stopped during the Great Depression after receiving bad press that women's morals were being corrupted by displaying themselves publicly in bathing suits (Savage 1998). In 1935, Lenora Slaughter was hired as the first female director of the tournament. Under her strong leadership, it was revived and emerged with a new name, the Miss America pageant. During these early years, the contest added a talent competition and winners received Hollywood screen tests and Hollywood agents (Pageant Center 2007).

The Miss America pageant persisted through World War II, with the public supporting it and believing that it brought hope to American troops (Savage 1998). In 1945, Ms. Slaughter implemented a scholarship program to help contestants enter college, a dream most American women could not achieve. Despite the protests of newspaper reporters in 1948, Miss America was now crowned in a gown, instead of a bathing suit. The debate over the necessity of bathing suit appearances became hotly contested again in 1951, after Yolanda Betbeze, the newly crowned Miss America, refused to do promotions in a bathing suit, maintaining that she was a classical opera singer and not a pinup girl. Catalina swimwear, the major sponsor of the pageant, ended its partnership after Betbeze's refusal and began its own pageant, Miss USA, as well as its international sister pageant, Miss Universe. All three pageants continued to thrive in the 1950s and as American society became enamored with British royalty, the pageant beauty queens, who were crowned with tiaras and adorned with roses, were themselves elevated to a comparable level. Another major development in pageant history occurred when the Miss America competition aired live on television for the first time on September 10, 1954, bringing in a record-breaking 27 million viewers, accounting for 39 percent of the television audience (Miss America Organization 2007).

1960s TO THE PRESENT: BEAUTY PAGEANTS AND WOMEN'S LIBERATION

The 1960s and 1970s brought the first strong and enduring criticisms of pageants. In 1968, in the early stages of the women's liberation movement, approximately 200 feminists staged a rally on the boardwalk in front of the Atlantic City venue of the Miss America pageant. They demanded an immediate end to beauty pageants, alleging they were sexist, racist, and a vehicle for corporations to continue the capitalist patriarchy. Because the pageant is a media magnet, the protest surrounding it quickly gathered infamy and alerted the world to the presence of feminists and other women who would no longer participate in enslavement to idealized beauty standards (Morgan 1970). It was not until 1970 that an African American woman, Cheryl Browne, won a state title, allowing her to compete in the Miss America competition. It would be another 20 years before African American women held national titles for an entire year: Carol Gist was Miss USA and Debbye Turner was Miss America in 1990 (Pageant Center 2007).

The 1960s and 1970s also spawned spin-offs of pageants for younger girls. Little Miss... pageants and Miss Teenage America both began in the early 1960s. These pageants continue to be controversial and are critiqued for their portrayal of sexualizing young girls, as the children often wear heavy make up and dress in adult-style fashions. The child-pageant industry has evolved into a force all its own, however, contributing approximately $5 billion annually to the American economy (Giroux 1998). A glaring spotlight was shown on the child pageant

---

MISS AMERICA 1926, NORMA SMALLWOOD

Did you know that Miss America 1926, Norma Smallwood, made more than $100,000 in appearance fees? Her income was higher than both baseball superstar Babe Ruth and the President of the United States (American Experience 2007).

---

industry after the 1996 sexual assault and murder of six-year-old "beauty queen" JonBenet Ramsey. As details emerged about the child's involvement in pageantry, the media exploded with stories of alleged child abuse related to pageant participation.

CURRENT CONTROVERSIES AND TRENDS

In recent years, there have been a series of scandals among pageant winners that have again caught the media's attention. The most famous scandal centered on Vanessa Williams, the first African American woman to win Miss America. Her crown was removed in 1984 after nude photos of her that were taken three years before were published half-way through her reign. The most current scandal involved Miss USA 2006, Tara Conner, who is alleged to have participated in underage drinking (she was only 20 when crowned), cocaine use, and promiscuous sex. This is particularly ironic, as Miss Conner's platform issue was drunk driving.

Pageants have also created international sensation and debate, which unfortunately turned deadly in 2001. The Miss World contest (Miss Universe's rival), which is the globe's largest live annual television event, with viewing figures topping 2 billion across more than 200 countries, was to be held in the Nigerian capital of Abuja that year (Olsen 2002). Approximately 12 days before the pageant, a newspaper suggested that Islam's founding prophet, Muhammad, would have likely chosen a wife from among the contest. Outraged, some fundamentalist Muslim groups denounced the pageant for promoting sexual promiscuity and indecency and angry mobs responded, leading to widespread rioting that resulted in the death of between 50 and 100 people (Olsen 2002). The event was quickly moved to London. It can no longer be said that pageants are simply harmless fun.

ADVOCATES OF BEAUTY PAGEANTS

Although many believe that beauty pageants no longer have a place in today's society, their supporters contend that pageants "are in the business of making dreams come true" (Bivans 1995, 1). They believe that pageants are not just for showcasing a woman's beauty, but also her intellect and talent. Furthermore, they think that pageants allow women extraordinary opportunities to develop both personally and professionally. The Miss America Organization states that it has "maintained a tradition for many decades of empowering American women to achieve their personal and professional goals, while providing a forum in which to express their opinions, talent, and intelligence" (Miss America 2007).

Many women enter beauty pageants for the financial gain that comes with winning a crown. Each year, the Miss America Organization awards more than $45 million in cash and scholarship assistance (Miss America Organization 2007). Lenora Slaughter, who initiated the scholarship program with only $5,000 in 1945, said she began it because she couldn't finish college herself as a result of the Great Depression and it was the dream she never achieved. Her dream has been recognized for the women who win her contest at least. Many winners of Miss America and other pageants are now able to pay for their entire college and graduate school education with their prize money. They have gone on to become professors, doctors, lawyers, pharmacists, entertainers, and politicians, among other professionals.

Also, titleholders at state and national levels can earn high personal incomes for their appearances during their reign. In addition to appearance fees, many winners receive prize packages, publicity, or corporate contracts (e.g., Miss America, Miss USA, and Miss Universe each receives a one-year contract with their sponsoring organization and represents their company during that time; perks include first-class travel and luxury accommodations, hosting charity events, new wardrobes, jewelry, etc.). A large number of contestants use the pageants to launch their careers in entertainment. Former beauty queens include media moguls Diane Sawyer, host of *60 Minutes* and *Prime Time Live* (former America's Junior Miss) and Oprah Winfrey (former Miss Fire Prevention and Miss Black Tennessee), as well as actresses Cybill Shepard, Sharon Stone, Morgan Fairchild, Halle Berry, and Vanessa Williams (Bivans 1995).

Pageants also provide women with the opportunity to develop strong communication skills and to "sell" themselves, skills they likely need to make themselves marketable employees in their chosen career fields. In 1989, the Miss America Organization founded the platform concept, which "requires each contestant to choose an issue about which she cares deeply and is of relevance in our society" (Miss America Organization 2007). Once Miss America is chosen, she uses her title to advance the platform issue during her reign. The Miss Universe and Miss USA pageants have devoted their titleholders to attend to two of the major health crises facing contemporary women: breast/ovarian cancer and the global AIDS pandemic. Titleholders have made real advancements for people in their communities related to these issues. For example, Mpule Kwelagobe, Miss Universe 2000, created a not-for-profit foundation during her reign that funded and built a 400-bed pediatric AIDS hospital and orphanage in her native Botswana, which has been ravaged by the AIDS epidemic (Miss USA 2007).

Although all of these benefits lead young women around the world to participate in pageants, there is something to be said about being deemed the "most beautiful," which may be enough of a reason for some to participate. And being the most beautiful is no simple task. For some pageant participants, a national or international title is the ultimate goal. They spend years refining their appearance, some choosing cosmetic surgery to enhance their natural beauty while others use professional coaches to aid them on their quest for the crown.

For pageant participants, parents, judges, and promoters, success is the final word. They believe that pageants create successful women. A study published by *USA Today* linked pageant participation with increased personal development (Bivans 1995). Ann-Marie Bivans, a renowned Miss America judge, states, "The bottom line is that the quest for the crown is not about the tearful victory-walk down an illuminated runway with the crown and roses. Pageantry, ultimately, is about using the process of competition to pursue and achieve an extraordinary life personally and professionally" (Bivans 1995, 10).

CRITICAL PERSPECTIVES ON BEAUTY PAGEANTS

At their heart, beauty pageants are a paradox. On the one hand, pageants glorify an idealized female physicality and sexuality, and on the other hand they demand contestants' participation in enforcing a conservative morality about female sexuality (i.e., contestants must act in "moral" ways, they must not be married or divorced, they must not have any children, etc.). It is no wonder then that as long as beauty pageants have existed, so, too, has criticism of them.

The 1920s are often held as the "first wave" of American feminism, as the hard work of suffragists finally paid off and women were granted the right to vote in federal elections. Women shed the shroud of Victorian-era sexual politics that relegated them to the home. Many began working, and it was not uncommon to find young women cutting their hair into the flapper style and dancing the night away at jazz clubs. It was this new generation of women who were bold enough to enter bathing beauty competitions (Savage 1998). As women's roles at this time continued to shift, so did their fashion choices. They began to show more skin and initial criticism of beauty pageants centered on this impropriety. In fact, a woman could still be sent to jail in the 1920s for baring too much of her legs (Savage 1998). Then came the Great Depression followed by years of war. A backlash to early feminism began as men demanded their jobs back from women when they returned to the home front. For American women in the 1950s, opportunities were again limited and pageants were popularized as a way for women to achieve the life they would normally not be able to. But a backlash to the backlash had begun, and the 1960s ushered in the strongest wave of feminism yet. The Miss America pageant became one of its launching pads.

The infamous 1968 Atlantic City protest of the Miss America pageant was begun by a small group of radical women from New York City. On the boardwalk in front of the Convention Hall, approximately 200 women participated in a pageant of their own making where they crowned a sheep, hurdled oppressive feminine materials into a Freedom Trash can (e.g., girdles, curlers, false eyelashes), and held a women's liberation rally at midnight, when Miss America was being crowned (Savage 1998). They released a 10-point manifesto that

MISS AMERICA AS DREAM EQUIVALENT TO—?

"In this reputedly democratic society where every little boy supposedly can grow up to be President, what can every little girl hope to grow up to be? Miss America? That's where it's at. Real power to control our own lives is restricted to men, while women get patronizing pseudo-power, an ermine clock, and a bunch of flowers; men are judged by their actions, women by their appearance." This is the ninth principle of the 1968 feminist protest of the Miss America pageant (Morgan 1979, 523–524).

laid out the principles of their protest and included a focus on the connections between "ludicrous beauty standards," racism, militarism, popular culture, and capitalism (Morgan 1979). Miss America (and all beauty pageants) were seen as the perfect symbol of female oppression in this country supported by both racism and capitalism. It had long been noted that the women who wore the sashes on stage did not represent just themselves. "The women who are parading around... are being displayed to someone else's glory and profit... their sashes do not say Ms. Jane Doe, but Miss Fresno, Miss Huntington Beach. They are displayed as exemplary products of the economy of their home town." (Savage 1998, 2).

African American women first began their opposition to mainstream beauty pageants like Miss America by staging their own beauty pageants, which were often sponsored by the local branch of the National Association for the Advancement of Colored People. And even though these contests were popular among African Americans, black women thought that they were relegated to second-class status because they could not participate in all-white pageants. They began to organize and started to put political pressure on corporate sponsors to allow African American women to participate in pageants that discriminated against them. You will recall that it was not until 1984 that an African American woman, Vanessa Williams, temporarily held the Miss America crown. Although seeking equal participation in pageants was one form of protest, some African American women opposed them all together, perceiving a stronger relationship between racism and sexism. They believed all women were oppressed by pageants, regardless of whether the crowned queen was black or white.

Although the protests in general continued into the 1970s, they really didn't seem to have a large-scale effect until 1977, when ratings for both Miss America and Miss Universe plummeted. By 1984, the historic year when Vanessa Williams was crowned Miss America, the pageant had only half its typical audience remaining (Savage 1998). It is still debated whether this was the effects of feminism catching up to mainstream society or whether people were just getting tired of pageants and what some viewed as their "outdated" fashions and acts. Even former beauty queens themselves had turned on pageantry. In 1985, Ann Simonton, a model and former crowned beauty queen, was arrested for attempting to incite a riot after she and another protestor splashed their own blood on a sidewalk outside of the Miss California pageant. Simonton's perspective on beauty pageants and their media connections drastically changed after she was gang-raped on her way to a photo shoot some years earlier. She has since founded *Media Watch,* a nonprofit organization dedicated to exposing racism, sexism, and corporate propaganda in the media (Savage 1998).

Criticism of pageants continued in the 1990s, gaining attention again after the murder of JonBenet Ramsey. All of this has resulted in lower ratings every year for beauty pageants. In 2004, for which the last ratings were released, only 9.8 million people tuned in to watch Miss America. The live televised event was cut by one-third its usual airtime.

CONCLUSION

In response to their critics, Miss America and other pageants revamped their identities and now hold themselves to be organizations focused on scholarships and empowerment for women. Even the beauty queens themselves admit, though, that a beauty pageant is still about idealized female beauty. Miss America 1993, Leanza Cornett, contends, "I used to tell everyone, 'it's not a beauty pageant…it's not a beauty pageant…' but hey, if it looks like a duck and walks like a duck, it is a duck" (Savage 1998, 117). Although ratings for televised beauty pageants are at their lowest ever, pageants persevere and new pageants are regularly added to the local, state, national, and international levels. America's love/hate affair with this cultural institution continues and the new century will likely determine its fate.

See also Barbie and the Feminine Ideal of Beauty; Beauty Industry; Femininities and Masculinities; Media Images of Women: Television and Film.

Further Reading: *American Experience,* "Miss America," available at: http://www.pbs.org/wgbh/amex/missamerica/timeline/index.html, accessed February 12, 2007; Bivans, Ann-Marie, *101 Secrets to Winning Beauty Pageants* (New York: Citadel Press, 1995); Craig, Maxine Leeds, *Ain't I a Beauty Queen: Black Women, Beauty, and the Politics of Race* (New York: Oxford University Press, 2002); Giroux, Henry A., "Nymphet Fantasies: Child Beauty Pageants and the Politics of Innocence," *Social Text* no. 57 (Winter 1998): 31–53; Morgan, Robin, ed., *Sisterhood Is Powerful: An Anthology of Writings from the Women's Liberation Movement* (New York: Vintage Books, 1979); "The History of Pageants," available at: http://pageantcenter.com/history.html, accessed February 12, 2007; The Official Site of Miss USA and Miss Universe, available at: http://www.missusa.com, accessed February 12, 2007; The Official Site of the Miss America Organization, available at: http://www.missamerica.org, accessed February 12, 2007; Olsen, Eric, "Nigerian Riots Kill at Least 100," 2002, available at: http://blogcritics.org/archives/2002/11/22/103248.php, accessed February 12, 2007; Savage, Candace, *Beauty Queens: A Playful History* (New York: Abbeville Press Publishers, 1998); Watson, Elwood, and Darcy Martin, eds., *"There She Is, Miss America:" The Politics of Sex, Beauty, and Race in America's Most Famous Pageant* (New York: Palgrave McMillan, 2004); Wolf, Naomi, *The Beauty Myth: How Images of Beauty Are Used against Women* (New York: William Morrow and Company, Inc., 1991).

Jeanette Koncikowski

BIRTH CONTROL

In the twenty-first century, women face numerous options for controlling their fertility, from barrier methods to hormonal contraceptives. Yet despite an increase of choices, birth control remains controversial and fraught with complications. More and more women have come to rely on hormonal methods, which are highly effective in terms of preventing pregnancy, but also introduce new health risks and side effects into otherwise healthy patient populations. In addition, the question of "choice" has become more complex, as individuals and groups debate the safety and legitimacy of certain types of hormonal contraceptives, as well as their use on minority populations and the disabled.

BACKGROUND

The term *birth control* was coined by Margaret Sanger, the leading activist in the United States for contraceptive prevention in the twentieth century. In Sanger's view, the movement began on the day that one of her patients, Sadie Sachs, died from an induced abortion. At that time, Sanger was a 29-year-old mother of three, working as a public health nurse in New York City's lower East Side. Specializing in obstetrics, she witnessed women struggling to deliver and raise baby after baby in crowded urban conditions with little money or power. She recalls the number of women who begged her to tell them the "secret" to preventing conception. All she could recommend, however, were condoms or withdrawal, both of which required the cooperation of the male partner. One day, she was called to the home of a young Jewish immigrant living in a tenement on Hester Street. Sadie Sachs, mother of three, was suffering from complications of a self-induced septic abortion. Sanger recalled the accompanying doctor's response to Sachs's plea not to have another child: to tell her husband to "sleep on the roof" (Chesler 1992). Three months later, Sanger was again called to the home of Sadie Sachs, pregnant again and dying of septicemia.

Sanger retold this story frequently over the course of her activist career, in part to emphasize class-based restrictions on fertility control. It was the poor women, the ones most in need of education and access to birth control, who were the least likely to get it. She vowed to make this her lifelong crusade—making birth control accessible to all women. She began publishing *The Woman Rebel* in 1914, a magazine intended for working women to educate them about sexuality and contraception. She also used it to challenge the Comstock Law, in effect since 1873, which prohibited the importation and mailing of contraceptive information and devices in the United States. It was in her magazine that she chose the term *birth control* to replace more awkward phrases such as *family limitation* or *voluntary motherhood.* (Chesler 1992). After seven issues of the magazine, the paper was shut down, deemed "unmailable" by the U.S. Post Office (under the Comstock Obscenity Laws).

But Sanger was not to be deterred. She then published a pamphlet entitled "Family Limitation" to be distributed to poor women. The pamphlet provided information about barrier methods, including condoms and cervical caps. Again in trouble for producing and disseminating literature labeled obscene by the federal government, she fled to Europe, leaving her husband to distribute 100,000 copies. In her absence, husband William Sanger was arrested for violation of the Comstock Law. Ironically, it was one of the last arrests Anthony Comstock would make; at Sanger's trial, Comstock caught a cold and died of pneumonia shortly thereafter (Tone 2001).

Margaret Sanger returned from Europe interested in opening the first birth control clinic in the United States, but she still faced several challenges. The main obstacle was the continued illegality of contraceptive marketing and

SUFFRAGISTS AND "PROMISCUITY"

Even many feminist activists did not believe that promoting women's right to sexual freedom would further their cause in the early twentieth century. For example, both the National Woman's Party and the League of Women Voters (LWV) refused to support birth control because it "clashed with their conceptions of femininity, maternity, and progress." In 1924, the LWV voted to study sterilization of the unfit as a strategy to reduce degeneracy, but it refused to include birth control as part of the study, owing to its controversial nature. Because opponents attacked women's suffrage as a threat to family life, suffragists wanted to avoid any controversial issues that "smacked of promiscuity" (McCann 1994).

distribution. The most effective contraceptive devices currently available in Europe could not be legally transported to the United States. Nonetheless, she opened the first birth control clinic in Brownsville, New York, in 1916. Although it did not stay open for long, the experience made her realize the importance of obtaining medical support for birth control, and so she began to shift strategies.

THE MEDICALIZATION OF BIRTH CONTROL

Although birth control was not openly discussed in public in the early twentieth century, there was plenty of evidence that it was already in use, at least within certain socioeconomic groups. College-educated middle-class white women demonstrated by a dramatic drop in fertility that they were practicing some form of birth control in the 1920s. Katharine Bement Davis's massive 10-year study (published in 1929), *Factors in the Sex Lives of Twenty-two Hundred Women,* revealed the extent to which certain women were familiar with forms of birth control. A total of 74 percent of 1,000 college-educated women queried admitted to using some form of contraception, despite the fact that information on birth control had "virtually been driven underground."

Many middle-class social reformers couched their concern in eugenic terms, fearing that the Anglo-Saxon population would soon be overcome by immigrants and African Americans. Over the course of the century, the white middle-class birthrate had dropped by nearly half, from seven to just over three children. Teddy Roosevelt and others had sparked a widespread concern about "race suicide" at the turn of the century, but the white middle-class birthrate dropped even lower in the 1920s. The rate of childlessness reached a record high in the 1920s and 1930s, and the birth rate would not actually begin to increase until the postwar era (May 1995).

Although the declining birthrate demonstrated that many (predominantly in the middle and upper classes) still managed to gain access to birth control, it was not widely talked about in public. Most professionals, including physicians and even feminists, avoided such a controversial topic, which they believed might undermine their credibility. "I regret to say that I cannot give the use of my name in connection with your work," psychologist G. Stanley Hall explained to the Massachusetts Birth Control League in 1916. "If you want to know why, I will tell you frankly that I have borne my share of *odium sexicum*.... I have done my bit in this movement and now I am retiring and am going to have a rest from this trouble for the remainder of my life" (Reed 1978).

Physicians, as James Reed points out, had "no strong motive for a positive attitude toward birth control," often because they, too, were concerned about the declining birth rate and the change in sexual mores. As a result, they "betrayed a startling reticence and lack of information on the subject." They often perceived contraceptives as both morally and physically dangerous. Since its antiabortion campaign in the 1870s, the profession regarded itself as "the gatekeepers of women's virtue" (Reed 1978, Chesler 1992).

Given the reluctance of medical professionals (and even many feminists) to support her cause, Sanger took another approach. Rather than directly challenging the Comstock Law, she sought to reform it. She toned down her argument that women had a right to control their own bodies, instead marketing her crusade as a public health campaign. She began pushing for a "doctors only" bill that would exempt doctors from criminal prosecution. Eventually, this strategy would prove effective. With massive financial background from her wealthy second husband, Noah Slee, Sanger helped to establish the first birth control firm that would sell birth control devices directly to doctors, the Holland-Rantos Company (Tone 2001). This encouraged more doctors to support the medicalization of birth control, providing a financial incentive. For example, they could purchase diaphragms directly from Holland-Rantos, then prescribe them to their patients at a profit. In the 1930s, for example, doctors marked up the price of individual diaphragms anywhere from 75 cents to more than $3, depending on the design (Tone 2001).

Two events in the 1930s further legitimized the use of physician-controlled contraceptive use. First, in a landmark decision, the Comstock Law was modified in 1936 to allow physicians (only) to order contraceptives through the mail. Second, the American Medical Association voted in the following year to endorse physician-prescribed contraceptives. As a result, birth control gained legitimacy in the eyes of many. In the process, however, birth control fell under the direction of doctors rather than women, a far cry from what many had envisioned.

HORMONAL CONTRACEPTIVES

The medicalization of birth control remains today. If anything, the introduction of hormonal contraceptives has guaranteed that birth control will remain steadfastly under the control of doctors and the regulation of the Food and Drug Administration (FDA). With the introduction of the FDA-approved birth control pill in 1960, debates about contraceptive use took on a whole new turn. Emerging at the dawn of the sexual revolution, the pill raised expectations that women were sexually available. By 1965, more than 6 million women had taken oral contraceptives. Planned Parenthood noted that 70 percent of all women using its services for birth control chose to get a prescription for the pill. By

1990, more than 80 percent of American women born in the postwar era had tried it (Watkins 1998). The pill offered many advantages over barrier methods of birth control: it was highly effective, convenient, and entirely separated from the act of intercourse. It also did not require the consent or even awareness of a male sexual partner. Both doctors and female patients initially expressed enthusiasm for this new form of birth control.

Yet by the end of the 1960s, many had lost confidence in this new form of birth control. The first pill, Enovid, contained approximately 10 times the amount of progesterone and four times the amount of estrogen used in later doses. As a result, many women suffered from severe side effects, including blood clots and heart attacks. In 1969, the U.S. Senate conducted hearings on the safety of the pill, resulting in a requirement that makers of the product include a patient package insert warning of potential side effects of the pill. Pill use subsequently dropped by 20 percent, but it remained the most popular contraceptive.

THE DEPO-PROVERA DEBATE

Other controversies continued to complicate the debate surrounding hormonal contraceptives. Growing cynicism and a rising women's health movement raised new questions regarding the validity of prescribing hormonal contraceptives to millions of healthy women. Many accused scientists and doctors of using women as guinea pigs whose health was expendable in the name of scientific research. Nowhere did this seem more evident than in the clinical trials of Depo-Provera at Grady hospital.

From 1972 to 1978, the Grady Family Planning Clinic in downtown Atlanta, Georgia, was the largest site for U.S.-based clinical trials of Depo-Provera, an injectable hormonal contraceptive manufactured by the Upjohn Company beginning in 1967. Dr. Robert Hatcher, known to his friends and family as "Captain Condom," oversaw the trials as director of the clinic and remains on the faculty at Emory University, in the department of obstetrics and gynecology (http://gynob.emory.edu/familyplanning/hatcherbio.cfm). Approximately 9,000 mostly poor African American women were injected with Depo-Provera as part of the study, before it was terminated by the FDA in 1978. The Grady trials, along with investigational drug itself, quickly became controversial. Supporters and opponents, policymakers, researchers, activists, and users of the drug constructed competing narratives about the drug's true nature beginning in the 1970s. They debated whether Grady patients were victims of racist policies that endangered their health or recipients of a "superb contraceptive," in Dr. Hatcher's words (Hatcher 1978). More generally, they questioned whether Depo-Provera was a dangerous tool for population control advocates or a crucial form of birth control for women in need of greater choice.

Depo-Provera was certainly not the first controversial form of birth control, nor would it be the last. But its potential for abuse as an irreversible injectable, and its long limbo status—25 years between its initial marketing and FDA approval in 1992—speak to its significance in the history of drug regulation and women's health, and to the power of protest to dramatically lengthen the FDA approval process. The controversy erupted in a decade of scandals, running from Watergate to flammable children's pajamas, to a consumer audience now quite familiar with the politics of deception and well versed in the language of rights. It was fueled by the recent health scandal surrounding the pill, which lay the groundwork for widespread suspicion that pharmaceutical companies were not to be trusted, particularly when it came to contraception and women's bodies.

The debate over Depo-Provera spoke to the increasing complexity of reproductive regulation. In the 1970s, consumers demanded access to and involvement in regulatory decisions previously considered beyond their purview. Women's health activists, newly armed with political, legal, and medical expertise, introduced new evidence to the process: patient testimonials. They thus guaranteed that women's experiences, rather than just those of beagle dogs and rhesus monkeys, became part of the scientific testimony presented before the FDA on numerous occasions. They also altered the process of risk-benefit analysis by challenging the notion of value-free, objective science. Weighing the risks and benefits of a drug, particularly one prescribed to millions of healthy patients, required not just statistics but stories, they argued. Consider one woman's assessment: "I still think of those long dark months of trying to cope with the effects of a drug that I would never knowingly have allowed in my body, a drug that has such limited use that it should not be allowed on the market, lest it be used and abused on other women such as myself" (patient testimony, FDA hearings).

At the Grady clinic, patients were offered Depo-Provera "cafeteria-style," along with birth control pills, intrauterine devices, diaphragms, foams, and condoms. Despite the fact that it was an investigational new drug, it was offered to patients as one of many birth control options. But Dr. Hatcher stressed that Grady patients received detailed instructions and signed a consent form before choosing the drug. "Education is a very, very important component of our family planning activities at Grady," he emphasized. "We not only make efforts to assure that our patients understand the contraceptives they choose to use, but we expect them to act as the captain of their own health team—to be, as it were, their own best friend in a medical sense." (Hatcher 1978). Such language suggests that he had learned much from the women's health movement, although his use of Depo at Grady was chastised by many health feminists. Assuming that all patients really read and understood the consent form, they were aware of its purpose—to prevent pregnancy—that it required repeated injections of the synthetic progesterone every 90 days, that large doses of it had caused breast cancer in some beagle dogs, that other, nonexperimental methods were available, and that they might experience some severe side effects.

In his own analysis, Hatcher found that Grady patients were quite enthusiastic about the drug, stressing its convenience and reliability during interviews conducted in 1978. "I want the 'shot,'" stated one. "I don't want to use the pill or anything else. I'd go crazy; I'd worry all the time about getting pregnant. If they said no more Depo I'd cry. I used it for five years, stopped and got pregnant one year later. I've been using it again now for one year. It's the only thing I trust." Far from sounding like a victim, this patient clearly felt empowered by her ability to receive the injections. "The shot's the best for me, announced another Grady patient. "I've used it for two years; if they stopped it I'd go through the floor... It's our choice, not the Government's." Note her emphasis on choice, suggesting not only that she was *not* coerced into receiving Depo injections, but that she believed accessibility was central to reproductive choice.

But opponents defined reproductive choice differently, particularly when it came to investigational drugs. At a 1979 conference on the ethics of reproductive technology on a Depo-Provera panel, academic Joyce Berkman suggested that "we need to think about setting limits to the notion of absolute reproductive choice and a completely free cafeteria situation" (Holmes et al. 1981:13). Health activist Gena Corea put it even more strongly when she testified before an FDA-appointed scientific board of inquiry that women who believed they were freely choosing Depo were victims of a patriarchy that controlled consciousness, rendering "vital facets of reality" invisible (Corea 1983). In other words, they were duped; there was no real "choice" here.

For health feminists and consumer activists, the Grady trials were a call to arms. The National Women's Health Network launched a campaign for drug safety against Depo. They issued news alerts, placed ads in women's magazines such as *Redbook* encouraging so-called victims to participate in their Depo-Provera registry, sent letters to radio stations and black newspapers, and staged news conferences. Together with Public Citizen's Health Research Group and the Black Women's Health Project, they fought to keep Depo-Provera from being approved as a form of contraception.

Those arguing both for and against the FDA approval of Depo-Provera beginning in the 1970s were forced to simplify a complex problem involving gender, race, class, reproductive technology, and drug regulation into a basic yes-or-no question: Should Depo-Provera be made available to women in the United States as a contraceptive? The most effective way to answer the question, initiated first by women's health activists, was to turn to the patients themselves, whose stories vividly portrayed the way in which Depo had either saved or destroyed their lives. In the process, these two groups, supporters and opponents, found themselves inextricably polarized, but not into simple categorizations. Some poor working-class women loved Depo, and some powerful doctors opposed it.

CONCLUSION

Although Depo-Provera finally received FDA approval in 1992, the story did not end there. FDA announced a label change for Depo as a result of data on the drug submitted by now-owner Pfizer. Included a black box warning linking prolonged use with loss of bone density (and thus the potential to develop osteoporosis), and a warning that Depo-Provera should not be used for more than two years "unless other birth control methods are inadequate" (FDA 2004). New evidence continues to raise questions about cancer risks, and of course, the side effects remain a problem for many users. The question of whether women should have freedom from Depo or freedom to use Depo continues to be pervasive in American society. More generally, this case study illustrates the complex nature of birth control in

American society. In addition to potential health risks from certain types of birth control, the question of how to balance accessibility with protection from abuse on certain patient populations continues to divide the feminist community.

See also Abortion; Birthing Practices; Population Policy.

Further Reading: Brodie, Janet, *Contraception and Abortion in Nineteenth-Century America* (Ithaca: Cornell University Press, 1997); Chesler, Ellen, *Woman of Valor: Margaret Sanger and the Birth Control Movement in America* (New York: Doubleday, 1992); Corea, Gena, "Depo Provera and the Politics of Knowledge," testimony, FDA hearings, January 1983; D'Emilio, John, and Estelle Freedman, *Intimate Matters: A History of Sexuality in America* (Chicago: University of Chicago Press, 1998); FDA (Food and Drug Administration), "Black Box Warning Added Concerning Long-Term Use of Depo-Provera Contraceptive Injection," FDA Talk Paper, November 17, 2004, http://www.fda.gov/bbs/topics/answers/2004/ANS01325.html, accessed October 3, 2007; Gordon, Linda, *Woman's Body, Woman's Right: Birth Control in America* (New York: Penguin Books, 1990); Hatcher, Robert, "The Depo-Provera Debate," hearings before the select committee on population, August 8, 1978; Holmes, Helen, Betty Hoskins, and Michael Gross, eds., *Birth Control and Controlling Birth: Women-Centered Perspectives* (Totowa, NJ: Humana Press, 1981); May, Elaine Tyler, *Barren in the Promised Land: Childless Americans and the Pursuit of Happiness* (New York: Basic Books, 1995); McCann, Carole, *Birth Control Politics in the United States, 1916–1945* (Ithaca: Cornell University Press, 1994); Reed, James, *From Private Vice to Public Virtue: The Birth Control Movement and American Society since 1830* (New York: Basic Books, 1978); Tone, Andrea, *Devices and Desires: A History of Contraceptives in America* (New York: Hill and Want, 2001); Watkins, Elizabeth, *On the Pill: A Social History of Oral Contraceptives, 1950–1970* (Baltimore: Johns Hopkins University Press, 1998).

Wendy Kline

BIRTHING PRACTICES

In contemporary United States, birthing has become largely medicalized and takes place in hospitals. Supporters of medicalized childbirth contend that appropriately applied technology can enhance the birthing experience and act as a life-saving tool for both mother and baby. In contrast, some mothers and practitioners argue that the use of technology and medical intervention in birth negatively affects women's birthing experiences and therefore advocate for alternatives to the medical model.

BACKGROUND

Birthing entails the beliefs and customs surrounding how, where, and with whom women give birth. Birthing practices vary extensively cross-culturally; location, social structures, access to technology, and cultural or religious beliefs contribute to the social and biological nature of birth. As a rite of passage, or transition from one life phase to the next, in all cultures the ways in which women experience childbirth reveals a great deal about how women are regarded in each society (Davis-Floyd 1992; Jordan 1983; van Gennep 1960; Kitzinger 1978). Feminist debates surrounding childbirth are generally located within critiques of medicalized approaches to pregnancy and labor and the ways in which women are able to subvert or challenge these dominant discourses (Oakley 1980, 1984; Rothman 1988; Martin 1992; Mitford 1992; Davis-Floyd 1992; Zodoroznyj 2001). Supporters of medicalized childbirth contend that appropriately applied technology can enhance the birthing experience, empower women, and act as a life-saving tool for both mother and baby. Many pregnant women desire and even require the presence of technology and intervention during birth. In contrast, feminist scholars argue that the use of technology and medical intervention in birth negatively affects women's birthing experiences. For example, it is often argued that the techniques and technologies of biomedicine are privileged over women's bodily knowledge. Ann Oakley (1980, 1984) argues that women who experience high degrees of intervention (for example, the use of forceps or pain-killing drugs) during labor are less satisfied with their birth outcomes and are more inclined to experience postnatal depression as a result.

BIRTHING: A BRIEF HISTORY

Historically, birth has been a social event. Women gave birth at home with the aid of midwives or other female family members. With industrialization during the late nineteenth and early twentieth centuries, pivotal changes transformed the American lifestyle. Urbanization, new modes of transportation, shifting social and political values, the increase in life expectancy, and decrease in maternal and infant mortality paved the way for medicine to become intimately associated with broader social life. As childbirth fell under the domain of obstetricians, women's bodies were increasingly perceived as pathological or "sick" and in need of medical management by male doctors. For example, in 1900, fewer than 5 percent of women gave birth in hospitals, whereas approximately 99 percent of American women deliver in hospitals today (Davis-Floyd 1992).

This shift in attitude toward the medicalization of women's bodies stems from historical notions of women's bodies as being associated with "nature." Women are seen as being prone to more physical illness under male medical definitions. This is an example of how medical definitions are gendered. Medicalization occurs when a medical definition or treatment is used for the management of a problem. The pathologizing of women's bodies has been attributed to class differences between women, as well as to the economic or commercial self-interest of obstetricians. For example, poor and working-class women were more immune to extensive medical intervention during pregnancy and birth because they had less leisure time and fewer resources to pay for medical treatment even though they were much more susceptible to hazards with pregnancy resulting from sickness, exhaustion, and even death from complicated labor or multiple births (Ehrenreich and English 1978). The bodies of middle- and upper-class women became the targets of medical intervention as a result of their "nervous" and "fragile" conditions arising from a refined lifestyle.

By the mid-1800s in the United States, more women went to hospitals for childbirth as medical advances invited reliance on doctors and technology to manage pregnancy and labor. In particular, it was the perceived loss of control of the body and the pain of birth that motivated many upper-class women to give birth in hospitals under total anesthesia. The pain-relieving drug scopolamine was introduced in Germany in the 1930s and was widely used until the 1950s when tales of its abuse became rampant in women's magazines (Davis-Floyd and Sargent 1997). The drug did not cause women to become unconscious but supposedly induced women into animal-like fits of rage and hysteria. The 1960s brought with it the Lamaze method of controlled breathing to manage the pain of labor and encouraged women's awareness during childbirth. The feminist and natural childbirth movements of the late 1960s through the 1980s promoted "natural" and unassisted birth, bringing the issue of women's reproductive rights and "choice" to the forefront of American politics. Feminists argued that providing women with more information about their choices in childbirth would empower them. With these social movements came the active involvement of fathers in pregnancy and birth, the resurgence of breastfeeding, and interest in midwifery. By the 1990s, however, medically managed childbirth was and still is a dominant and authoritative force in the United States. Although many women are cautious of interventions in birth and advanced technology, the majority of women desire and accept technology as part of a "normal" birth and see the use of technology in birth as a positive reproductive choice. Many feminists argue that "choices" with regard to reproductive choice are circumscribed primarily by race and class and are based on unequal access to relevant medical knowledge

MURPHY BROWN AND THE POLITICS OF SINGLE MOTHERHOOD IN AMERICA

In May 1992, American television's wildly popular, strong-willed, and intelligent sitcom character, Murphy Brown, gave birth to a son in one of the most widely viewed episodes about childbirth. An estimated 38 million Americans watched Murphy Brown (played by Candice Bergen) give birth out of wedlock, sparking a fierce debate surrounding one of the most controversial issues of the late 1980s and early 1990s in American politics: single motherhood. Airing in concert with the 1992 American presidential campaign, Vice-President Dan Quayle criticized the popular sitcom for supporting single mothers at the expense of fatherhood. Quayle famously stated that Murphy Brown was "mocking the importance of fathers, by bearing a child alone, and calling it just another 'life-style choice' " (*Time* 1992). Quayle's comments ignited a media firestorm; feminists, political commentators, and everyday Americans panned Quayle as being out of touch with modern family values and the rising proportion of American single mothers. The creators of *Murphy Brown* responded to the Quayle speech in a later episode in September 1992, celebrating the diversity of American families and mocking Quayle's remarks (IMDB 2006). As a result of the backlash, Quayle qualified his statement by saying he "had the greatest respect for single mothers" (*Time* 1992).

"Dan Quayle vs. Murphy Brown: The Vice President takes on a TV Character over 'Family Values'," *Time Magazine*, June 1, 1992, 28.

(Haraway 1991). Yet, as the appropriateness of the biomedical model for birth is increasingly questioned globally, more holistic birthing practices are becoming preferable alternatives. Today, less than 10 percent of American women rely on holistic birthing practices (homebirth, midwives, birthing centers) compared to 90 percent of women who give birth in hospitals, indicating the overwhelming dominance of the medical model.

THE MEDICAL MODEL OF BIRTH

American childbirth is typically characterized by medical management. Pregnant women are treated as patients in hospitals under the care of obstetricians or doctors that specialize in birthing. A medicalized birth is also characterized by the use of advanced medical technology and pain medication during delivery.

Medical intervention in childbirth has resulted in a number of positive benefits for childbearing women as a result of advancing medical technology. For example, obstetricians argue that the use of fetal ultrasound during pregnancy, aside from its valuable diagnostic benefits, facilitates a sense of emotional connectedness between mother and fetus. Many pregnant women feel reassured by seeing visual images of the fetus as "proof" that the pregnancy is viable. Ultrasound also allows family members to become more fully engaged with a woman's pregnancy. Moreover, modern obstetric medicine has allowed women to relieve themselves of the pain of childbirth; pain relief can be empowering for birthing women when administered appropriately. Obstetricians also suggest that the advent of hospital birthing has allowed women to deliver safely, especially for those women that are unable to give birth at home or who have serious preexisting medical conditions that require more significant monitoring (for both mother and fetus). Fetal monitoring has significantly reduced morbidity and mortality in the third trimester for women with high-risk pregnancies (ACOG 1999).

As a result of access to higher quality prenatal care, the American infant mortality rate has diminished dramatically since 1965. In 2001, the infant mortality rate was 6.9 deaths per 1,000 live births (Maternal and Child Health Bureau 2003). Hospital birthing has also lowered the rate of maternal mortality significantly to 9.8 deaths per 100,000 live births in 2001 (Maternal and Child Health Bureau 2003). Maternal and infant mortality rates have declined as a result of improved nutrition and hygiene practices, along with new medication, incubators, and surfactants to help premature babies breathe. Also, medical recommendations to put babies to sleep on their backs, as well as encouraging the intake of folic acid during pregnancy to lower rates of spina bifida, have both contributed to lowered infant mortality. There still remains a longstanding discrepancy between Anglo American and African American infant and maternal mortality rates, however, primarily as a result of African American women's poor access to quality medical care. For example, the infant mortality rate of African American babies is nearly 2.5 times that of Anglo American babies (Maternal and Child Health Bureau 2003).

Critics argue that in the medical model, obstetricians become agents of social control, meaning that they hold primary access to specialized technical knowledge. Feminists suggest that birth is treated as a form of production in the medical model, much like a factory. For example, obstetrical literature refers to the uterus as the functional muscle that does the work of labor. The amount of time in labor and the strength of the contractions are used to determine the pace of production (Martin 1992). In this production model, a woman's body is the "machine," the obstetrician is the "mechanic," and the baby is the "product" of labor. The description of childbirth as mechanical establishes the idea that the female body is abnormal and defective and constantly in need of manipulation as it is held against a male standard of health. Many feminists argue that the mechanical medical model is problematic in two ways. First, this model insists on a separation of the mind and the body, also known as Cartesian dualism (Martin 1992). The separation of mind and body suggests that women's bodies are primarily acted on medically through monitoring and assisted delivery while their emotional needs and well-being are secondary. Second, the medical model dichotomizes or separates the mother's body and that of the fetus by positioning them hierarchically; the fetus is privileged as the inherently more interesting patient both technically and medically. Feminists argue that when the mother and fetus are treated as separate patients, the rights of the mother are potentially compromised. The mother should *want* to sacrifice her body, and even her life, for that of the fetus.

Ultimately, with the redefinition of pregnancy and childbirth as a public medical event, American women's reproductive capacities became strictly controlled. A number of contemporary scholars argue that increased technological intervention in pregnancy and childbirth is unnecessary except in high-risk pregnancies and instead reflects a power imbalance between women and doctors, a loss of female agency in reproduction. Some argue that the overwhelming majority of babies are delivered in hospitals because women feel like there are not as many safe alternatives. It is important to note that these scholars do not necessarily think that all technology in birth is inherently "bad"; it is the way in which technology is used in childbirth and its capacity to manage or control women's birthing bodies that is of concern. Essentially, the focus on the baby, or the product of birth, and not the process of childbirth is argued to undermine the experience of birth for the mother (Martin 1992). The health of a newborn baby reflects quality of care; prenatal screening technologies such as amniocentesis, ultrasonography, and monitoring of the fetal heart rate are now routine and necessary components of pregnancy. It is the perception of birth as a "dangerous" process that perpetuates the American cultural perception that a birth that is not medically managed reflects a dangerous disregard for the safety of both mother and baby. Biomedicine encourages women to conform to the tenets of medical knowledge by offering a means to a healthier child, and therefore making women better, more responsible mothers. This suggestion is especially relevant for women 30 years and older who are considered to be at higher risk for birth complications. Older mothers are offered a number of prenatal screening tests such as ultrasound and amniocentesis to ensure the health of the fetus.

CESAREAN BIRTH

As the use of technology during birth (for example, new forms of surveillance and monitoring equipment such as ultrasonography) becomes increasingly more common, feminists worry that the deployment of technology is normalized in pregnancy and birth. For example, this is evidenced by the increasing rates of cesarean sections in "normal" or uncomplicated births. This is the most extreme cultural attempt to legitimate surgical procedure in childbirth. During a cesarean section, an incision is made in the women's abdomen and uterus to remove the baby. Cesareans are usually performed in an emergency as a consequence of unforeseen complications that prevent a vaginal delivery, but some women opt to have an elective or prescheduled surgery.

Many feminists are wary of the rise in cesarean births in many Western countries, especially the United States. This procedure requires the most active management by the obstetrician and the least physical labor by the mother. As forceps, an instrument similar to tongs to aid in delivery, were used previously to speed the delivery process and have largely fallen out of favor in the birth community, the cesarean section has replaced this procedure in upholding the ideology that women are dependent on technology. Previously, the cesarean section was used only in high-risk pregnancies or as a life-saving procedure. Now, as a result of the belief that cesarean sections improve birth outcomes, are more convenient in allowing a woman to control exactly when she will deliver, and avoid the pain of labor, many women elect to have a cesarean section in an uncomplicated pregnancy. For instance, 27.6 percent of births in 2003 were cesarean sections of the 4 million babies born in that year, the highest rate ever recorded. This is an increase from 22.8 percent in 1989 (National Center for Health Statistics 2003). The World Health Organization suggests that cesarean rates between 10 and 15 percent are average, and anything above that in any region is inordinately high (www.who.int). Moreover, the safety and necessity of cesarean births are still under investigation. The risk of maternal death associated with cesarean delivery is 26 times greater than vaginal delivery and the extreme discomfort after a cesarean section, categorized as major abdominal surgery, is often more debilitating and requires far more recovery time (at least 6 weeks) compared with the recovery associated with vaginal delivery. As biomedicine argues for the use of the cesarean section because it is convenient, safe, and eliminates the pain of childbirth, and increasingly more American women are choosing to undergo the procedure, many feminists argue that the protection of certainty and medical control constitutes a cultural prescription for what childbirth *should be* and uses scientific data or technology rather than women's bodily knowledge to support its use.

ALTERNATIVE APPROACHES TO BIRTH

Despite the predominance of medically managed births, a growing number of American women are not reassured by technology and biomedicine. Resistance to medicalized birth has come in many forms: the homebirth movement, family birthing centers, and midwifery. Whereas the medical model is characterized by the power of medical authority, these alternative models aim to redress the

DID YOU KNOW?

"Lotus birth" is the practice of leaving the placenta attached to the baby until the cord falls off (sometimes up to a few days!). Some mothers argue that leaving the cord uncut results in a less traumatic birth experience for the baby and represents a secure connection to the mother.

biomedical suggestion of incompatibility of the mother and fetus using more holistic and woman-centered approaches to pregnancy and childbirth. Initially, it was the "men with tools" (for example, forceps) that removed childbirth from the domain of female midwives; however, woman-centered birth has always existed as a challenge to the medical model, primarily in home birth or the "natural" childbirth movements.

Midwives generally promote women's reproductive right to have a natural birth that is not controlled by medicine or obstetricians. Women who choose midwives (about 6 percent of American women) often do so because they see a hospital as an obstacle to a meaningful birth experience and the midwife as more than a medical support but an emotional support as well. Midwives aim to empower women during childbirth and see childbirth as a process that ought not to be controlled or managed. For instance, most midwives do not rely heavily on medical measures during the pregnancy, particularly with regard to weight gain or invasive testing.

Midwifery is becoming increasingly professionalized as midwives are being educated in obstetrics and formalizing their "traditional" knowledge as a means of working within and outside of biomedicine and challenging the dominance of the medical model. Midwives are able to work with women in a number of settings other than a woman's own home; many midwives are employed by hospitals and birthing centers. This position of being both outside of and within the medical model can create internal ideological or philosophical struggles for midwives trained to encourage holistic birthing practices while in a modern hospital filled with sophisticated medical technology. Supporters argue that midwifery care generally results in lower rates of intervention during birth, better psychological benefits for women, and lower associated costs than obstetric care (midwives have a 19 percent lower infant mortality rate than obstetricians).

Midwives are predominately involved in home births, which offer women the chance to give birth in the comfort of a familiar environment and the opportunity to practice rituals or relaxation methods with the support of family and friends. Home birth is considered to be as safe as hospital birth with the support of a qualified and knowledgeable midwife or nonmedically trained birth attendant (commonly known as *doula*, originating from the Greek meaning a woman who personally serves another woman) and with a low-risk pregnancy. Women who choose to have a home birth generally avoid technology (for instance, ultrasound) and medical intervention as much as possible. Some women who give birth at home may do so in a birthing pool, known as a water birth. A woman experiences the birth in a pool of body temperature water as a more gentle way of giving birth and introducing the baby into a familiar environment (like the amniotic fluid in the womb). Women can still have a holistic or "natural" birth at a birth center, often a more comfortable alternative for women who do not feel completely assured of the safety of giving birth at home. Despite being affiliated with hospitals, birth centers rely on the knowledge that women's bodies should be trusted during pregnancy and labor and encourage as little intervention as possible during both of these periods. Birth centers encourage the active participation of families in health-related decisions in a familiar and relaxing environment and continuity of care with the support of midwives. Women can have their babies in these facilities safely with the knowledge that medical equipment is available if necessary.

PAIN RELIEF

Generally, women who are supported by midwives often feel that having a natural birth without pain-killing drugs is preferable. This is a direct challenge to the preponderance of pain-relieving drugs, referred to as analgesics (for example, epidural or pethadin), concurrent with vaginal delivery in hospitals where it is assumed that pain of childbirth is negative and must be avoided. Feminists argue that obstetricians in the West encourage pain management because pain is perceived to be a sign of weakness (Davis-Floyd 1992). According to biomedicine, women's bodies are weak and fragile. The pain of childbirth is perceived as being too intense for such inadequately equipped bodies. Returning to the mechanical metaphor, if machines cannot feel pain, women giving birth should not either (Davis-Floyd 1992). Midwives and proponents of natural birth argue that even the word "labor" is a part of medical rhetoric that encourages the mechanistic model. Feminists suggest that obstetricians are sometimes overly willing to administer analgesics without a woman fully understanding the effects of the drugs. For instance, instead of providing support when the labor becomes more difficult, medication is encouraged as a means to avoid contending with the woman and her heightened emotional and physical state. Midwives argue that analgesics distance women from their bodies and their babies and that the use of analgesics reinforces the Cartesian dualism that the body can survive and function without the mind.

Hypnobirthing, or self-hypnosis during birth, is a relatively new technique used by many women who want to avoid pain-killing drugs. Hypnosis is a naturally induced state of relaxation. By using hypnobirthing techniques during pregnancy, women learn to create a natural anesthesia during labor in order to be active participants in birth. Midwives argue that if women are permitted to experience the pain of childbirth, it makes for a more personal and empowering experience; women should try alternative methods for pain management such as walking, yoga, meditation, hypnosis, massage, showers, or controlled breathing. It is argued that pain medication can slow down the labor, lower blood pressure, and possibly put the baby in distress. By completely surrendering to the process of childbirth, proponents of natural childbirth contend the pain of the process is accepted as a birthing force, rhythm, or surge and not a contraction as it is referred to in medical discourse.

Although more natural or noninterventionist methods of childbirth are preferable to a growing number of American women (currently, just under 10 percent), nevertheless, it is problematic to imply that a "natural" childbirth with no pain relief necessarily creates a more meaningful birthing experience for all women. Some feminists argue that the "natural is better" philosophy is equally as prescriptive as the medical model and essentializes women to their reproductive biology. For many women, the use of analgesics or pain relief is preferable and makes birth a less stressful experience. On the other hand, analgesics do not provide complete relief and women who believe that they will feel no pain at all may be feeling like they were misinformed (Davis-Floyd 1992). Ultimately, women have the right not to be in pain and there is a significant cultural pressure for women to avoid pain relief, implying that women who use pain relief have somehow "failed" in their first job as a mother.

CONCLUSION: WHICH BIRTHING PRACTICE IS BEST?

As much as the medical model modifies the bodily knowledge of pregnant and birthing women, women also modify technology and biomedicine. Women are not passive recipients of medical knowledge, and women often need technical information to make informed choices during pregnancy. Obstetricians are becoming increasingly more in tune with women's needs during pregnancy and birth and are encouraging intervention only when necessary. After all, advances

---

THE BOSTON WOMEN'S HEALTH BOOK COLLECTIVE AND *OUR BODIES, OURSELVES*

A feminist classic, *Our Bodies, Ourselves: A Book by and for Women,* arose out of discussions between women about their bodies in 1969 and inspired the women's health movement in the United States. Frustrated with condescending doctors, women from various backgrounds created the nonprofit organization, Boston Women's Health Book Collective, and researched health topics relevant to women. The first full edition of *Our Bodies, Ourselves* was published in 1973; its 12th edition was published in 2005. More than 4 million copies have been sold and the book has been translated into 17 languages and Braille. From the start, *Our Bodies, Ourselves* was based on the model that women's knowledge about their bodies should be made central to their medical experiences, a revolutionary concept for the early 1970s. Thus in each edition, women's personal stories have been included alongside traditional forms of medical knowledge about issues pertaining to women's health. The collective continues to deliver groundbreaking discussions of pregnancy, birth control, and abortion by encouraging women to think about pregnancy and parenthood as issues of choice rather than destiny. Their Web site (http://www.ourbodiesourselves.org) continues to serve as an important educational and advocacy site for women and health practitioners.

---

in medical technology have saved thousands of women and their babies from unnecessary death. A natural approach is understandably powerful and increasingly preferable for some women, but it is important to recognize that women do have choices in childbirth, for example, choosing to have pain-killing drugs during labor or having a baby in a hospital. These choices, however, are often circumscribed by a number of factors including race, class, and sexuality. As feminist scholar Donna Haraway (1991) argues, perhaps there is not a particularly feminist way of understanding reproductive technology or reproductive rights. Rather, understanding how biomedicine is constructed and sustained is a more reasonable project as each woman experiences technology and intervention (or lack thereof) during childbirth differently.

See also Birth Control; Breastfeeding; Fetal Rights; Medicine and Medicalization: Views on Women's Bodies.

Further Reading: American College of Obstetricians and Gynecologists, "Antepartum Fetal Surveillance," *ACOG Practice Bulletin* 9 (1999): 1–11; The Boston Women's Health Book Collective, *Our Bodies, Ourselves: A Book By and For Women* (New York, Simon and Schuster, 2005); Davis-Floyd, R., *Birth as an American Rite of Passage* (Berkeley: University of California Press, 1992); Davis-Floyd, R., and C. Sargent, eds., *Childbirth and Authoritative Knowledge: Cross-cultural Perspectives* (Berkeley: University of California Press, 1997); Ehrenreich, B., and D. English, *Complaints and Disorders: The Sexual Politics of Sickness* (New York: The Feminist Press, 1973); Gennep, A. v., *The Rites of Passage* (London: Routledge and Kegan and Paul, 1960); Haraway, D., *Simians, Cyborgs, and Women: The Reinvention of Nature* (New York: Routledge, 1991); Internet Movie Database (IMDB), "Murphy Brown," 2006, available at: http://www.imdb.com/totle/tt0094514, accessed August 27, 2007; Jordan, B., *Birth in Four Cultures: A Crosscultural Investigation of Childbirth in Yucatan, Holland, Sweden and the United States* (Montreal: Eden Press, 1983); Kitzinger, S., *Women as Mothers* (Oxford: Martin Robertson, 1978); Martin, E., *The Woman in the Body: A Cultural Analysis of Reproduction* (Boston: Beacon Press, 1992); Maternal and Child Health Bureau, "Child Health USA 2003," U.S. Department of Health and Human Services, Health Resources and Services Administration, 2003, available at: http://mchb.hrsa.gov; Mitford, J., *The American Way of Birth* (London: Goliancz Ltd., 1992); National Center for Health Statistics, "National Vital Statistics Reports," U.S. Department of Health and Human Services, Centers for Disease Control and Prevention, 2003, available at: www.cdc.gov/nchs; Oakley, A., *Women Confined: Towards a Sociology of Childbirth* (Oxford: Martin Robertson, 1980); Oakley, A., *The Captured Womb: A History of the Medical Care of Pregnant Women* (Oxford: Basil Blackwell, 1984); Rothman, B. K., *The Tentative Pregnancy: Prenatal Diagnosis and the Future of Motherhood* (London: Pandora, 1988); World Health Organization, "Making Pregnancy Safer," 2006, available at: www.who.int; Zodoroznyj, M., "'Birth and the 'Reflexive Consumer': Trust, Risk and Medical Dominance in Obstetric Encounters" *Journal of Sociology* 37, no. 2 (2001): 117–141.

Meredith Nash

BISEXUALITY

Bisexuality is contested as an authentic sexual identity category by heterosexuals, gays, and lesbians alike. Opponents argue that the sex/gender binary does not support bisexuality; proponents argue that the sex/gender binary is rigid, limiting, and serves only to reinforce biases about bisexuality.

BACKGROUND

Although *gay, lesbian*, and *heterosexual* are commonly recognized in the West as legitimate categories for conceptualizing individual sexual identity, the concept of bisexuality remains contested as an acceptable way to describe one's sexuality. Skeptics ask whether *bisexual* can be a legitimate category in a binary sex/gender structure, whether people who call themselves bisexual are, in actuality, simply in the process of making the transition to a stable gay or lesbian identity or heterosexuals simply "experimenting," and whether bisexual interests should be considered in conjunction with gay and lesbian concerns. Those who consider themselves bisexual argue that theirs is a legitimate sexual identity category, that they face discrimination and invisibility in both heterosexual and gay/lesbian environments, and that bisexual identity is radical in its implications for social life.

WHAT IS BISEXUALITY?

In its broadest sense, the term *bisexual* contains at least three distinctive connotations: (1) to be of two sexes, (2) to engage in sexual behavior with members of two sexes, and (3) to regard an aspect of one's self or one's identity as bisexual. Merl Storr (1999) includes in the range of historical bisexual conceptualizations in the academic literature the additional possibility that one is, psychologically, simultaneously masculine and feminine. In its most common contemporary usage, the term *bisexual* evokes considerations of sexual behavior and sexual identity, and the terms *intersexed* and *transsexual* are more commonly used to describe the experience of having physical characteristics or social identities that include both male and female aspects of biology, and *androgyny* refers to a psychological identity incorporating both masculine and feminine traits. Although the embodied forms of bisexuality attract conflict and controversy, bisexuality-as-behavior and bisexuality-as-identity have provoked nearly continuous and heated debate in both the academic literature and popular culture over the course of the last century. More fundamental than questions about the significance of bisexuality for culture and society are the following three questions about bisexuality: (1) Does bisexuality truly exist? (2) Are there "real" bisexuals? and (3) Are people who call themselves bisexual either confused or in transition to a heterosexual, lesbian, or gay identity?

Contributors to this debate recognize that sexual behaviors and sexual identities may be independent of one another. For example, a woman may identify as lesbian but behave bisexually; conversely, she may identify as bisexual but have sexual relationships with members of only one sex. Although there is much evidence of bisexual behavior cross-culturally and trans-historically, only in modern Western history has an identity formation crystalized around bisexuality. As a result, we may talk about the bisexual behavior of historical figures without defining them as bisexual. In some contexts, women's primary sexual attractions and preferences may be toward women, but social pressures require them to

BISEXUALITY AND STRESS

In a news story reported by the Gay.com/PlanetOut.com News Network in May 2002, there are indications that bisexuals are more likely than straight or gay people to develop mental health difficulties. This conclusion is based on research conducted in Australia and reported in the May 2002 *British Journal of Psychiatry.*

In a three-year study of 4,824 young and middle-age adults, researchers discovered that bisexually identified participants reported "the deepest feelings of anxiety, depression and negativity." According to Gay.com news, the researchers speculate that "It is possible that having neither a clear heterosexual or homosexual orientation is an important stressor, in addition to the social pressures of having a different sexual orientation to the majority."

engage in sexual relationships with men; objectively, their behaviors are heterosexual, but their identities or attractions may be lesbian or bisexual. In other instances, women may acknowledge their attractions to both sexes while limiting their sexual experiences to one sex or the other; objectively, their behaviors appear to be heterosexual or lesbian, but their identity may be bisexual.

In recent decades, controversy has centered on both bisexual identity and bisexual activity. In popular culture, questions of the ontological status of bisexual identity are common. "Do bisexuals really exist?" "Are bi people just afraid to come out?" "Are bisexuals just in a transitional phase?" These questions remain common, as well as vexing, to both those who identify as bisexual and those who are disturbed by the idea of bisexual identities. Independent of concern about the existence of bisexual identity, conflict and controversy about bisexual behavior in the United States in the late twentieth century evolved from the epidemiology of the AIDS crisis, which made clear that the relationships among sexual identities and sexual behaviors are often indeterminate, porous, and unpredictable. To understand bisexuality, bisexual identity, and conflict and controversy attached to them more fully, it is important to examine four broad areas of debate, each fraught with confusion and consternation among those to whom the concept of bisexuality, however defined, makes sense, and those to whom it does not.

ARE WE ALL ESSENTIALLY BISEXUAL IN THE BEGINNING?

Early contributors to the Western conversation on bisexuality were mostly rooted in Europe, where sexology became a serious academic discipline in the late nineteenth and early twentieth centuries. Sexologists first used the term *bisexual* to describe the state of physically possessing traits of both sexes, then to describe being psychologically both masculine and feminine, then, eventually, to describe being attracted to members of both sexes (Ellis 1915). Psychoanalyst Sigmund Freud (1897, 1905) most significantly became associated with the idea of bisexuality in the United States, when his work was translated, sometimes questionably, into English and read widely in this country. Freud theorized bisexuality as an inherent, innate, infantile state in human beings; he argued that all people are born with the capacity for sexual attraction to a wide range of people and objects, but that through a series of crises and discoveries and experiences in early childhood, sexuality is usually shaped by parents and others so that it is directed at the opposite sex. According to Freud, the typical developmental situation requires that people repress their attractions to members of the same sex to conform to the psychological and social expectations of the society around them. From Freud's perspective, sometimes individual sexuality is not directed either toward the opposite sex or toward one sex alone, with the result being that an individual's sexuality is gay or lesbian or, alternatively, bisexual. Freud's theory of fundamental bisexuality became popular among those experimenting with alternative lifestyles in the United States in the "Roaring Twenties," during which the "free lovers" used it to justify more sexually experimental behavior than was commonly accepted at the time (D'Emilio and Freedman 1988).

Although Freud's theoretical insights fell into disfavor in many circles over the course of the twentieth century, the idea that bisexuality is common received support from a less theoretical, more empirical source at mid-century. Alfred Kinsey's name became familiar to most Americans in association with his groundbreaking research on sexuality. Kinsey (Kinsey, Pomeroy, and Martin 1948) constructed a now famous six-point scale bearing his name on which he asked people to rate themselves as "exclusively homosexual" to "exclusively heterosexual" in their attractions. After thousands of men and women had engaged in the process of self-rating, Kinsey determined that the majority of people are to some degree bisexual, at least in their attractions and fantasies. A smaller minority of people are exclusively heterosexual or gay/lesbian in their behaviors, attractions, and fantasies. The term a *Kinsey 3* has come to be a common reference point among bisexual people as a way of signifying a balanced degree of attraction to both men and to women; someone identifying himself or herself as a *Kinsey 4* is attracted to both sexes, but slightly more often finds members of the opposite sex appealing.

Kinsey's research, however, ultimately focused on behavior more than identity. His research answered the questions "do people behave bisexually?" and "are people attracted to members of both their own and the opposite sex?" His research did not answer the questions "do people consider themselves bisexual in identity?" or "does this society acknowledge bisexual identity as one of the options?" Evidence of the answers to both of those questions has been found in broader studies of bisexual identity and in writing by bisexually identified individuals. During the 1970s, in concert with the emergence of the New Left, the gay liberation movement, and the free love movement, a number of bisexual organizations appeared across the country, emphasizing an end to all sexual categories and an emphasis on bisexuality as a behavioral potential (Uddis-Kessler 1996); many of these organizations closed their doors by the beginning of the 1980s (Weinberg, Williams, and Pryor 1994), just as the AIDS crisis was emerging. Throughout the 1980s and 1990s, the bisexual category reappeared, this time with an emphasis on identity instead of behavior; many formerly "gay and lesbian" organizations became "lesbian, gay, and bisexual" organizations, as a result of pressure from an increasingly visible bisexual population for gay and lesbian communities to accept and create coalitions with bisexuals. At the heart of this development was controversy around bisexual people, both within the dominant culture as it experienced the AIDS crisis, and within the lesbian and gay communities, in which the tensions between lesbians and bisexual women were especially noteworthy (Ault 1996a, 1996b; Faderman 1991; Rust 2000).

BISEXUALITY AS A THREAT TO THE DOMINANT CULTURE: HIV/AIDS

Mainstream America became interested in bisexuality during the beginning of the first decade of the HIV/AIDS crisis. Initially, AIDS in the United States was seen as a "gay disease"; infection and mortality rates were high among men both identified as and perceived as gay. Because a great stigma was still attached to being gay, the government remained silent on the issue for several years, instead of following the leads of other industrialized countries, which actively and quickly worked to educate their citizens about infection mechanisms and prevention. Heterosexual Americans became more concerned about the disease when it became clearer that it did not infect only gay men, but that heterosexual men and women were vulnerable as well. The epidemiology of AIDS eventually made clear that men who had been infected by men were sometimes also sexually active with women, and that men who were married to women also sometimes engaged in sexual relations with other men, as well as with their wives and other women. Medical researchers began to refer to "gay and bisexual men" in their reports on the spread of HIV/AIDS, and reactionary conservatives began to identify bisexuals as a source of threat to the well-being of the heterosexual population. Bisexuals were widely demonized as sources of infection, even as "murderous." In one famous instance, the host of a national news program asked a man dying of AIDS whether he felt he had in some way "murdered his wife" because he had been sexually active with her after he was infected by a man.

Although both medical and media attention focused on bisexual men, the most vocal response to the demonization of bisexuals came from feminist women (Uddis-Kessler 1996). By using feminist discourses on individual's rights to sexual self-determination, sexual liberation and empowerment, and sexual choice, feminist bisexuals published several collected volumes on bisexuality dedicated to documenting the realities of bisexual lives, the legitimacy of bisexual identity, the forms of erasure and discrimination faced by bisexuals, and the ways in which the oppression of bisexuals is related to the oppression faced by lesbians and gay men (Ault 2006b).

BISEXUALITY AS A THREAT TO MARGINALIZED CULTURE: LESBIAN FEMINISTS AND BISEXUALITY

Although feminist bisexual women articulated a response to the mainstream effort to demonize bisexuals, feminist lesbians were not always receptive to the argument that bisexual people experience forms of oppression similar to those

SEXUAL IDENTITY TIMELINES

In a large-scale quantitative study of sexual minority women, sociologist Paula Rust (2000) documented the nuances in the processes through which women come to define themselves as either lesbian or bisexual. One of her most interesting findings is that although lesbian and bisexual women tend to experience similar events in the process of questioning their heterosexuality, they do so on differing timelines. On average, women who ultimately define as bisexual begin to question their heterosexuality and experience attraction to women a few years later than those who define themselves as lesbian.

experienced by lesbian and gay people. Social scientists and popular commentators alike noted lesbian hostility toward bisexual women. Many lesbians saw bisexual women as enjoying "heterosexual privilege," defined as the many benefits people in a heterosexist society receive for being, or being perceived as, heterosexual. Lesbians accused bisexual women of "passing," and of "going straight when the going gets tough." Many lesbian women hostile to bisexual women reported that they didn't want to date or have partnerships with bisexual women because they predicted that bisexuals would either leave them for men or that they would bring diseases they got from sexual relations with men into the lesbian community, in an argument similar to that made by conservatives afraid bisexuals were a threat to the heterosexual population (Ault 1996a).

BISEXUALITY AS SEXUAL LIBERATION

Bisexually identified people faced controversy and stigmatization in both mainstream society and marginalized sexual minority groups during the first decade of the AIDS crisis. In response, they worked to address both stereotypes around bisexuality and to advance their own theories about bisexuality and its meaning for society. At a theoretical level, bisexuals argued that recognizing bisexual identity as a legitimate way of describing oneself created the possibility of revolutionizing narrow, constraining, and outdated ways of conceptualizing sexuality; some argued that to be "monosexual," or interested in only one sex, was a limited way of interacting with others. They further asserted that if people acknowledged the fundamental bisexuality posited by Freud or the wide-ranging bisexuality documented by Kinsey, our society would be more tolerant and loving. People would not have to work so hard to prove their heterosexuality, for example, by restricting their closeness with people of the same sex. Bisexuals also worked to demonstrate that when they are in relationships with people of the same sex, they face the same kinds of oppression and discrimination experienced by lesbian and gay people, and that lesbian and gay political interests are closely related to their own. Finally, bisexual people worked to clarify the difference between identity and sexual fidelity, noting that these are independent features of an individual's character. Many bisexual people are monogamous, and many heterosexual, gay, and lesbian people are nonmonogamous.

CONCLUSION

Although it is not without controversy today, bisexual identity has become increasingly accepted as a legitimate sexual identity category. National, state, community, and school-level organizations devoted to lesbian and gay issues and rights typically include the word *bisexual* in their names, even if they do not offer specific services for bisexuals or political initiatives devoted exclusively to bisexual issues. Some may, indeed, find the bisexual label best describes their sexuality during their formative years and choose to identify as straight or gay or lesbian at other points in their lives—and vice versa. Although it appears unlikely that the monosexual "straight" and "gay/lesbian" categories will be eliminated in favor of the idea of universal bisexuality in the near future, it also appears that the category of bisexual identity has become widely enough institutionalized that it is a permanent part of our sexual culture.

See also Heterosexism and Homophobia; Lesbian, Gay, Bisexual, Transgender, and Queer Movements; Sexual Identity and Orientation.

Further Reading: Ault, Amber, "Hegemonic Discourse in an Oppositional Community: Lesbian Feminist Stigmatization of Bisexual Women," in *Queer Studies,* ed. Brett Beemyn and Mickey Eliason, 204–216 (New York: New York University Press, 1996a); Ault, Amber, "Ambiguous Identity in an Unambiguous Sex/Gender Structure: The Case of Bisexual Women," *The Sociological Quarterly* 37, no. 3 (1996b): 449–463; Clasen, Jan, *Apples and Oranges* (Boston: Houghton Mifflin Company, 1999); D'Emilio, John, and Estelle Freedman, *Intimate Matters: A History of Sexuality in America* (New York: Harper Perennial, 1988); Ellis, Havelock, "Extracts from Studies in the Psychology of Sex, Volume I: Sexual Inversion (1897) and from Studies in the Psychology of Sex, Volume II: Sexual Inversion (1915)," in *Bisexuality: A Critical Reader,* ed. Merl Storr, 15–19 (New York: Routledge, 1999); Faderman, Lillian, *Odd Girls and Twilight Lovers* (New York: Columbia University Press, 1991); Freud, Sigmund, "Extract from Three Essays on the Theory of Sexuality: 1. The Sexual Aberrations (1905)," in *Bisexuality: A Critical Reader,* ed. Mer Storr, 20–27 (New York: Routledge, 1999); Garber, Marjorie, *Vice Versa: Bisexuality and the Eroticism of Everyday Life* (New York: Simon and Schuster, 1996); Kinsey, Alfred, Wardell B. Pomeroy, and Clyde E. Martin, "Extracts from Sexual Behavior in the Human Male," in *Bisexuality: A Critical Reader,* ed. Merl Storr, 31–37 (New York: Routledge, 1999); Rust, Paula C., "Neutralizing the Political Threat of the Marginal Woman: Lesbians' Beliefs About Bisexual Women," in *Bisexuality in the United States,* ed. Paula Rust, 471–497 (New York: Columbia University Press, 2000); Storr, Merl, "Editor's Introduction," in *Bisexuality: A Critical Reader,* ed. Merl Storr, 1–12 (New York: Routledge, 1999); Uddis-Kessler, Amanda, "Identity/Politics: Historical Sources of the Bisexual Movement," in *Queer Studies,* ed. Brett Beemyn and Mickey Eliason, 52–63 (New York: New York University Press, 1996); Weinberg, Martin S., Colin J. Williams, and Douglas W. Pryor, *Dual Attraction: Understanding Bisexuality* (New York: Oxford University Press, 1994).

Amber Ault

BREAST CANCER

The causes and treatment of breast cancer, which disproportionately afflicts women, have been debated on the grounds of where research should focus, what environmental factors cause it, who is responsible for managing what may be controllable risk factors, and whether corporations' interests or cancer patients' interests prevail in its current commercialization.

BACKGROUND

Breast cancer disproportionately affects women, and different populations of women present with different rates of breast cancer and different survival rates. In recent years, breast cancer has received a lot of commercial attention through efforts such as the Susan G. Komen "Race for the Cure" and through businesses that donate a portion of their earnings to breast cancer research, outreach, or prevention education (King 2006). Some advocates have been critical of the medical research and commercialization of breast cancer on the grounds that corporate interests prevail over women's own interests in their health and well-being.

WHAT IS THE MEDICAL RESEARCH?

Cancer rates in industrialized nations are much higher than in nonindustrialized nations, a yet unexplained relationship. Cancer rates of groups that migrate from nonindustrialized to industrialized areas rise to meet the higher industrial rates within one to two generations (Coyle 2004). This correlation evidences some type of environmental cause, not, for example, a difference in genetics between different ethnic or racial groups.

Geographical and socioeconomic factors contribute to rates of contracting cancer and to survival rates for women who present with breast cancer. In the United States, African American women are less likely than white women to contract breast cancer but more likely to die from it. Because of racism in the medical profession and other barriers to access, African American women tend to present later in the progression of breast cancer, which greatly reduces their survival rates. Lower socioeconomic status increases the likelihood that one's breast cancer will be detected later and that one's treatment will be insufficient to prevent recurrence and mortality.

WHAT ARE THE ENVIRONMENTAL RISK FACTORS?

Because of the difficulty in isolating specific carcinogens, researchers look for risk factors, anything that indicates a greater or lesser chance of developing a disease. Risk factors may be genetic, lifestyle, or environmental type risks. Genetic factors cannot be changed, but only 10 percent of women who present with breast cancer have a known family history with the disease (NBCC 2007). Nonetheless, more time and money have been devoted to genetic research, to the exclusion of environmental causes.

Of the possible environmental causes, increased exposure to estrogen is a well-established risk factor for breast cancer; the use of DES, a synthetic estrogen given to pregnant women during the 1970s, is one example. Most potential environmental breast cancer carcinogens are chemicals that act as estrogen in women's bodies. The use of hormone [estrogen] replacement therapy (HRT) during and after menopause prolongs a woman's lifetime exposure to estrogen. Many women use HRT to alleviate some of the negative symptoms of menopause.

According to some observers, gender, class, and other factors contribute to what is researched and how and why. For example, the symptoms of menopause and many other life experiences of women are considered "disorders" in medical discourse and not seriously considered as conditions in need of serious research. Individual women have very little control over their exposure to environmental estrogens because corporations introduce possible breast cancer carcinogens into the environment when governments do not restrict use of the carcinogens. The lack of proof of environmental causes of breast cancer allows corporations to escape responsibility for disseminating possible carcinogens and avoid restrictions on their use. Governments and corporations are major funders of breast cancer research and have little motivation for supporting research that could prove their culpability.

WHAT SHOULD BE DONE?

The debate over breast cancer research, then, concerns why so much time and money have been spent on genetic causes for breast cancer when they account for at most 10 percent of breast cancer cases. Critics of the conventional medical model ask, where does the responsibility lie for managing lifestyle and environmental risk factors? Healthy diets and exercise can lower a woman's risk of developing breast cancer. Many occupations and their chemicals are correlated with higher rates of breast cancer. For example, chemicals used in dry cleaning have been found to increase breast cancer rates, so the question arises, should women be restricted from working in the dry cleaning business or should companies use different chemicals? One could argue that women should not work in industries that use possibly carcinogenic chemicals, but companies often do not educate their employees about health risks, and restricting where women may work has negative economic effects.

A healthy diet and exercise decrease breast cancer risk, which points to the individual woman's responsibility for that aspect of her health, but is she the only one who is responsible for barriers such as the unaffordability of healthy food? When a woman is disproportionately responsible for the extra hours of unpaid labor in her home and community, is it entirely her fault that she does not have time to exercise? Who, then, is responsible for the prevention, detection, and treatment of breast cancer? These are big questions that are often difficult to answer.

CONCLUSION

Breast cancer prevention is one important step toward addressing these questions. The multiple causes of breast cancer require multiple levels of prevention, risk management, detection, and treatment. Whatever the manifestation of the detrimental effects of a chemical or other element, many observers would agree that its use should be eliminated or reduced as much as possible. Research could continue to support prevention efforts by looking for modifiable risk factors. Because breast cancer exists, detection and treatment technologies such as mammography, radiation, and chemotherapy must be made available and accessible to everyone; even this continues to be an obstacle in equitably treating all breast cancer patients.

See also Medicine and Medicalization: Views on Women's Bodies.

Further Reading: Coyle, Yvonne Marie, "The Effect of the Environment on Breast Cancer Risk," *Breast Cancer Research and Treatment* 84 (2004): 273–288; King, Samantha, *Pink Ribbons, Inc.: Breast Cancer and the Politics of Philanthropy* (Minneapolis: University of Minnesota Press, 2006); National Breast Cancer Coalition, available at: http://www.natlbcc.org/, accessed July 27, 2007; Potts, Laura, "Narratives of Risk and Collective Identity," *Auto/Biography* 14 (2006): 116–133; Susan G. Komen Breast Cancer Foundation, available at: http://www.komen.org; Sutton, Amy, ed. *Cancer Sourcebook for Women* (Detroit, MI: Omnigraphics, 2006); Wolff, Mary, Julie Britton, and Valerie Wilson, "Environmental Risk Factors for Breast Cancer among African-American Women," presented at the Summit Meeting on Breast Cancer Among African American Women, Washington, DC, September 8–10, 2000.

Chana Wolfson

BREASTFEEDING

There are multiple views of breastfeeding, informed by women's experiences, science, public health, and politics. Current debates on breastfeeding involve scientific claims on the superiority of breast milk, whether responsibility for policy and advocacy lies with governments or individuals, and sexualized versus utilitarian views of women's breasts.

BACKGROUND

Breastfeeding is many things: an evolutionary means of infant survival and child spacing, a cultural practice embedded in female bodies and sexualities, a form of mother-infant relationship, a morally and politically laden option for infant feeding. Throughout history and across cultures, humans relied on breast milk or alternatives to sustain infant life. Alternatives included wet nursing (a lactating woman breastfeeding another woman's child); the use of other species' milk (cow, goat, sheep); or pap, a mixture of gruel and water. In the United States, the development of pasteurized formula in the 1930s, along with safe water and sterilization techniques, reduced infant mortality rates of prior decades and physicians began promoting formula use (Wolf 2002). Modernization, immigration, urbanization, the influence of science, and the rise of pediatricians as experts contributed to a steady decrease in U.S. breastfeeding rates throughout the 1940s to 1970s. By 1971, only 24 percent of mothers breastfed at least once, the lowest point in history (Wolf 2003).

Many factors contributed to declining breastfeeding among American mothers. Women whose lives were affected by immigration and urbanization often abandoned "traditional" practices in their quest for modern American lifestyles informed by science (Litt 2000). The transition to hospital birth included new pain relief technologies (e.g., scopolamine), leaving women groggy and unable to breastfeed. The common practice of separating newborns from mothers interrupted hormonal exchanges, which aid successful breastfeeding. In the 1970s, women's health advocates achieved limited reforms in hospital birth and infant care practices that supported women's desires to birth without interventions and breastfeed on demand. Women and allied physicians legitimized these reforms using scientific, religious, and maternal politics in the absence of widespread cultural or medical support (Ward 2000).

BREASTFEEDING ADVOCACY AND CONTROVERSIES

In recent years, there has been renewed advocacy for breastfeeding, informed by new scientific evidence that breast milk is the optimal nutrition for infants up to one to two years of age, as recommended by the American Academy of Pediatrics and the World Health Organization, respectively. Current U.S. breastfeeding policy is informed by *Healthy People 2010* objectives of the Department of Health and Human Services (DHHS) to increase breastfeeding initiation and duration rates. Although overall breastfeeding rates are increasing, by 2004 only 14 U.S. states achieved the *Healthy People 2010* objective of 75 percent of mothers initiating breastfeeding (CDC 2004). Fewer than five states achieved the goals of 50 percent of mothers breastfeeding children at six months of age and 25 percent of mothers breastfeeding their children at one year. Only two states, Oregon and Utah, achieved all three of these *Healthy People 2010* objectives.

In light of this outcome, and with data showing that breastfeeding is less likely among women of low socioeconomic status, the U.S. DHHS Office on Women's Health launched a national campaign in June 2004 designed to encourage first-time mothers to breastfeed exclusively for six months. The campaign used a new tactic: it highlighted the health risks of *not* breastfeeding, using the tagline, "Babies were born to be breastfed." Such health risks include chronic diseases such as obesity, diabetes, asthma, and acute illnesses (e.g., ear infections) (Steingraber 2001). The economic benefits to state-funded health care programs were undoubtedly a factor in the campaign.

Controversies over how and whether to advocate breastfeeding as national policy are concerned with how messages are conveyed and to whom. Feminists argue that a focus on primarily individual change obscures the need for widespread social, institutional, and economic support for breastfeeding mothers (Behrmann 2005; Hausman 2003). A focus on public health unduly places infant feeding as a personal decision, and in the face of racial and class disparities, this "choice" is available to some, but not all, women. Currently, older, educated, employed, white women are most likely to breastfeed (Hausman 2003). These controversies have racial and class undertones: Whereas breastfeeding is seen as "good" and linked to "good mothers" (i.e., white, middle class, heterosexual), the use of formula is seen as "bad" and linked to "bad mothers" (i.e., poor, working class, typically nonwhite, often single) (Hausman 2003).

BREASTFEEDING: MEDICAL, ECONOMIC, AND CULTURAL PERSPECTIVES

Medical professionals do not always have accurate and supportive information regarding breastfeeding. Economic incentives in marketing formula to medical professionals, hospitals, and government food programs have had an impact on medical education in regard to breastfeeding. The $3 billion formula industry is tied to commercial interests of pharmaceutical companies. In the past 20 years, a new occupational niche, the lactation consultant, has emerged in response to mothers' need for skilled, knowledgeable breastfeeding support. To date, few insurance policies cover these services.

The work environment affects breastfeeding. Unlike most countries, the United States has no national maternity leave policy; therefore individual employers decide how and whether to offer such benefits. Full-time work among mothers with young children is associated with lower breastfeeding rates. Low-income women, among whom women of color are overrepresented, are more likely to return to work earlier and have jobs less amenable for pumping and storing breast milk. Many employers do not understand the ease and low cost in providing support to breastfeeding workers, or how such support can reduce costs associated with employee illness and productivity. Exhorting women to breastfeed as the healthy choice without also providing structural changes in employment and state policies to support breastfeeding leaves out social solutions by governments and businesses.

Breastfeeding is deeply connected to cultural meanings of the female breast. Breastfeeding advocates note that in the United States, breasts are overwhelmingly portrayed as sexual objects, as opposed to their evolutionary purpose for infant feeding. Women's own experiences are diverse and complex. Some enjoy breastfeeding as a sensual and satisfying, physical and emotional relationship with their infants. For others, breastfeeding feels like a coercive use of their bodies, and they are repulsed by the physical act or the public display of breastfeeding. Many states have enacted legislation granting women the right to breastfeed in public, but the recent case of a breastfeeding woman ejected from a Delta airliner shows that this right is not available to all. Thus breastfeeding, like other reproductive practices, has always been influenced by complex configurations of cultural, economic, political, and scientific factors and holds different meanings among different groups of women (Solinger 2005; Baumslaug and Michels 1995; Berhmann 2005).

CONCLUSION

Both science and notions of "good mothering" shape current debates on breastfeeding. As in previous generations, when science valued formula over breast milk, science continues to play a role in influencing women and state policies. Indeed, most, if not all, parenting decisions are laden with moral, cultural, and evaluative components, and debates on breastfeeding practices will surely continue.

See also Birthing Practices; Medicine and Medicalization: Views on Women's Bodies.

Further Reading: Baumslaug, N., and D. L. Michels, *Milk, Money and Madness: The Culture and Politics of Breastfeeding* (Westport, CT: Bergin and Garvey, 1995); Berhmann, B. L., *The Breastfeeding Café: Mothers Share the Joys, Challenges and Secrets of Nursing* (Ann Arbor: University of Michigan Press, 2005); Centers for Disease Control and Prevention (CDC), Department of Health and Human Services, "National Immunization Survey: Breastfeeding Practices among Children Born in 2004" (Atlanta: CDC, 2004), available at: http://www.cdc.gov/breastfeeding/data/NIS_data/data_2004.htm; Hausman, B. L., *Mother's Milk: Breastfeeding Controversies in American Culture* (New York: Routledge, 2003); Litt, J. S., *Medicalized Motherhood: Perspectives from the Lives of African-American and Jewish Women* (New Brunswick, NJ: Rutgers University Press, 2000); Solinger, R., *Pregnancy and Power: A Short History of Reproductive Politics in America* (New York: New York University Press, 2005); Steingraber, Sandra, *Having Faith: An Ecologist's Journey to Motherhood* (New York: Perseus Publishing, 2001); U.S. Center for Disease Control, available at: http://www.cdc.gov/breastfeeding/data/NIS_data/data_2005.htm; Ward, J. D., *La Leche League: At the Crossroads of Medicine, Feminism, and Religion* (Raleigh: The University of North Carolina Press, 2000); Wolf, J. H., "Low Breastfeeding Rates and Public Health in the United States," *American Journal of Public Health* 93, no. 12 (2003): 2000–2010.

Christine H. Morton

C

CHILD CUSTODY AND PARENTAL RIGHTS

The "special treatment/equal treatment" debate over custody policy is between two groups who are both committed to gender equality but who have different visions of how to achieve it. On one side, *maternalists* believe mothers deserve "special treatment" in custody cases and that women should be empowered within their traditional caregiving roles. On the other side, *equal-parenting advocates* believe parenting should be done equally by men and women and this should be the goal of child custody decisions.

BACKGROUND

Custody policy decisions are made on contested gendered battlegrounds and ignite our deepest beliefs about parenting. Custody decisions impact the majority of U.S. citizens at some point in their lives. The U.S. divorce rate more than doubled between 1965 and 1980 and an estimated 40 to 50 percent of all marriages now end in separation or divorce, affecting more than 1 million children annually. Child custody disputes form the largest percentage of domestic-relations cases and account for close to one-quarter of all legal filings, making it the largest category of court action.

In the United States, until the mid-19th century fathers were granted custody of their children because children were considered their property. During this Puritan-influenced time, wives were expected to show "reverence," defined as a mixture of fear and awe, toward their husbands. Custody laws did not begin to change until the late 1800s when a capitalist market economy reorganized work into separate spheres of home and men's market work outside of it and created a close linkage of masculinity with breadwinning. The emergence of the tender-years doctrine thus arose because childrearing became reconceptualized as something mothers were uniquely suited to do, in the privacy of their homes, away from the "selfish and calculating" world of the market.

Beginning with the feminist movement of the 1960s, virtually all jurisdictions determined that maternal preference by case law or statute was sexist and thus eliminated it. By the mid-1980s, the trend toward presumptive joint custody emerged, which exists when both parents legally share responsibility for the child. The new standard was a gender-neutral custody determination in the "best interests of the child." This was viewed as a victory by equal-parenting advocates who welcomed the change in custody law that stressed that there was no "real" difference between the sexes and that differentiation that does exist only reflects sex-based stereotypes. Equal-parenting advocates believe that once "special treatment" and discrimination are removed from a maternal preference, the gender-neutral best interest standard will allow women to achieve equality through equal competition in the social and economic marketplace. On this view, any hint of maternal presumption in custody is understood to push women back into the caregiver role and pull men out of it.

In contrast, maternalists worry that a gender-neutral best interest standard ignores the fact that women do the lion's share of child care and housework and are marginalized in market work because of it. Maternalists argue that there is little evidence that a joint custody standard changes the behavior of fathers or that courts have the resources to turn fathers into active parents. Recent statistics reveal a sexual division of labor in parenting patterns. According to Rose Kreider and Jason Fields, in their 2005 report *The Living Arrangements of Children,* between 1970 and 1990 the proportion of children living only with their mother doubled from 11 percent to 22 percent. In 1960, father-absent families numbered 10 million in the United States; today it stands at 24 million. Ironically, this historically unprecedented shift in family composition occurred at the same time the gender-neutral best interest standard took effect.

TYPES OF CHILD CUSTODY

Legal custody refers to parental authority over children. *Sole custody* means that one parent has the right to make major decisions for their child(ren) including decisions regarding education, medical care, and religion. *Joint legal custody* means that both parents share in major decisions but individually make the day-to-day decisions when the child(ren) are with him or her. *Physical custody* refers to the time children actually spend with their parent(s); and primary physical custody means children spend the majority of their time with one parent and "visit" their "nonresidential parent."

In working out a joint custody arrangement, efforts may be made to divide the child's time equally between parents (generally an average of two overnights per week). Parents with joint physical custody (about 100 overnights per year) have lower child-support obligations in most states. Maternalists point out that fathers frequently threaten to fight for joint custody to gain better divorce property settlements and enforce joint physical custody in court (but not in life) in order to pay less child support. Maternalists fear that if joint custody does not enforce obligations of fathers but gives them significant rights to command how mothers do virtually all of the family work, the symbolic message is that divorced fathers are entitled to control their children without doing any of the day-to-day work of raising them. On this view, eliminating entitlements for caregivers is not a desirable feminist strategy given that there are significant power differentials between men and women. Maternalists dismiss the idea that the goal of "equality" ought to be based on accepting maleness as the norm and a denial of equality to women who are unable or unwilling to assimilate to that norm.

Equal-parenting advocates, on the other hand, believe that joint physical custody will encourage a redefinition of domesticity. Domesticity is currently gendered and divides family work from market work. According to an analysis of supplemental 1998 U.S. Census data, about 65 percent of mothers have sole physical and legal custody, 10 percent had sole physical and joint legal custody, 11 percent of fathers had sole physical custody (with either joint or sole legal custody), 9 percent of parents had joint physical and legal custody, and 5 percent had split custody (Child Trends 2002). Equal-parenting advocates argue that unless fathers and mothers are allocated equal joint physical custody, the current gendered organization of domesticity will continue to be justified, sustained, and reproduced.

THE CUSTODY DEBATE

When parents cannot decide on a parenting plan postdivorce/separation and head to family court to seek a custody solution, they may enter court with vastly different ideas of how custody should be allocated. On the one hand, maternalists enter court with the belief that because children have likely received primary caregiving from their mothers whose lives are framed by powerful social forces that lead them to "choose" to become marginalized and cut off from most social roles that offer responsibility and authority, children should be "awarded" to mothers who have sacrificed economic gain to engage in carework. Maternalists argue that a *sole custody* model serves the best interest standard because relationships between children and their mothers should be central to the best interests of the child test.

Maternalists believe that formal legal equality undervalues the gendered division of carework, household labor, and domestic violence, and limits mothers' right to restrict contact with fathers while imposing no obligation for contact on fathers. Also, they point out that joint custody identifies the child's right to contact with both parents only in the postseparation family and not in the preseparation family and ignores the problems of fathers seeking revenge, retribution, and control through custody. Furthermore, maternalists find that increased paternal involvement does not automatically mean improved child outcomes nor that biological fathers provide such unique nurturance that it can not be provided by substitute caregivers. On this view, the role of custody law should recognize existing gendered inequality and move beyond the simplistic equality paradigm.

In contrast, equal-parenting advocates argue that joint custody better serves the best interest standard because it keeps fathers attached to their children and increases the frequency of child support payments. Also, because market work structures encourage paternal absence in terms of actual parenting and fathers have no control over this, they should not be punished for it in a custody decision. Equal-parenting advocates also argue that fathers are necessary for children's healthy development and should have an equal right to custody regardless of their history of caretaking. And finally, mental health professionals and custody evaluators frequently favor presumptive joint custody; and as recent Congressional fatherhood bills argue that "fatherlessness" is the "most consequential social problem we confront" no one should deny custody to fathers who want it.

Equal-parenting advocates interpret women's desire for sole custody as contributing to a culture of gender inequality and the perpetuation of traditional gender roles. Equal-parenting advocates seek to undermine traditional gender roles and defend their proposal by reference to the law's expressive function—its ability to express and change social expectations and norms. They argue that joint physical and legal custody will ignite a gender-neutral norm of parenting that involves fathers as much as mothers. Equal-parenting advocates want to destabilize domesticity's gender roles and restructure the relationship between market work and family work so that all parents can engage in both without becoming marginalized in either. On this view, gender neutrality is necessary in child custody decision making because it is consistent with general liberal notions of equality. On a symbolic level, making equality the organizing concept underlying custody decision making ensures a more just society.

FEDERAL AND STATE RESPONSES

In the United States, the parents of a child born within a marriage are joint guardians of that child and the rights of both parents are considered equal: each parent has an equal right to the custody of the child when they separate. The federal Constitution allows a state to interfere with this right only to prevent harm or potential harm to the child. In *Meyer v. Nebraska,* 262 U.S. 390, 399, 401 (1923), the Supreme Court held that the "liberty" protected by the due process clause includes the right of parents to "establish a home and bring up children" and "to control the education of their own." According to *Reno v. Flores,* 507 U.S., at 304 (1993), "as long as a parent is fit there will normally be no reason for the State to inject itself into the private realm of the family to further question the ability of that parent to make the best decisions concerning the rearing of that parent's children."

Maternalists see the lack of federal intervention in the family as gross neglect of women and children and interpret the state's "hands off" approach to "the private realm of the family" as discrimination against unpaid family work, most of which is done by women. Maternalists argue that affirmative action principles should be applied to the family context and that without a well-funded federal institutional structure of available child care and health care services, as well as adequate social and economic support systems that enable men and women to nurture and rear their children, formal equality is understood to hurt women. Because market work is stacked against mothers, calculations of child or spousal support in which courts assume that the father and mother have had equal access to the breadwinner role, on this view, are unfair. Maternalists argue that advocacy of equal treatment denies difference, requires women to adhere to masculine life patterns, and ignores evidence that equal treatment harms women.

The Uniform Marriage and Divorce Act (1979) suggests that the following be considered in determining the "best interests" standard: (1) the wishes of the children and their parent(s); (2) the interaction and interrelationship of the children and their parent(s), siblings, and any other person who may significantly affect the children's best interests; (3) the children's adjustment to their home, school, and community; and, (4) the mental and physical health of all individuals involved. Although the Uniform Marriage and Divorce Act (1979) underlies the "best interests" standard, custody laws differ from state to state. Emery, Otto, and O'Donohue (2005) point out some idiosyncratic norms considered by judges in different states. For example, South Carolina takes into account the religious beliefs of the parents, and Alabama, Florida, Michigan, North Dakota, and Utah consider parents' "moral character" to be relevant to children's best interests. Equal-parenting advocates fear that the "best interest of the child" legal standard is vague, founded on values and beliefs grounded in sex differences between mothers and fathers, allows judges to make custody decisions in keeping with their own and the local community's prejudices about what a child needs and what a family is, and perpetuates a gendered division of labor.

PROBLEMS WITH THE "BEST INTEREST" STANDARD

Because the "best interest of the child" legal standard is so vague, judges across the United States have turned to child custody evaluation experts and frequently rely on the findings of their clinical assessment instruments. Custody evaluators routinely rely on IQ tests, clinical interviews, direct observation, "friendly parent" measures, "parental alienation" measurement instruments, children's wishes, and psychological tests. Placing custody decisions in the hands of social scientists, however, has been sharply criticized. Emery et al. (2005) find that there is no scientific evidence to support most of the psychological instruments and practices of mental health professionals who serve as custody evaluators. They argue that the state of psychological science is too limited to reach valid, replicable, and reliable measures to reach clear conclusions about controversial topic such as children's wishes, overnight visits, and joint custody decisions.

Maternalists interpret the widespread use of mental health professionals in custody hearings as an excuse for judges to ignore the significant power differentials between mothers and fathers. Maternalists suggest that it is less risky politically for a judge to make a custody decision based on the "professional" opinion of a mental health professional rather than on the "nonprofessional" opinion of the primary caregiver. Maternalists argue that women, as mothers, need concrete legal protection and the law's expressive function should offer this and leave in tact the gendered allocation of childrearing to mothers. They charge that mental health professionals care more about protecting a few caregiving men than the large majority of caregiving women and that judges find it easier to impose joint custody across the board than to determine who has sacrificed social status and economic independence to accommodate child care.

AMERICAN LAW INSTITUTE'S "APPROXIMATION RULE"

The American Law Institute (ALI) is a national nonprofit group of lawyers and legal scholars who make recommendations for state legislation. For the first time, in 2002, ALI issued recommendations for states' laws on family dissolution titled *Principles of the Law of Family Dissolution: Analysis and Recommendations.* They argue that the "best interests" standard is met by facilitating planning and agreement, continuity of parent-child attachments, meaningful contact between children and each parent, caretaking relationships with adults who know how to care for a particular child's needs, security from conflict and violence, and expeditious and predictable legal decision making. ALI finds that the best interest test, as currently practiced in most jurisdictions, is not in the best interest of children if it involves a prolonged legal contest with a parade of competing psychological experts, other witnesses, and delays to custody decisions.

ALI proposes judges rely on an "approximation rule" to make custody decisions. The approximation rule means that caretaking and decision making be allocated in roughly the same proportion it was when the family was intact and that states establish what that minimum time is: they mention six days a month as a rough idea. ALI also seeks to alleviate inequality among children by their list of "prohibited factors" that courts may not consider when ordering parenting plans. This list of factors includes: (1) the race or ethnicity of the child, parent, or other household member; (2) the sex of the parent or child; (3) the religious practices of a parent or child, except to prevent severe harm to the child or to protect the child's right to practice a religion that has been a significant part of the child's life; (4) the sexual orientation of a parent; (5) the parent's extramarital sexual conduct, except were it harms a child; and, (6) the parent's earning capacities or financial circumstances (except where combined finances of parents set practical limitations to custodial arrangements).

CONCLUSION

The "approximation rule" appears to offer a middle ground for both maternalists and equal-parenting advocates. It stresses that custody laws ought to be designed to protect caregivers regardless of sex. It does not include maternal presumption but rather a caregiver presumption. The custody debate between maternalists and equal-parenting advocates reaffirms the importance of treating men and women the same, but shows that avoiding discrimination in custody policy requires treating parents the same by extending benefits traditionally based on sex and linking them instead to *gender,* making custody available to men as well as women who play the primary caregiver role.

To enact fair guidelines for determining custody when parents cannot reach agreement, formal equality must be combined with an analysis of gender and power. According to ALI, the advantage of the approximation rule is that it is a clear, determinative standard. There is a lot of support for the "approximation rule" whereby the postdivorce division of the children's residential time between the two parents should match, as far as possible, the "respective involvement of the parents in the childrearing during the marriage." Clear guidelines will help families know what to expect when entering custody negotiations. The "approximation rule" is drafted as gender rather than sex-linked and therefore respects carework and avoids eliminating entitlements for caregivers in the name of equal-parenting goals. On the other hand, an "approximation rule" that is designed around gender rather than sex presents the risk that courts will apply it in a way that reflects and perpetuates male power over women. So far, no state has implemented the approximation rule.

See also Childcare; Family Values; Fatherhood Initiatives.

Further Reading: Allen, M., and N. Burrell, "Comparing the Impact of Homosexual and Heterosexual Parents on Children: Meta-analysis of Existing Research," *Journal of Homosexuality* 32 (1996): 19–35; American Law Institute, "The Allocation of Custodial and Decision Making Responsibility for Children," in *Principles of the Law of Family Dissolution: Analysis and Recommendations* (Philadelphia: America Law Institute, 2002): 92–408; Child Trends, *Charting Parenthood: A Statistical Portrait of Fathers and Mothers in America* (Washington, DC: Child Trends, 2002); Edin, Katherine, and Maria Kefalas, *Promises I Can Keep: Why Poor Women Put Motherhood Before Marriage* (Berkeley: University of California Press, 2005); Emery, Robert E., Randy Otto, and William O'Donohue, "A Critical Assessment of Child Custody Evaluations: Limited Science and a Flawed System," *Psychological Science in the Public Interest* 6, no. 1 (2005): 3–31; Fineman, Martha, *The Illusion of Equality: The Rhetoric and Reality of Divorce Reform* (Chicago: University of Chicago Press, 1991); Fineman, Martha, *The Neutered Mother and the Sexual Family* (New York: Routledge, 1995); Hays, Sharon, *Flat Broke with Children* (New York: Oxford University Press, 2003); Mason, Mary Ann, *The Custody Wars* (New York: Basic Books, 1999); Mason, Mary Ann, *From Father's Property to Children's Rights: A History of Child Custody in the United States* (New York: Columbia University Press, 1994); Riseman, Barbara, *Gender Vertigo: American Families in Transition* (New Haven, CT: Yale University Press, 1998); Smart, Carol, *Child Custody and the Politics of Gender* (New York: Routledge, 1989).

Lynn Comerford

CHILD SEXUAL ABUSE

Stemming from the longstanding cultural view of women and girls as the property of men, child sexual abuse has been acknowledged as a widespread social problem only since the late twentieth century. As the view of women and girls as property has shifted, messages of victim blaming have surfaced, alleging that adult men abuse young girls because they are flirting or sexually enticing men. The belief that perpetrators are solely responsible for their behavior is fairly recent and still often challenged.

BACKGROUND: WHAT IS CHILD SEXUAL ABUSE?

Child sexual abuse is a devastating phenomenon resulting in life-changing consequences for survivors. Sex offenders are cunning and calculating in their acts of abuse, and frequently engage children in secrecy by using tactics such as shaming, fear, threats, and intimidation. Many factors contribute to the shroud of secrecy and victim blaming surrounding sexual abuse including societal messages that privilege men over women and boys over girls.

Broadly defined sexual abuse is sexual contact or activities perpetrated against a child by an adult or older child. Prevent Child Abuse America (PCAA) provides a more specific definition:

> Sexual abuse of a child is inappropriately exposing or subjecting the child to sexual contact, activity or behavior. Sexual abuse includes oral, anal, genital, buttock and breast contact. It also includes the use of objects for vaginal or anal penetration, fondling or sexual stimulation.... In addition, exploitation of a child for pornographic purposes, making a child available to others as a child prostitute, and stimulating a child with inappropriate solicitation, exhibitionism, and erotic material are also forms of sexual abuse. (2006, 1)

Girls are disproportionately victims of sexual abuse, and 90 percent of victims are abused by someone they know. Statistics indicate that 20 percent of girls and 5 to 16 percent of boys in the United States will be sexually abused before age 18 (PCAA 2006). These statistics challenge the stereotype of child sexual abuse as an uncommon occurrence by a stranger who tries to lure a child into his car with candy.

RECOVERED MEMORIES: THE DEBATE

Throughout the literature are examples of adult survivors of sexual abuse experiencing amnesia to the abuse until years later. In these cases a child remembers the abuse during childhood, but the mind, in order to protect itself, forgets or "blocks out" the traumatic memories at some point. Years after the abuse, when the mind is ready to start remembering, certain situations may begin to trigger the memories. The resulting journey can be devastating as survivors navigate the journey of uncovering the layers of hidden memories. In the early 1990s, a controversy developed about whether these recovered memories were genuine, or planted in the heads of vulnerable adult survivors through hypnosis or other techniques by therapists looking to further their own agenda. This controversy occurred before the widespread acknowledgement of men as victims, and therefore it was almost always women's memories that were called into question. In a patriarchal society where men's memories and voices are valued above women's, the survivors' statements were often dismissed as vindictive and untrue. For some time, there was a public spotlight on this issue, causing an extreme amount of distress for adult survivors who remained unsure of the veracity of their memories. The battle played out in the media and in the courts, with several public cases of therapists being sued by clients or their families for alleged false accusations of abuse resulting from memories "recovered" in therapy (e.g., *State of New Hampshire v. Hungerford 1997, Wilson v. Phillips 1999*). The American Psychiatric Association published a "Statement on Memories of Sexual Abuse" that discusses abuse survivors' use of coping mechanisms, which may include the lack of conscious awareness of the abuse over periods of time (APA 1993). After time, the spotlight swung elsewhere, and a consensus came in the mainstream mental health community that many adult survivors do repress memories as a way to survive the abuse as a child. Many research studies that looked to independent sources to verify the accuracy of memories (e.g., perpetrator confessions, accounts from others involved) backed this assertion (e.g., Williams 1995; Loftus 1994), and some studies found that as many of 38 percent of adult survivors forget at least some of their abuse histories (Loftus 1994). In addition, survivors gained more credibility with the emergence of the sex abuse scandal in the Catholic Church, which began increasing the public statements of male survivors discussing recovered memories. These statements by men also served to legitimize women's memories. Nonetheless, there remains a quiet wariness in the general public about adult survivors reporting recovered memories, and adult survivors still remain, grappling with the stories of their trauma and working to heal.

CHILD SEXUAL ABUSE: A GENDERED DEBATE

Traditionally, children were considered property and could be treated in whatever way their fathers saw fit. Little attention was given to the idea that children should not be hurt by adults until 1874 when the phenomenon of child abuse came to public light with the case of Mary Ellen, a young girl who was being severely beaten. Concerned citizens brought the case to court, noting that existing laws made it much easier for animals to be protected than children. As a result, Mary Ellen's stepmother was convicted of assault and battery and the Society for the Prevention of Cruelty to Children was founded. The focus remained on physical abuse until the 1970s, however, when child advocates and feminists worked together to bring the problem of child sexual abuse to the awareness of the public. The phenomenon gained widespread public attention with the 1984 case of the McMartin Day Care Center, where the adults were found to have abused many children over a period of 10 years (Loseke 2005). As the awareness of child sexual abuse rose in U.S. society, the main focus was on the sexual abuse of girls. It is only recently that focus has come to boys as victims as well. Girls are still abused at higher rates that boys, however, and gendered societal messages reinforce the secrecy and shame surrounding sexual abuse.

SEX OFFENDERS AND THE CYCLE OF ABUSE

Child sexual abuse is perpetrated overwhelmingly by offenders known to the victim. Sex offenders cross racial, age, cultural, and socioeconomic boundaries. Offenders are men in 90 percent of child sexual abuse cases and are often seen by children and parents alike as the "perfect" parent or mentor to children. Societal views of men as protectors of women and children, as well as the general surprise and delight that often accompany fathers and adult men showing affection to children, further create an environment where sexual abuse of children can occur unacknowledged. Sex offenders are often charming and work to gain the trust of children and adults before creating opportunities to be alone with children. The 10 percent of sex offenders who are women focus on manipulation and persuasion as opposed to force or threat of force (PCAA 2006). Sex offenders engage in a process of preparing their victims for abuse called grooming, where they gain the trust of the child and often the parent/guardian (or, in the case of a parent offender, the trust of the nonoffending parent), slowly and carefully encroach on the child's boundaries, and may use tactics such as pornography, alcohol, or drugs to introduce the child to sexual material and lower inhibitions before engaging in more intensive forms of abuse such as physical touching or intercourse. Offenders also use coercion, manipulation, deceit, and threats of force to engage the child in secrecy (Johnson 2006). This level of manipulation leads to self-blame and shame experienced for years after the abuse, which is further reinforced by victim-blaming messages, particularly targeted at girls.

THE IMPACT OF CHILD SEXUAL ABUSE

The impact of child sexual abuse on children, families, and society is no less than devastating. Sexual abuse robs children of their trust, safety, and comfort in the world. The cost to society is huge. Research indicates the annual cost of child abuse and neglect is more than $94 billion a year (Fromm 2001). In addition, child sexual abuse results in both immediate and long-term effects for victims and their families. Physical effects may include physical injury, sexually transmitted diseases, genital pain, and possible pregnancy. Most investigations, however, yield no physical evidence of otherwise substantiated sexual abuse because of the less invasive abuse methods used by many sex offenders. Emotional effects include feelings of self-blame, shame, guilt, betrayal, confusion, fear, depression, and anxiety. These emotional effects can be manifested by behaviors such as nightmares, regression (e.g., returning to younger behaviors such as bed wetting or thumb sucking), change in school performance, problems concentrating, sexual acting out or age-inappropriate sexual knowledge, clinginess to nonoffending adults, irritability, and outbursts of anger (Kendall-Tackett 1993). In general, children who have been sexually abused demonstrate more behavior problems than their peers (Dubowitz 1993). In contrast, some children follow the rules almost too well, anxiously trying to become invisible by fading into the background.

Resiliency

Resilience is "the power or ability to return to original form or position after being bent, compressed, or stretched, as well as the ability to overcome adversity, survive stress and rise above disadvantage" (Valentine 1993, 222). Resiliency factors for sexually abused children include the number of incidents of abuse, the relationship of the perpetrator to the child, at what point in the process the child chooses to tell (if s/he ever tells at all), and, in particular, how the disclosure is received. A positive response to the initial disclosure resulting in the end of abuse and the continued support of loving, patient, nonabusive adults (ideally a nonoffending parent in the home) is an indicator for increased resiliency (Valentine 1993). Research has identified traits that appear to be characteristic of resilient children and adults including above average intelligence, talent, creativity, and ability to see meaning in their experiences. Gender also affects resiliency for sexual abuse survivors. Victim-blaming messages, resulting in part from socialized messages that women and girls are to blame for the faults of men, can greatly hinder resiliency. Also, girls seeking out relationships with adults are often labeled as needy and attention-seeking, and then ignored or discouraged as a result, which may create further barriers to building relationships that foster resiliency.

Self-Blame and Shame: "A Girl Problem"

Not only do many survivors distrust others, they often distrust themselves. Most survivors feel as if the abuse is in some way their fault, or as if they deserved the abuse because of a perceived internal flaw (e.g., "I deserved it because I wasn't strong enough to stop it"). Abusers, however, often use these tactics as a form of manipulation and control by making the child feel like an active participant, complicit in keeping the secret. During the course of the abuse, this tactic is often reinforced by threatening or blaming statements by the perpetrator, such as, "Now if you weren't so pretty, I wouldn't want to do this to you" (Johnson 2006). Women, in particular, are socialized to engage in self-blame for any perceived flaw. The gendered nature of self-blame is entrenched in traditional gender role messages, which only reinforces perpetrators' blaming messages. Men are taught to be self-confident, to make the decisions in relationships, and to avoid any appearance of self-doubt. Women, on the other hand, are socialized to constantly think of the needs and comfort of others before themselves, to keep problems inside, and not to cause trouble. When things "go wrong" for women, they are taught to look inward for the cause.

Difficulties with Intimacy and Sexuality: "A Women's Problem"

Many adult survivors of child sexual abuse struggle with intimacy and sexuality later in adolescence and adulthood. Some survivors go to great lengths to avoid sex and situations that may involve intimacy to keep themselves safe from perceived future victimization (Maltz 2001). Others respond to childhood trauma by taking charge of their bodies and engaging in frequent sexual activity, believing if they initiate sex, no one will be able to victimize them. Both of these behaviors are common in adult survivors, with most people swinging to one end of the spectrum or the other. Intimacy and relationship problems in particular result in societal and self-blame on the part of women, who receive message that they are to take care of men and please them sexually at all costs. Messages around sexuality carry a double standard: women who do not engage in sexual activity are considered frigid, and those who do are considered promiscuous. Yet men receive positive social reinforcement for the same sexual activity. Society's shaming messages to women about sexuality further isolates women survivors struggling with intimacy and may make it more difficult to discuss these concerns with male partners.

Coping Skills and Dissociation: "Women Get All the Blame"

Every person develops coping skills to help them navigate daily life. These skills assist with managing difficult emotions and situations and allow for problem solving, taking a break from coping with long-term stress, and asking for help. Adult survivors of sexual abuse often developed coping skills that were effective in childhood but do not work as well in adulthood. One example of this is a skill called dissociation. When young children are abused they may adapt by pushing the memories of the abuse out of their thoughts. If the child does not remember the abuse, the resulting impact to his or her daily functioning is reduced. All people dissociate to an extent. Most people have had the experience of driving home, then suddenly realizing they have arrived at home, but have no memory of most of the trip. Dissociation occurs on a continuum, from forgetting the drive home on one end, to actually "splitting off" the psyche to keep traumatic memories hidden from the conscious mind. Dissociation is an adaptive and resourceful solution that enables a small mind to handle a devastating situation, but often creates problems for navigating every day life in adulthood. Often, dissociation and other coping skills developed by women are seen by society in the context of gender roles and stereotypes. For example, a married woman who copes by working many hours at a high stress job, metaphorically "running" from memories of abuse, may be see by society as neglectful of her husband or children. However, a male survivor of child sexual abuse who copes the same way may be seen as a "go-getter" and good provider for his family. The validity of women's coping mechanisms are often called into question. For women, dissociation is pathologized; adult women survivors of child sexual abuse who disclose in adulthood receive messages that they are "making it up" or trying to ruin the lives of male perpetrators, who are often seen as role models and leaders in the community. Alternatively, men who dissociate and later discuss traumatic material, such as combat experiences in a war zone, are seen as strong and brave for persevering in the face of such adversity. Even the very fact of speaking out is scrutinized. As the child sexual abuse scandal has emerged in the Catholic Church, the survivors, who are mostly men, are seen as brave for telling their stories, yet the motives of women who disclose similar abuse from male relatives are questioned.

Posttraumatic Stress Disorder: "Men Get All the Credit"

Posttraumatic stress disorder (PTSD), according to the Diagnostic and Statistical Manual of Mental Disorders (DSM-IV 1994) can develop when a person experiences a traumatic event that "involved actual, or threatened death or serious injury, or a threat to the physical integrity of self or others" and the person's response "involved intense fear, helplessness or horror" (American Psychiatric Association (APA) 1994, 428). PTSD was first identified as a disorder because of patterns of symptoms observed in returning Vietnam combat veterans. The same symptoms had been pathologized in women for centuries, most notably by Sigmund Freud, but it was the acknowledgement of these symptoms in men as a result of combat trauma that resulted in reduction in societal stigma and the development of effective treatment for women survivors of child sexual abuse. The National Institute of Health Co-Morbidity Study (2002) indicated that 12.2 percent of men and 26.5 percent of women who were molested develop PTSD. Symptoms experienced by survivors include hypervigilance, flashbacks, nightmares, exaggerated startle response, mood swings, intrusive memories or thoughts of the abuse, feelings of helplessness, and dissociation. PTSD resulting from sexual abuse is diagnosed more often in women than men. This may be due in part to the fact that U.S. society and mental health professionals more readily acknowledge and pathologize such symptoms in women. Women may also be more likely to seek out treatment than men.

CONCLUSION

Child sexual abuse occurs overwhelmingly to both men and women, but it is seen largely as a women's issue. Gender socialization and pathologized stereotypes of women's sexuality result in societal stigma and self-blame for sexual abuse survivors. Women have indisputably demonstrated an ability to survive in adversity, however, and sexual abuse survivors remain a testimony of the incredible ability of the mind to survive horror and thrive in healing.

Nonetheless, the circumstances requiring such strength and resiliency should not exist, and only interventions at a societal level will see a decrease in the incidence of child sexual abuse. Protecting children needs to become a societal priority. Myths about child sexual abuse, such as the portrait of abusers who are strangers, create conditions in which perpetrators can abuse children to whom they are close. Myths that girls make up stories of sexual abuse create an environment in which children are not believed. And sexualized images of young girls and teenagers in the media create a society in which "sexy" portrayals of children are considered normal and even appealing. Silencing messages such as "children should be seen and not heard" need to be challenged. And above all, society must speak with a collective voice that any behavior that leads to the sexual abuse of children is unacceptable.

See also Intimate Partner Violence; Sex Trafficking; Sexual Assault and Sexual Harassment.

Further Reading: American Psychiatric Association, *Diagnostic and Statistical Manual of Mental Disorders*, 4th ed. (Washington, D.C.: American Psychiatric Association, 1994); American Psychiatric Association, *Statement on Memories of Sexual Abuse* (Washington, D.C.: American Psychiatric Association, 1993); Dubowitz, Howard, Maureen Black, Donna Harrington, and Anna Verschoore, "A Follow-Up Study of Behavior Problems Associated with Child Sexual Abuse," *Child Abuse and Neglect* 17, no. 6 (1993): 743–754;

Fromm, Suzette, *Total Estimated Cost of Child Abuse and Neglect in the United States: Statistical Evidence* (Chicago, IL: Prevent Child Abuse America, 2001); Johnson, Scott Allen, *Physical Abusers and Sex Offenders: Forensic and Clinical Strategies* (Boca Raton, FL: CRC Press, 2007); Kendall-Tackett, Kathleen A., Linda M. Williams, and David Finkelhor, "Impact of Sexual Abuse on Children: A Review and Synthesis of Recent Empirical Studies," *Psychological Bulletin* 113, no. 1 (1993): 164–180; Loeske, Donileen, Richard J. Gelles, and Mary M. Cavanaugh, *Current Controversies on Family Violence* (Thousand Oaks, CA: Sage Publications, 2005); Loftus, Elizabeth E. F., M. Garry, and J. Feldman, "Forgetting Sexual Trauma: What Does it Mean When 38% Forget," *Journal of Consulting and Clinical Psychology* 62 (1994): 1177–1181; Maltz, Wendy, *The Sexual Healing Journey: A Guide for Survivors of Sexual Abuse* (HarperCollins Publishers, 2001); National Institute of Health, "National Institute of Health Co-Morbidity Study," 2002; Prevent Child Abuse America, *Fact Sheet: Sexual Abuse of Children* (Chicago, IL: Prevent Child Abuse America, 2006); Singer, Mark I., David Hussey, and Kimberly J. Strom, "Grooming the Victim: An Analysis of a Perpetrator's Seduction Letter," *Child Abuse and Neglect* 16 (1992): 877–886; *State of New Hampshire v. Hungerford,* 1997 No. 95-429, Supreme Court of New Hampshire; Valentine, LaNae, and Leslie L. Feinhauer, "Resilience Factors Associated with Female Survivors of Childhood Sexual Abuse," *The American Journal of Family Therapy* 21, no. 3 (1993): 216–224; Williams, L. M., "Recovered Memories of Abuse in Women with Documented Child Sexual Victimization Histories," *Journal of Traumatic Stress* 8 (1995): 649–673; *Wilson v. Phillips,* 1999 No. G019891, California Court of Appeals, 4th District.

Kathryn Woods

CHILDCARE

Controversies concerning childcare in the United States, which center on who should take responsibility, have moved in and out of the spotlight for more than 150 years. Social and moral issues concerning appropriate childcare are motivated primarily by the dilemma of public versus private responsibility for the well-being of children.

BACKGROUND

Although many people may believe that the issue of childcare is relatively new, this issue has been part of our national landscape for quite some time. In fact, the first recorded formal daycare began in 1854 in New York City (Rose 1999). At that time, these centers were called "day nurseries." The nurseries were modeled after the formal French daycare centers called *crèches*. The primary purpose of the day nurseries was centered on issues of child neglect as opposed to a childcare service. In the beginning, day nurseries were not federally funded ventures and instead tended to be funded by settlement houses and local service agencies.

During the Great Depression of the 1930s, however, childcare use and offerings were greatly expanded as part of the Works Progress Administration (WPA) (Rose 1999). The major purpose for the inclusion of childcare under WPA was to create jobs—in this case, jobs as childcare workers. An even bigger expansion of childcare occurred in 1943 under the Lanham Act. This expansion was necessary because of the incredible increase of women in the workforce during World

War II. Because childcare offerings weren't readily available during this era, the federal government funded more than 3,000 daycare centers for approximately 60,000 children as part of this act. This expansion of childcare extended to private business as well. During World War II, for example, the Kaiser Shipbuilding Corporation in Oregon was the first known employer-sponsored childcare offering. This offering consisted of two daycare centers that operated 24 hours a day. When the war ended, so did the need for women in the workforce; thus childcare services greatly decreased at that time.

The 1950s decade brought with it a continued allegiance to a more traditional mother's role—that is, one that is primarily focused on raising children. The 1950s ideology was questioned beginning in the 1960s, however, when a more liberal view of women's roles prevailed. At that time, more women were entering the workforce and that in turn influenced the amount of childcare that was necessary. Since the 1960s, childcare offerings and use have increased dramatically. This is so even in light of the demise of the first Comprehensive Child Development Bill in 1971. This bill would have authorized more than $2 billion specifically for childcare services. President Nixon vetoed the bill stating that, "for the Federal Government to plunge headlong financially into supporting childcare development would commit the vast moral authority of the National Government to the side of communal approaches to child rearing" (Robertson 2003, 7). Despite the President Nixon veto in 1971, both federal and state governance have been major contributors to childcare definitions, regulations, finance, and structure.

WHAT IS CHILDCARE?

Typically, childcare is defined as care provided for children by those who are not the children's parents/guardians. Most often, the caregiving work for children is financially compensated. The federal government has attached an age requirement for its definition of childcare that spans from birth through 12 years of age. The age category specifies eligibility of childcare subsidy and tax credits regulated at the federal level.

Childcare structure occurs in several differing arrangements: relative care, daycare center care, family daycare, and in-home care. Relative care is care provided by a family member outside the immediate family, most often by the grandmother of the child. Even though the grandparent or other family relative may be a blood relative to the child, financial compensation may still be part of the arrangement. In the past, relative care had been the most utilized style of childcare arrangement. Today, daycare centers are the most common style of childcare used.

A daycare center arrangement is care provided by a nonrelative that occurs in a public setting much like a school setting. In fact, daycare centers are often part of school systems but also can be part of a workplace setting, as well as a freestanding facility. The increased popularity of daycare center care is due in part to the education environment it commonly offers. Traditionally, daycare centers deliver childcare services to a large number of children of wide-ranging ages. Because daycare centers normally operate as a business venture, that is, occurring in a public setting and with a trained and fully compensated staff, daycare centers tend to be described as the most reliable style of childcare arrangement.

Family daycare offerings are commonly located in the childcare provider's home. Normally, a family daycare provider serves as few as one child but usually not more than six children because of licensing regulations. Family daycare tends to be used by families with younger children because the setting is considered more "homelike" than the more institutionalized form found in daycare centers. Thus the transition for very young children from home to daycare, it is reasoned, will be somewhat less stressful, as the care setting tends to be similar to a child's own home.

In-home childcare is the least used style of childcare arrangement mainly because it is the most expensive form. In-home childcare is care by a nonrelative that occurs in the child's home. This style of arrangement is also commonly known as care performed by a nanny or au pair. The childcare provider provides care to a single child or family of siblings. Babysitting is not included in formal childcare arrangements, as babysitting services are more likely those that are retained while a parent is involved in errands or other functions not associated with the workplace.

Another area used to describe childcare is based on licensing status. Childcare is regulated by individual states. Although some subsidies originate from the federal government, each state sets standards for childcare delivery usually in the form of childcare licensure. The states use regulation standards through the licensing of childcare providers. The issue at hand is that much childcare exists in an "underground" fashion, that is, as unlicensed. Estimations of unlicensed childcare in the United States range from 50 percent to as high as 80 percent (Clark-Stewart & Allhusen 2005). Because unlicensed childcare is virtually impossible to detect and thus regulate, issues such as child safety and the quality of care they receive are major concerns. Beyond the issue of licensing, a crucial component of childcare involves the responsibility of caregiving.

OPPOSITIONAL TERRAINS

The private responsibility debate suggests that children are best cared for within the "family," preferably when the mother provides the hands-on daily care of her child(ren) (Robertson 2003). The assumption is that the rearing of children is a private matter and caregiving is a natural purview of women generally and of mothers specifically. This ideology stems from the concept of, the "cult of true womanhood." Here, women's highest calling is rooted in caregiving. That is, to be a woman means caregiving and that in turn means mothering.

Arguments supporting the private responsibility debate often center on the issue of children's developmental health. This focus claims that children are likely harmed developmentally in daycare settings. For example, children may have higher levels of aggressive behavior such as bullying or classroom disruptions when they have spent more time in daycare (Robertson 2003). This perspective originates from infant attachment theory posited by John Bowlby in 1951 in his highly influential work, *Maternal Care and Mental Health.* His work suggested that these harmful behaviors are found in children who have not had adequate

THE COLUMBINE HIGH SCHOOL SHOOTINGS: A CASE FOR STAY-AT-HOME PARENTAL CHILDCARE

Unsupervised children indulged by affluent parents is a recipe for disaster, and disaster is exactly what transpired at Columbine High School. Opponents of daycare suggest that it was precisely this combination that was the root cause for the Columbine atrocity. Klebold and Harris came from homes where both parents worked outside the home, with the boys enjoying considerable autonomy and freedom. Although warning signs existed about the upcoming shootings, such as the videotapes explaining the plans, fascination with violent video games, and reports from school authorities about the boys' aggressive and threatening behavior, these signs appeared to go unnoticed by their parents. Harris's voice on a video saying, "thank God my parents never searched my room," offers support to these allegations of inattentive parenting. Moreover, Klebold describes a great deal of anger surrounding daycare experiences such as being teased and mocked. These experiences continued and were magnified during high school, and interestingly he pens an essay in his creative writing class about a daycare center in hell that was operated by Satan (Robertson 2003). Examples such as these contribute to the private responsibility debate whose proponents contend that often the investment in a dual-career family occurs at the expense of children because little time exists to properly attend to the monitoring and well-being of children.

opportunities to bond with their mothers because the children are in daycare settings instead of at home with their mothers.

The public responsibility debate centers on the notion that children are the collective responsibility of communities, states, and of the entire nation. Collective responsibility extends to the social, political, educational, and economical realm. Thus this perspective suggests that childrearing is akin to education. Whereas education is funded and regulated at both the state and national level, so also should childcare. This ideology gained momentum and notoriety with Hillary Clinton's book, *It Takes a Village.* (1996).

Clinton (1996) argued that to create a strong and thriving nation, communities must be fully committed to children in every sense. Moreover, families need support and resources to grow strong children who are contributing members of our society. Applied to the issue of childcare, the contention is that childcare must be made available and financed so that children are not left unsupervised and are not subjected to substandard childcare venues. Thus as part of our societal offerings and commitment to children, childcare needs to be widely available, of high quality, and affordable.

CHILDCARE AND MEDIA INFLUENCE

Although both the public and the private responsibility debate have merit, these dichotomous perspectives have been reduced to a clash between working and stay-at-home mothers. This controversial and very public debate, however, encompasses the much more complex issue of, what is women's proper role in society?

Perhaps one of the best examples of this clash is one that played out in the media in the 1990s. The case of Jennifer Ireland garnered national attention and the media spotlight after she gave birth to her daughter when she was a 16-year-old high school student (Frost-Knappman and Cullen-Dupont 1997). The father of the child, Steven Smith, was also a high school student. After graduating from high school, Ireland was a recipient of a college scholarship at the University of Michigan. In 1993, Ireland attended the university and at that time enrolled her daughter in the university-affiliated daycare center. In 1994, Smith sued Ireland for custody of the child, claiming that she was an unfit mother. Part of the claim centered on the assertion that Ireland was more interested in her academic career than in her daughter because she chose to put her child in daycare while she attended to her studies.

Initially, Smith won the case. Smith, who also was attending college, resided with his parents, explaining that his mother would provide care for his daughter while he worked and attended classes. The judge, Raymond Cachen, agreeing with Smith, concluded that a child, "raised and supervised by blood relations" as opposed to being "supervised a great part of the day by strangers" would be the better arrangement for the youngster (Frost-Knappman and Cullen-Dupont 1997). A public uproar ensued over the decision. Allegations of a backlash against women, specifically career women, were declared. A year later, the decision was overturned on appeal. The *Ireland v. Smith* case brought the daycare debate into the media spotlight, as well as into public discourse.

A precursor to the Ireland case, the McMartin Preschool scandal likely wielded considerable influence in the original Ireland decision, as well as to public opinion surrounding the issue of childcare. This case was first filed in 1983 with allegations of sexual abuse of a child while the child attended the McMartin Preschool/daycare center (Douglas and Michaels 2004). The case grew from abuse of a single child to more than 125 children, with accusations extending from torture and satanism to secret tunnels existing beneath the daycare facility. The children's silence surrounding the abuse was allegedly coerced through the viewing of atrocities such as cutting the ears off live rabbits, smashing baby turtles, and beating a horse to death. Children reported abuse over an approximate 10-year span and/or including many members of the McMartin family in their allegations. After a lengthy trial, the allegations were found to be unsubstantiated, and the case was dropped by 1990 after an unsuccessful retrial. The impact of the unsupported allegations of nightmarish and perverse atrocities against young children lingered in the media and likely in many parents' minds as well. Since the McMartin case, cadres of other similar daycare abuse cases have been played out in the media and consequently on a national platform. Some of the claims were certainly founded, but many others were reported to be pure fabrication. The media influence of the McMartin and Ireland cases, in part, explains the hypervisibility of childcare. To have a full understanding of childcare issues, however, an overview of the challenges families face in the provision of care for their children is necessary.

CHILDCARE CHALLENGES

Formalized childcare has often been described as a "patchwork" system of caring for children. This description of childcare is used because there is no formal or comprehensive style of caring for children outside of the immediate family. Parents, especially mothers, often feel immense frustration, as few options and conversely many gaps exist in securing childcare. For example, oftentimes, licensed childcare simply does not exist after 6 P.M. This can be an insurmountable problem for women whose work hours do not fit the typical 9-to-5 workday.

The securing of infant care can also add to the challenge of childcare. Normally, infant care is quite time intensive for providers, and they must subsequently reduce their childcare load to care for an infant. Because of this situation, providers are less likely to engage in infant childcare, as they can earn higher incomes caring for toddlers and preschoolers. The very issue of childcare cost continues to add to the challenges of childcare. The cost of caring for children is staggering. For a single child in 2003, full-time childcare costs averaged $4,000 to $6,000 per year and is significantly higher for infant care (Clark-Stewart and Allhusen 2005).

The issues of childcare gaps presented here, as well as childcare cost generally, create the market for unlicensed childcare that currently exists. Although many parents may feel they have no other options than to use unlicensed childcare, it is important to note that unlicensed childcare is not eligible for childcare subsidies or tax credits. A parent, for example, may use a licensed daycare center for one child and unlicensed care for her infant because either licensed care is not available or is too expensive. Because daycare centers typically do not offer services beyond 6 P.M., the same mother may also need to employ yet another person to pick up the childcare slack should her workday extend beyond 6 P.M. As mothers "patch" together many different styles of childcare to successfully complete their childcare needs, the patchwork system will likely be less stable and can be

---

THE DEVALUING OF PUBLIC CHILDCARE

It is surprising that childcare provider pay is among the lowest of all professions given the fact that childcare cost is often described as exorbitant. In fact, it is commonplace for childcare providers to earn wages far below poverty rates. Gas station attendants, zoo employees whose primary job is feeding animals, and bank employees responsible for counting money command higher wages than do childcare providers. These startling examples provide motivation for childcare providers to seek other employment out of financial desperation. Provider turnover rates are estimated to be 30 percent (Clark-Stewart and Allhusen 2005). This rate is among the highest of all professions and more than four times that of teachers. Many childcare experts caution, however, that what we call turnover, children experience as loss. Thus turnover represents the loss of someone who is important in the lives of children, to whom children may have developed an important emotional attachment.

---

prone to last-minute cancellations and changes. In the previous example, only one of the three arrangements need to fail, causing her to scramble to locate another last-minute arrangement. The alternative is that the working mother misses work, which also may translate to less money—money that is likely critical to the maintenance of the family.

The patchwork system of childcare provision is a compelling one, but proponents of stay-at-home parental childcare suggest that the struggle is rooted in how federal government organizes tax subsidies. At issue is the increasing of options to families as opposed to increasing the offerings of formal childcare. This perspective focuses on working parents' discomfort with formalized childcare, despite their uneasiness, feel forced to participate in a dual-career formulation. Instead, they seek financially viable opportunities as an avenue to providing daily care for their children (Robertson 2003).

The challenge becomes an economic one for families who prefer stay-at-home parental childcare. To begin addressing this concern, it is proposed that corporations should be encouraged to provide family-friendly policies such as flextime, part-time, and job-sharing options, as well as priority scheduling and telecommuting opportunities for parents. These offerings would provide families with choices to be able to construct workdays that promote direct caregiving to their children.

Moreover, the government can continue to increase options by raising the personal exemption allowance. This would reduce the tax burden on families, thereby allowing for one parent to remain at home to care for children. A more direct measure would include the expansion of the dependent care tax credit to extend beyond families who use formal childcare to parents who provide stay-at-home parental childcare. Currently, subsidy exists only for families who use formal childcare and this, it is argued, occurs at the expense of stay-at-home parents. Thus the organization of tax subsidy literally compels families to pay others to care for their children.

CONCLUSION

Whether, "it takes a village" or a "stay-at-home mom" and exactly what serves the best interests of children are still unknown. How children may be hindered developmentally or helped educationally is a controversy with a long history. The debate over public versus private responsibility to children will likely continue to be portrayed in the media and pondered within the home. As families continue to grapple with this issue, it is likely that communities, states, and the federal government will as well. Nonetheless, the struggle over women's appropriate role in contemporary society remains an active site of contention for all Americans.

See also Child Custody and Parental Rights; Family Values; Fatherhood Initiatives.

Further Reading: Clark, Alison, and Virginia Allhusen, *What We Know About Childcare* (Cambridge, MA: Harvard University Press, 2005); Clinton, Hillary, *It Takes a Village*

(New York: Simon and Schuster, 1996); Douglas, Susan, and Meredith Michaels, *The Mommy Myth: The Idealization of Motherhood and How it Has Undermined All Women* (New York: Free Press, 2004); Family Research Council, 2006, available at: http://www.frc.org; Fox, Isabel, and Norman Lobsenz, *Begin There: The Benefits of a Stay-at-Home Parent* (Hauppage, NJ: Barrons Educational Series, 1996); Frost-Knappman, Elizabeth, and Kathryn Cullen-Dupont, *Women's Rights on Trial: 101 Historic Trials from Anne Hutchinson to Virginia Military Cadets* (Detriot: Gale, 1997); Jackson, Mick, *Indictment: The McMartin Case* (HBO Home Video, 1995, 132 min); Robertson, Brian, *Day Care Deception: What the Child Care Establishment Isn't Telling Us* (New York: Encounter Books, 2003); Rose, E., *A Mother's Job: A History of Day Care 1890–1960* (New York: Oxford University Press, 1999).

Lori McNeil

COLONIALISM AND IMPERIALISM

The interrelated processes and discourses of colonialism and imperialism have been viewed by some as empowering to women and by others as oppressive. Current debates concerning the effects of colonialism and imperialism on women involve whether women benefit economically, politically, and/or socially from the material and ideological effects of these historical relationships between rich and poor countries and between the East and West.

BACKGROUND

The terms *colonialism* and *imperialism* are often used interchangeably to refer to the various forms of political, economic, and cultural control by a greater power over less powerful territories. These terms are typically used to describe a period beginning in the mid-nineteenth century, when the industrializing European nations and the United States colonized the nonindustrialized territories and directly ruled their indigenous populations in an attempt to secure access to cheap resources and labor and markets for manufactured products. By and large, these formal colonial empires broke up after World War II. Because the former colonial powers have still maintained their dominance on the world stage, albeit often through less direct mechanisms such as political influence, threat of military intervention, and various forms of economic leverage, however, the concepts of imperialism and colonialism are still relevant today. Many authors use the terms *neoimperialism* and *neocolonialism* to refer to this continued, less formal domination of the West over many parts of Latin America, Africa, and Asia. Of particular concern to analysts of neoimperialism in the latter half of the twentieth century is the role that Western and particularly U.S.-based multinational corporations play in controlling the economic fate of many areas in the global South.

In addition to being a synonym for imperialism, the term *colonialism* also refers specifically to cultural misrepresentations regarding the superiority of the West and corresponding backwardness of all other regions. Colonialism often relies on racist and ethnocentric ideas that place Europeans at the highest level of civilization and all other peoples on a lower rung on the hierarchy as a result of their supposed natural, social, technological, and/or cultural deficiencies. Such Eurocentric portrayals have more often than not served as implicit justification for Western imperial ambitions. The "backwardness" of the nonindustrial territories was generally seen by Europeans as fueling "barbaric" social practices and economic inefficiencies. People in these territories could be saved from these ills, it was argued, only through direct contact with the civilized West via colonization. This salvation narrative of superiority, in which colonialism becomes a civilizing mission, relies on exaggerated and essentialized notions of difference between the colonizing and colonized regions. For instance Edward Said, a well-known scholar of colonialism and cultural imperialism, states that colonial ideas often portray the non-West as the backward, irrational, weak Other that can be contrasted with, and needs to be saved by, the liberated, rational and strong West (Said 1978). This dualistic formation, Said emphasizes, exaggerates both the backwardness of the non-West and liberation and rationality in the West in ways that fail to capture colonial realities.

Without question, the various economic, political, and cultural mechanisms of imperialism and colonialism have had an enormous impact on women's lives. Yet until recently, the gendered aspects of imperialism have been absent from most historical, economic, and cultural analyses. Most scholars were preoccupied with male domains and experiences and did not consider questions of women and empire. Thankfully, since the 1980s, a number of feminist studies have begun to explore the complex relations between gender and imperialism (e.g., Chaudhuri and Strobel 1992; McClintock, Mufti, and Shohat, 1997; Midgely 1998). This feminist work offers insight into the gender implications of imperial power, especially how colonial practices rearranged gender relations and affected women's social status. It examines how gender relations played a special role in framing the West's civilizing mission. It pays attention to the intersections of gender with race, ethnicity, and class across various sites of imperial encounters. It looks at how exploitative relations of neoimperialism continue to affect women's lives in the global South. It also challenges contemporary colonial scripts that portray non-Western women as victims of cultural backwardness who need salvation from the supposedly more civilized Western societies.

GENDER RELATIONS IN THE COLONIES AND IMPERIALISM'S CIVILIZING MISSION

As many observers have noted, the economic goal of direct forms of imperialism in the nineteenth and early twentieth centuries was aimed at controlling the resources, labor, and markets of colonial territories. But concerns about unequal gender relations in those territories were often used to legitimize colonization, and a discussion of these concerns provides a good entry point for understanding the impact of imperialism on women. Colonial administrations explicitly targeted gender relations in many of their policies and laws, and debates about how to best "save" colonized women from "savage" men's treatment of them raged in many European and American social circles (Enloe 2000, 27).

One example of how this civilizing mission played out can be seen in the ways that the British colonial administration attempted to transform gender relations in India. Among many nineteenth-century British social reformers, the comparative lack of women's rights in India implied that it was in need of Britain's civilizing influence through colonization. As British political economist James Mill wrote in *History of India,* "among rude people the women are generally degraded, among civilized people they are exalted" (Mill 1817, cited in Enloe 2000, 48). Descriptions of patriarchal practices such as *sati,* in which Hindu widows from a relatively small segment of Indian society immolated themselves on their husbands' funeral pyres, shocked Victorian sensibilities. These limited events were turned into a practice associated with all of India, and thus served as the moral ground on which the civilizing mission of empire could be launched. As outsiders, the British portrayed themselves as interceding on behalf of Indian women, and, as feminist scholar Gayatri Spivak so famously put it, saw themselves engaged in a colonial project of "saving brown women from brown men" (Spivak 1985, 121).

The changes in legislation put in place by British and other colonial administrations to achieve this civilizing mission certainly resulted in a reorganization of gender relations, although not always in the direction of increased rights for women. For example, the British colonial state at first refused to ban the practice of *sati,* claiming that it was based in Hindu religious texts and thus beyond law. *Sati* was then made illegal in 1829, but this law was rarely enforced, and later in the century, the practice was decriminalized (Mani 1999). British officials also passed legislation that raised the age of legally permissible sex for girls from 10 to 12 years old, gave women some inheritance rights, and allowed widows to remarry (Midgely 1998). But laws were also enacted that imposed a system of prostitution so that British soldiers would have access to sexual relations with Indian women, and that gave prison sentences for those wives who refused to meet their marital sexual obligations (Enloe 2000, 49).

Further, the passing of these laws often turned on debates between male colonizers and anticolonial traditionalists in which the subjects of law—the women themselves—were marginalized. For example, debates about *sati* between British administrators and Indian traditionalists before 1829 turned on whether this practice was sanctioned by Hindu scripture, and not on the rights of women as human beings (Mani 1999).

Laws enacted to "save brown women from brown men" in other colonial contexts also failed to take local women's desires and concerns into account, which often resulted in policies that did not necessarily benefit or liberate colonized women. For instance, when the French colonized Algeria in the 1830s, part of their self-declared civilizing mission involved outlawing the veil (Hélie-Lucas 1987). During the late nineteenth-century colonization of Egypt by Britain, colonial officials, often supported by male and female reformers back home, also challenged the practice of veiling, but to use a more correct term, *hijab. Hijab* literally translates into "modesty" but generally refers to a woman covering her hair and/or face with a scarf or other covering. In both the Algerian and Egyptian cases, the needs and desires of the colonized women themselves were marginalized. For instance, European women who incorrectly denounced "the veil" as representing the depravity of the harem rarely took the time to find out about the thoughts and lives of colonized women. Further, despite not yet having the vote or other basic political rights themselves, these European women often traded in misrepresentations of the meaning behind *hijab* in ways that portrayed themselves as free and powerful vis-à-vis Algerian and Egyptian women (Chaudhuri and Strobel 1992). Ultimately, the more that colonizers attempted to ban *hijab* in the name of promoting civilization in Algeria and Egypt, the harder it was for colonized women to control debates around the practice. Instead, the Europeans created a reaction in which local anticolonial elites became increasingly focused on controlling women's behavior in an attempt to preserve threatened traditions. Women who did go into public with their heads uncovered were made to seem complicit with the imperialist project (Enloe 2000, 53). Thus although the stated goal of colonial reforms was to increase women's rights, these reforms often failed for various reasons. They did not accurately understand the nature of gender relations in the colonized territories, preferring instead to trade in crude stereotypes that mostly served to make European women look liberated in contrast to these Others. And they also failed because they did not take the actual desires and goals of local women into account in the creation of laws and policies (Ahmed 1992).

Nonetheless, the attempts by colonizing forces to civilize local populations and "save brown women from brown men" continue to have an enormous impact on women's lives in the former colonies to this day. As local elites began to challenge colonization through independence movements in the early to mid-twentieth century, and then set up postcolonial states, responding to the colonizers' views of the "proper" role of women became a central concern. Sometimes, postcolonial elites would rearticulate the European civilizing mission. For instance, India borrowed language from the British and recriminalizing *sati* (Mani 1999). Iran and Turkey maintained the colonial ban on women wearing *hijab* to show that they were modern, "civilized" countries. Just as common, though, were postcolonial movements that called for women's return to "traditional" roles, and highlighted the need to defend traditional gender roles against the degradation of outside forces. In nearly all cases, moving from colonial rule to postcolonial self-rule often encompassed a "complex inter-relationship of contest and collusion between indigenous patriarchal norms and those held by administrators" (Sangari and Vaid 1993, 7). Women have a particularly hard time challenging some of these calls to return to so-called traditional gender roles when they are posed as if traditions are immutable, when in fact traditions are often contested and/or reinvented activities. Further, when women do ask for more social justice, they are often told that they are importing a Western ideology and thus reproducing the former social relations of colonization. In this manner, the colonial civilizing mission did not lay the groundwork for women's emancipation as much as it made the context of feminist struggle more difficult to navigate in the colonies and former colonies.

THE IMPACT OF IMPERIALISM ON WOMEN'S ECONOMIC AND POLITICAL STATUS IN THE COLONIES

In contrast to the Europeans' stated goal of improving gender relations in the colonies, much of the feminist research on this topic shows that imperialism often exacerbated or created gender inequalities. For example, the Seneca tribe in what is now western New York, USA, was one in which women had a great deal of power. But when North America was colonized, this power waned because the Europeans refused to trade with women, thus giving Seneca men exclusive access to the increasingly important money economy (Rothenberg 1980). In parts of southern Africa, the inculcation of European norms of femininity and family organization through religious and/or cultural indoctrination decreased the power that women had obtained through matrilineal notions of kinship (Ferguson 1999). In West Africa, the assignment of formerly communally held land rights to men by colonial administrators decreased women's control over food production and distribution (Leacock and Etienne 1980). In Dutch colonies in Indonesia, colonial administrators decreased local women's access to economic means so that they would be available to serve as prostitutes to local plantation workers, and concubines to Dutch migrant workers. Often, plantation companies would hire women at half the rates paid to men, which was not enough to meet their needs, in an explicit attempt to give them incentives to provide sexual services to male plantation workers. This was done by design and not by accident, for the Dutch believed that local men would not do plantation work if they were not provided with female sexual services. Concubinage occurred through a similar mechanism, and was planned by local administrators to meet migrant workers' sexual and domestic needs in a time when few Dutch women were willing to migrate to the new colonies. Not only did concubinage meet the sexual needs of the migrant workers from the Netherlands, but it allowed the plantation companies to keep salaries of these workers low because the local women did domestic work that the Dutch would have otherwise had to pay for (Stoler 1997). These practices were justified through a colonial script in which the Indonesian were portrayed as less civilized than the Dutch. As one writer on the colonies in Indonesia put it, using local women to meet sexual needs was a "necessary evil" that involved no emotional attachments, because for Indonesian women, "the meaning of our word 'love' is entirely unknown" (Ritter 1856, cited in Stoler 1997, 368).

Even when European women did migrate to the colonies, there was a steady demand for domestic servants, and many local women worked as servants or nannies in the homes of European settlers. These relationships were hardly the ground on which alliances could be built between European women and local women, however. Indeed, the relationship was often based on, and maintained, an exaggerated notion of difference and power among women, in which the European woman was the civilized, respectable feminine ideal to which the colonized domestic servant might aspire but could never quite reach. European women often treated local women as childlike creatures who, despite many attempts at instruction regarding the proper way to make tea, raise children, or set a table would never be able to grasp the trappings of civilization. In fact, as feminist political scientist Cynthia Enloe puts it, this "paternalistic relationship between the white mistress and her local servants was frequently held up as an example of what the colonizing mission was all about" (Enloe 2000, 182). Further, there was much at stake in maintaining the differences of class and race that separated the European women from the local women who worked as servants in their homes. Such cultural codes and practices have had an effect on relationships between women of European descent and local women in the colonies to the present day. For example, many women in South Africa are still trying to negotiate and overcome the power differentials that were constructed through the paternalistic "black maid/white madam" relationships that were first developed under colonialism (Enloe 2000, 182).

IMPERIALISM, NEOIMPERIALISM, AND WOMEN'S LABOR

When tracing the broad contours of how women's labor has been used for economic gain in colonial and neocolonial regimes, and how this has affected women's lives, a couple of points stand out. First, women's subsistence work was often exploited by the colonial administration to keep wages of male laborers low. Thus there was pressure to maintain this subsistence economy, even as there was the counterpressure of the profit motive to integrate women into the market system and make them wage workers. This issue was first raised in the early twentieth century in Rosa Luxemburg's theory of imperialism with regard to how the peasantry in general served as a source of cheap nonwage goods and a market for capitalist products (Luxemburg 1913). But while Luxemburg considered only a nongendered category of peasants, later theorists showed how the subsistence labor of women in particular was at times viewed as essential to the profitability of empire. For example, Maria Mies, in an essay in the book *Women: The Last Colony,* emphasizes how colonizers relied on women's noncapitalist subsistence activities such as raising food and caring labor in the household. Using case studies from India, she argues that imperialism often increases sexism and ideas about "women's rightful place in the home" to maintain access to this subsistence and caring labor, often negatively affecting women's overall economic well-being (Mies, Von Werlhof, and Bennholdt-Thomsen 1988). Thus Mies et al. argue that neither class relations nor patriarchy alone is the dominant oppression for women in the colonies and former colonies, and advocate for an anti-imperialist feminist struggle that can confront both issues simultaneously.

A second major point is that processes of neoimperialism in the late twentieth and early twenty-first centuries have included capital expansion in which women were often targeted as the "ideal workers" in the new multinational factories. Since the 1970s, multinational firms have increasingly relocated production from Europe and the United States to Asia and Latin America. Many of the jobs in these factories consist of labor-intensive assembly work, and most of the workers in these plants are women. This transnational dispersion of production is often viewed through the lens of imperialism (or neoimperialism) because U.S.- and European-based corporations have relocated to these regions to take advantage of low-wage labor. Further, they are often able to use their greater power (and the greater power of their governments) to sidestep environmental, health, minimum wage, and other labor regulations in these countries. Because the spread of multinational capital involves political, economic, and cultural control by a greater power over less powerful actors on the world stage, and because it represents an attempt to secure access to cheap resources and labor, many analysts refer to it as a phase of economic imperialism, albeit a less formal one in the sense that these other countries are not directly ruled by Western nations.

The impact of multinational corporations and factory work on women's lives is context dependent. Although the increased availability of jobs in the regions where these factories relocate is often touted as an opportunity that women can use to improve their lives, the evidence shows mixed results. Research on the Caribbean and Latin America suggest that it is the low wages of women that attract multinational firms, and that these firms work in concert with local governments and local male elites to maintain low wages for women (Safa 1995). When factories first moved to many parts of Southeast Asia, women's wages were 20 to 50 percent lower than men's for comparable jobs in these factories, even in cases where male productivity is lower (Elson and Pearson 1981, 148). Feminists who research women's experience as workers in multinational firms often emphasize the powerful role of patriarchal and colonial assumptions that non-Western women are less skilled and thus deserve a lower wage, and contend that these assumptions, in concert with unequal power relations on the world stage, play a large role in women's low pay and economic exploitation.

In addition to providing a source of cheap labor, non-Western women are attractive to multinational firms because of colonial and patriarchal assumptions that they are more dexterous and docile than men (or for that matter, Western women). For instance, a brochure created by the Malaysian government to entice multinational corporations to locate in their country states that "the manual dexterity of the oriental woman is famous the world over. Her hands are small, and she works fast with extreme care" (cited in Elson and Pearson 1981, 149). The biased assumption here is that Asian women are more suited to tedious, delicate, and/or repetitious work. It is also believed that these women will be more passive and less likely to complain because of their docility; however, the supposed docility of these women has been challenged by a number of studies. Aihwa Ong's study of Malaysian factory workers is one of the most well-known of these. She recounts the manner in which these women gained control over the pace of their work by claiming that their machines were possessed by spirits and telling the Western managers that they had to shut down the machines to eliminate these spirits through time-consuming rituals, which was analogous to a sit-down strike (Ong 1987). Ong's study provides not only a challenge to colonial stereotypes of passive Asian women but also a reminder that women's forms of resistance can be multiple and varied.

There has been significant debate over whether the expansion of capital across borders has improved the lives of non-Western women. Does working in a factory in a multinational corporation increase women's exploitation, or does it make them better off? Has the spread of capital and with it certain Western cultural norms increased women's freedoms, or has it led to a decline in women's access to resources and power? These questions lie at the heart of every analysis of neoimperialism and its impact on women. They also echo debates about imperialism and neoimperialism more generally, in which some theorists say that progress is moved forward by contact with capitalism and the West, and others say the opposite (Brewer 1990). Many feminist economists believe that the movement of women out of nonwage work and into the capitalist labor market is their best hope for fighting gender oppression by gaining income and thus leverage in the home (e.g., Kabeer 1994). Once women are integrated into the labor market, it is argued, then the system of patriarchal domination will break down. Some studies bear this out. For example, anthropologist Helen Safa reports that women factory workers in export manufacturing firms in the Caribbean use their earnings to bargain for increased authority within the household (Safa 1995). Other studies demonstrate that different outcomes can occur. Social scientist Fauzia Ahmed's research in Bangladesh shows that factory work does not increase women's bargaining power at home, but it does increase their overall exploitation (Ahmed 2004).

Anthropologist Maria Patricia Fernández-Kelly's (1983) landmark study of women factory workers in Mexico in the early 1980s provides an account in which multinational capital can be shown to affect women's lives in complex and contradictory ways. These workers face long hours and terrible working conditions, and are offered little in terms of job security. They take the jobs, however, because many of them are single mothers and they have few other opportunities. This lack of other options certainly makes them vulnerable to exploitative labor practices in the factories. At the same time, however, they are able to break free of sometimes stifling patriarchal relations by having access to their own income. They are also able to develop a sense of solidarity by working together, which provides a base to challenge male authority in the plant and in their communities. Considering the complex interactions between capitalism, patriarchy, and imperial and colonial processes that are possible, then, many researchers contend that it would be best to examine the effects these have on women on a case-by-case basis, locating where it intensifies gender oppression in some cases, challenges it in others, and transforms it in still others (e.g., Elson and Pearson 1981; Mohanty 1991). Others have added the insight that attention must be paid to how neoimperialism has differing effects on different groups of women in a particular region, for instance benefiting upper class women in Mexico City while decreasing the well-being of very poor women (Benería and Roldan 1987).

COLONIAL REPRESENTATIONS OF NON-WESTERN WOMEN AND CONTEMPORARY POLITICS

A final issue regarding colonialism's impact is the existence of colonial stereotypes about non-Western women that continue to circulate within, and inform, contemporary power relations on a global scale. As discussed previously, the politics of representing non-Western women as passive victims in need of salvation from the West is part of a long history of colonialism. Unfortunately, such stereotypes continue to have salience, even in some feminist circles. For instance, many political and social reformers who are concerned about women's human rights around the globe portray the average non-Western woman as poor, backwards, and a victim of tradition. Anticolonial feminist scholar Chandra Talpade Mohanty has provided a well-known challenge to these representations by showing that they are produced by a colonial mindset that defines these women as the oppressed Other to the supposedly liberated Western woman (Mohanty 1991). Mohanty argues for an alternative analytical framework that begins with recognition of colonial misrepresentations in order to avoid them. She also calls for an appreciation of the heterogeneity of women's experiences in both the West and the non-West, particularly as this would call into question the dualistic framework of West/liberated, non-West/victim. Mohanty also stresses the importance of recognizing non-Western women's capabilities and strengths in providing solutions to their own problems, instead of having these solutions imposed on them (Mohanty 1991).

A particularly salient example of how colonial representations of non-Western women still circulate and affect global politics, and why Mohanty's pleas are important, is in how Afghan women have been represented in the United States by politicians and the news media, particularly after the events of 9/11. As many people know, Afghan women did suffer significant limits and oppressive violations to their basic human rights under the regimes of the U.S.-backed Northern Alliance in the early 1990s, and later under the Taliban. Far fewer are aware, however, that there has been an organized feminist struggle in Afghanistan against these human rights abuses by groups such as the Revolutionary Association of Women of Afghanistan (RAWA). This lack of awareness is at least in part due to colonial representations of Afghan women as victims that need to be saved, which downplays and marginalizes the role of these groups and their struggles. For example, in the late 1990s, RAWA became frustrated with some well-known feminist organizations in the United States such as the Feminist Majority, which argued for Western intervention in Afghanistan to save Afghan women, even offering a roadmap of what that intervention should look like, but gave no credit or recognition to RAWA (Farrell and McDermott 2006). A few weeks after the events of 9/11, the arguments made by these U.S. feminist groups were used in a radio address by first lady Laura Bush as a legitimating source for why the United States needed to pursue aggressive foreign policy in Afghanistan: "Civilized people throughout the world are speaking out in horror not only because our hearts break for the women and children in Afghanistan, but also because in Afghanistan we see the world the terrorists would like to impose on the rest of us" (cited in Farrell and McDermott 2006, 49). Here we see a return to the binary in which the West must undertake a civilizing mission to save non-Western women. There is much that is lost in such binary thinking, including any recognition of Afghan women's own needs and desires, or the fact that Afghan women were already actively fighting back, and, in the words of RAWA, needed "money and moral support, not instructions" (RAWA 1994, cited in Farrell and McDermott 2006, 33).

CONCLUSION

As these examples illustrate, it is difficult to claim that colonialism and imperialism are entirely "good" or "bad" for women, although many scholars highlight the negative impacts of these processes and ideologies on women's lives. As long as there continue to be daunting inequalities between rich and poor countries, poor women in particular will continue to be vulnerable to changes in the global economy, and so long as poor and/or "non-Western" countries are seen as inferior to the industrialized West, conflicts will continue regarding the various consequences of these global political and economic arrangements.

See also Gender and Globalization: Free Trade Zones; Gender and Globalization: Trends and Debates; Gender and International Development.

Further Reading: Ahmed, Fauzia, "The Rise of the Bangladeshi Garment Industry: Globalization, Women Workers and Voice," *NWSA Journal* 16, no. 2 (2004): 34–45; Ahmed, Leila, *Women and Gender in Islam: Historical Roots of a Modern Debate* (New Haven, CT: Yale University Press, 1992); Benería, Lourdes, and Martha Roldan, *The Crossroads of Class and Gender: Industrial Homework, Subcontracting, and the Household Dynamics in Mexico City* (Chicago: University of Chicago Press, 1987); Brewer, Anthony, *Marxist Theories of Imperialism: A Critical Survey* (London: Routledge Press, 1990); Chaudhuri, Nupur, and Margaret Strobel, eds., *Western Women and Imperialism: Complicity and Resistance* (Bloomington: Indiana University Press, 1992); Elson, Diane, and Ruth Pearson, "The Subordination of Women and the Internationalization of Factory Production," in *Of Marriage and Market: Subordination in International Perspective,* ed. Kate Young et al., 144–166 (London: CSE Books, 1981); Enloe, Cynthia, *Bananas, Beaches and Bases: Making Feminist Sense of International Politics,* 2nd ed. (Berkeley: University of California Press, 2000); Farrell, Amy, and Patrice McDermott, "Claiming Afghan Women: The Challenge of Human Rights Discourse for Transnational Feminism," in *Just Advocacy?: Women's Human Rights, Transnational Feminisms, and the Politics of Representation,* ed. Wendy Hesford and Wendy Kozol (New Brunswick, NJ: Rutgers University Press, 2006); Ferguson, James, *Expectations of Modernity: Myths and Meaning of Urban Life on the Zambian Copper Belt* (Berkeley: University of California Press, 1999); Fernández-Kelly, Maria Patricia, *For We Are Sold, I and My People: Women in Industry on Mexico's Frontier* (Albany: State University of New York Press, 1983); Hélie-Lucas, Marie Aimée, "Against Nationalism: The Betrayal of Algerian Women," *Trouble and Strife* 11 (1987): 27–31; Kabeer, Naila, *Reversed Realities* (London: Verso, 1994); Mani, Lata, *Contentious Traditions: Debate on Sati in Colonial India* (Berkeley: University of California Press, 1999); Leacock, Eleanor, and Mona Etienne, eds., *Women and Colonization: Anthropological Perspectives* (New York: Praeger Press, 1980); Luxemburg, Rosa, *The Accumulation of Capital* (London: Routledge, Kegan and Paul, 1913); McClintock, Anne, Aamir Mufti, and Ella Shohat, eds., *Dangerous Liaisons: Gender, Nation and Postcolonial Perspectives* (Minneapolis: University of Minnesota Press, 1997); Mies, Maria, Claudia Von Werlhof, and Veronika Bennholdt-Thomsen, *Women: The Last Colony* (London: Zed Press, 1988); Midgely, Clare, ed., *Gender and Imperialism* (Manchester: Manchester University Press, 1998); Mohanty, Chandra Talpade, "Under Western Eyes: Feminist Scholarship and Western Discourses," in *Third World Women and the Politics of Feminism,* ed. Chandra T. Mohanty, Ann Russo, and Lourdes Torres (Bloomington: Indiana University Press, 1991); Ong, Aiwah, *Spirits of Resistance and Capitalist Discipline: Factory Women in Malaysia* (Albany: State University of New York Press, 1987); Rothenberg, Diane, "The Mothers of the Nation: Seneca

Resistance to Quaker Intervention," in *Women and Colonization: Anthropological Perspectives*, ed. Eleanor Leacock and Mona Etienne (New York: Praeger Press, 1980); Safa, Helen, "Gender Implications of Export-Led Industrialization in the Caribbean," in *Engendering Wealth and Well-Being*, ed. Rae Blumberg et al. (Boulder, CO: Westview Press, 1995); Said, Edward, *Orientalism* (New York: Vintage Books, 1978); Sangari, Kumkum, and Sudesh Vaid, eds., *Recasting Women: Essays in Indian Colonial History* (New Delhi: Kali for Women, 1993); Spivak, Gayatri, "Can the Subaltern Speak? Speculations on Widow Sacrifice," *Wedge* 78 (1985): 120–130; Stoler, Ann Laura, "Making Empire Respectable: The Politics of Race and Sexual Morality in Twentieth-Century Colonial Cultures," in *Dangerous Liaisons: Gender, Nation and Postcolonial Perspectives*, ed. Anne, McClintock, Aamir Mufti, and Ella Shohat, 344–373 (Minneapolis: University of Minnesota Press, 1997).

Suzanne Bergeron

COMPARABLE WORTH

Comparable worth as a means to bring pay equity to women in the workplace has been controversial since it began to be broadly discussed in the 1980s. Supporters believe that pay equity between men and women for jobs performed predominately by women will be achieved only through the use of intervention strategies like comparable worth. Opponents argue that comparable worth is an inefficient model that interferes with the marketplace and actually results in a loss of jobs for women workers.

BACKGROUND

Comparable worth strategies are based on the notion of "equal pay for equal work." First proposed by policymakers, politicians, and activists in the late 1970s and early 1980s, comparable worth is based on the belief that when jobs filled mostly by women, such as childcare, cleaning hotel rooms, and secretarial help, pay lower wages than jobs filled mostly by men, such as janitorial work, truck driving, or meat packing, policies should be put into place to ensure that wages are equal and the gender gap in pay is eliminated. As national studies have demonstrated, professional, skilled, semiskilled, or unskilled labor jobs that are disproportionately held by men earn significantly more money then professional, skilled, semiskilled, or unskilled labor jobs that are disproportionately held by women (Sorensen 1994). Enacting comparable worth policies is seen as a way to end discrimination in pay between men and women and to finally close the gender pay gap.

If comparable worth policies were enacted, employers would be obligated to pay wages based on the *worth* of a job. Worth could be determined in several ways but most likely happens through studies that evaluate job attributes, skills, work conditions, and educational requirements that would determine the worth of the labor being supplied to the workforce. For example, janitors and hotel maids may be deemed to be comparable worth positions and therefore should receive equal pay or women's and men's basketball coaches at universities should receive equal pay for doing jobs of comparable worth for their universities.

THE GENDER WAGE GAP AND COMPARABLE WORTH

According to the U.S. Bureau of the Census, in 2003 women earned 75.5 cents to every dollar earned by men, based on median annual earnings of full-time men and women workers. In 1988, the wage gap was approximately 70 cents to the dollar. The latest statistics show that as of 2005, the gap was 77.1 cents (Institute for Women's Policy Research 2007). Progress to completely close the wage gap has stalled and research indicates that progress made toward pay equity in recent years has been the result of men's wage increases slowing at a faster rate than women's. It seems that market forces have not been able to achieve what opponents of comparable worth had hoped, that if the market was left alone, as more women entered the workforce, the gender wage gap would close.

Washington state passed a law in 1983 that required all state jobs to achieve comparable worth by 1993. By 1992, when the U.S. General Accounting Office evaluated the program, almost 60,000 employees had been classified into more than 3,000 jobs. The evaluation determined that in lower-paying female-dominated positions, the gender wage gap improved from 80 to 90 percent. In higher paying jobs the gap closed very little.

THE DEBATE: FOR AND AGAINST COMPARABLE WORTH

Supporters of comparable worth argue that the gender pay gap is a result of discrimination and cannot be closed without corrective strategies that are imposed on a gender-biased labor force system, either through government regulation or voluntary participation. Comparable worth would not only help to close the gender wage gap but it would also raise the value of women's work instead of pushing women into male-dominated work places (Blum 1991). Blum argues that in contrast to affirmative action policies, which she views as pushing women into male-dominated work places, comparable worth actually looks for real gender equity, in that women's work is expected to be equally valued and compensated for in the marketplace. She also argues that comparable worth strategies could create and strengthen important links between labor and feminist movements.

Opponents of comparable worth strategies argue that measures to place a value on jobs is subjective, expensive, and difficult to implement. Furthermore, the process interferes with supply and demand in the marketplace and the end result would be worse, as fewer jobs are available for women as higher rates of pay are mandated. In addition, employers would become more vulnerable to litigation based on the outcomes of arbitrary formulas and point systems created to implement comparable worth.

CONCLUSION

Comparable worth as a strategy for reducing the gender wage gap largely lost favor in the last 10 years. Advocates of gender equity more commonly pressed for more flexible "family friendly" work environments, sought to help women succeed in male-dominated professions, and fought to raise the minimum wage.

With the persistence of the wage gap, however, some argue that it may be worth reconsidering a comparable worth strategy. At the very least, it is clear that it will be difficult to end the gender wage gap and maintain a commitment to fair pay without a cultural shift that equally values women's and men's labor.

See also Affirmative Action; Equal Rights Amendment; Feminization of Poverty; Glass Ceiling; Work: Paid versus Unpaid.

Further Reading: Blum, Linda, *Between Feminism and Labor: The Significance of the Comparable Worth Movement* (Berkeley, CA: University of California Press, 1991); Chavez, Linda, "Comparable Worth: Liberals Pillory John Roberts for Having Opposed a Silly Idea," *Wall Street Journal*, editorial page, August 27, 2005; The Institute for Women's Policy Research, *Wage Gap Persists: New Government Data Show No Progress in Closing the Gender Wage Gap*, April 24, 2007, available at: http://www.iwpr.org/pdf/C350release.pdf, accessed May 24, 2007; Sorensen, Elaine, *Comparable Worth: Is it a Worthy Policy?* (Princeton, NJ: Princeton University Press, 1994); United States General Accounting Office, *Washington State's Efforts to Address Comparable Worth: Report to Congressional Requesters* (Washington, DC: General Accounting Office, 1992).

Stephanie Brzuzy

CRIME AND CRIMINALIZATION

Although traditionally viewed as more likely than men to be *victimized* by crime, women are increasingly being identified as *perpetrators* of crime. Debates concerning women's involvement in crime involve cultural and racialized perceptions of women as docile or, conversely, as prone to violence and gender discrepancies in the criminal justice and penal systems.

BACKGROUND: WOMEN IN THE CRIMINAL JUSTICE SYSTEM

Women can be both victims and perpetrators of crime. The majority of women who are currently being identified as criminals and prosecuted by the criminal justice system are poor and nonwhite. Based on the 2005 Bureau of Justice Statistics data, women represent just 7 percent of all inmates currently held in state and federal facilities, but their rate of incarceration is now twice that of men owing to their increased involvement in drug crimes, violent crime, and fraud. According to *The Sentencing Project,* which tracks parody and trends in sentencing decisions across U.S. courts, drug crimes, in particular, are carrying ever-tougher sentences as a result of the "war on drugs," and these sentences ensure that women and men prosecuted for drug charges spend longer periods in prison facilities. Adding more women to the prison system is raising many issues for departments of correction. Women's facilities must be expanded. Issues of children and families need to be managed. The majority of incarcerated women are mothers, and this raises unique issues for wardens and prison staff in terms of how visitors are to be handled and what freedoms the female inmates well have to interact with their children. Also, propensities in our society toward paternalism are enacted as prison staff attempt to regulate their inmates sexuality during visits by significant others. Although such management of the intimate happens in men's facilities, there is seemingly more effort to monitor and control female inmates in this respect. For instance, the Supreme Court ruling *Turner v. Safley* (1987) clarified that prisons cannot take longer to approve women's marriages if they allow men's marriages, which is what Missouri wardens have been doing in an effort to "protect" their female inmates. Based on ethnographic research, it is still clear, when touring prison facilities and talking with staff, that many still adopt this view, often clarifying that they strongly encourage inmates—and especially the female inmates—in lower security facilities where there are women and men in close proximity to avoid intimate relationships (Lea 2007).

WOMEN, AGGRESSION, AND CRIME

American cultural patterns generally deny women the externalized expression of aggression (while condoning, if not sanctioning, it for men), and thus aggressive behavior is characterized as masculine (Henry and Short 1954). Such normative expectations muddy our very conceptualization of aggression (Widom and Stewart 1986). For instance, a woman living within a Victorian setting might be more inclined than one living in modern times to appropriate the role of a "black widow." A Victorian lady had little opportunity to earn a living on her own; she was dependent on her male "caretakers." If she were to murder a wealthy husband or father, however, she would legally acquire his wealth and maintain the security of a widowed woman's social position. This was one of the few means by which a Victorian lady could gain independence. Researchers, of course, have little means of knowing how often such a tactic was used, but perusal of the historical record of female criminals (Newton 1993) makes it clear that there were many more incidents of black widowhood and of other lone-woman-perpetrated murder (usually of other victims who were the woman's kin) recorded in the United States before 1950 than after 1960 when divorce became more accessible and equitable for women. If we consider the Lizzie Borden (see Sidebar Lizzie Borden and the Chivalry Hypothesis) case in this light, for example, it seems quite possible that she might have killed her parents (her father and her stepmother) so as to gain independence. Her father, part of the Borden milk lineage, is said to have been very stingy with his financial resources. Lizzie, still unmarried by her thirties, would have been completely dependent on him.

Schur (1984) notes that women, when they do exhibit aggression, are quite likely to act out of frustration in the home environment, against a spouse or child. This, again, dovetails with the idea of an opportunity structure within which one might engage in crime. It is quite plausible, then, that some women might engage in criminal acts that go undetected because we are not asking the right questions about such things as spousal abuse, child abuse, and so forth. In some studies, for instance, research indicates that women actually report engaging in partner abuse at least as much as do men (Newburn and Stanko 1994; Lottes and Weinberg 1997; Lea 2007). As Greven (1991) observes in his

LIZZIE BORDEN AND THE CHIVALRY HYPOTHESIS

If the O.J. Simpson trial can be called the trial of the twentieth century, then the Lizzie Borden trial might reasonably be called the trial of the nineteenth century. In many ways, the two cases are quite similar. Both Simpson and Borden were accused of brutal double homicides—and both went on to live many years as a free (if scrutinized) citizen after a very public trial. Borden was accused of murdering her father and stepmother with an axe. In the case of Borden, however, that acquittal was afforded by what amounted to a chivalrous jury.

In that time, juries were composed of middle-class males. Middle-class women were viewed as keepers of the hearth and home. They were idealized as innocent, loving, and kind-hearted. The idea that a woman might commit a crime—let alone murder—was anathema to the ideals of the era. That a woman might murder by poison or possibly by gunshot might have been considered, but the idea of a woman killing by axe was unimaginable. This was especially the case given Ms. Borden's social standing. She came from an affluent, powerful Fall River, Massachusetts, family; she was a lady. A lady simply could not do such a thing. And so, it is reasonable to think that the Borden jury might have acquitted her simply to avoid the awkwardness of acknowledging that, in all likelihood, Borden was guilty. Instead, an immigrant, who had been convicted of committing the only other axe murder to have ever occurred in Fall River, Massachusetts, was convicted (although he had not even moved to the United States by the time the Borden murders occurred; the axe murder he seems to have actually perpetrated occurred several months after the Borden murders). No matter, he served as a good scapegoat for settling the Borden crimes.

The propensity of male juries, judges, prosecutors, and police officers to "go lighter" on middle-class women (note that this only applies to middle-class or upper-class women—not to working-class, nonwhite, or poor women) is known as the chivalry hypothesis and has been explored by journalists such as Patricia Pearson (1997) and by academics such as Grabe et al. (2006). Examples include a jury acquitting Borden because it seems unimaginable that a woman could have done such a crime, a police officer allowing a female motorist off with a warning, or a judge, such as the one handling the Louise Woodward case, letting a young female babysitter who shook a baby to death off with a light, one-year "time served" sentence.

---

book, *Spare the Child: The Religious Roots of Punishment and the Psychological Impact of Physical Abuse,* child maltreatment by caregivers—and not just the obviously abusive examples but also the more generic behavior of spanking—is likely responsible for much of the violent behavior we see within our society. Drawing the link that women surely perpetrate much of this child maltreatment is not made by Greven, perhaps because it is so difficult to conceptualize mothers as being aggressive toward their children. This is so antithetical to our cultural notion of a mother. We see this happen sometimes in public places, but it is often behavior that is kept behind closed doors.

STUDYING CRIME: WHERE ARE THE WOMEN?

Most classic studies of delinquency and criminal behavior focused nearly exclusively on boys and men (e.g., Chambliss 1973; Glueck and Glueck 1950; Cohen 1955; Sampson and Laub 1993). Women were dismissed as not being particularly prone to crime or deviance. If considered at all, women were analyzed as potential sexual deviants and scrutinized for such things as promiscuity. That most researchers were men surely contributed to this marginalization. Theories based on research that considers only men are no more universal or generalizable than are clinical studies of heart medications that are designed for men or women but tested only on men. It is crucial to consider the characteristics of women and crime independently, but much research has considered women and crime only in terms of men's patterns of criminal behavior.

Messerschmidt (1997) suggests that crime is, in effect, an expression of masculinity, a means by which those deprived of traditional means of social success might gain social clout and respect. Steffensmeir and Allan (1998) go on to argue that, because crime is so stigmatized vis-à-vis women, those women who do act out criminally tend to actually be more deviant than their male counterparts. These women are generally motivated by the same kinds of things that motivate their male counterparts such as, finances, social clout, or respect. Some of these women may have been victims of incest or other sexual abuse and have adopted a "tough" persona by which to compensate—and even, possibly, put off would-be male suitors. In fact, the very terms we use for criminal identities tend to have masculine connotations: thug, mugger, killer, etc. (see Heise [1979, 2007] and MacKinnon [1994] for a discussion of such linguistic connotations per affect control theory, which reasons that words that represent identities carry not only cognitive meaning but also affective sentiments). Thus we may have difficulty even conceptualizing or categorizing a deviant or violent woman, although they may be equally prone toward deviant or violent behavior. Brock (2000) echoes this sentiment in her exploration of law as a gendering process, arguing that (1) the ability to conceptualize a person as a potential perpetrator of a given crime is crucial to convicting that individual, and (2) the rubric by which lawyers, juries, judges, and the broader public interpret a case is anchored by gendered notions and norms. It is easy, she argues, to conceptualize a woman as a victim, a nuisance, or even a fallen woman; but it is not so easy to imagine a woman in the more active, aggressive role of a perpetrator.

WHY WOMEN DO CRIME

The theory that women are more likely to engage in crime at rates similar to that of men is called the liberation hypothesis (Schur 1984). This theory supposes that as women have gained more social equality and have more equal opportunity to that of men, they will do more of the things that men do—including engaging in crime. The very dramatic Manson case of the late 1960s likely gave rise to the idea that, as women gained more autonomy and sexual freedom, they were, indeed, becoming more like men. Although Charles Manson's "right hand man" was a man (Charles "Tex" Watson) and although Watson did most of the killing, several of "Charlie's Girls" did a lot of very bloody killing at two different crime sites, known together as the Tate-LaBianca killings. The idea that women could do *anything* chilled many Americans. The girls yielded from middle-class backgrounds but were transformed, it seemed, into violent killers by Manson. It is worth noting, however, that the "Manson girls" had to be actively coached and pushed by Manson and Watson to participate in these killings, suggesting perhaps that women are less motivated toward "senseless" violent crime than are men. Women who murder without male prompting are most likely to have been motivated by romantic interest or revenge or by self-defense against a violent partner (Jones 1996).

Some theorists such, as Chesney-Lind (1997) contend, however, that even with greater equality, women will be more obedient to social norms because they are more actively socialized to internalize them. Theorists imagined that women were traditionally only more inclined to avoid crime because of external structures such as parental control that prohibited them from being in situations wherein they might do crime. Less external controls should, then, result in more female crime. Lagrange and Silverman (1999) explored self-control measured against opportunity structures, comparing men and women. Curiously, they found that, given similar opportunity structures, women still exhibit more self-control and demonstrate a lower rate of rule-breaking behavior. Chesney-Lind (1997) argues that a woman's obedience may be more a function of much greater monitoring and surveillance of girls by parents and other authority figures than some abstract propensity for girls to obey. Hagan (1991) suggests, for instance, that parents may enact gender preferences regarding risky behavior. Because many delinquent acts are fun, exciting, and pleasurable, it seems reasonable to think that girls may not be so free to pursue these endeavors. Also, when they do and are caught, authorities are more likely to respond in a patronizing manner, asking the girl why a "good girl" like her is not at home with her family, for instance. Thus even with greater liberation, girls may still be more highly monitored by adult authority figures and thus may be more inclined to internalize the norms of their society. Quite possibly, however, there may be differences by subculture or socioeconomic strata in the extent to which girls internalize social norms. Or, alternatively, some girls may internalize subcultural social norms that run counter to mainstream norms and face reprimand by mainstream authority structures.

Theories of gender and crime that emphasize opportunity structure and women's liberation yield from a liberal feminist perspective. Those theories were challenged by more radical feminists, who focus more on how power is constructed and dominated by males in society. Specifically, radical criminology focuses less on social roles and more on how the capitalist economic system fosters crime via the creation of a patriarchal and sexist society. In such a system, argue radical feminists, women are defined in terms of family and reproduction. One might consider also, then, the idea of opportunity structure in terms of economic marginalization, as Naffine (1987) does. Naffine argues that, barring meaningful economic opportunities, women are more likely to do as many men do and to pursue criminal pursuits so as to make ends meet.

WOMEN AND VIOLENT CRIME

Overall, then, although many more men than women engage in crime, the rate of women's involvement is increasing more quickly than is men's involvement. Even in cases of more extreme violence, women have gradually been demonstrating more parity with men. For instance, few people realize that one of the first school shootings in the United States was perpetrated by a woman. Brenda Spencer, 17, of San Diego, California, received a rifle for Christmas and then used it to wound eight students and a police officer at an elementary school across from her home. Two men were killed trying to protect the children at the school. Although women do not usually engage in mass murder, there have been a few notable exceptions within the past several years. In January, 2006, 44-year-old Jennifer Sanmarco, who had been placed on leave for psychological problems, killed six people and then shot herself at a postal facility in Goleta, California. In June 2001, Andrea Yates drowned her five children one morning in Houston, Texas. Yates had also been suffering from psychological illness. In each of these high-profile cases, the female perpetrators yielded from white, middle-class backgrounds, as do the men who engage in similar sorts of crime.

These high-profile incidents raise an interesting point. It is evident from crime data that technology has equalized women with regard to access to fraud and computer crime. They *are* doing more of that. As discussed previously, it is not so clear whether this is really the case with violent crime or if, instead, there is simply a fascination with the idea that women might be doing more violent crime. In her article, "The Myth of Girl Gangs," Batchelor (2001) reports on a study exploring violent behavior from the perspective of girls. She found that violence *by* girls was not a major social problem but that the media response to the possibility that girls were perpetrating violence was profound. Press reports mischaracterized the study, which intended to explore violence from girls' points of views, as instead being a study of violent girls. Media even went so far as to misquote from it. Although there is some evidence that the rate of female-perpetrated violence is increasing, women are still much more likely to hurt themselves than to do violence toward others.

There is also an immense amount of psychological deflection generated at the idea of a woman—and especially a girl—engaging in violent behavior. Unless a woman can somehow be characterized as "hard" or "bad"—perhaps yielding from a lower social class or a disadvantaged minority group, the concept of a woman doing violence is difficult for many people to imagine and accept. This may also be why people so demonize those women such as Andrea Yates or Susan Smith, who do cross that line; it is the only way most people can psychologically manage the idea that, for instance, a mother might kill her own children. Alternatively, however, women who commit heinous crimes and can then construct themselves as reformed can potentially gain much public sympathy, particularly, it seems, if they are white and pretty such as, for example, Karla Faye Tucker in Texas. Tucker had pick-axed a former boyfriend and his lover one summer night while high on several drugs. She found the Lord in prison and a grassroots campaign sprang up to spare her from execution; such

AILEEN WUORNOS: THE FIRST FEMALE SERIAL KILLER?

Aileen Wuornos is suspected of having killed at least seven people, mostly male strangers, between 1989 and 1991. Her much-publicized case led to her being considered by some observers as the "first female serial killer" in modern times. But was Aileen Wuornos the first female serial killer? Some scholars disagree. Michael Newton, in his 1993 anthology of female serial killers, *Bad Girls Do It!*, clearly shows that there have been many female serial killers active in the United States before Wuornos. The most prolific of them was Dorothea Puente, born in 1959, who is thought to have killed as many as 25 elderly boarders in Sacramento, California, between 1986 and 1988. Puente killed the boarders to obtain their Social Security income.

Wuornos claimed that many of the murders she perpetrated were effected in self-defense, that these men were trying to rape or kill her during tricks that had gone wrong while she was prostituting herself. A telling of events that is sympathetic to Wuornos's version of the story was depicted in the 2003 film, *Monster*. Wuornos was sentenced to death by the State of Florida in 1992 and was executed by lethal injection on October 9, 2002.

In fact, the first known female serial killer in all recorded history was Erzsebet (or Elizabeth) Bathory, daughter of an aristocratic soldier and the sister of Poland's reigning king. Born in 1560, Bathroy was from one of the oldest noble houses in Hungary, which was peppered with alcoholics, murderers, sadists, and satanists. During her adolescence, Elizabeth was introduced to satanism by one of her uncles. As was common to the time, Elizabeth married young; however, she did not conceive. Instead of raising children, she busied herself having love affairs with both men and women and torturing servant girls for her entertainment. She would poke these girls with pins and needles—on the lips and nipples, and beneath the fingernails. She would strip them, smear them with honey, and then expose them to attacking ants and bees. She would even drench them in water and then put them out in the freezing cold. As she aged and found no curtailment by authorities of her sadist endeavors, her actions became increasingly violent and murderous. Eventually, however, her targeted victims were not just hapless peasants but lesser nobles, and this brought the legal system down on her. In 1610, she was apprehended and brought to trial. It is estimated that she killed between 300 and 650 victims; it is impossible to know a certain figure. She died while awaiting execution and is thought to have inspired some of the vampire legends of southeastern Europe. For instance, she is rumored to have maintained her youth by drinking the blood of young virgins.

---

campaigns seem less common on behalf of the many black and Latino men on Texas's death row.

WOMEN AS VICTIMS OF CRIME

The groups most likely to fear crime often are the least likely to be a victim. They are elderly and middle-class white women. In fact, most crime in the United States occurs intraracially, typically between young, nonwhite males

(Bureau of Justice Statistics 2007). In addition, children are the most likely victims of crime. Shows like Lifetime TV's *Snapped*, however, makes an enterprise of depicting young girls who have enacted very brutal crimes, often against their parents. In fact, girls are in most danger in their own homes and are most likely to be victimized by friends and intimates.

When white, middle-class women are victimized in especially horrific ways, these cases become extremely high profile. Consider the case of Laci Peterson, a pregnant, white woman who disappeared on Christmas Eve in Modesto, California. Her husband, Scott, was convicted of her murder after her body (and that of her unborn son Conner) was discovered in the San Francisco Bay. The case made international headlines, although husband-wife murders are hardly uncommon. There have, of course, been other pregnant women who have vanished and turned up dead; LaToyia Figueroa, for instance, was pregnant and disappeared on August 20, 2005. She was of African American and Hispanic origin, however, and thus did not receive the kind of press coverage that a missing white woman would receive. This discrepancy has come to be referred to as the missing white woman syndrome. *Essence* magazine and other media outlets have noted how mainstream news programs such as CNN devote hours, days, and even weeks of coverage to cases that feature a missing white girl or woman. The examples are seemingly endless: Laci Peterson, Natalee Holloway, Elizabeth Smart, Chandra Levy, and even Patty Hearst in the mid-1970s.

Not only do missing white women generate extensive media coverage, their cases also prompt legislation. The Peterson case, for instance, generated the passage of Laci and Conner's Law, which has been ratified by many states and the federal government and which makes it a double homicide to kill a pregnant woman. In the specific case of Peterson, where Laci was eight months pregnant, such a law seems reasonable to many people—there is a unique horror in imagining how someone could murder a very pregnant woman. There was the same reaction to the murder of Sharon Tate by the Manson "family" 30 years earlier. If a woman is only three or four months pregnant, however, this is perhaps a different situation. Also, it has been observed that this legislation opens the gateway for challenges to *Roe v. Wade* (1974) by way of how and when personhood, in the legal sense, is defined.

Other examples of parent-driven crusades based on the deaths or injury of middle-class white children include Megan's law, which was inspired by the murder of 7-year-old Megan Kanka and which generated the sex offender registry; the Amber Alert system, which is used to advise police and citizens of missing persons and which was inspired by Amber Hagerman, a 9-year-old who was murdered in Arlington, Texas; the efforts by Carolyn McCarthy to pass gun control legislation after her husband was killed and her son badly wounded by a gunman on the Long Island Railroad; and even the Mothers Against Drunk Driving crusade.

CONCLUSION

Women's rate of criminal activity has increased over the last couple of decades. Some theorists credit this increase to changes in the social status of women, that is, women's liberation. It is often women from poor and nonwhite backgrounds who engage in crime, motivated usually by poverty and sometimes by frustration, revenge, self-defense, or prior sexual abuse. Ironically, the liberation of women in the United States has least benefited these women, who are likely to have very low wages, work many hours, and have children depending on them. These stressors can provide strong motivation to engage in crimes such as identity theft or fraud. What is not clear from research is whether such women are likely to engage in such criminal behavior on their own or in collusion with men.

Our understanding of crime is deeply gendered. Violent crime, in particular, is conceptualized as a masculine act. Women do, of course, engage in violent crime; however, it seems that there may be more of a hype and imagination regarding violent women than there is an actual explosion in the number of women who do actually engage in violent crime. One thing is certain: the 24-hour news industry loves sensation—whether it be the woman who drowns her five young children or the latest missing white woman. And although such cases may make exciting copy, they keep too many women running scared of the serial killer in the shadows who is unlikely to appear anywhere other than on the movie screen.

See also Feminization of Poverty; Race and Racism: Social Stratification in the United States; Sex Work.

Further Reading: Batchelor, Susan, "The Myth of Girl Gangs," *Criminal Justice Matters* 43 (2001): 26–27; Brock, Deborah, "Victim, Nuisance, Fallen Woman, Outlaw, Worker?" in *Law as a Gendering Practice,* ed. Dorothy E. Chunn and Dani Lacombe, 79–99 (Don Mills, Ontario: Oxford University Press, 2000); Bureau of Justice Statistics U.S. Department of Justice, 2007, available at: http://www.ojp.usdoj.gov/bjs/; Chambliss, William, "The Roughnecks and the Saints," *Society* (November/December, 1973): 24–31; Chesney-Lind, Meda, *Girls, Delinquency, and Juvenile Justice* (Belmont, CA: Wadsworth, 1997); Cohen, Albert K., *Delinquent Boys: The Culture of The Gang* (New York: Free Press, 1955); Gluek, Sheldon, and Eleanor Gluek, *Unraveling Juvenile Delinquency* (New York: Commonwealth Fund, 1950); Grabe, Maria, K. D. Trager, Melissa Lear, and Jennifer Rauch, "Gender in Crime News: A Case Study Test of the Chivalry Hypothesis," *Mass Communication and Society* 9, no. 2 (2006): 137–163; Greven, Philip, *Spare the Child: The Religious Roots of Punishment and the Psychological Impact of Physical Abuse* (New York: Alfred A. Knopf, 1991); Hagan, John, "A Power-Control Theory of Gender and Delinquency," in *Crime in Canadian Society,* 4th ed., ed. R. Silverman, J. Teevan, and V. Sacco, 130–136 (Toronto: Butterworths, 1991); Heise, David R., *Expressive Order: Confirming Sentiments in Social Actions* (New York: Springer, 2007); Heise, David R., *Understanding Events: Affect and the Construction of Social Action* (New York: Cambridge University Press, 1979); Henry, Andrew, and James Short, *Suicide and Homicide* (New York: Arno Press, 1954); Jones, Ann, *Women Who Kill* (New York: Beacon Press, 1996); Lagrange, Teresa C., and Roberta A. Silverman, "Low Self-Control and Opportunity: Testing the General Theory of Crime as an Explanation for Gender Differences in Delinquency," *Criminology* 37, no. 1 (1999): 41–72; Laub, John H., and Robert J. Sampson, *Shared Beginnings, Divergent Lives: Delinquent Boys to Age 70* (Boston: Harvard University Press, 2003); Lea, Suzanne Goodney, *Delinquency and Animal Cruelty: Myths and Realities about Social Pathology* (New York: LFB Scholarly Publishing, 2007); Lea, Suzanne Goodney, *Touring Prisons with Students:*

Insights, Awkward Moments, and Reflections upon the Value of this Tactic of Instruction (in progress); Lottes, Ilsa, and Martin S. Weinberg, "Sexual Coercion Among University Students: A Comparison of the United States and Sweden," *Journal of Sex Research* 34 (1997): 67–76; MacKinnon, Neil J., *Symbolic Interactionism as Affect Control* (Albany: State University of New York Press, 1994); Messerschmidt, James W., *Crime as Structured Action: Gender Race, Class, and Crime in the Making* (Thousand Oaks, CA: Sage, 1997); Naffine, Ngaire, *Female Crime: The Construction of Women in Criminology* (Boston: Allen and Unwin, 1987); Newburn, T., and Elizabeth A. Stanko, "When Men Are Victims," in *Just Boys Doing Business? Men, Masculinities and Crime,* ed. T. Newburn and E. A. Stanko (London: Routledge, 1994); Newton, Michael, *Bad Girls Do It!* (Port Townsend, WA: Loompanics Unlimited, 1993); Pearson, Patricia, *When She Was Bad: Violent Women and the Myth of Innocence* (New York: Viking, 1997); Sampson, Robert J., and John H. Laub, *Crime in the Making: Pathways and Turning Points Through Life* (Cambridge, MA: Harvard University Press, 1993); Schur, Edwin M., *Labeling Women Deviant: Gender, Stigma, and Social Control* (New York: Random House, 1984); The Sentencing Project, available at: www.sentencingproject.org; Steffensmeir, Darrell, and Allan, Emilie, "The Nature of Female Offending: Patterns and Explanations," in *Female Offenders: Critical Perspectives and Interventions,* ed. R. Zupan, 5–30 (Gaithersburg, MD: Aspen Publishing, 1998); *Turner v. Safley,* 482 U.S. 78 (1987), available at: http://www.law.umkc.edu/faculty/projects/ftrials/conlaw/turnervsafley.html; Widom, Cathy S., and A. J. Stewart, "Female Criminality and the Status of Women," *International Annals of Criminology* 24 (1986): 137–162.

Suzanne Goodney Lea

D

DEPRESSION

Women are twice as likely as men to be diagnosed with depression. Some argue that this is true because women and men report symptoms differently and diagnostic categories of depression are more stereotypically associated with women. Others argue that women's disproportionate exposure to trauma, violence, and lack of resources creates the cluster of symptoms most closely associated with depression.

BACKGROUND

According to the World Health Organization, depression is the most common mental health problem in women and one of the world's most untreated diseases (WHO 2002). By most accounts, women outnumber men two to one in the lifetime prevalence of depression. In any given year, 10 to 14 million people experience clinical depression; women 18 to 45 years old account for the largest proportion of this group (National Alliance on Mental Illness 2003).

Why do so many more women than men suffer from this debilitating condition? The answer depends on who you ask. Does it have something to do with a woman's "weaker constitution," as was suggested in the early days in the field of psychiatry (Ehrenreich and English 2005)? Is it, as was written extensively about in the 1960s, symptomatic of "the housewife syndrome," a role expectation wrought with dissatisfaction and unfulfilled dreams? What about the biology of women, that imperfect physical system of dysregulation, inadequacies, and failing parts described for centuries by leading male physicians?

What seems to be clear is that untreated depression in women places an enormous burden on society. Depression not only affects women's health and well-being but also puts a strain on their families, especially children, thereby involving future generations of parents and children. It affects families, communities, and the economy, and it is the leading cause of disability among women worldwide.

DEPRESSION: A WOMAN'S DISEASE?

So, why the gender gap? Recent studies point to several plausible explanations. One is the way men and women experience and report the symptoms of depression and the manner in which professionals inquire about them. Studies have shown that physicians tend to inquire about depressive symptoms more often when treating women than when treating men (WHO 2006). In addition, when presented with identical symptoms, physicians diagnose depression in women more often than in men, leading to the probable overdiagnosing of the condition in women and underdiagnosing in men. There are important differences in the way men and women report symptoms as well. Men tend not to recall depressive symptoms even when others have objectively observed them. Men also are more likely to abuse substances, which may mask depressive symptoms and appear as the primary diagnosis. Men present for diagnosis and treatment at later stages of depression. In contrast, women report more symptoms that closely align with recognized symptoms of depression such as overwhelming sadness or emptiness, feelings of failure, anhedonia (loss of feeling of pleasure), intense feelings of guilt, helplessness, hopelessness, worthlessness, isolation/loneliness, and/or anxiety. Women also tend to seek treatment in earlier stages, use outpatient services more than men, are more aware of the effects on marital or relationship adjustment, are more likely to experience distress as a result of their symptoms, and volunteer symptoms of depression to family physicians more often than men.

Perhaps the overrepresentation of women with depression lies in the definition of depression itself. "Depression" as a cluster of symptoms may fit the stereotypical female more than her male counterpart. In his book, *Irritable Male Syndrome,* psychotherapist Jed Diamond (2004) asserts "extreme irritability," the most prevalent symptom of depression in men, is inexplicably left out of the Diagnostic and Statistical Manual of Mental Disorders (DSM). The definition of depression accepted by mental health professionals (American Psychiatric Association 2000) often does not fit men's own experience of depression.

CONCLUSION

Factors such as those described here have led some to conclude that the condition of depression has no gender bias; rather, social conditions that affect both men and women largely are responsible for the difference in the rate of depression (Pavlovich-Danis 2004). For example, the same bias that occurs in physicians' assessments of depression occurs in family members' as well. A study of the role of gender bias in families concluded that women were more likely to be identified as having depression when symptoms were identical to that of men, and family members were more likely to attribute depressive symptoms to internal factors in women (motivation, grief, weak constitution, etc.) as opposed to external factors in men (job, money, life stages, etc.) (Brommelhoff, Conway, Merikangas, and Levy 2004). Researchers, therapists, and feminist health activists continue to debate the reasons why women are considered to experience depression more often than men.

See also Medicine and Medicalization: Views on Women's Bodies; Mental Health: Gender Biases in Diagnoses of Women.

Further Reading: American Psychiatric Association, *Diagnostic and Statistical Manual of Mental Disorders* (Washington, DC: APA, 1952, 1987, 1994, 2000); Brommelhoff, J., K. Conway, K. Merikangas, and B. Levy, "Higher Rates of Depression in Women: Role of Gender Bias within the Family," *Journal of Women's Health* 13, no. 1 (2004): 69–76; Diamond, Jed, *The Irritable Male Syndrome: Managing the Four Key Causes of Depression and Aggression* (Emmans, PA: Rodala Books, 2004); Doyal, Lesley, *What Makes Women Sick: Gender and the Political Economy of Health* (London: Palgrave MacMillan, 1995); Ehrenreich, Barbara, and Deidre English, *For Her Own Good: Two Centuries of the Experts' Advice to Women* (New York: Second Anchor Books, 2005); Lennon, M., J. Blome, and K. English, *Depression and Low-Income Women: Challenges for TANF and Welfare-to-work Policies and Programs* (Research Forum on Children, Families and the New Federalism, National Center for Children in Poverty, 2001); National Alliance on Mental Illness, *Depression and Women*, 2003, available at: http://www.nami.org/Template.cfm?Section=By_Illness&template=/ContentManagement/ContentDisplay.cfm&ContentID=17627; National Institute of Justice/Centers for Disease Control and Prevention, *Prevalence, Incidence, and Consequences of Violence Against Women: Findings from the National Violence against Women Survey,* 1998, available at: http://www.ncjrs.gov/pdffiles/172837.pdf; National Institute of Mental Health, *Depression: What Every Woman Should Know*, 2005, available at: http://www.nimh.nih.gov/publicat/dep womenknows.cfm#ptdep4; Pavlovich-Danis, S., "Real Men Do Cry: Depression Has no Gender Bias," *NurseWeek* (2004), available at: http://www.nurseweek.com/news/Features/04–09/DepressionInMen.asp; U.S. Census Bureau, *Current Population Survey*, 2006, Annual Social and Economic Supplement, available at: http://pubdb3.census.gov/macro/032006/pov/new01_000.htm and http://pubdb3.census.gov/macro/032006/pov/toc.htm; World Health Organization, Gender and Women's Mental Health, *Gender Disparities and Mental Health: The Facts,* 2002, available at: www.who.int/mental_health/resources/gender/en/; World Health Organization, *Gender and Health, Modules in Review, Gender and Depression, Gender Differences in diagnosing depression*, 2006, available at: www.genderandhealth.ca/en/modules/depression.

Lanai Greenhalgh

DIGITAL TECHNOLOGIES

Virtual communities historically have been dominated by men. Whether the Internet and World Wide Web will serve women's interests in a liberating way, contribute to women's oppression, or do both is now up for debate.

BACKGROUND

The Internet and the World Wide Web are not the first virtual communities to exist. Scholars of virtual reality note that first the book, then radio, and then television created opportunities for people spread across wide expanses of geographic distance to share common experiences: the experiences of reading the same text; hearing the same speech, news, or music; and seeing the same programming. These experiences created a common context of culture, education, and conversation that allowed people who did not directly physically connect with one another on a regular basis to share a virtual common reality. The obvious difference between these forms of virtual reality and the World Wide Web is the degree to which the audience has the capacity to shape, send, and control messages, rather than simply to receive them.

Virtual communication has been heavily male dominated. Women have often been deprived access to the resources to develop literacy, and those women who have become writers, for example, have often been denied access to the benefits of having their work published. Radio and television, too, have been controlled by men, both financially and programmatically, and have largely served to reinforce unequal power dynamics between men and women. Because new forms of communication in the form of the Internet and World Wide Web allow users to communicate directly with other users, both individually and in mass numbers, scholars are now asking whether women's status in this form of virtual community is greater than in previous forms of mass communication.

WOMEN AND THE INTERNET: PROS AND CONS

On the surface, it would appear that the World Wide Web and the Internet are populist forms of media, and that this would benefit women. Boys and girls have access to computers in schools; people can "hop on-line" for free at their local libraries; and educational, public, and commercial spaces increasingly offer access to "free wireless Internet" service. Nonetheless, access to hardware and even software doesn't guarantee the development of skill in using technology, and research indicates that boys and men, on the whole, are more aggressive in their development of technical literacy with computers, as well as in their involvement with computer programming. The information technology industry is male-dominated, making it predictable that men's interests would be overrepresented in the development of services, programs, and vehicles for communication on the Web.

Feminist scholars have argued that the Internet creates exciting possibilities for women, alongside its potential as a vehicle of exploitation. The Internet has allowed women to build support networks across time and space around issues that concern them, ranging from domestic labor, to breast cancer treatment, to dealing with depression. It has provided opportunities for marginalized groups—from bisexual women to sex workers, third world activists, to stay-at-home mothers—to organize in the "virtual world" in ways that have often translated into political action in the embodied world, and has allowed women to organize and participate in progressive responses to public events in the realm of politics. It has also allowed women to start home-based businesses that give them greater access to income than they would have in store-front shops, as well as greater flexibility with their time. In addition, the Internet has offered women who know how to use it access to immense amounts of information previously inaccessible to most people.

Conversely, the Internet, the World Wide Web, and the computer industry are troubling to feminists for many reasons. At the level of the industry, analysts distinguish among "hardware," the physical components of computers; "software," or computer programs; and "wetware," the embodied people that produce programs and hardware. Within the computer industry, the most poorly paid workers tend to be women who work in component factories in Third-World countries, and who often do not enjoy access to computers, the Web, or the education to use these resources. Because of this, coupled with impressive differences between groups on a global scale—men and women, whites and people of color, people in early and late industrializing nations—scholars are concerned about a "digital divide" that will shape economic and cultural relationships between those who have access to and control over these new technologies and those who do not have the educational or financial resources to put them to use.

EXPLOITATION AND THE INTERNET

Another area of concern and contention for feminists is the Internet's potential to exploit women and to promote violence against women. In the United States, a history of social and legal commitments to free speech leads some to argue that the Web should be an open space tolerant of a broad expression of sexual and political behavior in its virtual spaces. Others argue that easy access to pornography, along with easy access to misogynist (and racist and homophobic) rhetoric on the Web reflects and expresses the exploitation of women, and actively promotes it. These debates echo older feminist controversies regarding free speech and the relationship between pornography and the "real time" embodied exploitation of women (Dworkin 1991; Mackinnon 1998). When a person in a virtual chat room describes "himself" as violating another person's sexual boundaries, should we regard this as real rape, virtual rape, or a literary description of sexual exploitation? If young people pose clothed with friends in their MySpace photos or YouTube videos in ways others regard as sexually exciting, are the youth engaged in pornography? If a man "impersonates" a woman in a virtual space, is he engaged in gender play consistent with the culture of cyberia, or is he engaged in an unethical deception?

CONCLUSION

Feminists are concerned that the Internet and the World Wide Web, while offering women greater opportunities to connect and to organize, also offer various governments and commercial concerns greater opportunities to monitor and therefore control women's lives. Few people consider, when they sit down to e-mail a friend, that e-mail technology was developed by the military, or that the Homeland Security Act passed in 2001 granted the U.S. government the right to conduct surveillance on the e-mail messages millions send daily. With women residing on the "wrong side" of the digital divide, they may be less educated about the ways the Internet and the information they share there may ultimately make them more vulnerable to exploitation.

See also Media Images of Women: Advertising; Media Images of Women: Television and Film.

Further Reading: Cherny, Lynn, and Elizabeth Weise, *Wired Women: Gender and New Realities in Cyberspace* (Seattle: Seal Press, 1999); Dworkin, Andrea, *Pornography: Men Possessing Women* (New York: Plume Press, 1991); Harcourt, Wendy, *Women and the Internet: Creating new Cultures in Cyberspace* (London: Zed Books, 1999); Kramarae, Cheris, *Technology and Women's Voices: Keeping in Touch* (New York: Routledge, 1998); MacKinnon, Catherine A., *In Harms Way: The Pornography Civil Rights Hearings* (Boston: Harvard University Press, 1998); Turkle, Sherry, *Life on the Screen: Identity in the Age of the Internet* (New York: Simon and Schuster, 1997).

Amber Ault

DISABILITY AND GENDER

Scholars and practitioners hold competing views on the causes and understandings of disabled versus nondisabled persons in society. Whereas some draw from a medical model and attribute the gendered experience of disability to scientific factors, others draw from a social model and attribute this experience to socially constructed categorizations of physical and mental normalcy.

BACKGROUND

Western culture defines masculinity as strength, speed, rationality, self-reliance, determination, virility, fortitude, and perseverance (Smith and Hutchison 2004). In contrast to the standards set for the male body, women in Western culture are expected to be graceful, nurturing, beautiful, and docile. Women are expected to appear healthy and attractive, or at least to protect onlookers from any sight of failure to meet these standards (Miner 1997). These cultural expectations pose high standards for the bodily performance of a male with a disability and the bodily presentation of a female with a disability. The medical model, which focuses on disability as a singular bodily deficit, and the social model, which addresses disability as a culmination of societal barriers, help shed light on how gender and disability interact to result in the experience of multiple intersecting oppressions.

The very word *disabled* linguistically carries societal negative connotations. The process of deconstructing the word *disability* reveals that the prefix *dis* means absence of, opposite of, or deprived of, according to the *American Heritage Dictionary.* Putting the word back together leads to the conclusion that a person with a disability has absence of ability, encompasses the opposite of ability, or is deprived of ability.

As many scholars have pointed out, being measured against a norm divides subgroups on the basis of difference and quantifies normalcy and deviancy. The very process of defining disability by comparing the "impaired" to the "normal" encourages the exaggeration of difference between people with disabilities and nondisabled people, making disability seem exceptional and uncommon. This tendency may stem from the knowledge that disability is an all-inclusive club that does not discriminate membership on the basis of ethnicity, race, religion, gender, socioeconomic status, or sexuality. The push for clear demarcation between people with disabilities and nondisabled people is a defensive strategy that relies on the natural tendency to deny human frailty (Davis 2005).

Scholars point out that people with disabilities serve as a constant reminder that illness and discomfort are part of the life experience, especially as our bodies age. Acquiring a disability is not so much a question of whether but when. To admit and acknowledge the reality of just how vulnerable we all are to illness and disability is frightening and unpleasant. To segregate people with disabilities through defining them as "other" allows nondisabled people a false comfort of everlasting health, strength, and well-being. Portraying disability as unusual and rare allows for society to overlook, ignore, or deny the needs and rights of people with disabilities (Davis 2005).

THE MEDICAL MODEL OF DISABILITY

The medical model of disability developed in conjunction with the field of modern medicine and the enhanced role of the physician in the nineteenth century. The medical model redefined disability as an organic disturbance within the human body, rather than the historical explanation of disability as the outcome of moral failings or spiritual transgressions of the afflicted. Useful for the healthcare world, this model guides doctors, nurses, and other medical professionals in approaching disability management with a focus on medical interventions, drug regimens, and a diagnostic classification of symptoms. Such medical advancements lengthen lifespans, lessen pain and suffering, and improve quality of life.

Under the medical model, disability is viewed solely as a deficit residing within the individual. Disability is something to be contained or alleviated and its symptoms are deemed as the "enemy" (Taylor 1999). The disabled body is viewed through biological and mechanical lenses, ignoring the ways in which the same disease can be experienced differently psychologically and socially by different people, often varying by social class and ethnic cultural background (Charmaz and Paterniti 1999).

Persons with disabilities are seen as "patients" and are expected to fulfill the "sick role." The concept of the sick role equates disability to illness, portraying the expectation that persons with disabilities should be passive, dependent, and grateful for expert advice. This notion deepens the stereotype of persons with a disability as inferior, deficient, and pitiable The cultural demand for official medicalization of disability veils social forces that influence health and well-being. When disability is located as a problem within the individual, the responsibility of overcoming societal, architectural, and legal barriers is placed on the person with the disability.

THE SOCIAL MODEL OF DISABILITY

In contrast to the medical model, the social model specifically delineates disability as a social construction and identifies society as the creator of disability. The barriers that persons with disabilities face are believed to be constructed through oppressive societal attitudes, policies, and practices. Such institutionalized forms of ableism (discrimination against persons with disabilities) result in adverse social, political, and economic consequences for persons with disabilities, which limit their opportunities for success.

The social model is a rally cry for people with disabilities everywhere to come together and fight against their social oppression: disabling stereotypes, objectification by healthcare professionals, and a social welfare system that keeps people with disabilities dependent on a power structure. The shift from seeing an impairment as a personal disabling characteristic to recognizing and challenging disabling social exclusion from education, employment, and recreation became empowering. Disability, rather than being reduced to individual deficit, came to be perceived as an element of human diversity around which a proud sense of culture has formed. Such coalition building has resulted in tremendous success and ongoing efforts toward societal and political change.

DEFINING DISABILITY: STRADDLING THE MEDICAL AND SOCIAL MODELS

There is no universally agreed on definition of disability. Identifying who is "disabled" is as confounding as delineating any other identity status. Indeed, the World Health Organization (WHO), the United States Social Security Administration, and the Americans with Disabilities Act (ADA), among others groups, are continually refining their attempt to precisely define disability, signifying the complexity of this exercise (Kafer 2003). One broadminded definition is that one is disabled if one says she or he is (Linton 1998). When identity claims might result in collecting from the government for medical care, however, legal protection, pensions, or workers' compensation, distinct definitions, and boundaries of disability are insisted upon (Fox and Kim 2004).

The process a government, organization, or agency goes through in naming, defining, and categorizing disability has great political, financial, legal, social, and personal implications. Definitions of disability result in the difference between securing and being denied assistance or entitlements for education, training, equipment, transportation, home healthcare, and medical supplies (Wendell 1996).

Disability policy in the United States straddles the medical and social models. Although the definition of disability as explicated by the ADA was designed to

AMERICANS WITH DISABILITIES ACT

The Americans with Disabilities Act of 1990 (ADA) was designed to ensure equal opportunity for people with disabilities to live independently, achieve economic self-sufficiency, and fully participate in the community. It is the most widespread equal opportunity act passed since the 1964 Civil Rights Act. The ADA defines a person with a disability as someone:

a. who has a disability that substantially affects one or more daily life activities, or
b. who has a history of having such a disability, or
c. who is considered to have such a disability.

Certain conditions are excluded, including transsexuality and substance abuse. Conservative critics have argued that conditions such as clinical depression should not be afforded the same legal protections as more serious physical disabilities. Others have pointed out that this legislation has had the unintended consequence of influencing employers not to hire people with disabilities, as they are viewed as an economic or social burden in the workplace. Some studies even indicate that there has been a drop in hiring people with disabilities after the passage of the 1990 Act.

take into account the lived experience of disability (see Sidebar Americans with Disabilities Act), it relies on the medicalization of an impairment as a necessary prerequisite for legal protection and access to often scarce resources. When discrimination protection comes into question under the court of law, people who have a disability are covered, provided they possess diagnostic medical authentication of such a disability as designated by the medical profession. This practice completely discounts an individual's lived experience of ableism, which according to the social model, is the creator of disability. Doctors become the gatekeepers to the classification "disabled" and, in effect, are considered the single valid credible authority on whether an individual experiences disability (Francis and Silvers 2000). Oppressive practices are inherent in the very arrangement of one group of privileged people being entrusted to define the characterization of group membership of another group of less powerful people (Davis 2005).

Also, the media largely contributes to the socially constructed image of what disability is. Human-interest stories portray persons with disabilities as either sick and needy or as superheroes. It is rare that financially, occupationally, and emotionally successful women with disabilities are publicly portrayed. Disability is always portrayed as "different," visually or otherwise, from nondisabled people.

"NORMAL" ABILITY

The WHO differentiates between impairment and disability. Impairment is defined as a loss or abnormality in bodily or physiological function, or body structure. Disability is defined as a lack of ability, resulting from an impairment, to perform an activity in the manner or within the range considered *normal* for a human being. Advocates of the social model of disability revolted against this definition, which implies that the participation restriction is the cause of individual pathology. Consequently, WHO added the caveat that disability is not an attribute of an individual, but rather a complex collection of conditions, many of which are created by the social environment.

WHO definitions overtly refer to "normal" as a yardstick against which to measure individuals. Such classifications and gauges enable comparisons of levels of health and participation of people and allow for the identification of individuals who need accommodations or direct assistance to participate or survive in society. The explicit reference to "normal," however, implies that there is a concrete universal, biological standard of human structure, function, and ability. Although there certainly would be advantages if this fictitious "norm" did exist, the insinuation presents real dangers to people with disabilities worldwide. (Wendell 1996).

"NORMAL" GENDERED ABILITY

Failure to meet societal and cultural standards of "normal" for a man, lacking a strong, nearly immortal male body, threatens a male's perceived manliness. In a capitalist society, men are judged by their capacity to provide for themselves and their families by working productively, energetically, and diligently in a way that meets these cultural norms (Francis and Silvers 2000). Meanwhile, the social construction of disability signals passivity, dependence, and tentativeness. Thus in an ableist society, having a disability deprives a man of his masculinity, rendering him less than a man (Smith and Hutchison 2004).

Hegemonic masculinity preaches risk taking and pain suppression, making it difficult for men who experience pain and physical limitations on a daily basis to acknowledge, express, and treat their discomfort. Emotions that frequently accompany the disability adjustment process, such as depression, anger, grief, fear, anxiety, and guilt, are also expected to be repressed under the auspices of masculinity (Smith and Hutchison 2004). Indeed, the societal cultural expectation of stoicism in the face of discomfort or distress is continually reinforced.

The social construction of "normal" is restricting for women with disabilities in a different way. Western culture's obsession with the physically perfect body, particularly for females, emits insidious pressure to strive to be more "normal" (Stone 1995). Undeniably, concealing bodily imperfection is a multimillion-dollar industry as people strive toward elusive physical and psychological flawlessness, whether that be slimmer, richer, or happier (Davis 2005, Stone 1995). In such a society that values women exclusively for their appearance and servitude, being expensive, dependent, and lacking in beauty, women with disabilities disrupt the normative standards of appropriate feminine behavior and appearance (Weiss 1985).

The WHO distinguishes a handicap from an impairment and a disability by defining it as a disadvantage resulting from an impairment that limits or prevents the fulfillment of a role that is normal, depending on age, sex, and social and cultural factors for that individual. A handicap refers to the problems an individual may experience in life situations when an individual's participation is compared to what is expected of an individual without a disability in that culture or society. Qualifying "normal" based on sex, among other factors, is troubling. Although differences between male and female biological bodies certainly exist, this caveat leaves room for sexism and patriarchy (Wendell 1996). A patriarchal value system renders the disabled woman who violates norms of femininity virtually invisible and, as a result, at greater risk for unemployment, poverty, and medical neglect.

Social acceptance is influenced by any view of what it means to be normal. When an elusive norm-based standard exists for all human beings in terms of how they should look, act, and what they should be able to do, people who deviate from these standards are viewed as lacking in some way. An emphasis on normalization is oppressive to people with disabilities. With an idea of "normal" in mind, any actions taken on behalf of people with disabilities will be to change them into more normal beings rather than to integrate and accept them into society as a natural part of community (Linton 1998).

WOMEN WITH DISABILITIES: INTERSECTION OF MULTIPLE OPPRESSIONS AND THE FEMINIST MOVEMENT

The feminist movement has been engaged in a longstanding battle against the patriarchal idea that a woman's individual worth is based on how closely and how favorably her bodily appearance comes to the value-based ideal. Attention is called to the inequality women face in comparing their income, educational, and employment opportunities to that of men. This inequality is compounded for women with disabilities, who are more quickly and frequently cut off from productive work than men with disabilities (Fine and Asch 1988) and thus more likely than men with disabilities to rely on government support.

Feminism has been accused of leaving its disabled sisters behind in the struggle for equality (Fine and Asch 1988). Because women with disabilities are often perceived to be needy, dependent, and passive, they represent stereotypical feminine qualities. Women with disabilities were abandoned for the aim of projecting an image of autonomy, strength, and competence (Fine and Asch 1988). Several feminists involved in disability studies, such as Adrienne Asch, Michelle Fine, Barbara Hillyer, Susan Wendell, Jenny Morris, and Rosemarie Garland-Thomson, have loudly called attention to the neglect of disability issues within the feminist movement and have brought to light many overlaps between the fight for women's liberation and the fight for disability rights. Similarly, there is a growing movement to recognize and address the presence of racism, ageism, heterosexism, and classism within both the feminist and disability rights movements (Vernon 1999).

Women with disabilities experience significantly more oppressive practices than both nondisabled women and men with disabilities, implying that bodies that are both female and disabled are doubly devalued (Fine and Asch 1988; Smith and Hutchison 2004). Being identified as "disabled" becomes a master status, which dominates other identifying characteristics resulting in the ignored intersection of multiple oppressions. The experience subjugation based on race, ethnicity, religion, sexual orientation, and/or social class, in addition to gender and disability, has been overlooked in research and service programming (Fine and Asch 1988; Vernon 1999). The social consequence of the experience of multiple oppressions—for example, being a lesbian of color with a disability—is frequently poverty. Living in poverty with a disability means experiencing a substandard level of basic necessities, like food and shelter, combined with a lack of disability-related necessities like medication, personal-care attendants, accessible transportation, or technological aids (Wendell 1996).

The Medical Model and Women

The medical model, which focuses solely on the biological processes of the body, methodically medicalizes the female body, including naturally reproductive functions like pregnancy, childbirth, menstruation, and menopause. As a result, females are innately "impaired" by unstable bodies, an assumption that underscores patriarchal superiority of the male body over the female body. The problematization of women's bodies also serves to maintain an unbalanced power dynamic between male doctors over their female patients.

Powerful economic, social, and cultural forces are imposed on the autonomy of women and even more so when disability is involved (Sherry 2004). Each encounter that women with disabilities have with medical professionals requires testimony of biological, cognitive, sensory, or psychological deviation from the norm. Her inferiority is regularly reestablished through the obligatory revelation of intimate, private, and even humiliating personal details (Davis 2005).

Traditional Female Roles

Although women with disabilities may be accused of being too stereotypically feminine by the feminist movement, they are simultaneously banned from fulfilling the ideals of femininity by society. Women with disabilities are frequently seen as unfit to be sexual partners, which may contribute to their reports of rape being ignored by professionals (Fine and Asch 1988). Fine and Asch report that women with disabilities are less likely to be married, more likely to marry later, and more likely to be divorced than both men with disabilities and nondisabled women. More frequently than nondisabled women, they stay in abusive relationships. Also, when women with disabilities are seen in public with a nondisabled male partner, he is frequently lauded as saintly, but nondisabled women in relationships with men with disabilities are perceived as dominant and controlling (1988, 155–160).

Because women with disabilities are perceived as asexual, infertile, and unattractive, their ability to fulfill otherwise female roles, like motherhood, is called into question (Smith and Hutchison 2004). In fact, until relatively recently, many states in the United States mandated forced sterilization of women with histories of certain disabilities and impairments (Fine and Asch 1988). Women with disabilities frequently report a total lack of professional counseling and information on sexuality, birth control, pregnancy, and childbirth (Fine and

Asch 1988). The counseling they do receive urges them away from motherhood through routine persuasion that their own health will be jeopardized or that their own impairments will keep them from being a good mother by harming, depriving, or burdening their children. Women with disabilities frequently experience barriers in adopting, foster caring, and winning child custody (Fine and Asch 1988). Abortion is frequently presented as a "solution" to both non-disabled and disabled women when the birth of a baby with a disability appears imminent (Kafer 2003; Sherry 2004). This forceful suggestion relays the message that life in a disabled body is not worth living, and the conception of the disabled body should be prevented at all costs (Wendell 1996).

Women with disabilities who require personal care attendants defy the societal expectation that females are inherently nurturing caregivers. In a society that so clearly values independence, the relationship between one who needs personal care assistance and one who gives such assistance is complicated. It is women who most frequently serve as personal care attendants for people with disabilities, whether through socialization or exploitation. People who serve as caregivers often help with daily tasks, such as shopping, cleaning, cooking, toileting, bathing, dressing, and eating. Oftentimes, they take on the responsibility of carrying out unpleasant tasks such as administering medications that cause adverse side effects, performing painful procedures in the name of therapy, or accompanying care receivers to hospital visits for painful or frightening treatments (Wendell 1996). Although it is personal care attendants who have daily contact with the person with a disability and provide the most intimate care, they are often paid the least (if at all) compared with the other members of the healthcare team, and their voiced insights carry little authoritative weight, if acknowledged at all (Hillyer 1993).

JUDY HEUMANN, DISABILITY RIGHTS ACTIVIST

Judy Heumann is a contemporary female leader in the disability rights movement. Born in 1947, she contracted polio at age 18 months. Her public school system refused her attendance, claiming her wheelchair was a fire hazard. As a result of her mother's advocacy, she began attending school in fourth grade. Years later, she took up a similar battle and successfully sued the New York City Board of Education for refusing her a teaching license solely because of her disability.

Heumann helped develop the Individuals with Disabilities Education Act and helped draft the Americans with Disabilities Act. She has created and served on several organizations, including Disabled in Action, Center for Independent Living, World Institute on Disabilities, and the American Coalition of Citizens with Disabilities. In 1993, she was appointed as the assistant secretary of education in charge of the Office of Special Education and Rehabilitation. She is currently the World Bank Advisor on Disability and Development. Heumann has paved the way for women and people with disabilities through her dedicated advocacy and political action.

Persons with disabilities have had to fight for their right to select and purchase personal care services; hire, manage, and fire personal care attendants; and assert authority over procedures administered to them. The dichotomization between the perspectives of personal care attendants and persons with disabilities who need personal care attendants conceals the often reciprocal nature of caregiving relationships (Wendell 1996).

THE PLACE OF CHRONIC ILLNESS

Chronic illness is a major cause of disability, particularly among women . The relationship between chronic illness and disability is complicated. The crusade of the disability rights movement has been to separate the notion that disability equals sickness; many people with disabilities do not suffer and enjoy an utmost level of health and wellness (Wendell 1996). The medical model recognizes pain and fatigue as significant aspects of illness and disability, but the social model, which identifies the cause of disability as oppressive social structures, excludes the experience of people who are sick and who are disabled by the painful, fatiguing, or nauseating symptoms of their illness.

Further complicating the relationship between people with chronic illness and disability is the hidden nature of many forms of chronic illness. To the public eye, a person with a chronic illness may look the picture of health and is often expected to fulfill the role expectations of a nondisabled person. As a result, people with chronic illness are faced with a constant decision: to tell or not to tell (Goffman 1963). Each new encounter requires another decision and the costs and benefits of concealing or disclosing the diagnosis are continually mentally weighed.

Often people with a chronic illness experience immense pressure to avoid showing any sign or symptom of the disability. They may not be accessing necessary accommodations to avoid skepticism or drawing attention to the existence of the illness (Taylor 1999). As a result, bodily limitations might be ignored or minimized, leading to exacerbation of the condition. Symptoms may be attributed to something other than disability, people or places might be withdrawn from, and engaging in behaviors that might reveal a symptom may be avoided. This often means limiting the depth of relationships and reducing contact with friends or other members of the community, furthering isolation from larger social systems.

Disclosing the existence of chronic illness renders it visible, which can be a liberating process, but can also make one vulnerable to discrimination and social rejection (Myers 2004). When a person has a disability that is not apparent, or when acute symptoms are present one day and few or none are present the next, support system members often unknowingly minimize the experience or give an impression that the condition is not believable (Charmaz and Paterniti 1999). Many family members and friends openly question the reality and severity of the condition.

Strangers often express dissatisfaction with stares, frowns, silent disapproval, and outright verbal questioning when one accesses special accommodations

(Taylor 1999). One then faces the additional burden of explaining or proving to others why a particular service is needed. Even health professionals might minimize one's experience and compare it to more visible disabilities (Charmaz and Paterniti 1999).

CONCLUSION

Neither the medical nor the social model accounts for the entirety of the lived experience of disability, but each sheds a unique light on the origination and current place of disability and ableism in our society. Disability activists have successfully pushed through revolutionary legislation to protect the ability of persons with disabilities to fully participate in community life, employment, and education; but there is still evidence of significant attitudinal, legal, architectural barriers that persons with disabilities face (NOD/Harris 2000). This is compounded for women with disabilities, who are affected by oppressive social consequences of a patriarchal society and ableist conditions. Ultimately, to fight for civil rights for one group of individuals, all revolutionary-minded groups must band together to fight against oppression for all citizens.

See also Disability and Sexuality; Medicine and Medicalization: Views on Women's Bodies.

Further Reading: Americans with Disabilities Act of 1990 (ADA), PL 101–336, (July 26, 1990) Title 42, U.S.C. 12101 et seq: Us. Statues at Large, 104, 327–378; Berger, Peter L., and Thomas Luckmann, *The Social Construction of Reality: A Treatise in the Sociology of Knowledge* (New York: Free Press, 1966); Charmaz, K., and D. A. Paterniti, *Health, Illness, and Healing: Society, Social Context, and Self* (Los Angeles: Roxbury Publishing Company, 1999); Davis, N. A., "Invisible Disability," *Ethics* 116 (2005): 153–213; Fawcett, Barbara, *Feminist Perspectives on Disability* (London: Prentice Hall, 2000); Fine, M., and A. Asch, *Women with Disabilities* (Philadelphia: Temple University Press, 1988); Fitzgerald, M. H., "'You Look so Well': The Multiple Facets of Hidden Disabilities," *Society for Disability Studies Quarterly* 20 (2000): 254–258; Fox, M. H., and K. Kim, "Understanding Emerging Disabilities," *Disability and Society* 19, no. 4 (2004): 323–337; Francis, L. P., and A. Silvers, *Americans with Disabilities: Exploring Implications of the Law for Individuals and Institutions* (New York: Routledge, 2000); Garland-Thomson, R., "Integrating Disability, Transforming Feminist Theory," *NWSA Journal* 14, no. 3 (2002): 1–32; Goffman, E., *Stigma* (Englewood Cliffs, NJ: Prentice-Hall, 1963); Hillyer, B., *Feminism and Disability* (Norman: University of Oklahoma Press, 1993); Kafer, A., "Compulsory Bodies: Reflections on Heterosexuality and Able-bodiedness," *Journal of Women's History* 15 (2003): 77–89; Linton, S., *Claiming Disability: Knowledge and Identity* (New York: New York University Press, 1998); Miner, M., "'Making up the Stories as We Go Along': Men, Women and Narratives of Disability," in *The Body and Physical Difference: Discourses of Disability,* ed. David Mitchell and Sharon Snyder, 283–295 (Ann Arbor: The University of Michigan Press, 1997); Myers, K. R., "Coming Out: Considering the Closet of Illness," *Journal of Medical Humanities* 25, no. 4 (2004): 255–270; National Organization on Disability/Harris, "The 2000 N.O.D./Harris Survey of Americans with Disabilities: Survey Program on Participation and Attitudes," available at: www.nod.org; Sherry, M., "Overlaps and Contradictions between Queer Theory and Disability Studies," *Disability and Society* 19, no. 7 (2004): 769–783; Smith, Bonnie, G., and Beth Hutchison, *Gendering*

Disability (New Brunswick, NJ: Rutgers University Press, 2004); Stone, S. D., "The Myth of Bodily Perfections," *Disability and Society* 10, no. 4 (1995): 413–424; Taylor, S., *Living Well with a Hidden Disability: Transcending Doubt and Shame and Reclaiming Your Life* (Oakland, CA: New Harbinger Publications, 1999); Vernon, A., "The Dialectics of Multiple Identities and the Disabled People's Movement," *Disability and Society* 14, no. 3 (1999): 385–398; Weiss, J., "Issues/Questions/Strategies: Disabled Women," *Resources for Feminist Research* 14 (1985): 4–5; Wendell, S., *The Rejected Body: Feminist Philosophical Reflections on Disability* (New York: Routledge, 1996).

Aimee Burke

DISABILITY AND SEXUALITY

Women with disabilities have often been depicted in the media and treated by medical professionals and able-bodied people as asexual, resulting in part from the controversial historical belief that they should not reproduce and are incapable of sexual expression. Recently, disability advocates have worked to counter this stereotype by promoting sex education and rethinking the meanings of *ability* and *normalcy*.

BACKGROUND

Historically, sexuality among women with disabilities has long been discouraged by medical professionals and the dominant able-bodied culture. Extreme examples include forced sterilizations and sex segregation to prevent mingling, both common practices in the United States and Europe throughout the early to mid-twentieth century. White (2000) documents that institutions for the blind used to segregate the sexes to prevent intermarriage and sexual misconduct. There was a belief that two blind people being intimate or marrying was "immoral or sexually perverse." Attempts were made to prevent such unions legally (White 2003). Margaret Sanger, a controversial birth control advocate in the early twentieth century, promoted eugenics—the belief that controlled reproduction would improve the human race—for people with disabilities, as did the Nazi regime in its overall program to eliminate "undesirables" in Germany and throughout Europe. Because the common belief has been that people with disabilities should not reproduce, women with disabilities, in particular, have faced obstacles concerning their ability and right to express themselves sexually.

Until today, a common misconception by medical professionals and the dominant able-bodied majority is that women with disabilities either have no sexual or romantic impulses, or that their disability prevents them from having a sexually healthy and satisfying life. As Wilkerson states, "Just as homosexuality, long considered an illness, was treated for year with drugs, castration, hypnotherapy, psychoanalysis, and aversion therapy, people with various kinds of disabilities have also faced medical denial of their sexualities" (Wilkerson 2002, 33). Despite this denial of sexuality by able-bodied people, women with disabilities are fully aware of their sexual and romantic impulses. It is how they are taught about sex and sexuality through the media and other means that makes the difference between living the stereotype and living a sexually healthy and satisfying life.

MEDIA DEPICTIONS OF SEX AND DISABILITY

The media provide an important example of how women (and men) with disabilities are viewed, either as asexual and dependent or as autonomous beings with desires like everyone else. Two examples of U.S. cinema serve to illustrate variations in media depictions of people with disabilities in regard to sex and sexuality. In the 1999 film, *The Other Sister,* the story centers on a young woman who is mentally handicapped, and after returning home from a special boarding school, decides that she wants to be independent and live on her own. This is difficult for her able-bodied parents to handle, for they believe that she is completely incapable of taking care of herself. She then falls in love with a young man who also happens to be mentally handicapped and thus shatters her parents' perception of her inability to have a relationship. There is much arguing among the family about whether or not she is capable enough to live on her own, and not-so-surprisingly, it is her lesbian sister who, also unaccepted by their parents, rallies on her behalf. In the end, the young woman gains her independence and is allowed to marry the young man.

At first thought, this sounds like a positive portrayal of disability and an encouraging tale of a mentally handicapped woman who overcomes her disability and finds independence and love. Given the parents' initial reaction of astonishment and anger, however, one sees the culturally shared tendency to think of disabled people as asexual, as not capable of being in a romantic, let alone sexual, relationship.

The 2005 film, *Murderball,* provides another contradictory example of how disability is portrayed on the screen and in popular culture. Although it focuses on men rather than women, the film speaks to how traditional constructions of sexuality are used to understand the lives of the disabled. *Murderball* focuses on the men of a quadriplegic rugby team who overcome unimaginable obstacles to compete in the Paralympic Games in Athens, Greece. Like *The Other Sister,* this is an inspirational tale of people with disabilities overcoming their handicap and living their lives like "normal" people; however, it also reveals the cultural implications and stereotypes of being disabled. In dealing with the stereotype that disabled men are weak and nonsexual, the creators of this film have created super strong, sexually aggressive, heterosexual men as their characters. This implies two contradictory notions. First, the filmmakers attempt to break down the stereotypes of disabled men, but then they reestablish the presumed missing masculinity of disabled men. Although the film is not meant to patronize the experiences of disabled men, scholars of disability studies point out that these super masculine characters encourage the idea that only strong, athletic, heterosexual men can be considered "real men." For example, in the film the statement is made that playing rugby gives these men a new sense of purpose, Although this may be true to some degree, it also reinforces the stereotype that being disabled is a bad thing, and if one has a disability then one is inherently unhappy with one's life. Eli Clare (1999) says it best when talking about the media exploitation of people with disabilities: "These 'supercrip' stories reinforce the superiority of the non-disabled body and rely upon the perception that 'disability' and achievement contradict each other and that any disabled person who overcomes this contradiction is heroic" (quoted in Ware 2002, 144).

CONCLUSION

Disability advocates have both supported and critiqued these media representations of sexual expression among disabled people. Supporters point out that these media depictions create an important space for women with disabilities to identify with media representations that have rarely existed for them in the past. At the very least, they are allowed the right to sexual expression, an important step, given the scientific community's historical emphasis on preventing their reproduction. On the other hand, critics charge that these representations do not go far enough; they tend to reinforce specific notions of femininity, masculinity, and sexual identity that are not always achievable or desirable among women with disabilities, thereby limiting their imagined forms of sexual expression even more than those media representations available to able-bodied women. The emphasis on traditional sexual and gender roles arguably liberates these characters to some degree yet also places them in a contradictory bind that reinforces traditional stereotypes about women (and men) with disabilities as less than "normal," an issue that will continue at a societal level so long as "ability" and "normalcy" remain unchallenged in law, policy, science, and popular culture.

See also Disability and Gender; Media Images of Women: Television and Film; Sexual Identity and Orientation.

Further Reading: Clare, Eli, *Exile and Pride: Disability, Queerness and Liberation* (Boston: South End Press, 1999); Kaufman, Miriam, Cory Silverberg, and Fran Odette, *The Ultimate Guide to Sex and Disability* (San Francisco: Cleis Press, 2004); Ware, Linda P., "A Moral Conversation on Disability: Risking the Personal in Educational Contexts," *Hypatia* 17, no. 3 (2002): 143–172; White, Patrick, "Sex Education; or, How the Blind Became Heterosexual," *GLQ: A Journal of Lesbian and Gay Studies* 9 nos. 1–2 (2003): 133–147; Wilkerson, Abby, "Disability, Sex Radicalism, and Political Agency," *NWSA Journal* 14, no. 3 (2002): 33–57.

Emily Joy

E

EATING DISORDERS

Diagnosis and treatment of eating disorders typically are relegated to psychiatry, although cultural critics and feminists have pointed out that culture, rather than merely individual psychology and home environment, may also play a role in causing eating disorders. The majority of people diagnosed with eating disorders are white women, although the number of eating disorder patients that are women of color and men is growing, which further complicates the debate on the cultural vs. psychological causes.

BACKGROUND

Eating disorders, most notably anorexia nervosa and bulimia nervosa, are common in Western cultures, although they occur with increasing frequency in poor and/or non-Western societies as well. Anorexia nervosa was first considered a disease, and one specific to women, during the mid-1800s; the first cases occurred in educated, middle class, white women. Social historicists such as Joan Brumberg, author of *Fasting Girls,* see the rise in eating disorders among women at that time as a silent protest against expectations for the roles those women would play in society as passive, submissive women confined to the private sphere. Considering not only anorexia but also bulimia and other related eating disorders, explanations for their occurrences in women range from the pressure of having so many options that historically had not been available to women and the fear of making the wrong choices or failing to live up to expectations, to desperation to be as thin as possible in order to meet and exceed the social norms for female beauty, to more individual concerns such as hating one's body because of sexual abuse or punishing the body because of a lack of coping method for feelings of anxiety, anger, or even happiness and success.

These ideas about eating disorders inform and are informed by the clinical criteria for determining whether someone has an eating disorder and what kind is established in the *Diagnostic and Statistical Manual of Mental Disorders* (DSM), a book of diagnostic criteria for mental illnesses, compiled by the American Psychiatric Association. Anorexia was the first eating disorder to be included in the DSM in the mid-1950s. The DSM added bulimia as a distinct category in 1980, and in 2000, a new category, Eating Disorder Not Otherwise Specified (ED-NOS), was added to assist doctors in diagnosing those who suffer from disordered eating but do not meet all the criteria for anorexia or bulimia. There are two other disorders that are not recognized in the DSM: binge eating disorder (BED) and compulsive overeating disorder (COE), both of which are thought by some professionals to deserve their own entries in the DSM's next edition, which will appear in 2011. Sufferers of both disorders are characterized by periodically going on large binges without purging and tend to be overweight, but the difference between BED and COE is that individuals with COE have an "addiction" to food. Both types of individuals, however, are said to use food and eating as a way to hide from emotions, to fill inner voids, and to cope with daily stresses and problems. Common for both disorders is also a desire to hide behind the physical appearance of obesity, using it as a blockade against society.

TIMELINE

1870: British physician, Sir William Gull, first identifies and describes anorexia nervosa as a disease in itself rather than as a symptom of other diseases that include loss of appetite

1952: Anorexia nervosa is given its own entry in *The Diagnostic and Statistical Manual of Mental Disorders (DSM).*

1978: Hilda Bruch publishes *The Golden Cage*, the first book solely devoted to discussing the treatment and causes of anorexia.

1979: Formation of Anorexia Nervosa and Related Eating Disorders, Inc., the first nonprofit group devoted to education about and recovery from eating disorders.

1980: Bulimia is given its own entry in the DSM.

1983: Popular singer, Karen Carpenter, dies from complications of anorexia. Actress Tracey Gold and Princess Diana of Wales go public with their eating disorder struggles.

1985: The first residential eating disorder clinic, The Renfrew Center, opens in Philadelphia.

1987: First National Eating Disorder Awareness Week (NEDAW) is held.

DEBATES ON THE CAUSES OF EATING DISORDERS

Psychological Explanations

There are many theories explaining how and why women develop eating disorders. Most explanations before the 1980s and 1990s constructed the problem and solution as being largely individual for each patient and her immediate family environment. In the classic psychoanalytic model, eating disorders are manifestations of a woman's psychosexual development. In that case, a woman or girl refuses to eat because she rejects her womanly body and what its health represents—sexual fertility. Along this line of thinking then, a compulsive overeater may seek to cloak her sexuality in body fat.

These ideas subtly speak to cultural expectations for women's bodies and the judgment of what is beautiful or desirable in a woman, causing a second generation of critics to notice that the way in which social systems operate to reinforce negative messages to women about their bodies points toward patriarchy, defined as a system of interrelated social structures and practices in which men dominate, oppress, and exploit women. These social values are specific to our capitalistic society, in which the so-called cult of thinness supports food, diet, and health industries. "Weight concerns or even obsessions are so common among women and girls that they escape notice. Dieting is not considered abnormal behavior, even among women who are not overweight. But only a thin line separates 'normal' dieting from an eating disorder" (Hesse-Biber 1996). Twiggy, the waifish British fashion model of the 1960s, and the popular Mattel doll, Barbie, are often cited as icons of the impractical expectations society has for the size of women's bodies. It is commonly known that the average model during the 1950s wore a size 8 and the average woman a size 10; today the average model wears a size 2, and in contrast the average woman now wears a size 12. The rise in disparity between model size and real women's bodies parallels the rise of eating disorders, although experts are divided on the degree to which society is responsible. Joan Brumberg and most leaders of the eating disorder conversation agree that these images play a key role in the development of eating disorders, but psychiatrists say these coincidences might instigate disordered eating behaviors, but are not enough to completely explain the development of the diseases anorexia and bulimia.

Biological Explanations

In this model, eating disorders are related to depression and bipolar disorder—both of which may be caused by chemical imbalances and thus corrected with medication. The only drug that has been approved by the U.S. Food Drug Administration for the treatment of eating disorders is Prozac, to be used in bulimia patients. There are many studies into medication for anorexic patients, and some trials have yielded individual successes, but because the anorexic's body chemistry is abnormal because it is in starvation mode, many drugs have little or no effect. Hesse-Biber criticizes the disease model of eating disorders, because that model locates the problem as being within the individual, rather

HOW PREVALENT ARE EATING DISORDERS?

According to Anorexia Nervosa and Related Eating Disorders, Inc.:

- Over one-half of teenage girls and nearly one-third of teenage boys have tried to control their weight by skipping meals and fasting, vomiting, and taking laxatives.
- For females between 15 and 24 years old who suffer from anorexia nervosa, the mortality rate associated with the illness is 12 times higher than the death rate of all other causes of death.
- One percent of female adolescents have anorexia, four percent of college aged women have bulimia, and one percent of all American women suffer from BED.
- Twenty percent of untreated eating disorder cases result in death, and two to three percent of patients treated for eating disorders do not survive.

than being located outside oneself. She acknowledges that the disease model is good in that it frees patients from guilt, but then notes at the same time that this model benefits the healthcare industry—replacing a potential feminist view that society needs to be healed with a medical view that the victim needs professional treatment.

Family and Home Environment Explanations

Yet another model posits that eating disorders arise as symbolic representations of family dynamics. In this case, a power struggle between parent and child, especially the mother, may motivate a girl to find power over one thing she can control—what she eats. In this case, treatment and diagnosis involve the entire family. Feminist psychoanalyst Kim Chernin argues that eating disorders primarily develop as a response of overly controlling parents or environments that do not nurture a girl's journey from childhood to womanhood; psychiatrist Mary Pipher views eating disorders as responses to our culture's social dictate that a good woman is passive, quiet, and takes up very little space. Chernin and Pipher do agree, however, that eating disorders develop in situations that prevent the victim from saying or acknowledging to herself what she thinks, feels, or wants. In this way, then, eating disorders can be seen as survival strategies in response to emotional, physical, and sexual abuse; sexism; classism; homophobia; or racism—in other words, responses to trauma. Contemporary researchers and scholars mostly agree that eating disorder behaviors are coping mechanisms that give the sufferers a feeling of empowerment. By refusing to eat, bingeing, or bingeing and purging, a woman gains some influence over her environment. Control over the body becomes a substitute for control a woman may wish to have over her economic, political, or social circumstance. Thus weight loss or gain may not be a primary motivation for disordered eating.

INCREASED RECOGNITION OF EATING DISORDERS AMONG RACIAL MINORITIES

African American singer, Dinah Washington, died as result of an overdose of diet pills and alcohol; Puerto Rican poet Luz Maria Umpierre-Herrera writes about her struggle with anorexia; and African American writer Gloria Naylor writes about generations of eating disordered women in *Linden Hills* (Thompson 1996). According to Becky Thompson's research on minority women, many of them were taught to diet, binge, and purge by older relatives, who had done so themselves, which suggests that although statistics show that eating disorders are on the rise in American minority cultures, this may simply be the result of more careful research rather than an actual, sharp increase. Health professionals assume and are taught that eating disorders are a white women's disease, so in women of color eating disorder symptoms would be dismissed or treated as something else. Particularly because Hispanic and black women are culturally stereotyped as plump or obese, whereas Asian women are stereotyped as very thin, doctors would ignore those visual cues as signs of eating problems. Exacerbating this situation is that most minority women also see eating disorders as a "white" problem, so they are more reluctant to recognize signs of disorder in themselves or seek help. This explains why most women of color who are treated for eating disorders are in more severe states than white women with the same disorders.

Women in African American and Hispanic communities have traditionally been larger than women in white communities, and minority communities have been more tolerant and even celebratory of the large female body as a symbol of health and wealth. One explanation for their larger size is food custom, but researchers have found that women in those communities also exhibit compulsive overeating behaviors, using bingeing as a way to cope with stress. Bingeing then is a "cheap" way to find temporary relief from oppressive social and economic conditions such as sexual abuse, poverty, racism, and sexism. Since the 1980s, eating disorder diagnoses, particularly of anorexia, have risen among the African American population. Some experts note that this rise parallels the increasing affluence of middle class black families, who find themselves embracing traditionally white values, including the obsession with thinness. This trend is also noted among upwardly mobile young Hispanic women and adolescents who see thinness as a key to success. A study conducted among a diverse selection of college-age women revealed that minority women who identified with their ethnic groups had fewer obsessions with thinness and realistic body goals, compared to women who rejected their cultural identities and also subscribed to the thin ideal for themselves, resulting in a much larger percentage of eating-disordered behaviors (Abrams 1993).

INCREASED RECOGNITION OF EATING DISORDERS AMONG MEN

The ratio of women to men with eating disorders is 9:1, although some researchers suspect that more men suffer from eating disorders and go untreated,

FASHION WEEK IN MADRID

Madrid's 2006 Fashion Week was the first of its kind to place a ban on models with a Body Mass Index below 18, a move that Australia's Fashion Week followed. A 5-foot 9-inch model weighing 125 pounds would have a body mass index of 18, which is the lowest healthy body mass range. This ban resulted in the turning away of 30 percent of the models scheduled to participate in the fashion week. Madrid's decision was a result of lobbying from groups such as Spain's Association in Defense of Attention for Anorexia and Bulimia, who argue that young women develop eating disorders as a result of trying to be as thin as the underweight fashion models. One turning point in the debate over model size for Madrid was the death of 22-year-old South American model Luisel Ramos, who suffered a heart attack after stepping off a runway in August of that year. She had been counseled that her career would jump start if she lost weight, so for three months she had been on a diet of green leaves and Diet Coke. Reactions to the ban from the fashion industry were mixed. Some designers refused to participate in Madrid's Fashion Week; others lauded the spirit of the ban. Most felt, though, that the fashion industry was being scapegoated for mental illnesses, when fashion merely reflects values society already holds. For eating disorder activists, this ban was seen as a major step toward having the fashion industry represent beauty at healthy weights and also having it assume a degree of responsibility for the health of its models, who so often starve themselves and are told by designers and agents to lose weight.

particularly with bulimia, because it is easier to hide than anorexia (Crawford 1990). Like women of color, men with eating disorder symptoms may go unnoticed by physicians because they do not fit the classic diagnostic and treatment models, which tend to focus on women. Men who are more vulnerable to developing eating disorders participate in athletic activities that have regular weigh-ins, such as wrestling. Disordered eating and overexercising is sometimes ordered by a coach so that a team member will be a certain weight for a tournament, and this unnatural obsession over weight and control over can lead to the wrestler using starvation as a means of weight control. Gay men may also be more susceptible to eating disorders because of the importance of appearance in gay culture. In a study comparing gay and straight men, homosexual men have been found to be more preoccupied with their body sizes and appearances and more likely to suffer from body dysmorphia than their heterosexual counterparts (Crawford 1990). Experts forecast that eating disorders in all men will continue to rise as the marketing of men's health and beauty products becomes increasingly aggressive with "metrosexual" men, straight men who are overly concerned about their grooming, clothing, and overall appearance; and they, too, seek to make their bodies conform to the thin standard already set for women (Patterson 2004).

CONCLUSION

Debates will continue regarding whether eating disorders stem from biological, psychological, environmental, or structural factors. What researchers do know is that women of various socioeconomic backgrounds are disproportionately represented in the diagnosis and treatment of eating disorders, as defined by the DSM. Many eating disorder activists argue that the so-called cult of thinness requires a more critical look at our culture at large, including gendered patterns of family life, girls' and boys' socialization, and the effects of various forms of oppression on individuals. Thus some activist-scholars argue that stopping the cycle of girls being socialized into the cult of thinness is a public, not a private, enterprise (Hesse-Biber 1996). Activism such as boycotting companies and products whose marketing includes the use of the thinness ideal is one approach that has been used by the Boston-based Boycott Anorexic Marketing group, which was effective during the mid-90s in getting Coca-Cola and Kellogg to portray athletic instead of waifish women. More recently, this kind of activism has been taken on by marketers themselves, particularly with Dove's ad campaign that features women's bodies with "real curves." Groups such as the Eating Disorder Coalition have been lobbying the U.S. Congress to provide more money for eating disorder research and to force insurance companies to cover medical treatment. In addition, new research results continue to be released that point to other factors contributing to the prevalence of eating disorders among white, middle class women, as well as among men of various backgrounds and women of color, research which will surely shape future debates on their causes.

See also Barbie and the Feminine Ideal of Beauty; Beauty Industry; Medicine and Medicalization: Views on Women's Bodies; Self-Injury and Body Image.

Further Reading: Abrams, S. K., Allen, L., and Gray, J., "Disordered Eating Attitudes and Ethnic Identity," *International Journal of Eating Disorders* 14 (1993): 49–57; ANAD, National Association of Anorexia Nervosa and Associated Disorders, 2006, available at: http://www.anad.org; Bruch, Hilde, *The Golden Cage: The Enigma of Anorexia Nervosa* (Cambridge, MA: Harvard University Press, 1978); Brumberg, Joan Jacobs, *Fasting Girls: The History of Anorexia Nervosa* (Cambridge, MA: Harvard University Press, 1988); Chernin, Kim, *The Obsession: Reflections on the Tyranny of Slenderness* (New York: HarperPerenial, 1981); Crawford, David, *Easing the Ache: Gay Men Recovering from Compulsive Disorders* (New York: Dutton, 1990); Greenfield, Laura, *Thin* (HBO Documentary, 2006); Hesse-Biber, Sharlene, *Am I Thin Enough Yet? The Cult of Thinness and the Commercialization of Identity* (New York: Oxford University Press, 1996); Maine, Margo, *Body Wars* (Carlsbad: Gurze Books, 1991); Patterson, Anna, *Fit to Die: Men and Eating Disorders* (Chapman: Paul Educational Publishing, 2004); Pipher, Mary, *Reviving Ophelia: Saving the Selves of Adolescent Girls* (New York: Random House, 1994); *Something Fishy Website on Eating Disorders,* CRC Health Corporation, 2006, available at: http://www.somethingfishy.org/; Thompson, Becky W., *A Hunger so Wide and Deep: A Multiracial View of Women's Eating Problems* (Minneapolis: University of Minnesota Press, 1996).

Cynthia Childress

EDUCATION

The status of women in education has progressed to a point where women are more successful in schools than men, yet arguments over how men and women learn and why men and women have differing levels of achievement perplex many.

The place of women in the American education system has changed dramatically throughout history. When public schools first began in the nineteenth century, girls were educated only if necessary. It was believed that girls should be taught only the skills to keep house and raise children. With the women's rights movement, women began demanding equal educations and moved out of the home and into the workforce. Today, boys and girls are equally enrolled in elementary schools, and women receive more high school and college degrees than men.

Women's place in education has changed, and these changes have brought about increased controversy. With girls excelling in schools and boys seemingly "falling behind," some ask do boys and girls learn in different ways? Where are the gender gaps in schools, and why do they exist? Should alternative ways to teaching children be considered?

HOW DO BOYS AND GIRLS LEARN?

A debate in the field of education and in the general public is whether boys and girls learn differently. Some believe that boys' and girls' brains develop at different times and in different ways advantaging boys in certain subjects and skills and advantaging girls in others. Others argue that girls and boys, despite so-called brain differences, are socialized, or taught, by parents, schools, and society to behave and excel in different subjects. This argument leaves the question, how do boys and girls learn?

BIOLOGICAL DIFFERENCES

Many argue the reason why boys and girls excel at different levels in schools may be a result of natural, biological differences between the male and female brain. Pointing to biological differences is not considered politically correct to some, yet research suggests that men and women's brains are different. It is argued that gender differences in brain development begin six weeks after conception before birth (Moir and Jessel 1989). Neural and hormonal differences cause male and female brains to develop in different ways and at different rates. Basic developmental differences between male and female brains are said to explain girls' and boys' later learning differences.

Male brains excel at spatial activities and mathematical reasoning; female brains are able to understand more complexity, have stronger short-term memories, and are extremely active. In general, girls' brains mature at an earlier age than boys'. Because of this, girls develop verbal skills as much as a year earlier than boys. Girls digest more sensory data than boys, meaning their senses are stronger, causing them to hear and smell better and take in more from touch. Girls control impulsive behavior better than boys (Gurian 2001).

The strengths of males' and females' brains also lead to differing behaviors. Males are considered harder to teach and have more learning and discipline difficulties because of the wiring of their brains. Aggression and competition are

TITLE IX

A triumph for women in education was the passage of Title IX of the Education Amendments in 1972 (since renamed the Pasty T. Mink Equal Opportunity in Education Act). Title IX prohibits any discrimination in any educational activity based on sex. It states that no one can be excluded from, denied benefits of, or be discriminated against in any education program or activity that receives federal money on the basis of sex. The passage of Title IX meant the girls and women could not be denied funding, participation, or membership in any educational activity. In addition, Title IX forced educational institutions to integrate. This excluded traditionally male or female colleges, fraternities and sororities, traditionally male or female youth organizations, and beauty pageants. Title IX's biggest impact has been in sports.

With the passage of Title IX, many worried that male athletic teams would lose money or be eliminated to accommodate female teams; however, this is not the case. The purpose of Title IX was not to increase opportunities only for females, but to create a level playing field for both sexes. To ensure equality and fairness, as well as compliance, Title IX includes a three-part test. First, men and women's participation opportunities must be "substantially proportionate" to their school enrollment. Second, a school or college that has continually expanded programs and opportunities must continue expansions with the underrepresented sex in mind, creating opportunities according to their interest and ability. Third, a school or college is recognized as complying with Title IX when it has effectively accommodated the interests and abilities of female students, even when there are less female students participating in activities than male students. These tests guarantee that the same opportunities will be available for males and females.

Before Title IX, in high schools and colleges, women's sports received little to no recognition or money. Women were denied the opportunity to participate in sports.

According to the Department of Education's 1997 report on Title IX, the amendment has increased women's participation in college athletics four times since it began (U.S. Department of Education 1997). Women represent 39 percent of high school student athletes and 37 percent of college student athletes. Before Title IX, college scholarships were rare for women athletes. In 1964, Donna de Varona, an Olympic gold medal-winning swimmer, was unable to obtain a college swimming scholarship because they did not exist. In 1974, 100,000 men were attending college on athletic scholarships compared to only 50 women. Currently, women receive one-third of all academic scholarships. Women have not reached parity in participating in and receiving scholarships for athletics, but great strides have been made to ensure equal opportunities.

also a result of the male brain. Females' active brains lend to their success in the classroom.

Boys and girls learn in different ways. Boys are deductive learners, meaning it is easier for them to move from general principles and ideas to individual, specific cases; girls are inductive learners. Girls learn from concrete examples, which they then add to their repertoire of conceptualization and apply to other situations.

It is important to remember that the differences between male and female brains are based on generalities. Not every male brain excels at mathematical reasoning. Some may excel at vocabulary. Not every female brain is unable to learn spatial tasks. Researchers have found these general patterns of difference between the male and female brain, but this by no means dismisses a boy's ability to understand people's gestures and work in a people-oriented field or a girl's ability to understand complex math problems and achieve great success in the field of math.

Some point only to biological differences to explain the differing successes of boys and girls, but others argue that society and the way we teach and treat children guides them to perform and behave according to their gender. Gender socialization, or how society teaches behaviors and attitudes that correspond with one's gender, starts early.

GENDER SOCIALIZATION

When parents-to-be find out the sex of their child, family and friends begin to buy gifts according to gender. Girls receive pink clothing, and boys receive blue clothing. If parents choose not to know the sex of the child, generally clothing will be bought in "gender-neutral" colors like yellow and green. Buying babies' clothing in specific gendered colors begins the socialization process, which will continue when toys are purchased—dolls for girls, trucks for boys. The teaching of gender continues in society and carries over into schools.

Schools socialize students in multiple ways starting in kindergarten. Schools teach young students about the society they live in and their expectations of behavior. Citizenship is stressed in early education, through activities such as saying the pledge of allegiance and singing the national anthem. How to conduct one's self appropriately and listen to authority are also highly valued in early schooling. Much time is spent on sitting in your assigned seat, lining up properly, and learning to listen attentively to teachers (Thorne 1993).

Beyond these practical socializing factors, many researchers argue that schools also socialize according to gender. Teachers treat boys and girls differently based on different expectations of behaviors and intellect. Teachers tend to accept when boys "act out" more and justify boys' disruptions in the classroom as uniquely male features. Girls, however, are often reprimanded for similar behaviors, as teachers expect girls to be better behaved and less disruptive in class.

Teachers expect girls to be more studious and excel more in school, particularly in subjects like reading and writing; boys are favored in math and science.

Girls receive better grades than boys, and they also receive more favorable evaluations from teachers. Teachers seem to appreciate girls' cooperativeness and ease at communication and consistently rank girls higher on in-classroom behaviors. Girls may be better adapted to schools or may have different expectations than boys.

Young students are affected by gender socialization. In elementary school, boys and girls choose who is popular based on typical constructions of gender. Boys are thought to be popular when they are athletic and described as "tough" or "cool." Popular girls are chosen because of their physical appearance, social skills, and academic success (Adler, Kleiss, and Adler 1992).

THE FEMINIZATION OF TEACHING

A subtler way that schools reinforce gender is through the feminization of teaching. The feminization of teaching refers to the fact that the majority of teachers in the United States are women. Throughout elementary and high school, teachers tend to be female.

The field of education tends to replicate traditional gender hierarchies seen in other work environments, such as business. Although women dominate the status of teachers, a much higher percentage of education administrators, from principals and superintendents to positions in government, are male. Also, in colleges, a higher number of men are faculty members than women, particularly in math, science, and engineering fields.

The feminization of teaching has a long history in the United States. As early as 1880, 80 percent of elementary school teachers were women (Urban and Wagoner 2004). Schools originally hired women to teach because they could pay them less than men and were thought to be more nurturing and caring. It is arguable whether women make better teachers, but the high number of women teachers and the low level of female administrators shape how education is developed and taught, as well as how it is perceived by boys and girls.

What teachers and society expect of, teach, and demonstrate to children directly affects their opinions of themselves, their abilities, and what they are to hope for in school and the future. Girls may think they are supposed to be good writers but not good at math, or boys may think they should not be elementary school teachers because teaching is a female job. It is hard to disentangle whether girls and boys learn differently, or if they are taught to think that boys and girls are different from an early age.

WHERE ARE THE GENDER GAPS IN SCHOOLS?

Debates over how and why children learn and perceive themselves in different ways continue and evidence in schools shows that gaps exist between boys and girls in terms of achievement in the classroom, standardized tests, and completing schooling. These gaps vary. Some favor girls and others favor boys, beginning in elementary school and continuing throughout college and professional school.

Elementary School

Elementary school is the first formal schooling children receive, and it is primarily used to teach basic reading and math skills. In elementary schools, differences between boys and girls emerge. Since the 1950s, girls have consistently received higher grades in all elementary school subjects, even math and science, which are traditionally thought of as male subjects. (Alexander and Eckland 1974). Girls receive better ratings by teachers, better grades on report cards, and are less likely to repeat grades. Boys are more likely to repeat grades or drop out of school. (American Association of University Women 1998). Girls seem to excel in the early years of education; however, this is not the case when it comes to standardized testing.

On standardized tests, such as proficiency tests, gaps between boys and girls appear. Girls do significantly better on tests of reading and writing; boys do better on tests of science and math (American Association of University Women 1998). These gaps sometimes puzzle researchers who wonder why girls' abilities in the classroom do not translate to tests, and why boys' high-test achievement does not translate into the classroom.

High School

High school graduation rates suggest that girls are outpacing boys in schools and earning more degrees, but many obstacles stand in girls' ways for future success. Selection of classes becomes a cause of concern in high school. From early on, gaps in tests scores between boys and girls show that boys do better in math. The gap between math and science classes taken in high school is prevalent. Girls have increased their participation in math courses, but boys still take more advanced courses than girls. In science classes, boys are more likely to take all core classes, including biology, chemistry, and physics. Girls are less likely to take physics courses.

Conversely, girls take more English classes than boys and boys are more likely to be enrolled in remedial English courses. Girls also take more foreign language, fine arts, and social science courses. Over time, girls have been increasingly taking more math and science courses, but they still lag behind boys.

Postsecondary

Historically, more men than women attended and completed college education, but this trend has recently changed. By 1980, men and women enrolled equally in college and currently, more than 56 percent of undergraduate students in the United States are women (Freeman 2004). Women enroll and complete bachelor's degree at higher rates than men; however, women's increased enrollment and attainment in college do not mean that equity has been reached. Many inequalities still exist for women in college.

Majors in college are highly sex-segregated. Although women make up the majority of college students, certain fields seem regulated to males and females.

Men earn a large majority of engineering, physical science, and computer science degrees. Women earn only 20 percent of engineering and 28 percent of computer science degrees. Women earn 41 percent of physical science degrees. The fields of business, mathematics, social sciences, and history have relativity equal numbers of men and women earning degrees. Women dominate the fields of education, completing 77 percent of degrees, and health professions, completing 84 percent of degrees.

Of interest, the fields that are clearly dominated by men, engineering and computer science, have the highest starting salaries of all college degrees; the fields dominated by women, education and health professions, have much lower starting salaries. The starting salaries of males and females after college cause concern for some scholars who believe that majors are a way to segregate men and women financially.

SEXUAL HARASSMENT IN SCHOOLS

A pressing issue facing many students in American schools is sexual harassment. Recognizing and preventing sexual harassment are difficult for educators and students, but the issue needs attention. Often, sexual harassment is considered a problem that afflicts workers only, yet sexual harassment is common at all levels of schooling. Sexual harassment in schools does not exclusively affect girls. A study conducted by the American Association of University Women found that 83 percent of girls and 79 percent of boys in grades 8 to 11 report being sexually harassed at school. Also, 62 percent of women and 61 percent of men in colleges report experiencing sexual harassment.

Peers overwhelmingly conduct sexual harassment in middle and high schools. Girls in schools are likely to be harassed for different reasons than boys. The most common types of sexual harassment that occur in schools include having rumors spread about a person, being forced into sexual acts, or enduring verbal attacks about looks or sexuality.

In college, peers mostly perpetrate sexual harassment. Concerns over sexual relationships between students and instructors or professors have prompted many schools to forbid such relationships. These relationships are troublesome because the professor is in a position of power over the student, often a young female. Professors apparently can take on many roles in order to solicit relationships from young women, from threatening to decrease their grade, to acting like a counselor or mentor to the student (Dzeich and Weiner 1992).

Sexual harassment in schools is particularly harmful for women. The consequences of such experiences can cause girls emotional distress and is often associated with feelings of anger, fear, or embarrassment. Students who are sexually harassed may find it difficult to pay attention in class and their grades often suffer. In addition, they may skip class or drop out of school.

Although it is not likely to be a debate over whether sexual harassment is wrong, the issue is often overlooked or ignored in the education system. Affecting both boys and girls, sexual harassment should be discussed and addressed.

The types of degrees earned by men and women differ, as do the types of colleges and universities they attend. Even though women are more likely to be enrolled in college, the colleges that women enroll in are less likely to be prestigious, selective schools (Jacobs 1999). This group largely includes prominent engineering schools. Women are more likely than men to enroll in two-year institutions such as community colleges.

Graduate and professional schools, like college majors, are sex-segregated as well. Women are more likely to enroll in master's degree programs than men, but within these programs segregation similar to those seen in college occurs. The transition from master's to doctoral programs is less common for women, as they comprise only 45 percent of doctoral students. In professional fields, women's enrollment lags behind men. Roughly 39 percent of dentistry students and 43 percent of medical students are female. Law schools have almost reached parity in gender enrollment, with 47 percent of students being female.

INTERNATIONAL GENDER GAPS

Gender gaps in educational enrollment and completion of degrees exist in the United States, but what are the patterns of gender gaps in other countries? Similar gaps in standardized testing exist in other countries. In 2003, the Program for International Student Assessment tested 15-year-olds in math, science, and reading in 41 countries. Patterns similar to the United States are present in other countries. On average, boys performed better on tests of mathematics (OECD 2004). In 12 countries, however, the difference between boys' and girls' performance in math was not statistically significant. In all but one country, girls significantly outperformed boys on reading tests. In science tests, more variation occurs. In some countries, girls perform better than boys, but the opposite is true in other countries. On average, there is a minimal difference in science scores between boys and girls. Gender gaps seem to be consistent across countries, which is also true for educational enrollment.

In most industrialized countries, women have higher college enrollments than men. On average, they represent 53 percent of all students enrolled in tertiary education (OECD 2004). In some more conservative and traditional countries, such as Turkey and Germany, women still lag behind men in college enrollment, but in 13 industrialized nations, 55 percent of college students are women. In three countries, more than 60 percent of college students are female.

Gender gaps occur at all levels of schooling and across cultures, but the gaps do not always fall in one direction. Boys and girls have different advantages in schooling, creating a complex puzzle. Trends suggest that women have surpassed men, yet men still hold advantages in the work force. There is no clear answer explaining why girls excel in some areas and boys in others, and the controversies surrounding gender and education continue beyond how girls and boys learn and where they succeed.

SINGLE-SEX SCHOOLS

The debates over how boys and girls learn, and why they succeed in different ways, lead some to argue for single-sex schooling in the United States. Those in favor of single-sex schools believe that by schooling girls and boys separately, teachers can tailor their curricula according to gender. Opponents of single-sex schooling believe that there is no valid reason for segregating schools based on gender.

Single-sex schools have a complex history in the American education system. Founders of public schools wanted to segregate all schools based on sex, but it was expensive and inconvenient to do so; so public schools were integrated. Although many colleges were, and remain, single-sex institutions, an increasing number of elementary and high schools are becoming single-sex, but not without controversy.

It is estimated that 237 schools have single-sex classrooms and 51 public schools are completely single-sex in the United States (National Association for Single Sex Public Education, August 2006). Many experts, parents, and students argue that students learn better when not distracted by the opposite sex, but others counter that claim by reasoning that the real world is not segregated by sex and therefore single-sex schools do not prepare students for the actual work environment (McCollum 2004).

Those in favor of single-sex schools believe that boys and girls learn differently. Boys enjoy competition and working alone, whereas girls learn through cooperation. Boys and girls interact in the classroom differently, with boys shouting out answers and testing boundaries; girls are more likely to follow rules and thoroughly analyze questions before answering. By placing girls and boys in separate schools, they learn in environments tailored to their sex.

Researchers and educators believe that single-sex schools benefit girls more than they benefit boys, causing girls to develop higher self-esteem than they would in a coeducational school. Girls in single-sex schools are also found to be more likely to be leaders in life and to pursue advanced degrees. In addition, girls in single-sex schools are twice as likely to pursue careers in science compared to girls in coed schools.

Although single-sex schools seem to benefit girls, they have many opponents. Some question the benefits of single-sex schools, for they tend to benefit girls from wealthier backgrounds that could skew their positive effects. Mainly, opponents of single-sex schools believe that coeducational institutions can spark different kinds of learning for every student. The diversity of having both boys and girls is beneficial to the understanding of ideas and viewpoints. They will better prepare students to interact with a more diverse population. Some also questions whether single-sex schools violate the Fourteenth Amendment to the Constitution, stating that schools must be integrated.

Also, some believe that single-sex schools are being used as a type of quick fix to problems in the American education system. For example, in the 1990s California attempted to operate single-sex schools, which seemed to succeed at first. However, Over time, however, male-only schools became dumping grounds for boys with behavioral, educational, and emotional problems, which drove the schools to close. Although this case is extreme, the decision to implement single-sex schools is one that must be thoughtfully considered. In general, the majority of the American public does not believe in single-sex schooling (68 percent).

WOMEN IN THE FIELD OF SCIENCE

In early 2005, Harvard University's President Lawrence Summers suggested biological differences might be to blame for women's underrepresentation in the fields of science and engineering, pointing to statistical differences in standardized test scores. An immediate uproar over the remarks followed, launching a renewed interest in the controversy over women's performance in math and science. The debate has two contesting viewpoints. One view is that biological differences prevent women from being successful in science and engineering fields. The other view is that institutional forces and socialization prevent women from entering science and engineering fields.

The biological debate, discussed in this chapter, argues that men and women have different brains that have different specializations, which could benefit men in the participation in math, science, and engineering. The alternative argument, however, argues that the male-dominated fields, such as math, science, and engineering discriminate against women, which limits their participation and success. In a report produced by the National Academies Press on the position of women in science and engineering (2006), researchers found many obstacles that stand in women's way in these fields. First, they recognize that biological differences between the sexes may be present, but women are able to succeed in the sciences and have strong drives and motivations. Many women scientists have been extremely influential and successful in the sciences, such as Marie Curie, a physicist and chemist who was the first person to win two Nobel Prizes in different fields of science in 1903 and 1911. More recently, Linda Buck, a biologist, won the Nobel Prize in 2004 in the field of physiology.

Another obstacle for women in science is that at each educational transition, more and more women drop out of science fields. Women either opt out of or are "weeded" out of science programs as they progress through their education. Some suggest the presence of a science "pipeline" exists that disadvantages women. This pipeline refers to the trajectory that one must take to choose a science career. From elementary school to advanced degrees, women are not heavily placed on this pipeline. Also, within the fields of science and engineering, women face discrimination. Many science career and academic environments are traditionally male and favor males, making women feel uncomfortable or unable to be successful. Finally, most people have implicit biases that suggest women are not good at math, science, or engineering. Often employers will hire a man over a woman for a scientific job, even if they have the same qualifications.

These barriers to women in the field of science support those who argue that society and our education system disadvantage women who would like to participate in the sciences. The debate over women in science continues as researchers continues to study both brain differences between the sexes and the socializing processes and discriminatory practices that impede women's participation in the sciences.

CONCLUSION

Women's position in the education system is likely to keep evolving as women continue to succeed in schools. These changes will be closely monitored by researchers and the public as questions are asked about testing gaps and college completion differences. The controversy over how males and females learn will continue as debate over brain differences and social differences continue. A free and equal education is expected in the United States, but how do we feel when one gender seems to be benefiting more than others? Is there a middle ground between helping girls, who have traditionally been discriminated against in schools, succeed versus not wanting to diminish the success of boys?

See also Affirmative Action; Title IX and Women's Sports.

Further Reading: Adler, Patricia A., Steven J. Kleiss, and Peter Alder, "Socialization to Gender Roles: Popularity among Elementary School Boys and Girls," *Sociology of Education* 65 (1992): 169–187; Alexander, Karl L., and Bruce E. Eckland, "Sex Differences in the Educational Attainment Process," *American Sociological Review* 39 (1974): 668–682; American Association of University Women, "Gender Gaps: Where Schools Still Fail our Children," 1998, available at: www.aauw.org/research/girls_education/gg.cfm; *Beyond Bias and Barriers: Fulfilling the Potential of Women in Academic Science and Engineering* (Washington, DC: National Academies Press, 2006), available at: www.nap.edu/catalog/11741.html#toc; Dzeich, B. W., and L. Weiner, *The Lecherous Professor: Sexual Harassment on Campus* (Champaign-Urbana: University of Illinois Press, 1992); Freeman, C. E., *Trends in the Educational Equity of Girls and Women: 2004* (Washington, DC: National Center for Education Statistics, 2004); Gurian, Micael, *Boys and Girls Learn Differently! A Guide for Teachers and Parents* (Hoboken, NJ: Jossey-Bass, 2001); Jacobs, Jerry A., "Gender and the Stratification of Colleges," *The Journal of Higher Education* 70 (1999): 161–187; McCollum, Sean, "Single-Sex Schools: Solution or Setback?" *Literary Cavalcade* 57, no. 2 (2004): 18–19; Moir, Anne, and David Jessel, *Brain Sex: The Real Difference Between Men and Women* (Quince Cottage, England: Delta Publishing, 1989); National Association for Single Sex Public Education, 2006, available at: www.singlesexschools.org; Organization for Economic Co-operation and Development, "Learning for Tomorrow's World: First Results from PISA 2003," 2004, available at: www.oecd.pisa.org; Thorne, Barrie, *Gender Play: Girls and Boys in School* (New Brunswick, NJ: Rutgers University Press, 1993); Urban, Wayne, and L. Wagoner Jennings Jr., *American Education: A History* (New York: McGraw Hill, 2004); U.S. Department of Education, "Title IX: 25 Years of Progress" (June 1997), available at: www.ed.gov/pubs/TitleIX/Index.html.

Anne McDaniel

ENVIRONMENTAL JUSTICE

Debates concerning women and environmental justice focus on whether people who have less power in a society (e.g., racial minorities, low-income people, women) should be subjected to more pollution and health risks than those who have more power. Although many studies focus on environmental effects on racial minorities and poor communities, women in these communities have experienced gender-specific effects of pollution and health risks that are largely undocumented.

DEFINITION OF ENVIRONMENTAL JUSTICE

Environmental justice, as the term is used most frequently in the United States, focuses on the environmental problems (in terms of programs, policies, and/or activities) and the resulting health risks that are disproportionately faced by those with the least power (Fritz 1999). In the United States, these groups would be minority and low-income populations. Although the term *environmental justice* is the popular term, the focus really is on environmental injustice. The decision to use the term *justice* rather than *injustice* is interesting legally, socially and politically. *Environmental justice* pushes us to think about a negative situation by using a positive term. Other terms with the same positive ring are *environmental equity* or *human rights and the environment*.

Environmental injustice is sometimes called *environmental racism*. Environmental racism is a strong term chosen by those that think racism is frequently or always the root of an environmental problem. The decision to use a strong term may be based on the feeling that using a term like *environmental justice* to characterize a life-threatening environmental problem dilutes the central analysis of racism or might even keep an analyst from mentioning or thinking about the possibility of racism.

Some prefer the term *environmental justice* because what may have been a racist practice or decision initially has been perpetuated for reasons other than racism. Because environmental problems often develop over a long time and are complicated, these analysts may prefer to use both terms—*environmental justice* as a general term and *environmental racism* when a specific situation warrants the use of the term.

U.S. ENVIRONMENTAL JUSTICE TIMELINE

1964: The Civil Rights Act of 1964, through Title VI, prohibits the use of federal funds to discriminate based on race, color, and national origin.

1969: Ralph Abascal of the California Rural Legal Assistance files suit on behalf of six migrant farm workers that ultimately resulted in ban of the pesticide DDT.

1970: The United States Public Health Services indicates that lead poisoning was disproportionately affecting African American and Hispanic children.

1971: President's Council on Environmental Quality annual report indicates racial discrimination adversely affects urban poor and quality of their environment.

1979: *Bean v. Southwestern Waste Management, Inc.* is filed on behalf of Houston's Northeast Community Action Group.

1982: Warren County (North Carolina) residents protested the siting of a polychlorinated biphenyl landfill.

1983: U.S. General Accounting Office publishes *Siting of Hazardous Landfills and their Correlation with Racial and Economic Status of Surrounding Communities.*

1986: West Harlem Environmental Action (WE ACT) began organizing the community to combat the harmful impacts of the North River Sewage Treatment Plant. In 2003, Peggy Shepard, an African American, who is a co-founder and the executive director wins the Heinz Award for the Environment in 2003.

1987: The United Church of Christ Commission for Racial Justice issues a report, *Toxic Wastes and Race in the United States*

1990: The Indigenous Environmental Network is formed to address environmental and economic justice issues on a national level.

1990: The Southwest Network for Environmental and Economic Justice is established.

1991: The first National People of Color Environmental Leadership Summit is held, during which 17 Principles of Environmental Justice are adopted.

1992: The U.S. EPA creates what is now called the Office of Environmental Justice and releases *Environmental Equity: Reducing Risk for All Communities.*

1994: On February 11, President Bill Clinton signs Executive Order 12898, "Federal Action to Address Environmental Justice in Minority Populations and Low-Income Populations."

1994: Federal Interagency Working Group on Environmental Justice is established.

1998: United Church of Christ Commission on Racial Justice convenes an array of grassroots leaders to discuss Shintech's attempt build a PVC plant in Convent, Louisiana. Shintech suspends its efforts to build the plant in Convent.

2001: Residents of Anniston Alabama Sweet Valley/Cobb Town Environmental Task Force wins a $42.8 million settlement against Monsanto, a chemical company. The community is relocated because of PCB contamination.

2004: Margie Richard of Concerned Citizens of Norco, Louisiana, becomes the first African American to win a Goldman Environmental Prize. Richard led the battle to hold Shell Chemical accountable for her community's health problems.

2004: The EPA's Office of the Inspector General issues *EPA Needs to Consistently Implement the Intent of the Executive Order on Environmental Justice.* The EPA was found not to have fully implemented Executive Order 12898 nor consistently integrated environmental justice into its day-to-day operations.

2005: Environmental Action Now of Mossville, Louisiana, files a petition with the Organization of American States Inter-American Commission on Human Rights.

2006: The U.S. EPA's Inspector General issues *EPA Needs to Conduct Environmental Justice Reviews of Its Programs, Policies, and Activities,* which outlined the EPA's failure to comply with the requirements of Executive Order 12898.

THE CURRENT SITUATION

Minorities and low-income people have experienced serious problems in terms of environmental degradation (e.g., exposure to toxics) at home and at work. Increasing globalization, with the consent of governments, international financial groups, and large corporations, has put people of color, the economically poor, and economically developing nations at escalating risk, often with little protection and few prospects for individuals and communities to control their own lives.

Studies have consistently indicated that the burden of certain environmental problems is faced predominantly by those who are least able to effect the necessary changes. In the United States, a 1983 study, *Siting of Hazardous Landfills and their Correlation with Racial and Economic Status of Surrounding Communities,* was published by the U.S. General Accounting Office. The report indicated that three of four off-site commercial hazardous waste facilities located in one EPA region of the country were in African American communities. This was the case even though African Americans were just 20 percent of that region's population. In 1987, the United Church of Christ Commission for Racial Justice issued *Toxic Wastes and Race in the United States: A National Report on the Racial and Socio-economic Characteristics of Communities with Hazardous Waste Sites.* This was the first national study to correlate waste facility sites and demographic characteristics, and it pointed to substantial, unaddressed problems that minority communities face.

A 1992 U.S. Environmental Protection Agency (EPA) report, *Environmental Equity: Reducing the Risk for All Communities,* indicated that there were "clear differences between racial groups in terms of disease and death rates" and higher than average exposure of minority groups (in terms of race or income) to "selected air pollutants, hazardous waste facilities, contaminated fish and agricultural pesticides in the workplace." In 1999, a report from Institute of Medicine the National Academy of Sciences found that "the minority and low-income communities that it chose to visit have had disproportionately higher levels of exposure to environmental stressors compared with those for the general population... and (those communities) were least able to affect change." The committee urged policymakers "to exercise caution on behalf of the affected communities... taking reasonable precautions to safeguard against or minimize adverse health outcomes." In 2007, 20 years after the United Church of Christ's landmark study on toxic waste and race, researchers concluded that 9 of 10 EPA regions have racial disparities in the location of hazardous waste sites, and 40 of 44 states with hazardous waste facilities have disproportionately high percentages of people of color in the surrounding neighborhoods (Bullard, Mohai, Saba and Wright 2007).

It also should be noted that, although there are many studies linking toxicity and race, there are few that look at toxicity exposure in the workplace and gender. As many toxic workplaces around the world are highly gender segregated, it is important to examine women's toxicity exposure and the resulting health effects. Katsi Cook, a Mohawk woman, thinks of women as "the first environment," and she says the Mohawk women were "flabbergasted" when they realized that all the toxic chemicals "are stored in our body fat and excreted through breast milk... our sacred natural link to our babies" (LaDuke 1999, 18–19). As the Women's Foundation of California (2005) has noted, women's bodies are often:

> the markers of environmental contamination through diminished fertility, abnormal fetal development, increased rates of cancers and other

spiraling forms of environmental illness... Women, in essence, are the canaries of the coal mine.

WOMEN AS LEADERS OF ENVIRONMENTAL JUSTICE INITIATIVES

Communities and organizations have identified and fought against environmental injustice for more than 25 years. It is important when discussing the struggle for environmental justice to give special attention to women's voices. Women frequently predominate as members of neighborhood or community-based groups, and so it is no surprise to find that this may be the case in environmental justice groups where the issues are protecting the family, the children, the home, and the community. The women also frequently lead the neighborhood groups fighting for environmental justice and against environmental racism. Statistical data are not available regarding women's participation in environmental justice activities, but one analyst said, 10 years ago, that 90 percent of the active members of neighborhood environmental justice groups were women and another analyst noted that women "account(ed) for up to 60 percent of the leadership of people-of-color environmental justice organizations" (Stein 2004, 2).

In many countries, the backbone of a local environmental movement, including the environmental justice initiatives, has been women. Some women are rather well known but most are recognized only in their local areas. Among the better known is Hazel Wolf (1898–2000). She was born in Canada and "organized hundreds of organizers in hundreds of environmental projects and thus touched thousands" in the United States. Her biographer (Starbuck 2002, xiii) said that Wolf wanted her story published because "it would be a powerful argument for... social and environmental justice."

Diane Wilson, author of *An Unreasonable Woman: A True Story of Shrimpers, Politicos, Polluters and the Fight for Seadrift, Texas* (2005), is a fourth-generation shrimper and mother of five. In 1989, she read that her home county in Texas was the number one toxic polluter in the country. She began to discuss what the chemical plants were doing to the bay and became an environmental activist, taking on Formosa Plastics, Dow Chemical, and Union Carbide. Her work on behalf of Seadrift has earned her a number of awards including the National Fisherman Magazine Award and *Mother Jones*'s Hell Raiser of the month.

Finally, Kenya's Nobel Prize winner Wangari Maathai has been referred to as an "international eco-hero." She is the first woman in central or eastern Africa to earn a doctorate, and she has been the leader of the National Council of Women of Kenya. As head of the country's green belt movement, Maathai (2004) launched a campaign to plant ten million trees and most of these were planted by women.

The female role models in the environmental justice movement serve as activists, leaders of community and national organizations, analysts, and researchers. These women come from all kinds of backgrounds (e.g., ethnic, educational, economic and regional) to work on these issues. There is, for instance, Rose Augustine, a co-founder of Tucsonians for a Clean Environment and the

Southwest Network for Environmental and Economic Justice; Alicia Marentes, a labor organizer and farm worker; Sarah James, a member of the Gwitch'n nation in Alaska who wants to keep gas and oil exploration out of the Arctic National Wildlife Refuge; and Peggy Morrow Shepard, executive director of West Harlem Environmental Action and a former chair of the U.S. Environmental Protection Agency's National Environmental Justice Advisory Council.

Women have been leaders in organizing against unsafe practices in many areas of employment including the high-tech industry. There are organizations in the Silicon Valley (California), for instance, that are founded by women or linked to women's organizations including the Asian Immigrant Women's Advocates, Working Women's Leadership Project, and the GABRIELLA Network (Pellow and Park 2002).

We need to share the stories of the women activists in the environmental justice movement. The stories help keep us focused on resolving the problems our communities are facing and the stories help support women activists in other communities in their often isolated struggles. The stories also remind those community members who may not have even noticed the environmental work of women that women activists, analysts and/or scientists who work in support of environmental justice often do so under difficult circumstances. Policymakers who follow the initiatives of these women learn a great deal about the specifics of a community's environmental problems and also about particular theoretical frameworks (e.g., ecofeminism, standpoint theory, multicultural liberationist theory) that help explain their community's struggles for environmental justice in a challenging world.

CONCLUSION

A great deal of evidence shows that minority people, low-income populations and particularly women who are minority or low-income have health risks resulting from their exposure to toxics. Companies and governments that do not recognize environmental justice problems have said they are not supportive for a variety of reasons including: (1) there is no evidence that there is a problem; (2) there may be some evidence, but a decision to act should be made only after there is a considerable body of reliable scientific evidence; (3) people can move if they don't want to experience a problem; (4) it would cost too much to fix a problem; (5) the problem will be eliminated by advanced technology in the near future; and/or, (6) it is not the government or company's responsibility to fix a problem that may have many causes.

Addressing environmental justice problems is difficult, but not impossible. There must be both a recognition of the problem and a willingness to address it. We have made significant progress in calling attention to environmental injustice. We still have much more to do, however, in putting a human face on the outcomes of the problems. We need to let others know when there have been tragic outcomes for the people and/or the environment (including species loss and habitat destruction). We also need to showcase the communities that have made big steps in reducing problems and the ways in which they have done that.

In addition, we need to celebrate the efforts of those who have addressed these difficult community issues. As many of these community heroes are women, the more we publicize their efforts, the more we do to raise the status of women around the world.

As we call attention to the problems and our limited accomplishments, however, the world has changed. There is an amazing concentration of wealth and power and for the vast majority of the world's population, sustainability "is mostly about surviving until tomorrow and hoping there will be a tomorrow" (Stephens and Bullock 2004, 143). Globalization has meant that the "playing field" is no longer the nation-state, but a borderless world. This means that any justice provisions that are developed, implemented, and even enforced on a national basis may not apply or be seen as problematic in a borderless, global economy. We need, at least on an interim basis, to have campaigns that both appeal to the highest humanistic values that should be expected from our leaders (such as government officials and heads of corporations) and, at the same time, also publicize and embarrass those responsible for existing and developing environmental justice problems. In the long run, more attention and energy need to go into developing a shared vision of our future: creating a climate for the development and acceptance of treaties and documents that govern world activities and reallocating our resources to deal with our most important issues. We have a long way to go to create a world where ecology, health, cultural competency, and human rights are core considerations.

See also Gender and Globalization: Trends and Debates; Gender and International Development; Race and Racism: Social Stratification in the United States.

Further Reading: Bullard, Robert D., "Decision Making," in *Faces of Environmental Racism: Confronting Issues of Global Justice,* ed. Laura Westra and Peter S. Wenz (Lanham, MD: Rowman and Littlefield, 1995); Bullard, Robert D., Paul Mohai, Robin Saha, and Beverly Wright, "Toxic Wastes and Race at Twenty: 1987–2007, Grassroots Struggles to Dismantle Environmental Racism in the U.S." available at: http://www.ejrc.cau.edu/TWARTreport.htm, accessed March 6, 2007; Bullard, Robert D., and Damu Smith, "Women Warriors of Color on the Front Line," in *The Quest for Environmental Justice,* ed. Robert D. Bullard, 61–84 (San Francisco: Sierra Club Books, 2004); Cole, Luke W., and Sheila R. Foster, *From the Ground Up: Environmental Racism and the Rise of the Environmental Justice Movement* (New York: New York University Press, 2001); Fritz, Jan Marie, "Searching for Environmental Justice: National Stories, Global Possibilities," *Social Justice* 26, no. 3 (1999): 1043–1578; Institute of Medicine, *Toward Environmental Justice: Research, Education, and Health Policy Needs* (Washington, DC: National Academy of Sciences, 1999); LaDuke, Winona, *All Our Nations: Native Struggles for Land and Life* (Cambridge, MA: South End Press, 1999); Maathai, Wangari, "Nobel Peace Prize Acceptance Speech," City Hall, Oslo, Norway, December 10, 2004, available at: http://www.greenbeltmovement.org/a.php?id=34, accessed May 13, 2006; Pellow, David N., and Lisa Sun-Hee Park, *The Silicon Valle of Dreams: Environmental Injustice, Immigrant Workers, and the High-Tech Global Economy* (New York: New York University Press, 2002); Starbuck, Susan, *Hazel Wolf, Fighting the Establishment* (Seattle: University of Washington Press, 2002); Stein, Rachel, ed., *New Perspectives on Environmental Justice: Gender, Sexuality and Activism* (New Brunswick, NJ: Rutgers University Press, 2004); Stephens, Carolyn, and Simon Bullock, "Civil Society and Environmental Justice," in

Fighting for Human Rights, ed. Paul Gready, 134–152 (London: Routledge, 2004); United Church of Christ Commission for Racial Justice, *Toxic Wastes and Race in the United States: A National Report of the Racial and Socio-Economic Characteristics of Communities Surrounding Hazardous Waste Sites* (New York: United Church of Christ, 1987); United States Environmental Protection Agency, Environmental Equity: Reducing Risks for All Communities, EPA230-R-92–008 (June, 1992); United States General Accounting Office, *Siting of Hazardous Waste Landfills and Their Correlation with the Racial and Socio-Economic Status of Surrounding Communities* (Washington, DC: GAO, 1983); Wilson, Diane, *An Unreasonable Woman: A True Story of Shrimpers, Politicos, Polluters, and the Fight for Seadrift, Texas* (White River Junction, VT: Chelsea Green Publishing Company, 2005); Women's Foundation of California, *In the Shadow of Pollution: Southern California Women on the Front Lines* (San Francisco: Women's Foundation of California, 2005), available at: http://www.womensfoundca.org/, accessed March 6, 2007.

Jan Marie Fritz

EQUAL RIGHTS AMENDMENT

The Equal Rights Amendment (ERA), introduced in Congress as an amendment to the U.S. Constitution, aimed to provide equality for both women and men. Proponents argued that this bill would protect women against sex discrimination; opponents contended that women would be granted "special status" if they were to acquire this form of legal protection.

BACKGROUND

The ERA was first drafted by Alice Paul in 1923, soon after women acquired the legal right to vote in 1920. Paul argued that women needed more than the right to vote; they needed to have the same overall rights as men as citizens of the United States. The ERA requires that "equality of rights under the law shall not be denied or abridged by the United States or by any state on account of sex."

The ERA was introduced to Congress during every session in the 1923–1972 period; however, it failed to reach the floor for a vote until 1971. Early supporters of the ERA, including Paul, the National Women's Party, and professional women such as Amelia Earhart, argued that the legislation would guarantee "equal justice under law" to all women and men. Opponents of the ERA included reformers who had worked for protective labor laws, First Lady Eleanor Roosevelt, and the American Federation of Labor (AFL). In their view, the ERA would force women to directly compete with men in the labor market and place unwanted demands on government.

After 47 years, on October 12, 1971, Representative Martha W. Griffiths of Michigan introduced the ERA as House Joint Resolution No. 208. This time, at the height of the second wave women's liberation movement, the resolution passed the U.S. House of Representatives with a vote of 354–24. The resolution was then passed by the U.S. Senate on March 22, 1972, with a vote of 84–8. The ERA then had to be ratified by 38 states in accordance with a seven-year timeline. Only 35 states ever ratified it. From the time the ERA was passed in Congress to its final, extended deadline of June 30, 1982, both proponents and opponents organized to gain support for their stance.

OPPONENTS OF THE ERA

Opponents of the ERA successfully organized campaigns to prevent its ratification in states across the nation. One of the strongest opposition leaders during the time of the passing of the ERA in Congress in 1971 to its 1982 deadline was Phyllis Schlafly, a conservative Republican who established the Eagle Forum/ Stop ERA. Schlafly, fellow Republicans, and other opponents of the ERA felt that the passage of this amendment to the U.S. Constitution would have obliterated the traditional distinctions between the sexes. In her view, women would not be protected from being drafted by the military in times of war and they would not be protected by labor laws in manufacturing jobs. Critics of the ERA also claimed that state money could be used for medically necessary abortions because women's healthcare would have to be as comprehensive as the healthcare given to men. The Republican Party in 1980 removed ERA support from its platform, the same year that former California Governor Ronald Reagan successfully ran for the presidency of the United States. During this conservative period, opponents argued that the ERA would have granted more power to Congress and to the federal courts to legislate controversial policies and laws involving abortion, homosexuality, and the family.

SUPPORTERS OF THE ERA

Supporters of the ERA believed that it was and continues to be a necessary form of equal opportunity legislation; without it, they argue, persistent gender inequalities and forms of prejudice toward women will continue to persist. The National Organization for Women (NOW) was the most visible institutional supporter of the ERA. NOW worked to garner support from other organizations such as the League of Women Voters and the nation's largest labor organization, the AFL-CIO. Their chapters in unratified states organized to promote and elect pro-ERA candidates. As supporters of the ERA, they dismissed the argument by the opponents that traditional gender roles would be eradicated and viewed it as a scare tactic to promote disfavor toward the ERA. Supporters argued that its passage would promote freedom from legal sex discrimination and provide a constitutional guarantee of equal rights for men and women. NOW and ERAmerica, an umbrella support group, successfully organized to extend the seven year ratification deadline to 1982. Nonetheless, opposition groups prevented the ERA from ever being ratified by 38 states.

CONCLUSION

Although the debate between proponents and opponents of the ERA was most poignant when it went to the states for ratification in 1972, controversy concerning equal rights for women continues until today. For nearly a decade, supporters of the ERA lobbied their state representatives, marched, rallied, and picketed on behalf of this constitutional amendment. Women's groups and other organizations supported this constitutional amendment because they believed it would keep them from being discriminated against. Yet opponents also organized marches and lobbied their state representatives, perhaps more successfully than ERA supporters.

Although the intensity of the debate has passed, NOW continues its work in supporting the ERA. In the 1990s, NOW organized an ERA Strategy Summit to reinvigorate the language of the ERA. Furthermore, the ERA continues to be introduced into Congress, including in 2001–2002 when Senator Edward Kennedy from Massachusetts and Representative Carolyn Maloney from New York introduced it. It is still possible that the ERA will be ratified as the Twentieth Amendment to the U.S. Constitution.

See also Affirmative Action; Comparable Worth; Second and Third Wave Feminisms; Title IX and Women's Sports.

Further Reading: Becker, Susan D., *The Origins of the Equal Rights Amendment: American Feminism Between the Wars* (Westport, CT: Greenwood Press, 1981); Boles, Janet K., *The Politics of the Equal Rights Amendment* (New York: Longman Group, 1979); Critchlow, Donald T., *Phyllis Schlafly and Grassroots Conservatism: A Woman's Crusade (Politics and Society in Twentieth Century America)* (Princeton, NJ: Princeton University Press, 2005); Delsman, Mary A., *Everything You Need to Know About *ERA (the *Equal Rights Amendment)* (Riverside, CA: Meranza Press, 1976); Feinberg, Renee, *The Equal Rights Amendment: An Annotated Bibliography of the Issues, 1976–1985* (New York: Greenwood Press, 1986); Lee, Rex E., *A Lawyer Looks at the ERA* (Provo, UT: Brigham Young University Press, 1980); Mansbridge, Jane, *Why We Lost the ERA* (Chicago: University of Chicago Press, 1986); National Organization for Women, "Chronology of the Equal Rights Amendment, 1923–1996," 1995–2006, available at: http://www.now.org/issues/economic/cea/history.html; Schlafly, Phyllis, *The Power of the Positive Woman* (New Rochelle, NY: Arlington House, 1977); Schlafly, Phyllis, available at: http://phyllisschlafly.com; Slavin, Sarah, *The Equal Rights Amendment: the Politics and Process of Ratification of the 27th Amendment to the U.S. Constitution* (New York: Haworth Press, 1982); Steiner, Gilbert Yale, *Constitutional Inequality: The Political Fortunes of the Equal Rights Amendment* (Washington, DC: Brookings Institute Press, 1985).

Marcella Gemelli

F

FAMILY VALUES

Once considered a private concern, the term *family values* has emerged as a U.S. political term within the last 25 years, with growing use in recent elections. Now family values is understood to be analogous with Christian values and is associated with the opposition of gay rights and abortion, and the support of conservative social political policy.

BACKGROUND

The term *family values* became widely associated with politics only after a 1992 speech by then Vice President Dan Quayle, in which he explained the cause of the Los Angeles riots as a breakdown of family values (see sidebar The Historical Emergence of "Family Values"). Before this time, the term had been used by the Republican Party to attract conservative voters, and although it may have been used within the party, it was not an accepted part of the American lexicon. After Quayle's speech, the term gained popularity and has seen more frequent use in recent elections.

THE HISTORICAL EMERGENCE OF "FAMILY VALUES"

The Los Angeles riots were not the only thing attributed to a lack of family values during that May 19 speech in 1992. Then Vice President Dan Quayle also attacked a popular television show *Murphy Brown* for positively portraying a single mother under the umbrella of family values. "It doesn't help matters when primetime TV has Murphy Brown, a character who supposedly epitomizes today's intelligent, highly paid professional woman, mocking the importance of fathers by bearing a child alone and calling it just another lifestyle choice" (Quayle as cited in Blitzer 2002). This attack did face much countercriticism from liberal organizations as well as feminist and other media organizations, but it also illustrated the divide between the right and left in America. A large portion of the country was concerned with the maintenance of traditional gender roles in society and saw the media as implicit in dismantling these roles and as encouraging the American public to accept new radical notions of gender.

CONTEMPORARY USE AND TERMINOLOGY

Those who consider themselves members of the Republican Party, one of the two largest political parties in the United States, also vastly associate themselves with the term *conservative*, also known as *right* or *right wing*. According to the Unabridged American Dictionary, to be *conservative* one is "disposed to preserve existing conditions, institutions, etc., or to restore traditional ones, and to limit change." In contemporary political uses of the term, the theme of family values is support for, or a return to, traditional values, often with the understanding that tradition is dictated by biblical precedent. This includes the overarching understanding that a family requires its religion (implicitly Christian) to be a place from where family members' morality originates and that the nuclear family (a family unit composed of father, mother, and children) is the most important part of society.

The notion of religion being a place from where morality originates is not necessarily a recent phenomenon, but has recently become something the public views with more focus with the growth of the Evangelical Christian movement. Evangelical Christians are those Christians who emphasize their personal conversations with God and who also place a large importance on the word of the Bible. According to the National Association of Evangelicals (NAE), which was founded in 1942, the NEA represents 30 million people. Evangelical Christians have risen in number in recent years and are now considered to be a formidable political constituency. They can also be known as the Religious Right.

Since the 1980s, when the term *family values* was used to gather conservative Christian Republican voters to the party, the Republican Party has had a historical link with the religious American community. Currently, when seeking to understand social issues, from a Republican view, it is nearly impossible to understand them without considering the Christian perspective that informs so much of the Republican policy. The growing Evangelical Christian movement has advocated for a stronger religious influence in politics. According to the Christian Coalition of America, the self-titled leading grassroots American religious political organization, "today, Christians need to play an active role in government again like never before."

Within this context of the Republican Party, family values are associated with a number of political issues. Such issues include displaying the Ten Commandments, prayer in public schools, and the opposition of abortion, stem cell research, pornography, homosexuality, feminism, and cohabitation before marriage. These issues that fall under the subheading of family values do not all specifically appear in the Bible, but conservative Christians, and more recently Evangelical Christians, consider their stance on these issues to be preordained, or predetermined, by Jesus, as written in the Bible.

CRITIQUES OF THE CONSERVATIVE VIEW ON FAMILY VALUES

Conversely, the Democratic Party, the other major American political party, understands the term *family values* to encompass a number of different issues pertaining to families. This political party associates itself with the term *liberal*, which, according to the Unabridged American Dictionary, means, "pertaining to a political party advocating measures of progressive political reform"; other terms associated with this party are *left* or *left wing*. Democrats understand family values as those that encourage support of all families regardless of structure (including families made of single parents and same-sex couples), to promote access to safe and affordable birth control, and to encourage a living wage, universal healthcare, paid maternity leave, and sex education in schools.

CURRENT ISSUES UNDER DEBATE: ABORTION AND GAY MARRIAGE

To understand family values from any one perspective, it is important to understand that even a seemingly organized religious or political movement such as the Evangelical Christian movement, the Republican Party, or the Democratic Party, is not monolithic, that is acting as a single uniform group. Even a very small organization must allow for variation and the same is true of a 30-million member organization. So when thinking about any of these particular organizations, one must be careful not to overgeneralize the group, but rather to understand that these statements are true about many, but not all, members of each organization.

The two largest contemporary political issues considered to be family value issues are abortion and gay marriage. Looking at the Religious Right's, the Republican Party's, and the Democratic Party's stance on these issues can help one understand both the link between the Religious Right and the Republican Party and the difference in how each group views family values.

Regarding the political language of abortion, commons terms used are *pro-life*, meaning those against abortion, and *pro-choice*, meaning those in favor of reproductive choices, including abortion. According to the Christian view of abortion, the procedure is regarded as murder. Although there is no specific scripture verse citing the banning of abortion, according to the NAE the basis for considering abortion a political issue linked with the Bible comes from the understanding that citizens need to protect children. "We believe that God, Himself, in Scripture, has conferred divine blessing upon unborn infants and has provided penalties for actions which result in the death of the unborn." Looking to the Republican Party for an official stance on abortion, the language is different, but both stances support one another. According to their official

2004 platform, Republicans oppose abortion on the basis of protecting the life of unborn children as well. "As a country, we must keep our pledge to the first guarantee of the Declaration of Independence. That is why we say the unborn child has a fundamental individual right to life which cannot be infringed. We support a human life amendment to the Constitution and we endorse legislation to make it clear that the Fourteenth Amendment's protections apply to unborn children." Both groups focus on the rights of the unborn and the role of individual citizens as protectors of these rights, and they support legislation, or punishment, to those who do not protect the unborn.

In examining the official 2004 Democratic Party platform, however, one can see that the Democratic Party's reasons for supporting legal abortion differ from those given for the Religious Right's and the Republican's opposing it. "Because we believe in the privacy and equality of women, we stand proudly for a woman's right to choose, consistent with *Roe v. Wade*, and regardless of her ability to pay. We stand firmly against Republican efforts to undermine that right. At the same time, we strongly support family planning and adoption incentives. Abortion should be safe, legal, and rare." Democrats support abortion, or more specifically the *Roe v. Wade* court decision, which granted women the ability to choose abortion, based on the right of privacy (a deciding factor in the case). The Democrats argue the issue from a completely different perspective than the Religious Right and the Republican Party.

The next large issue included under the umbrella term of *family values* is gay marriage. This issue also comes with a number of additional terms. Most of these terms attempt to define the rights that accompany the various states of legal unions offered/advocated for. *Gay marriage* refers to the marriage of same-sex partnered couples and would afford them the same rights and responsibilities as any other married couple under federal law. Other terms used are *civil unions*, which are similar to marriages regarding rights and responsibilities but do not have the same name, and some argue prestige, as marriage, and also the term *domestic partnership*, which refer to rights that vary based on the location in which they are granted. Another term often associated with this issue is *homosexual agenda*; this term refers to the idea that lesbians, gays, bisexuals, and transgender persons (LGBT) are pushing a normative idea of their lifestyles through positive portrayals of themselves in contemporary media. According to the American Family Association (AFA) a nonprofit (501(c)(3)) organization founded in 1977 by Don Wildmon, which represents and stands for traditional family, the homosexual agenda is the successful attempt by the LGBT community to use the media to positively portray themselves, thereby "molding American culture in their own image." This term is understood as an attack on the LGBT community and is seen as a concern of the Religious Right.

The Religious Right is very firm about their stance regarding gay marriage, and through their interpretation of biblical scripture, they oppose gay marriage and see homosexuality as a sin. According to the NAE, "Homosexual activity, like adulterous relationships, is clearly condemned in the Scriptures. In Leviticus 18:22 God declares the practice of homosexuality 'an abomination in His sight. In Romans 1:26–27 the practice of homosexuality is described as a degrading and unnatural passion. I Corinthians 6:9–10 identifies [sic] the practice of homosexuality as a sin that, if persisted in, brings grave consequences in this life and excludes one from the Kingdom of God."

The Republican platform states their view on gay marriage in terms of federal rights and recognition, but still echoes the right's view as according to their 2004 platform, "legal recognition and the accompanying benefits afforded couples should be preserved for that unique and special union of one man and one woman which has historically been called marriage." Although the language is not specifically based on scripture, the statement does include mention of a "unique and special union," alluding to a spiritual or religious bond.

In looking at the Democratic Party's platform, again the issue is argued from a different standpoint. "We support full inclusion of gay and lesbian families in the life of our nation and seek equal responsibilities, benefits, and protections for these families. In our country, marriage has been defined at the state level for 200 years, and we believe it should continue to be defined there." Democrats ask that states make the decisions regarding whether they grant marriage rights, civil unions, domestic partnership, or no rights at all; but the party is clear that as a whole, they do support the inclusion of gay and lesbian families in American society on the basis of citizenship and equality, and refrain from making speculations on the basis of morality and religion.

This issue became especially important during the 2004 presidential election where the term *values*, or *voting values* took on an important new meaning. During this election incumbent Republican George W. Bush was running against Democratic challenger John Kerry. Among a number of domestic and foreign issues imbedded in each of the 2004 campaigns, gay marriage became one of the most important social issues. During this election 11 states—Arkansas, Georgia, Kentucky, Michigan, Mississippi, Montana, North Dakota, Oklahoma, Ohio, Utah, and Oregon—all passed amendments banning gay marriage as it codified marriage as a heterosexual institution.

With the presidential election running particularly close in the polls, this issue seemed to provide the voter turnout the Republican Party needed, speaking to those who felt similarly regarding the party's values. According to the Christian Coalition of America, this strategy may be used again in further elections because it was so successful: "It is expected that more states will have constitutional amendments on their state ballots during the 2008 presidential election and all of these are expected to pass overwhelmingly in addition to bringing out new pro-family voters in the presidential election." More important, however, this strategy publicly solidified the connection between the Religious Right and the Republican Party.

EMERGING ISSUES: STEM CELL RESEARCH

Interest in abortion and gay marriage are still important to the term *family values*, but one particularly interesting issue can be added to the list. Most recently stem cell research has been gaining interest in both parties, with a recent very close vote in Missouri (the stem cell initiative passed). This is the

Republican Party's take on the issue: We recognize that President Bush made a carefully considered decision to allow federal funding for stem cell research for the first time, and did not affect stem cell research in the private sector. We strongly support the President's policy that prevents taxpayer dollars from being used to encourage the future destruction of human embryos. In addition, we applaud the President's call for a comprehensive ban on human cloning and on the creation of human embryos solely for experimentation." The Religious Right is careful not to expressly contradict this statement, but it does state that although embryos are a human life given by God, scientific research can be done with them if overseen properly. The careful wording by both the Republicans and the Religious Right perhaps reflects the complexity of this issue. The stem cell initiative of Missouri perhaps marked one of the more recent times when the two communities faced a possible rift, as some Republican lawmakers supported the initiative, but most religious organizations were firmly against it.

The Democrats, who openly backed the bill in Missouri and claimed victory in the state in the majority of other races, openly support all forms of stem cell research. "President Bush has rejected the calls from Nancy Reagan, Christopher Reeve and Americans across the land for assistance with embryonic stem cell research. We will reverse his wrongheaded policy. Stem cell therapy offers hope to more than 100 million Americans who have serious illnesses—from Alzheimer's to heart disease to juvenile diabetes to Parkinson's. We will pursue this research under the strictest ethical guidelines, but we will not walk away from the chance to save lives and reduce human suffering."

The issue of stem cell research will be important regardless of whether it succeeds in forming a rift between the Republican Party and the Religious Right. If it does in fact succeed then it will be significant for having been the issue that ended the era of family values voting, which so firmly united the Religious Right with the Republican Party; and if it does not, it will be indicative of the extent to which each organization, the Religious Right and the Republican Party, is willing to change their politics to keep each other as constituents.

See also Abortion; Fatherhood Initiatives; Postfeminism; Right Wing Women's Movements; Same-Sex Marriage; Second and Third Wave Feminisms.

Further Reading: Albrecht, Gloria H., *Hitting Home: Feminist Ethics, Women's Work, and the Betrayal of "Family Values"* (New York: Continuum, 2002); Associated Press, *Stem Cell Proposal Splits Missouri G.O.P.,* March 12, 2006, available at: http://www.nytimes.com/2006/03/12/national/12stemcell.html?ex=1174363200&en=04c9238b565c431d&ei=5070, accessed March 5, 2007; Blitzer, Wolf, "Quayle: Ten Years After Murphy Brown," Interview with Wolf Blitzer, May 10, 2002, available at: http://archives.cnn.com/2002/ALLPOLITICS/05/09/quayle.cnna/, accessed January 28, 2007; Democratic National Convention Committee, *The 2004 Democratic Party Platform: Strong at Home, Respected in the World,* July 27, 2004, available at: http://www.presidency.ucsb.edu/showplatforms.php?platindex=D2004, accessed March 5, 2007; Henschen, Beth, and Edward Sidlow, *America at Odds,* 3rd ed. (Pacific Grove, CA: Wadsworth Thompson Learning, 2002); Inside Politics, *Quayle: Ten Years After Murphy Brown,* May 10, 2002, available at: http://archives.cnn.com/2002/ALLPOLITICS/05/09/quayle.cnna/ http://www.nae.net/, accessed March 5, 2007; liberal, *Dictionary.com Unabridged (v 1.1),* available at: http://dictionary.reference.com/

browse/liberal, accessed March 18, 2007; National Association of Evangelicals, *Issues,* March 18, 2007, available at: http://www.nae.net/index.cfm?FUSEACTION=editor.page&pageID=53&idCategory=8, accessed March 5, 2007; Peterson, Kaven, *50 State Rundown on Gay Marriage,* November 3, 2006, available at: http://www.stateline.org/live/ViewPage.action?siteNodeId=136&languageId=1&contentId=15576, accessed March 5 2007; Republican National Committee, *The 2004 Republican Party Platform: A Safer World and More Hopeful America,* August 26, 2004, available at: http://www.presidency.ucsb.edu/showplatforms.php?platindex=R2004, accessed March 5, 2007; Roberta Combs, *About Us,* March 18, 2007, available at: http://www.cc.org/about.cfm, accessed March 5 2007; Vitagliano, Ed, "Sodem's Solemn Warning: Defining the Biblical View of Homosexuality Pt.1," *American Family Association Journal* (November/December, 2003), available at: http://www.afajournal.org/2003/novdec/111203sodom.asp, accessed March 5, 2007.

Jessica Jennrich

FATHERHOOD INITIATIVES

Fatherhood initiatives believe that eliminating poverty and improving child well-being can be accomplished through father presence and marriage. Critics of this approach contend that poverty cannot be eliminated through father presence and marriage alone, and that problems experienced by children in single-parent homes are the result of many variables including a lack of adequate employment opportunities, healthcare and social support.

BACKGROUND

Fatherhood initiatives, which support the idea that fathers should play central roles in the lives of their children and families, began to be promoted in the mid-1990s. Typically, these initiatives have been promoted alongside marriage initiatives, which promote heterosexual marriage over cohabitation or single parenting, and have been promoted by both Democratic and Republican administrations. One important assumption made by supporters of these initiatives is that father presence and traditional marriage would help poor people escape poverty. Because of this belief, the federal government has incorporated responsible fatherhood and marriage initiatives into social welfare policies and programs, with the idea that if poor people are to receive public assistance, they must also acquire responsible parenting and marriage skills.

In 1996, former President William Jefferson Clinton (1992–2000) signed into law the Personal Responsibility and Work Opportunity Reconciliation Act, commonly referred to as the Welfare Reform Act, or simply as "welfare reform." Of importance, this act begins by stating, "Marriage is the foundation of a successful society" (Welfare Reform Act 1996, 110, as quoted in Silverstein and Auerbach 1999, 398–99). It was undertaken to "end welfare as we know it," according to President Clinton. He claimed the goals were to give families an opportunity to move from welfare to work. Critics saw welfare reform as a way to reduce government public assistance roles, regardless of the long-term outcomes for families, which they viewed as linked to state-provided social welfare.

FEDERAL FUNDING OF MEDIA MARRIAGE PROMOTERS

In 2004, Universal Press Syndicate columnist Maggie Gallagher was paid $21,500 to promote President George W. Bush's marriage initiatives. Gallagher was paid through the National Fatherhood Initiative, which was founded by Wade Horn, then Assistant Secretary for Children and Families at the Department of Health and Human Services. Gallagher had also received an additional $20,000 from the Bush administration in 2002 and 2003 to write the report, "Can Government Strengthen Marriage?" Gallagher wrote that report for the National Fatherhood Initiative as well, and it was used by supporters to back their policy initiatives.

During the debates to pass welfare reform legislation, fatherlessness was cited as one of the reasons for rising rates of juvenile delinquency, teen pregnancy, school dropouts, drug and alcohol use, and juvenile crime. Single-mother homes were compared to married homes, and it was concluded that welfare reform should promote marriage and father involvement as a means of reducing family poverty and the social ills that resulted. Critics argued that research showed father involvement programs, and marriage alone did not help poor families to rise out of poverty, nor did those programs and marriage promotion result in more marriages and more fathers becoming positive influences in their children's lives.

SUPPORTERS OF FATHERHOOD INITIATIVES

Supporters of fatherhood initiatives claim that since welfare reform was enacted in 1996, public assistance roles have decreased, more heads of household are working, and overall poverty statistics show decreases. They also note that there has been an increase in two-parent households, and rates of nonmarital childbirths have decreased.

A study of the role of fatherhood by Child Trends (1999), a nonpartisan research center that studies children and families, notes that fathers provide many benefits for children. Several studies have found that children benefit from increased time with fathers. Child Trends notes that children with fewer behavioral problems have fathers who provide higher levels of involvement in activities with their children that include eating together and homework assistance. These children also have a higher level of school performance.

Ron Haskins, a senior fellow at the Brookings Institute, a conservative think tank based in Washington, D.C., summed up the position of pro-marriage and fatherhood initiative advocates when he concluded in testimony before the Congressional Committee of Appropriations on May 3, 2006, that "children do best when reared by their married parents." He claimed that marriage reduces poverty by using statistics that show how female-headed houses have much higher rates of poverty than married households. According to Haskins, "in most years, children in female-headed families have poverty rates that exceed those of children in married-couple families by a factor of five or more." Thus he encouraged policymakers to promote marriage to reduce poverty.

Socioeconomic factors do play an important role in father-child relationships. Some studies show that levels of education play an important role in a father's engagement with their children. The higher the level of education, the more fathers stayed engaged with their school-age children. In addition, fathers who are financially capable of taking care of their children are more engaged in their lives regardless of whether they live in the same home.

OPPONENTS OF FATHERHOOD INITIATIVES

Researcher and author Stephanie Coontz examines father absence in her *Los Angeles Times* article, "Our Kids Are Not Doomed." She found that the "dire predictions of social decay" tied to divorce and single mother homes have not materialized. In fact, almost every negative social trend attributed to single mother households has declined. Coontz found that in the 1990s, teen birth rates actually fell by 30 percent and teen homicide rates also dropped. In addition, adolescent suicides decreased by 25 percent, and substance use by adolescents declined. The social decay that never materialized occurred during a time when cohabitation was on the increase and marriage was on the decrease. Coontz also notes that households headed by single mothers had increased at a rate of five times faster than the number of two-parent married households. This finding resonates with the U.S. Bureau of the Census 2005 American Community Survey, released in 2006, which reports that only 49.7 percent of all U.S. households are headed by married couples, the lowest figure in history.

Critics have also pointed out that the increase in two-parent households reflects an increase in nonmarital cohabitation, not legal marriage, as pro-marriage and pro-fatherhood advocates boast. In addition, the decline in teen pregnancies has caused the nonmarital child birth rates to fall; however, women in their twenties are having more children outside of marriage. Child Trends notes that research on fathers is limited and most studies that look at factors that positively impact children find no significant connection between father-child relationships and these outcomes; however, there is consensus that unemployment and economic difficulties for fathers do have detrimental effects on children.

Researchers have found that father absence depends as well on other relevant family characteristics such as the lack of an income from a male adult, the absence of a second adult, and the lack of support from a second extended family system. Drawing from the research of Vonnie McLoyd (1998), psychologists Louise Silverstein and Carl Auerbach have pointed out that "families without fathers are likely to be poor, and it is the negative effects of poverty, rather than the absence of a father, that lead to negative developmental outcomes."(1999, 399) They have also pointed out that "because single-mother families are overrepresented among poor families, it is difficult to differentiate the effects of father absence from the effects of low income" (1999, 403). Poverty and job status appear to be key factors regarding positive child outcomes in single-mother homes, not merely the presence or absence of a father. Katha Pollitt (2002) notes that research shows that women who are poor often date men who are poor and have additional problems that create difficulties for households, including problems such as high rates of unemployment, incarceration, substance abuse, and illness.

Critics also point out that statistics supporting pro-fatherhood and pro-marriage positions have a questionable background. Unfortunately, they argue, these statistics about fatherlessness have now become mainstream, promoted by groups like the National Fatherhood Initiative and the Children's Rights Council. In the mid-1990s, these statistics were first promoted by Fathers' Manifesto, an umbrella group of fathers' rights groups that denigrated single-mother homes. Fathers' Manifesto also called for the repeal of women's right to vote, as well as the right to father custody without exceptions. Although the research is flawed, fatherhood initiatives have received federal funding to support their pro-marriage cause, but funding for services to support poor women and their children have been cut. Services such as food stamps, housing assistance, health care, foster care, and childcare support have all seen budget cuts from the Bush administration. In other words, fatherhood and marriage initiatives have been framed largely from within a conservative approach to social welfare, despite the fact that liberal groups have also supported the general notion of promoting father participation in family rearing.

CHILD SUPPORT ENFORCEMENT

Federal and state fatherhood initiatives have focused primarily on collecting child support from what former President Clinton famously referred to as "deadbeat dads." In his 2000 State of the Union address, one of President Clinton's primary focuses was the enforcement of child support collection. The National Center on Fathers and Families (NCOFF) has noted that some fatherhood programs have been created to improve child support compliance and to address other negative behaviors related to child support collection in the judicial system. A mother who needs public assistance cannot collect benefits unless she names the father of her child or assists in establishing paternity. Supporters believe this is a first step toward establishing responsible fatherhood. Opponents argue that the purpose of these initiatives is not to bring fathers closer to their families. Rather, they claim, the state is mainly interested in acquiring reimbursement for money it pays to custodial mothers who need public assistance. According to their view, welfare reform has created a colossal mess of child support theory and collection. The slogan "child support is for the children" disguises the fact that child support is collected to reimburse the state with a minor pass through grant to mothers if payments are collected. Programs have not resulted in fathers taking a more active role in their children's lives. For example, an evaluation of the Colorado Parent Opportunity Project (1999), a fatherhood initiative focused on child support collection, found that the program experienced low participation rates and that many fathers dropped out of the program. Job compliance was mixed. Poor men were not likely to earn enough money to support a family or to lift that family out of poverty. Although participation rates were low, those who were in the program reported liking the program and the access they had to their children. The purpose of the program, however, was to find employment for poor fathers and to get them to pay child support regularly. The program was unable to effectively achieve these goals.

The National Practitioners Network for Fathers and Families (NPNFF) started a fatherhood initiative in the San Francisco Bay area. NPNFF also reported low participation rates. Fathers may have perceived that the purpose of the program was to get child support rather than help them establish better relationships with their children. Evaluators indicated that there was insufficient communication between counties, so ascertaining the effectiveness of this program was difficult. It was found, however, that illiteracy in mothers and fathers was a problem that affected their ability to get and hold a job and that staff who were hired to run the program were not sufficiently trained to help their clients be successful in finding and keeping employment. Here, too, responsible fatherhood was linked to a variety of factors, not just to the presence of fathers (or mothers).

FEDERALLY FUNDED MARRIAGE INITIATIVES

Since the 1996 welfare reforms, marriage initiatives have been implemented in tandem with fatherhood initiatives, as a way to bring poor families out of poverty. In 2004, reporters Maggie Gallagher and Michael McManus received funding from the U.S. Department of Health and Human Services (DHHS) to promote marriage initiatives in the media. They were severely criticized for doing so because the source of their funding was deemed unethical. Wade Horn, the Assistant Secretary for Children and Families at the Department of Health and Human Services, authorized the funding of the pro-marriage articles. Horn, co-founder of The National Fatherhood Initiative, is best known for his promotion of federal marriage and responsible fatherhood initiatives. His support of these initiatives is based on his ideological belief that fathers should be present in family life and that two-headed, heterosexual households are the most natural and efficient forms of familial social organization. He has admitted, however, that his writings about welfare reform and marriage are his opinion and not necessarily based on research.

TIMELINE: FEDERAL FUNDING FOR MARRIAGE INITIATIVES

1994: National Fatherhood Initiative (NFI) forms. NFI has been instrumental in promoting fatherhood in the media and to the federal government. NFI receives more than $3 million in funding to promote marriage and father presence in poor families. The funding comes from private family foundations.

1995: Fathers' Manifesto posts "fatherlessness" statistics on the Internet. Fathers' Manifesto is an umbrella group of right-wing father's rights groups that blame single and divorced-mother homes for social ills.

1996: President William Jefferson Clinton signs into law the Personal Responsibility and Work Opportunity Reconciliation Act, passing sweeping welfare reform legislation. The NFI begins lobbying to include fatherhood programs in welfare reform. The American Fathers Coalition submits a welfare reform paper that promotes father involvement, including the recommendation to switch custody from the mother to the father if the mother applies for public assistance.

1997: The Children's Rights Council (a father's rights group) promotes marriage as the answer to poverty. Fatherhood groups begin to promote marriage as a means of lifting poor single mothers out of poverty. Parents Fair Share is formed. Parents Fair Share is a welfare program sought to improve father involvement and to collect child support.

1999: The Fathers Count Act (H. R. 3073) provides $161 million in grants for programs that promote marriage and "responsible fatherhood." Temporary Assistance for Needy Families (TANF) program, created through the 1996 welfare reform legislation, promotes pro-marriage goals with federal funding.

2000: President William Jefferson Clinton proposes fatherhood initiatives.

2001: Wade Horn, former president of the National Fatherhood Initiative, is named assistant secretary for Children and Family Services at the Department of Health and Human Services under President George W. Bush (2000–2008).

2005: Head Start program adds fatherhood initiatives.

CONCLUSION

Debates concerning fatherhood and marriage initiatives are ideological as well as research-based. Supporters of these initiatives believe that father involvement and traditional marriage may help to lift poor families out of poverty. They argue that the presence of a father in children's lives will improve the lives of the children. The federal government, one of the largest supporters of these initiatives, has enacted welfare reform with this model in mind, including block grants awarded to states to promote employment, child support collection, father involvement, and marriage.

Critics of these programs have shown that marriage and a father's presence alone will not lift families out of poverty. They argue that these programs focus on draconian child support collection that does not collect enough money to lift poor families out of poverty. Fathers are often unemployed, in prison, or working in jobs that pay salaries too low to lift their families out of poverty. Rather than fund programs that promote marriage and father involvement, critics encourage the federal government to fund programs that provide single and divorced mothers with adequate child care, employment training, housing assistance, and help with addictions. These programs have already been proven to work, but they are being cut to fund unproven pro-marriage and pro-father involvement programs.

See also Child Custody and Parental Rights; Childcare; Family Values; Welfare Reform.

Further Reading: Berkowitz, Bill, "Wade Horn: The Marrying Man," in *Working for Change*, February 17, 2005, available at: http://www.workingforchange.com/article.cfm?itemid=18577; Blankenhorn, David, *Fatherless America* (New York: Basic Books, 1995); Child Trends, *Children and Welfare Reform Reauthorization: A Golden Opportunity or a Missed Opportunity*, April 2002, Washington, DC, available at: http://www.childtrends.org/Files/ChildrenWelfareReformFS.pdf; Child Trends, *How Do Social, Economic, and Cultural Factors Influence Fathers*, December 1999, Washington, DC, available at: http://eric.ed.gov/

ERICDocs/data/ericdocs2/content_storage_01/0000000b/80/10/f5/d3.pdf; Child Trends, *The Meaning Of Father Involvement For Children,* December 1999, Washington DC, available at: http://eric.ed.gov/ERICDocs/data/ericdocs2/content_storage_01/0000000b/80/10/f5/db.pdf; Child Trends, *What Do Fathers Contribute To Children's Well Being?* December 1999, Washington, DC, available at: http://www.childtrends.org/Files/dadchild.pdf; Clinton, William J., "State of the Union Address," *Washington Post,* January 27, 2000, available at: http://www.washingtonpost.com/wp-srv/politics/special/states/docs/sou00.htm; Coontz, Stephanie, "Our Kids Are not Doomed," *Los Angeles Times,* May 9, 2005, available at: http://stephaniecoontz.com/articles/article14.htm; Coontz, Stephanie, *The Way We Never Were: American Families and the Nostalgia Trap* (New York: Random House, 1994); Haskins, Ron, "Testimony," Committee on Appropriations, Subcommittee on the District of Columbia, May 3, 2006; Hochschild, Arlie, *The Second Shift: Working Parents and the Revolution at Home* (New York: Viking Press, 1989); Horn, Wade F., and Tom Sylvester, *Father Facts* (Lancaster, PA: National Fatherhood Initiative, 1996), available at: http://www.fatherhood.org/fatherfacts.asp; Horn, Wade, "Doing Something to Boost Marriages," *Jewish World Review,* October 26, 2000, available at: http://www.jewishworldreview.com/cols/horn102600.asp; Marshall, Joshua Micah, "Media Transparency Talking Points," January 25, 2005, available at: http://www.mediatransparency.org/recipientprofile.php?recipientID=252; McLoyd, Vonnie C., "Socioeconomic Disadvantages and Child Development," *American Psychologist* 53 (1998): 185–204; National Center on Fathers and Families, "Profiles of Public Support: Government Policies and Effort," in *Bay Area Fatherhood Initiatives: Portraits and Possibilities,* January 25, 2005, available at: http://www.ncoff.gse.upenn.edu/bayfids/bayfids-final-part2.pdf; National Fatherhood Initiative Website, 2006, available at: http://www.fatherhood.org/; National Practitioners Network for Fathers and Families, *Bay Area Fatherhood Initiative,* 2000–2001, available at: http://www.ncoff.gse.upenn.edu/bayfids/bayfids-final-part2.pdf; National Women's Law Center, Administration Rolling Back Progress for Women and Girls with Policies That Are Out of Sight and Out of Touch, April 8, 2004, available at: http://www.nwlc.org; Pearson, Jessica, and Nancy Thoennes, *An Evaluation of the Parent Opportunity Project,* Parent Opportunity Project, Executive Summary, 1999, available at: https://www.childsupport.state.co.us/siteuser/do/general/GetPDF?PDFNumber=28; Pollitt, Katha, "Shotgun Weddings," *The Nation,* February 4, 2002, available at: http://www.thenation.com/doc/20020204/pollitt; Popenoe, David, *Life Without Father* (Cambridge, MA: Harvard University Press, 1996); Silverstein, Louise B., and Carl F. Auerbach, "Deconstructing the Essentialist Father," *American Psychologist* 54 (1999): 397–407; Tanfer, Koray, and Frank Mott, *The Meaning of Fatherhood for Men,* prepared for NICHD Workshop, "Improving Data on Male Fertility and Family Formation" (Washington, DC: Urban Institute, 1997), available at: http://fatherhood.hhs.gov/CFSForum/apenc.htm; U.S. Department of Health and Human Services, *Promoting Responsible Fatherhood Resource*, 2006, available at: http://fatherhood.hhs.gov/; Wilson, William Julius, *When Work Disappears: The World of the New Urban Poor* (New York: Alfred A. Knopf, 1996).

Trish Wilson

FEMALE SEXUALITY AND DYSFUNCTION

Conflicting ideas surrounding women's sexual health and normal versus abnormal female sexuality constitute a central debate within feminist, medical, social, and psychological discourses of women's bodies. From historical views on hysteria to contemporary debates on sexual liberation, medical practitioners, scholars, and observers have long debated women's sexuality in terms of normal versus abnormal forms of behavior.

BACKGROUND: FROM THE VICTORIAN ERA TO SIGMUND FREUD'S RESEARCH ON PSYCHOANALYSIS

Ideas about sexual function and dysfunction have long governed social norms about female sexual health. Before the Victorian era (nineteenth century), women's sexuality was thought to be an important part of their overall health, and sexual freedom and expression were the norm. This included a generally positive attitude toward female orgasm, same-sex eroticism, and sex outside the conditions of reproduction (Foucault, 1978). When repression took hold in the West during the Victorian era, this shift dramatically changed the landscape of female sexuality, such that women's sexual desires were thought to be a sign of sickness. Physicians of this era claimed that women were naturally frigid, and that their only true sexual desire was to reproduce. Indeed, orgasm (administered to women under the care of a skilled physician) was thought only to be a "cure" for hysteria, a condition that doctors believed to be the result of the womb wandering throughout the body, thereby causing instability in the woman's nervous system. The Victorian era normalized lack of orgasm and women's distance from their sexuality, and it reinforced a new norm of sexual difference, where men experienced sexual desire in the pursuit of pleasure, whereas women could desire sex only for the purposes of sexual reproduction. These differences came to justify a variety of social inequalities, as female sexual desire was ascribed only to women of the working class. Women of the upper class were not to be troubled with feelings of sexual desire and pleasure-seeking behaviors. Instead, upper-class Victorian women became the symbolic representation of restraint, a carefully constructed (and politically significant) shift both for women's sexual health and for women's social and political status in society. Chastity became, for women, a symbol of status; lack of sexual desire linked womanliness with social mobility. Women who deviated from this Victorian exterior of purity and chastity were situated as cultural outsiders: madwomen, criminals, and disordered beings (Smith-Rosenberg 1985; Laqueur 1990).

HYSTERIA

Did you know that, from the days of Ancient Egypt until the nineteenth century Victorian era, the womb was thought to wander throughout the body if the woman was sexually unfulfilled, crowding other organs and causing tissue damage, suffocation, and hysterical symptoms? In fact, the word *hysteria* comes from the root *hyster* or uterus. Thus when we use the word *hysterical* to describe certain kinds of behaviors, we reify now defunct historical connections between women's bodies and mental illness. During the Victorian era, it was thought that the only way to cure hysteria was for a medical doctor to masturbate a woman until orgasm with a vibrator, thereby restoring her womb to its proper state of sanity.

Many theorists of sexuality have noted that this extreme embrace of repressive ideology during the Victorian era led, ironically, to an obsession with sex. In the public denial of women's sexual interests and desires, sexuality became a dominant and pervasive force. Arising out of the context of severe repression of women's sexuality, the work of Sigmund Freud sought to make visible the connections between repression of sexuality and obsession with sexuality, allowing psychoanalysis to take root both in Europe and in the United States. Suddenly, ideas about sexuality as a driving force of human behavior made sense. Like the sex research that was to follow psychoanalysis, the premise of psychoanalysis was to "rebel" against the repression of sexuality, and instead speak about sexuality in the public sphere. At the same time, these efforts to rebel against repression served both to free women's sexuality from the constraints of repression, while also simultaneously constraining it. Although Freud was not primarily concerned with female sexuality, psychoanalysis offered some complicated ideas about the nature of female sexual health. First, despite the fact that it functioned as the first "revolt" against the repressive discourses of the Victorian era, it nevertheless reified these repressive discourses by portraying women as naturally passive and domestic, and as having relentless "penis envy" (whereby women, having discovered their "lack" of penis, actively desired the penis as both a literal and symbolic symbol of power). And, despite bringing female sexuality into public discourse, psychoanalysis nevertheless kept female sexuality hidden and obscure by its overemphasis on male sexuality and masculine ideas of intercourse and penetration. Although psychoanalysis allowed for the existence of female sexuality, primarily by arguing that women could be sexual because they had the same instincts as men, it simultaneously maintained essential differences between men (as active, dominant, and phallic), and women (as passive, inferior, and envious) (Freud 1953; Buhle 1998).

ALFRED KINSEY'S AND MASTERS AND JOHNSON'S RESEARCH ON WOMEN'S SEXUALITY

Although psychoanalysis argued that both men and women were driven by unconscious sexual wishes and desires, American researchers Alfred Kinsey et al. (1953) and Masters and Johnson (1966) sought to study both male and female sexuality from an empirical perspective to prove that mainstream Americans were engaging in a wider variety of sexual behaviors and nontraditional lifestyles than previously thought. Kinsey was one of the first to study sexuality in a concrete, empirical manner (i.e., what people do sexually, how often, and in what ways), and he found that people engaged in masturbation, nocturnal sex dreams, intercourse with same-sex and opposite-sex partners, "petting," and, sometimes, animal contacts. This research brought sexuality into the public sphere and thereby normalized sexual variety, but it also sparked new norms of mandatory female sexual performance. Women suddenly faced a shift in public perception of themselves as relatively asexual and pure to a new definition of themselves as sexually obsessed (Freud) and sexually active in a diverse group of sexual behaviors (Kinsey; Masters and Johnson).

WOMEN'S SEXUALITY AND THE WOMEN'S LIBERATION MOVEMENT, 1960s+

As the Victorian era of repression and silence around sexuality gave rise to psychoanalysis and empirical sex research as revolts against repression, so too did the 1950s era of domesticity, passivity, and secret sexuality give rise to the women's liberation movement and the sexual revolution. These changes in climate around sexuality were, in part, nurtured by increasingly fervent criticisms of psychoanalysis (which naturalized women's passivity), anger and hostility about women's continued subjugation in the bedroom (brought to light most prominently by Simone DeBeauvoir and Betty Friedan, as well as many others), and increasing empirical evidence that despite efforts to silence public discourse about sexuality, Americans were engaging in a wide variety of sexual behaviors previously characterized as fringe behaviors (including homosexuality, oral and anal sex, group sex, and masturbation).

Activism around women's sexuality represented a central feature of the women's movement and the sexual revolution. It was at this point in history (the early 1960s) that women collectively fought against the legacies of repression that had so long denied women's pleasure and contained it within the discourses of propriety, decorum, modesty, and silence. In particular, women fought for orgasms—the right to have them, the right to talk about them, and the right to reject false assumptions that the vaginal orgasm was superior to the clitoral orgasm (Koedt 1973). Feminists also argued that heterosexual intercourse, given its infrequent contribution to female orgasm, was a patriarchal construct that contributed to the false belief in clitoral inferiority (both to the vagina and to the penis). Some feminists argued that if women did not prefer heterosexual intercourse, this was due to the institutionalization of patriarchal control over

---

VALERIE SOLANAS

First published in 1968, Valerie Solanas's *SCUM Manifesto* stands as testament to the innovation and creativity of radical feminist ideas about sexuality. Championed as "one of the most important spokeswomen of the feminist movement" and "the first outstanding champion of women's rights," Solanas argued for the removal of oneself from the sexual exchange with men, saying, "Sex is the refuge of the mindless. And the more mindless the woman, the more deeply embedded in the male 'culture,' in short, the nicer she is, the more sexual she is" (27). She called for a radical revision of sexual politics, and a complete upheaval of institutionalized heterosexuality, saying, "Sex is not part of a relationship; on the contrary, it is a solitary experience, non-creative, a gross waste of time.... [Woman] can easily—far more easy than she may think—condition away her sex drive, leaving her completely cool and cerebral and free to pursue truly worthy relationships and activities" (26). Solanas later became famous for her June 3, 1968 shooting of Andy Warhol, about which she declared, "I consider that a moral act. And I consider it immoral that I missed. I should have done target practice."

---

women, and that intercourse itself did not appropriately stimulate the clitoris. Some argued that sexual intercourse itself should be done away with, as it upheld men's power over women, denied women clitoral satisfaction, and reified heterosexist ideas and antilesbian vitriol. Women's sexual health and sexual function were portrayed in clitoricentric terms, as feminists encouraged women to embrace their sexual pleasure and reject anything that did not directly contribute to sexual empowerment and physical joy. One consequence of such a view was the championing of lesbian identification and lesbian sexuality, as well as a rejection of heterosexual coupling as the social ideal (Gerhard 2000).

As an outgrowth of the sexual revolution and the women's liberation movement, radical feminism garnered momentum, particularly in its attacks on conventional sexuality. Some radical feminists argued against both the tyranny of the vaginal orgasm *and* the championing of the clitoral orgasm, saying that both mandated female sexual performance in troubling ways. For example, the 1970s radical feminist group based in Boston, Cell 16, argued that patriarchy placed women in the midst of an "orgasm frenzy," obsessed with women's right to enjoy their bodies at the expense of a larger social critique. Others argued that sexual liberation in the 1960s and 1970s merely substituted one form of oppression (norms that forced women to have sex and orgasm frequently) for another (the norm of repression that dominated from the nineteenth century to the early 1960s), citing *The Joy of Sex* books, antilesbianism, and pornography as evidence. Radical feminists argued that this newfound sexual freedom to have lots of sex with lots of people simply ignored women's actual experiences of brutalization, rape, submission, and powerlessness in the bedroom (Jeffreys 1990). Rather than embrace frequent sex as a sign of sexual health, some radical feminists, including the Redstockings group as well as individual radical feminists, advocated an asexual lifestyle or a lesbian separatist lifestyle that would isolate women from men altogether (Solanas, 1968).

The sexual revolution and the women's liberation movement brought about a variety of important social changes that affected women's contemporary sexual lives. During that era, several important events occurred, including the advent of the birth control pill in 1960, the legalization of abortion, the passing of more complicated laws about divorce (coupled with more complicated views of divorce), more public displays of sexual variety (including lesbian sexuality), the increasing popularity of nontraditional lifestyles (e.g., free love, rootlessness, group living), and increasing antiwar sentiments inspired by Vietnam and the draft. These events coincided with a shift in the climate around sexuality, most prominently contributing to the split between sex-positive and sex-negative feminism that began in the 1980s and continued for the next two decades. This debate surrounding the discursive position of sex—that is, sex as violent and oppressive (sex-negative feminism) versus liberating and empowering (sex-positive feminists)—represented a central debate in thinking about women's sexuality and sexual health. Whereas sex-negative feminists located women's oppression in the act of intercourse itself (e.g., sex as rape), and specifically found fault with the circulation of pornography as a means of encouraging a culture of violence against women, sex-positive feminists embraced pornography, as well as a range of sexual acts, fantasies, and desires as central to women's freedom and expressiveness. Sex-negative feminists argued that, because sex cannot be equal between two partners, it rendered women powerless and submissive (Dworkin 1997; MacKinnon 1987). Sex-positive feminists argued that sex can, and should, be life-affirming, loving, and a positive aspect of women's lives (Nagle 1997). Such a debate continues to inform popular and medical discourses of female sexual health today.

CURRENT DEBATES

Today, women's sexuality is very much enshrouded in conflicting social norms about function and dysfunction. Within medical discourses, it is common for women to be labeled as pathological and dysfunctional if they do not regularly engage in heterosexual intercourse, and/or if they do not achieve orgasm frequently. Indeed, the *Diagnostic and Statistical Manual of Mental Disorders-IV-TR,* the most widely used and oft-cited classification system for mental illnesses, includes a substantial number of sexual disorders that categorize women as pathological if they do not have enough sexual desire, if they do not achieve orgasm regularly with a partner, and if they experience discomfort during sexual intercourse. The language of this manual includes phrases like "normal sexual arousal," without specifying any objective criteria for "normal" sexual expression. These medical diagnoses exist within a staunchly heterosexist framework, with the specific language of disorders including statements about intercourse as the sexual norm, and orgasm during masturbation as insignificant. The messages about female sexual function in these medical texts are clear: women should pursue sex as often as possible, enjoy sex when they have it, and define sex as vaginal intercourse. Sexual function, then, becomes directly defined by women's frequent sexual activity and frequent sexual desire for heterosexual intercourse.

Sexual dysfunction, in medical and psychological texts, is defined by women's inability to respond to appropriate partner stimuli and by women's aversion to sexual contact. Many medical studies have shown great concern with women's physical responsiveness to sexual stimuli, including their ability to produce "adequate lubrication" as well as their physical ability to achieve orgasm. Medical studies have frequently targeted women's hormones as a possible culprit in their often less-than-optimal sexual responsiveness, and have tested several hormone therapies as possible solutions to such problems. One such outgrowth of this viewpoint has been the increasing interest by several major pharmaceutical companies in developing a female version of the popular drug Viagra. Pfizer, for example, reported being frustrated by the failure of their company to develop a successful version of Viagra for women, citing the pill's inability to ignite female arousal patterns. They noted that, unlike male Viagra, female Viagra did not contribute to an increase in women's desire for sex, even if it did help to arouse women physically. This split between sexual desire and sexual arousal led to their eventual conclusion that they would instead need a pill to engender a sense of intimacy between men and women. These efforts have, to date, been unsuccessful (Harris 2004).

In response to the medical view of female sexual function and dysfunction as largely a physical phenomenon, feminists and sex therapists have been quick to situate women's sexuality within a sociocultural context. Many feminists have argued, for example, that women who do not regularly achieve orgasm or regularly engage in sexual activity may indeed be completely normal. They argue also that one must look not only at the woman's physical functioning, but also at the sexual skills of her partner(s). Too often, the context of sexuality is not fully considered when diagnosing sexual dysfunction, and therefore women are labeled as pathological without fully accounting for their psychological functioning, the experience and knowledge of their partner(s), and the context in which they function sexually and socially. One prominent feminist critic of the medical model of sexuality, Leonore Tiefer (1995), has argued that women experiencing sexual problems can benefit greatly from feminist-oriented sex therapy, in which sexual problems are explored in a social context. She argues that therapy should focus on the whole person, should not be too goal-oriented or too "genital," and should not limit or control women's sexuality by promoting patriarchal views of women's bodies. Instead, sex therapy should help women reclaim the language of sexuality, explore their sexual needs and desires, challenge a heterosexist worldview, and better understand the subjective sexual meaning of desire and satisfaction. Sexual function, then, is the demonstration of women's ability to fully integrate their sexual desires and sexual needs into their self-concept, such that they can experience and express themselves in ways that feel safe, pleasurable, and fulfilled. Tiefer and other feminist sex therapists also advocate an end to pharmaceutical treatments of sexual dysfunction, citing the medical model's overeagerness to situate women's sexual problems as a physical dysfunction. Rather, they argue, sexual dysfunction is a complex social phenomenon that occurs in the context of many different motives, scripts, emotions, sensations, and connections.

Other feminist critics, like Peggy Kleinplatz (2001), argue that sex therapists have not questioned the major assumptions of their field, such as "What is sex?" or "What is sexuality?" Such critiques have largely been relegated to the fields of queer studies and feminist studies, rarely entering into mainstream sex therapy debate. Also, the field of sex therapy has not established its major theoretical questions (e.g., what sex therapists hope to achieve, how the mind and body interact in sex, how fantasies and desires function, or what version of "normal" sexuality is prescribed), and consequently, the science of sex therapy exists in a theoretical vacuum. Kleinplatz has also argued that sex therapy too often reifies damaging and dangerous sexual myths, including the idea that couples seek therapy to help achieve orgasm, when in fact male more than female clients tend to express this concern. Feminist sex therapists have noted that this model of help-seeking affirms a patriarchal model of sexual function and dysfunction, whereby women's sexual function is determined by their partners rather than their own individual experiences. Both Kleinplatz and Tiefer have argued that one possible goal of sex therapy should be to help clients reimagine other aspects of sexuality that are meaningful and central to their sexual happiness. This can include intimacy, emotional closeness, and other models of physical connection. In general, feminist psychologists agree that an overemphasis on orgasm as a symbol of sexual maturity, as well as too much concern with women pressuring themselves to be "normal" in terms of sexual frequency and activity, leads to unhealthy attitudes about sexuality and reinforces a heterosexist, patriarchal model of women that denies their true sexual subjectivity.

See also Kinsey Scale of Sexual Behavior; Sadomasochism, Domination, and Submission; Sexual Identity and Orientation.

Further Reading: American Psychiatric Association, *Diagnostic and Statistical Manual of Mental Disorders,* 4th ed. (Washington, DC: American Psychiatric Association, 1994); Buhle, M. J., *Feminism and Its Discontents: A Century of Struggle with Psychoanalysis* (Cambridge, MA: Harvard University Press, 1998); Dworkin, A., *Intercourse* (New York: Free Press Paperbacks, 1997); Foucault, M., *The History of Sexuality: Volume 1* (New York: Vintage Books, 1978); Freud, S., "Five Lectures on Psycho-analysis," in *The Standard Edition of the Complete Psychological Works of Sigmund Freud,* ed. J. Strachey, 39 (London: Hogarth, 1953); Gerhardt, J., "Revisiting 'The Myth of the Vaginal Orgasm': The Female Orgasm in American Sexual Thought and Second Wave Feminism," *Feminist Studies* 26, no. 2 (2000): 449–476; Harris, G., "Pfizer Gives Up Testing Viagra on Women," *New York Times,* February 28, 2004, C-1; Jeffreys, S., *Anticlimax: A Feminist Perspective on the Sexual Revolution* (New York: New York University Press, 1990); Kinsey, A. C., W. B. Pomeroy, C. E. Martin, and P. H. Gebhard, *Sexual Behavior in the Human Female* (Philadelphia: W. B. Saunders Company, 1953); Kleinplatz, P., *New Directions in Sex Therapy: Innovations and Alternatives* (Philadelphia: Brunner-Routledge, 2001); Koedt, A., "The Myth of the Vaginal Orgasm," in *Radical Feminism,* ed. A. Koedt, E. Levine, and A. Rapone, 199–207 (New York: Quadrangle Books, 2001); Laqueur, T., *Making Sex: Body and Gender from the Greeks to Freud* (Cambridge, MA: Harvard University Press, 1990); MacKinnon, C. A., "Desire and Power," in *Feminism Unmodified: Discourses on Life and Law,* ed. C. A. MacKinnon, 48–62 (Cambridge, MA: Harvard University Press, 1987); Masters, W. H., and V. E. Johnson, *Human Sexual Response* (Philadelphia: Lippincott Williams and Wilkins, 1966); Nagle, J., *Whores and Other Feminists* (New York: Routledge, 1997); Smith-Rosenberg, C., *Disorderly Conduct: Visions of Gender in Victorian America* (New York: Oxford University Press, 1985); Solanas, V., *SCUM Manifesto* (San Francisco: AK Press, 1968); Tiefer, L., *Sex Is not a Natural Act and Other Essays* (Boulder, CO: Westview Press, 1995).

Breanne Fahs

FEMININITIES AND MASCULINITIES

Femininity and masculinity, terms that define gendered behavior, are typically tied to understandings of male and female bodies. Defenders of traditional forms of femininity and masculinity argue that gender roles are derived from biology and should not be changed. Critics contend that femininity and masculinity are socially constructed and subject to change over time, both within and among individuals and societies.

BACKGROUND

In Western societies, femininity and masculinity are binary concepts that define culturally appropriate gender behaviors, forms of expression, and expectations for women and men. These concepts are based on either biologically or socially constructed notions of gender, depending on the observer. According to those who hold the view that gender is directly derived from our biologies, expressions of masculinity and femininity stem directly from men's and women's innate biological characteristics; that is, their expressions of traditional gender identity are natural. Those who believe that gender is socially constructed argue that notions of femininity and masculinity are greatly influenced by social environment, including how we learn about our gender identities in families, the educational system, religious institutions, popular culture, and society at large. Many men and women experience their gender roles in terms of traditional notions of femininity and masculinity. At the same time, there are people of every culture who do not meet these expectations or feel that they fit into these traditional roles. As a result, they defy the taken-for-granted understandings of their gender roles, either voluntarily or involuntarily. Scholars have analyzed notions of masculinity and femininity as they affect the socialization of children and adults. Some argue that traditional notions of femininity and masculinity are binding for those who do not fit neatly into these categories; others argue that those who do not fit within prescribed gender roles are deviant or abnormal, and that traditional feminine and masculine forms of expression should not be changed or transformed.

JACKSON KATZ ON MASCULINITY AND INTERPERSONAL VIOLENCE

Jackson Katz has spent much of the past two decades speaking to boys and men about their role in domestic and sexual violence. Katz (2006) encourages men and boys to see domestic violence and sexual assault as a men's problem insofar as it concerns their socialization into norms that condone the denigration of women. In his book, *The Macho Paradox* (2006), Katz traces the cultural influences that frame masculinity in terms of power, control, dominance, and entitlement. These notions of masculinity are sexist, Katz argues, and are found throughout history on both institutional and individual levels.

Beginning at an early age, boys are socialized to discount the opinions of girls and women and to objectify them sexually. They learn that they cannot speak up against the gender norms of manhood or they will face something unacceptable: accusations of being gay or a sissy (i.e., less than a man). Males lose status if they speak up for females or if they don't join in subordinating them. Sexist treatment of women is so normalized in society, Katz argues, that many males fully incorporate degrading attitudes of women into their daily lives.

Katz argues that movies, television, wrestling, talk radio shows (e.g., Howard Stern, Tom Leykis, Rush Limbaugh), music icons like Eminem, and media coverage of high-profile sexual assault cases (e.g., Kobe Bryant) help to permeate the culture with anti-women messages. Athletics are an arena that bolsters the association of power and dominance with manhood at the expense of compassion and equality. Rather than bash these institutions, however, Katz suggests that men and boys should organize to rethink why so much value is placed on these masculine traits. His suggestions for boys and men to speak out, to support survivors of interpersonal violence, and to get involved in rape prevention and domestic violence movements are at the heart of his proposal. His work serves as a model of feminist-inspired activism by men working to end violence against women.

Debates on masculinity and femininity have escalated since the emergence of the second wave women's movement and the gay pride movement in the 1960s, as members of these movements have challenged essentialist (i.e., biologically deterministic) views on gender and sexual identity and have fought for their civil rights. Opponents of these movements argue that traditional expressions of women's femininity and men's masculinity are natural and the most appropriate or efficient in today's culture and market economy. The struggle over whether gender is rooted in biology or socialization continues at the level of academic scholarship, policy, and law.

TRADITIONAL GENDER IDENTITIES, ROLES, AND EXPECTATIONS

According to traditional cultural norms in U.S. society, females are expected to exhibit feminine qualities and to be soft, sensitive, delicate, nurturing, patient, collaborative, passive, beautiful, graceful, caring, gentle, and empathetic. In contrast, men are expected to exhibit masculine qualities such as being assertive or aggressive, physical, strong, rational, and goal-oriented, among others. Traditionally, this combination of traits is seen as a set of binary opposites; one can be feminine or masculine, but not both.

People express feminine or masculine qualities through speech, appearance, and emotions. For example, women and men are socialized to speak quite differently. Likewise, children are spoken to differently depending on their sex. Some studies show, for example, that men are more likely to sound assertive in their conversations, whereas women are socialized to maintain conversation through encouraging comments and questions (Brownmiller 1984).

In terms of appearance, traditional femininity stresses physical looks, especially in contrast to how men appear. For example, hair styles serve as a gender marker that help people to determine a person's gender at first glance. Historically in Western societies, hair has been viewed as one of women's "greatest assets," with long hair typically viewed as feminine and erotic (Weitz 2004). Beginning in sixteenth-century England, the view has been held that hair was given from God for women to cover themselves as a symbol of subjection and to be distinct from men. When Queen Elizabeth cut her hair and publicly announced her marriage to God, effectively calling off any possibility of marrying a man, this symbol went down in history as a sign of her strength and authority as the Queen of England. Popular images of fairy princesses typically represent them with long hair that is often blond. The cult of blondness itself speaks to how women are viewed as wholesome, fun, or sexy. At given historical times, when women have chosen to cut the hair, it has been seen as a sign of rebellion; the bob haircut of the Roaring Twenties, for example, was a sign of women's emancipation (Weitz 2004).

Feminist critics point out that although hair grows naturally on the body, it is the culture that determines and sends the messages where body hair is acceptable. For example, it is distinctly unfeminine for a woman to have hair on her face, under her arms, or on her legs, despite the fact that they naturally have hair in these places. European women with underarm hair are largely accepted,

CONCERNED WOMEN FOR AMERICA

Concerned Women for America (CWA), a conservative Christian group founded in 1979, focuses on preserving the traditional heterosexual nuclear family and on applying biblical principles to current social policy initiatives. Its founder, Beverly LaHaye, is a well-known conservative, antifeminist critic who has published extensively on issues pertaining to Christian women's lives. CWA began as an extreme right-wing organization with little support and has transformed into a relatively powerful lobbying group in the U.S. political system. Following LaHaye's published writings, CWA emphasizes women's traditional roles by asking women to nurture their maternal instincts. Since the 1990s, CWA has worked actively to oppose same-sex rights and support "pro-family" legislation. One irony of right-wing women's stances on preserving women's traditional gender roles is that many of the women leaders in CWA are themselves working women who do not stay at home and take care of their children on a full-time basis.

---

whereas in the United States women with underarm hair are not. In the United States, many women spend inordinate amounts of time shaving, plucking, and tweezing body hair, a fact supported by the overwhelming success of the nations' beauty industry (Chapkis 1986). Traditionally, gray hair on women has been perceived as unattractive, although this is changing as more and more women are opting not to die their hair but rather to leave it naturally gray.

Clear, fresh, firm, and youthful skin is also an attribute of the Western ideal of femininity. The skin of Snow White impresses on children the idea that to be feminine, one must have delicate, smooth, white skin (Chapkis 1986).The association between a hairless body, youth, and femininity is made through stories and advertising. It is often seen as unfeminine to sweat, have wrinkles, or have any body odors.

Clothing is also an important marker of one's gender identity, especially for women, who historically have been targeted as clothing consumers much more so than men. Based on the idea that women must perform their femininity through expressions of appearance, they more commonly concern themselves with dress and are more often targeted by industry. Researchers have pointed out gender differences in the production and usage of clothing. For example, women's clothing tends to be less functional than men's. The hoop skirts of the 1860s, hobble skirts of the 1880s, steel-ribbed corsets, whalebone stays, and high-heel shoes all restricted women's movement. The corset might exert 20 to 80 pounds of pressure on a women's frame and has resulted in fainting, broken ribs, or injured internal organs (Brownmiller 1984). Males may have altered styles, such as with cod pieces, elevated shoes, or padded shoulders, but these did not negatively affect their health in the same ways. Women have also used clothing as a marker of liberation, however; the image of women burning their bras during the 1960s women's liberation movement is just one example of this act of resistance to traditional notions of femininity, particularly as they are linked to women's inferior status in U.S. society.

Like appearance, emotions are also distinctly gendered, and women are typically associated with emotionality, whereas men are associated with rationality, a belief that stems back to early Western philosophers such as Plato and Descartes. Yet how women emote is also dependent on traditional notions of femininity, which assume that women are gentle, rather than assertive, as men are. Anger, viewed as an acceptable emotion is men, is seen as unbefitting of women who are judged as hard, mean, or unattractive when angry.

The view that women should be nurturing and the caretakers of others means that girls are socialized to be other-oriented. Motherly love and romantic love are in the purview of feminine emotion. Women can be sentimental "keepers of the heart"; for example, they are often responsible for remembering birthdays and anniversaries. They are seen as more emotionally attached (Gilligan 1982). Men, on the other hand, are seen as acting in their own self-interest rather than altruistically, as women do (Folbre 1994). They work outside the home, in the market economy, and act as benevolent fathers who provide for their families, a gender construction that many scholars have recently analyzed as one that is also oppressive to men who cannot fulfill these expectations (Faludi 2000).

Traditional models of mental health tend to be based on men's, rather than women's, personality traits. For example, in a classic study by Broverman and Broverman (1970), the stereotyped feminine traits were contrary to the psychologically healthy individual, whereas the masculine traits were listed as leading to positive mental health. A fully developed adult is viewed as one who is rational and acts independently, traits often associated with male breadwinners rather than with women who act altruistically for their families (Gilligan 1982). Research also shows how men and women respond differently to their frustrations or anger: Men tend to externalize their anger or frustration, arguably leading to high rates of violent crime, whereas women tend to internalize their anger or frustration, leading, for example, to high rates of depression (Faludi 2000).

STUDIES OF WOMEN AND FEMININITIES

Traditional feminist theories of femininity include Susan Brownmiller's (1984) groundbreaking book, *Femininity.* Brownmiller takes the critical view that femininity is "a nostalgic tradition of imposed limitations." She defines femininity as extending beyond specific biological traits of femaleness to include the cultural prerequisites and prescriptions of femininity. Hair, skin, voice, clothes, and emotion all help to mark standards of femininity. Feminist scholars like Brownmiller tend to view traditional femininity as problematic for women insofar as rigid gender roles have served historically to maintain women's second-class status in U.S. society. In this scholarship, very little is mentioned about men's roles or the meaning of masculinity in society, except where blame is placed on the patriarchal control of women.

Scholars of African American, Latino/a, Asian American, and Native American studies have pointed out that women of color, a political term used to describe the experience and epistemic location of nonwhite women, do not have access to traditional notions of femininity that are based on a white, middle class model.

For example, African American women have not necessarily been viewed as weak, delicate, or frail but rather as strong and either matriarchal or controlling, depending on one's view. Patricia Hill-Collins (2000) writes of the controlling images of black women who are widely portrayed as mammies, matriarchs, hot mamas, or welfare recipients. They are viewed as either hypersexual (e.g., hot mamas, welfare queens) or asexual (e.g., mammies). These images work to make inequalities of race, gender, and class seem natural and inevitable. According to these stereotypes, which many have proven to stem from the imaginations of whites rather than from African Americans' real, lived experiences (hooks 1994), African American women and other nonwhites are naturally unlike the dominant group.

Since the 1990s, in pointing out that Western gender binaries have been detrimental to those who do not fulfill prescribed gender and sexual roles, some groups of scholars have argued for an alternative way of viewing gender, either as a continuum or in multiple, rather than dualistic, form. Lori B. Girshick (forthcoming), for example, draws from queer theorists and puts forth a conceptualization of sex, gender, and sexual orientation that involves simultaneous parallel continuums. This conceptualization includes the possibility that someone can have a degree of maleness and a degree of femaleness. Femininity and masculinity are not in an inverse relationship; individuals can inhabit degrees of these qualities simultaneously. Individuals' identities can shift in a fluid manner over their lifetime. A male-bodied person could have a high degree of femininity, or a female-bodied person could have high degrees of both femininity and masculinity. This type of conceptualization, which has also been theorized by Judith Butler (1990) and Eve Sedgwick (1990), among others, allows for a range of gender expressions that diminishes the stigma for individuals who do not identify with traditional gender norms. This fluidity in itself encourages additional understandings of masculinity and femininity without necessarily replacing traditional masculinity and femininity. That general idea is that all expressions of femininity and masculinity should be respected and accepted, not just traditional forms.

Defenders of traditional femininity typically argue that femininity derives directly and naturally from women's biological and reproductive roles in human life. Critics of feminist theory of femininity include male and female conservative intellectuals as well as policymakers, politicians, and even the pope. For defenders of traditional femininity, women are meant to stay at home and take care of the children, whereas men are meant to work outside the home and provide financially for the family. Economist Gary Becker won the 1992 Nobel Prize in Economic Sciences for his research examining family structure and the market economy, in which he argues that the most efficient (and typically highest income) households are those where two heterosexual parents are present (Becker 1981). The flipside to his argument is that single-parented homes, same-sex households, and extended family households tend to be poorer and/or less efficient when it comes to both household maintenance and to the success or failure of household members in the market economy. Thus for Becker it is no coincidence that in communities where there is a high rate of single-headed and

DR. MARY EDWARDS WALKER

Dr. Mary Edwards Walker (1832–1919) was the founder of the Mutual Dress Reform and Equal Rights Association. She was a feminist, abolitionist, prohibitionist, surgeon in the Union Army, prisoner of war, and the only woman to receive the Medal of Honor.

In the mid-1800s, many women wore heavy corsets and long, heavy skirts that limited their activities and were often unhealthy for them. Along with other suffragist leaders such as Lucy Stone, Elizabeth Cady Stanton, and Susan B. Anthony, Dr. Walker began to wear Amelia Bloomer's famous design creation, bloomers, the popular dress and trouser combination that marked a revolutionary change in women's clothing. The bloomer costume did not compromise "feminine modesty" according to its users, although it created so much controversy that many suffragists stopped wearing them.

Dr. Walker wore the bloomer costume until the late 1870s, when she began dressing in men's clothing. She received her Medal of Honor in 1865 for her work in the Civil War, all the while wearing men's clothing, and felt that this honor gave her permission to continue to do so. Still, she was arrested for impersonating a man many times. Dr. Walker was an outstanding leader in many ways during her life, and her work for dress reform is only one of the many ways in which she was a role model challenging traditional norms of femininity.

extended-family households, they tend to be poorer overall and to remain poor over generations. In a similar vein, right-wing women have organized against feminism, in groups such as Concerned Women for America, as a way to defend their roles as housewives and mothers. Religious women's groups have also organized on this basis in the context of their religion.

STUDIES OF MEN AND MASCULINITIES

After the emergence of studies on femininities, which paralleled the second wave women's liberation movement of the 1960s and the growth of women's studies as an academic field, researchers began to observe more systematically how men, too, are influenced by their gender socialization. Studies of male violence have predominated these discussions, although work on male institutions such as fraternities, sports, and men's movements has also been done. These studies point out that men's lives and experiences should not be homogenized or viewed as merely or entirely "privileged" or "patriarchal." Rather, as men's studies scholars have pointed out, men of marginalized groups such as African American men and gay men do not have the same access to dominant ideals of masculinity as, for example, white, heterosexual, upper class men. R. W. Connell's (1987) groundbreaking work on "hegemonic masculinity" and "traditional femininity" has set an important agenda for rethinking femininities and masculinities from the perspective of both men's and women's experiences, rather than merely women's. Connell argues that we must understand masculinities as multiple and stratified. Hegemonic masculinity refers to those forms of masculinity that allow men full access to societal resources such as education, citizenship, class status and wealth, or professional success. This hegemony, or dominance, is structured throughout social and private life and defines not only gender expectations but sexuality; in this regard, hegemonic masculinity is heterosexual, patriotic, and nationalistic (Connell 1987). Men from working class backgrounds and men of minority racial status do not necessarily have access to hegemonic masculinity, according to Connell, although of course these men find ways to express their masculine identities, often in defiance of this stratified system (Majors 2004). Connell views masculinity among marginalized groups of men as a form of subordinated, rather than hegemonic, masculinity.

Subordinated forms of masculinity can be seen in how nonwhite men are represented in U.S. society and popular culture. For example, African American males have been hypersexualized throughout history, beginning with their treatment as slaves. Freed African slaves were feared for the very strength they displayed as slaves. The image of the oversexed and brutal black man served as a form of ideological and legal control for nervous whites. The "myth of the black male rapist," a notion that scholars such as Angela Davis (1981) and Patricia Hill-Collins (2000) have discussed, has served to create heightened law enforcement surveillance of black men, higher incarceration rates, and generalized fears of black men. During the 1960s civil rights struggles, the Black Panthers, a separatist group demanding black rights and dignity, exemplified black hypermasculinity as a form of resistance to white society, seen in their dress and demeanor. The Black Panthers called for the end to police brutality, poverty, and discrimination in their communities. Other subordinated groups of men, such as Latinos and Asian Americans, have also been hypersexualized and exoticized in ways that have been detrimental to their senses of self and personal security, a topic that has been discussed at length by scholars and activists (Mirandé 2004; Chua and Fujino 1999).

For Connell, the flipside of hegemonic masculinity is emphasized femininity. Emphasized femininity involves women who accommodate the interests and needs of men. It is based on their compliance with the hierarchical gender social order. As women define themselves according to dominant societal standards, which tend to view men as the "stronger sex" and women as the "weaker sex," they are arguably complicit in their own subordination. Other men's studies scholars such as Michael Kimmel point out that hegemonic masculinity is very much about males relating to other males and seeking their approval, respect, and acceptance. Research on male bonding Greek fraternities and sports documents this type of homoerotic behavior among men, and points to how masculinity is understood and negotiated by men in their daily lives.

Conservative views on men and masculinity have also emerged, especially since the 1990s. Conservative academics and policymakers argue that men have been victims of feminism and women's rights struggles insomuch as laws and policies favor women's "protection" over men's. This debate has been especially important in the context of struggles over defining policies and laws related to parental and custody rights, abortion and family planning, and workplace discrimination. Dalton Conley, a well-known sociologist at New York University, wrote an op-ed piece in the *New York Times* claiming that men should have equal say in whether or not a woman chooses to abort. According to Conley, if a man wishes to keep the child but the woman bearing the child does not, then the man should have equal right according to law to keep the child (Conley 2005). How this scenario would play out in court remains unanswered; nonetheless, suffice it to say that the conservative view on men's roles in family life emphasizes their rights as fathers (Silverstein & Auerbach 1999). According to this view, men are seen as oppressed by laws that emphasize women as the primary nurturers and therefore rightfully due custody in cases where all else is held equal. Much of this remains to be played out in future court cases.

CONCLUSION

When thinking about a gender binary of masculine and feminine traits, it is useful to remember that all people share 99.9 percent identical genetic material. That is, men and women are more alike than different, a fact often forgotten in contemporary discussions of gender relations in U.S. society. Whereas some believe that the binary of men's masculinity and women's femininity is natural and therefore unnecessary or inappropriate to challenge or change, others believe it is time to rethink the gender binary, for it negatively affects people who do not or cannot fulfill these traditionally prescribed gender roles and expectations. In her book, *The End of Gender,* Shari Thurer (2005) examines mainstream culture and demonstrates how "genders are leaking into each other." All around us, she states, in media, art, books, the Internet, and television, we are witnessing the end of traditional gender categories and the acceptance of new forms of gender expressions, or gender-bending, in daily life.

Ideas of masculinity and femininity are here to stay, but how they will be defined and whether they are used as categories to influence or control how people dress, act, and express their identities are topics that continue to bear great controversy in academic, legal, and policy arenas. Perhaps the question is best understood in terms of how certain forms of femininity and masculinity are viewed as acceptable and normal in our society, whereas other forms of expression are not. Debates over acceptable expressions of masculinity and femininity often concern long-held views on gender as natural and given, although critics continue to point out that people express their gender identities in multiple ways that defy the dualistic tradition.

See also Beauty Industry; Gender Socialization; Nature versus Nurture; Sex versus Gender.

Further Reading: Becker, Gary, *A Treatise on the Family* (Cambridge, MA: Harvard University Press, 1981); Broverman, I., and J. Broverman, "Sex-Role Stereotypes and Clinical Judgements of Mental Health," *Journal of Counseling and Clinical Psychology* 34 (1970): 1–7; Brownmiller, Susan, *Femininity* (New York: Fawcett Columbine, 1984); Butler, Judith, *Gender Trouble* (New York: Routledge, 1990); Chapkis, Wendy, *Beauty Secrets: Women and the Politics of Appearance* (Boston: South End Press, 1986); Chua, Peter, and Diane Fujino, "Negotiating New Asian-American Masculinities: Attitudes and Gender Expectations," *Journal of Men's Studies* 7 no. 3 (1999): 391–413; Conley, Dalton, "A Man's Right to Choose," *New York Times,* December 1, 2005; Connell, R. W., *Gender and Power: Society, the Person and Sexual Politics* (Oxford: Polity Press, 1987); Connell, R. W., *The Men and the Boys* (Berkeley: University of California Press, 2000); Davis, Angela, *Women,*

Race and Class (New York: Random House, 1981); Faludi, Susan, *Stiffed: The Betrayal of the American Man* (New York: Harper Perennial, 2000); Folbre, Nancy, *Who Pays for the Kids?* (New York: Routledge, 1994); Gilligan, Carol, *In a Different Voice* (Cambridge, MA: Harvard University Press, 1982); Girshick, Lori, *Transgender Voices: Beyond Women and Men* (Lebanon, NH: University Press of New England, forthcoming); Halberstam, Judith, *Female Masculinity* (Durham, NC: Duke University Press, 1998); Hill-Collins, Patricia, *Black Feminist Thought,* 2nd ed. (New York: Routledge, 2000); hooks, bell, *Outlaw Culture: Resisting Representations* (New York: Routledge, 1994); Katz, Jackson, *The Macho Paradox: Why Some Men Hurt Women and How All Men Can Help* (Naperville, IL: Sourcebooks, Inc., 2006); Kimmel, Michael, *Manhood in America: A Cultural History* (New York: Random House, 2005); Majors, Richard, "Cool Pose: Black Masculinity and Sports," in *The Masculinities Reader,* ed. Stephen M. Whitehead and Frank J. Barrett, 209–217 (Cambridge, UK: Polity Press, 2004); Messner, Michael, *Politics of Masculinities: Men in Movements* (Walnut Creek, CA: Altamira Press, 2000); Mirandé, Alfredo, "And Ar'n't I a Man?: Toward a Chicano/Latino Men's Studies," in *The Masculinities Reader,* ed. Stephen M. Whitehead and Frank J. Barrett, 341–350 (Polity Press, 2004); Sedgwick, Eve Kosofsky, *Epistemology of the Closet* (Berkeley: University of California Press, 1990); Silverstein, Louise B., and Carl F. Auerbach, "Deconstructing the Essential Father," *American Psychologist* 54, no. 6 (1999): 397–407; Thurer, Shari L., *The End of Gender: A Psychological Autopsy* (New York: Routledge, 2005); Weitz, Rose, *Rapunzel's Daughters: What Women's Hair Tells Us about Women's Lives* (New York: Farrar, Straus and Giroux, 2004).

Lori Girshick

FEMINIST ART PRACTICES

Artists have engaged in feminist art practices since the early 1970s, partly as a response to perceived sexism in artistic production and in the art industry. Controversies surrounding feminist art concern the often unequal representation of women artists in international art institutions and publications, the invisibility of gender in traditional artistic production, and the highly debated relationship between image and identity.

BACKGROUND: FEMINIST ART PRACTICES OF THE EARLY 1970S

Feminist art can be generally defined as artistic works that deal with aspects of women's status within society. Artists engaging in feminist art practices often intend to call attention to social, economic, and psychological forms of oppression suffered by women, with the purpose of initiating change in the social practices or beliefs that cause such oppressions through art.

The feminist art movement of the 1970s grew out of the women's movement, which took place in the United States in the late 1960s, and stemmed from the larger civil rights movement, also in full swing at that time. In response to the marginalization of women artists both in history, and at the time of its formation, as manifested in the lack of exposure female artists' work received in major public art institutions, and the perceived resistance to artworks dealing with themes of gender, and particularly femininity, in art academies, women artists engaged in the feminist art movement. They "asserted a new position for 'woman' in art, as subject rather than object, active speaker and not passive theme" (Broude and Garrard, 1993).

Consciousness raising played a major role in the creation of feminist art. Described as the practice of sharing personal experiences amongst women in hopes of raising awareness both as to the commonality of their experiences as women, and to the institutionalized patterns of oppression that they often fell victim to, artists used their artistic medium as a ground in which their own personal experience, and the more general political circumstances of women could be interwoven and brought to public attention. Thus artists actively engaged in feminist art practices saw their work as a direct employment of the feminist slogan, "The personal is political."

Judy Chicago, a sculptor, painter, and political activist had a tremendous impact on the shaping of the feminist art movement of the 1970s through her founding of the first Feminist Art Program at Fresno State College (now California State University, Fresno) in 1970. Through this program, Chicago developed a curriculum, which relied on feminist teaching methods that would prepare female art students to become professional artists and imbue them with the skills they would need to compete in the art world, which she perceived as decidedly hostile toward women. Housed in an anonymous studio space off of the college campus, Chicago addressed practical issues such as how to negotiate business transactions and instructed the students on how to construct their own studio space. Instead of structured classes, the feminist art program functioned in groups in which leadership responsibilities were rotated among the students on a weekly basis. Extensive feminist consciousness-raising activities encouraged the students to, first, think about and draw from their own personal experiences as a means of informing the content of their work, and second, on recognizing the similarities in others' experiences, to work collaboratively on larger art projects. Female sexuality became one of the most central issues confronted in the sessions, as well as in the artwork produced.

THE MOVE TO CALIFORNIA INSTITUTE OF THE ARTS

The feminist art program at Fresno created a unique environment for the training of women artists. It enabled participants to produce works that dealt with personal and political issues that might not have been produced if the circumstances were in any way altered. The separatist nature that the program took on, however, also had the drawback of limiting students' critical perspective and ultimately depriving them of a larger social context within which their works could be situated. As a means of solving this problem and gaining more critical and public exposure for the students, Chicago, in the fall of 1971, joined the faculty at the California Institute of the Arts and, along with the feminist painter Miriam Shapiro, already a member of the faculty, initiated a new feminist art program. Of the 22 female students enrolled in the program's first semester, seven were members of the original feminist art program at Fresno.

The program at CalArts could be distinguished from the one at Fresno in that students' work became more intertwined with feminist activism, and its critical focus narrowed to hone in on the representation of women in language, the media, art history, and popular culture. It sought to address the points of difference between the treatment of women art students and their male colleagues. Their concerns involved the concept of male genius or mastery as a necessity to the creation of artistic works, the lack of mentorship offered to female students, and the breaking down of traditional hierarchies of materials and methods taught in fine art institutions, which often relegated the skills and materials that female artists were traditionally trained in to the category of "craft."

All of the key issues that informed the foundation of the feminist art program at CalArts were engaged in the unique, collaborative project, *Womanhouse,* created by the students in the fall semester of 1971. The 22 students, along with Los Angeles artists Wanda Westcoast, Sherry Brody, and Carol Edson Mitchell, collaborated to transform an abandoned, condemned house in an urban neighborhood in Los Angeles into an all-encompassing art environment that focused on the lives of women within the private, domestic sphere.

Together the group extensively reconstructed the 17-room house, bringing it up to a workable condition, in which they could create the art environment. Each artist chose one of the spaces as her room, where she would create her installation, and at the same time small collaborative groups formed to prepare performances and other events that would take place during the exhibition. On the whole, *Womanhouse* is said to have made the problems expressed by Betty Friedan in *The Feminine Mystique* (originally published in 1963) come to life within the three-dimensional, all-encompassing space of the house, which highlighted and criticized culturally assumed connections between a woman's biology and her gender roles.

CRITIQUES OF EARLY FEMINIST ART PRACTICE: THE INCOMPATIBILITY OF FEMINISM AND ART

Self-proclaimed feminist artists of the early to mid-1970s created works that reflected political concerns and a particular ideological stance. Such artworks stand in direct opposition to the conception of the *artist* as a solitary male genius (promulgated by many canonical Western thinkers, such as Immanuel Kant), privy to otherworldly inspiration that is ultimately made manifest in the work of art. This conception of artist and artwork, often still used to this day, relegates the role of both the artist and the work of art to a realm outside of the real-life, social and political concerns faced by members of a society on a daily basis. Judy Chicago and other self-proclaimed feminist artists openly challenged that concept of the artist on various levels. First, their art sought to bring attention to serious social and political issues faced by women on account of the often unchallenged oppressions of patriarchal society. Second, these artists often worked collaboratively on large-scale projects (like *Womanhouse* or Chicago's *The Dinner Party*) in which each artist lent her personal skill to the overarching effort. Critics who find the combination of art and social or political concerns problematic have responded overwhelmingly negatively to the work produced by feminist artists of the 1970s, relegating their artistic practice to mere propaganda that seeks to "enforce common experience and crowd mental-

CONSERVATIVE OPPOSITION TO FEMINIST ART: JUDY CHICAGO'S *THE DINNER PARTY*

In 1990, Judy Chicago's installation, *The Dinner Party,* attracted the attention of the U.S. Congress, when the artist attempted to donate the massive piece to the University of the District of Columbia. Consisting of a triangular banquet table measuring 48 feet on each side, strewn with 39 place settings paying homage to a real or mythological woman in the history of Western civilization, the installation was first debuted at the San Francisco Museum of Modern Art in 1979. Despite the university's positive vote to accept the gift from Chicago, putting the piece on permanent display for the general public, debate ensued that eventually landed on the floor of the U.S. House of Representatives, because members of the public and members of Congress questioned whether the work's overt references to female genitalia was appropriate to show in the university setting. Representative Robert Dornan of California, among others, voiced the opinion that the particularly vaginal appearance of the dinner plates caused the work to appear "pornographic" and "obscene." Chicago was eventually forced to withdraw her offer. Fourteen years later, in 2004, *The Dinner Party* was given a permanent home by the Brooklyn Museum of Art.

ity" (Kuspit 1993). Art critics that take this position often put forth the critique that activist and political works, exemplified by feminist art practices, champion whatever issue is at hand, at the expense of work's artistic attributes; thus their creations cannot be seen as art, but merely political statements.

Feminist art has also attracted the negative attention of critics on account of its aesthetic appearance. To begin with, some critics see the use of what has been deemed traditionally feminine media, such as needlework and ceramics, typically used by feminist artists, as problematic. Opening up the often complex debate between high and low culture, critics have opined that artists' works that use such media appear too folksy or craftlike, and thus are not in line with the haute couture environment of the respected museum or art gallery.

In addition, feminist art work has received intense criticism on account of its often overt references to female sexuality. Chicago, in particular, has consistently created a stir with art critics on account of her use of (self-titled) central-core imagery. Such large-scale, multimedia projects as *The Dinner Party* and *The Birth Project,* which frequently feature openly vaginal forms have been labeled brash, crude, and even pornographic by critics, who see Chicago as an artistically untalented cult leader, relying on shear shock rather than artistic aptitude to get a rise out of her audience.

"POSTFEMINIST" ART PRACTICES: THE ISSUE OF AMBIGUITY

It was often the case that artists who came after the feminist art movement of the early 1970s refused to openly admit, or blatantly deny, an explicitly feminist ideology informing the work, even though they were consistently referred to as feminist by some critics and theorists,. This body of work, which is seen by some to reflect feminist concerns, is referred to as "postfeminist" art. The often ambiguous nature of postfeminist art practices has fueled the critique that the insights gained from the work of the feminist art movement of the early 1970s were taken for granted by women artists in later years. This ambiguity on the part of the artist has caused controversy as to the way in which such works can be read by art critics, theorists, and the general viewing public.

For example, in *Untitled Film Stills* (1976–1980), artist Cindy Sherman constructed false "film stills," actually still photographs, which featured herself as the main character of each scene. Often drastically altering her appearance to convincingly portray a vast array of female "characters," Sherman highlights the stereotypical portrayals of women in late-twentieth century popular culture, while at the same time demonstrating the disjunction between image and identity. Through her masterful masquerade in the guises of various pop culture "tropes," Sherman calls attention to the idea of the *self* as nothing more than various representations, ultimately disconnected from a single, stable identity.

Sherman's early artistic practice has generated diverse and often contradictory responses from feminist art critics and theorists. On the one hand, Laura Mulvey, a feminist film theorist, sees Sherman's work as a critical tool for feminists. She has expressed the view that Sherman's work, despite the artist's clear resistance to any theoretical alignments, presented a turning point, and indeed a refreshing change in feminist art practices. In contrast to the theoretical background knowledge required to make sense of feminist artwork like Mary Kelly's *Post-Partum Document,* Sherman's work took as its (general) reference female representation in the present day popular culture, and left the meaning open to be determined by the viewer. As Mulvey states, however, the shear popularity and publicity that Sherman has achieved with the series has "obscured both the work's interest for feminist aesthetics and the fact that the ideas it raised could not have been formulated without a prehistory of feminism and its theorization of the body and representation" (Mulvey 1991).

In sharp contrast, painter, writer, and participant in the feminist art program at CalArts from 1971–1972, Mira Schor, rejects the notion that Sherman's work

CINDY SHERMAN'S FINANCIAL SUCCESS

Because of the critical acclaim Cindy Sherman achieved at a young age, she has become one of the most financially successful female contemporary artists in the world. The Museum of Modern Art's purchase of the full *Untitled Film Stills* series in December 1995 for $1 million caused future auction prices of Sherman's work to jump considerably. In 1999, just one of Sherman's *Untitled Film Stills* sold at a Christie's auction for $190,000, and in 2000, she broke yet another auction record when her one of her art history portraits; an untitled 1989 self-portrait in a Renaissance costume sold for $269,750. As Sherman's artwork persistently remains in the public eye, both her critical acclaim and her financial success continue to grow in exponential proportions.

can be called feminist. Describing her work as "disturbingly close to the way men have experienced or fantasized women" (Schor 1997), Schor has put forth the position that Cindy Sherman's fame, critical acclaim, and financial success cannot be taken as a milestone by feminist artists who worked for years in the service of attaining greater visibility for female artists in the mainstream artistic community. Rather, Sherman and her images have been celebrated, according to Schor, "not because they threatened phallocracy but because they reiterated and confirmed it" (Schor, 1994).

The controversy surrounding Sherman's work on account of the artist's ambiguity, and more specifically, the desire of some feminists to lay claim to the work as an example of postmodern feminist art practice, or conversely, to reject the work outright as a step backwards in women's fight to transcend their position as the object of the male viewer's gaze highlights a more general matter that causes much debate in the understanding of contemporary feminist art practices. That is, what is the artist's role in the reception of the artwork? In other words, one must question whether artistic works can be "read" by the viewer as *feminist* only when the artist herself (or himself) makes the explicit claim to a feminist intent, or rather if the artist's intent is secondary to the dialogue that results from reading the work.

FEMINIST ART ACTIVISM AND ACTIVIST ART, 1980S TO THE PRESENT

The tactics adopted by feminist artists of the early 1970s to make public the unjust treatment of women in the art world were taken up again by artists and activist groups in the mid-1980s, and have continued up to the present. One group that has made messages about racism and sexism in the international art community very public is the Guerrilla Girls. This anonymous group of female activists first banded together in 1985, in reaction to a survey exhibition that opened at the Museum of Modern Art in New York that year. Billed as an up-to-date summary of the most significant contemporary art around the globe, it showcased 169 artists of which only 13 were women. After researching in galleries, and reading scores of articles and reviews on contemporary art in respected art publications such as *Art in America* and *The New York Times,* they realized a dramatic backslide in the representation of female artists and artists of color had occurred since the 1970s. On approaching some of the most prestigious institutions for an explanation, they found that no one would take responsibility for the lack of diversity in their collections or exhibitions, so the Guerrilla Girls decided to post the statistics publicly around New York City. Calling themselves "the conscience of the artworld" with the proclaimed intention of "making the f-word (feminism) fashionable again," the Guerrilla Girls have remained a very active and visible presence in the global art community ever since, working to get women and minority artists' work shown in a public context through posters, billboards, books, public appearances, letter-writing campaigns, bus ads, magazine spreads, and protest actions. To keep their identities anonymous, the group only appears in public wearing guerrilla masks, and each of the Guerrilla

Girls has adopted the name of a deceased female artist to retain their individuality in public appearances and interviews. Considering their mission to extend beyond the world of art, the Guerrilla Girls have expanded their focus over the years to publicly raise awareness about many different aspects of sexism and racism in Western culture at large, and have specifically taken on such issues as abortion rights, homelessness, and rape.

CONCLUSION

It is more difficult today to define what constitutes feminist art practices than it was, perhaps, in the early 1970s. Now the term is rather uncomfortably stretched to cover vastly varying conceptual frameworks and artistic positions, tied together through their concern for the oppression that women experience, but splintering in the racial, or class-based issues that the individual or group seeks to champion through their work.

In terms of breaking thematic taboos and increasing public exposure, however, feminist artists/activists have had an impact on the international art community, and women artists have achieved greater exposure in some of the most prestigious art institutions since the feminist art movement began in the early 1970s. Perhaps the most noteworthy milestones have taken place in the late 1980s and early 1990s, when the work of Jenny Holzer (1989) and Rebecca Horn (1993) were featured in solo exhibitions at the Guggenheim Museum. In 1990, Jenny Holzer was the first woman selected to represent the American Pavilion at the 44th Venice Biennale, where she received the Leone d´Oro grand prize for best pavilion. Also, in 1993, Rachel Whiteread became the first woman to win the prestigious Turner Prize at the Tate Gallery in London. Nonetheless, women artists still face obstacles in achieving a fair share of representation, funding, and public exposure in the international art community, and one of the greatest problems facing feminist art historians today is the task of preserving the work of women artists and incorporating it into the canons of art's histories.

See also Digital Technologies; Media Images of Women: Music; Second and Third Wave Feminisms.

Further Reading: Bailey, Courtney, "Feminist Art and (Post)Modern Anxieties," *Genders Online Journal* 32 (1997), available at: http://www.genders.org/g32/g32_bailey.html, accessed November 15, 2006; Broude, Norma, and Mary Garrard, *The Power of Feminist Art: The American Movement of the 1970s, History and Impact* (New York: Harry N. Abrams, Inc., Publishers, 1994); Chadwick, Whitney, *Women, Art, and Society*, 3rd ed. (New York: Hudson and Thames, 2002); Chicago, Judy, *Through the Flower: My Struggle as a Woman Artist* (New York: Penguin Books, 1975); Graham, Renee, "Why Judy Chicago is the Artist the World Loves to Hate," *The Boston Globe,* September 24, 1995, B27; Guerrilla Girls, *The Guerrilla Girls Bedside Companion to the History of Western Art* (New York: Penguin Books, 1998); Guerrilla Girls and Whitney Chadwick, *Confessions of the Guerrilla Girls* (New York: Perennial, 1995); International Feminist Art Journal, available at: http://web.ukonline.co.uk/n.paradoxa/; Krauss, Rosalind, *Bachelors* (Boston: MIT Press, 1999); Kuspit, Donald, "Crowding the Picture: Notes on American

Activist Art Today," in *Art in the Public Interest,* ed. Arlene Raven (New York: Da Capo Press, 1993); Meagher, Michelle, "Would the Real Cindy Sherman Please Stand Up? Encounters Between Cindy Sherman and Feminist Theory," in *Women: A Cultural Review* 13, no. 1 (2002): 18–36; Mullin, Amy, "Feminist Art and the Political Imagination," *Hypatia* 18, no. 4 (2003): 189–213; Mulvey, Laura, "A Phantasmagoria of the Female Body: The Work of Cindy Sherman," *New Left Review* 188 (July/August, 1991): 137–150; Pollock, Griselda, *Vision and Difference: Femininity, Feminism and the Histories of Art* (New York: Routledge Classics, 2003); Richard, Paul, "*Birth Project:* Fetal Visions," *The Washington Post,* May 28, 1985, D7; Schor, Mira, *Wet: On Painting, Feminism, and Art Culture* (Durham, NC: Duke University Press, 1997); Temin, Christine, "Judy Chicago's Unintended Horror," *The Boston Globe,* September 22, 1995, 51, available at: http://www.guerrillagirls.com/.

Kathryn Gentzke

FEMINIZATION OF POVERTY

The feminization of poverty speaks to the fact that a large proportion of the poor around the world are women. The reasons for the feminization of poverty are manifold and because it affects women and children, it has become one of the major issues regarding inequalities of gender, race, and class. The feminization of poverty is explained by political and cultural factors, which makes it a controversial topic.

BACKGROUND

The ideas around the feminization of poverty stemmed from a research paper written by Diana Pearce in 1978. She explored the notion that poverty was becoming "feminized" in the United States. Her work was based on statistics that almost two-thirds of the poor over the age of 16 were women. Pearce's work focused on the poverty of women in the United States; other researchers addressed the growing poverty among women around the world. Although some men are also affected by poverty, the gap between the poverty rates of men and women continues to grow. The reasons for men and women's poverty are often different, thereby establishing a need for investigating these reasons. The reasons for women's poverty are often seen as controversial and debatable.

According to Pearce, one reason for women's poverty is budget cutbacks in federal support programs. Women often rely more heavily on these programs and are employed by them more than men. Another reason for the feminization of poverty is the rise of single-parent, female-headed households. There are always debates about women having children outside of marriage and raising them without a father. A third reason for the feminization of poverty is the continuing wage inequality between women and men. Many people would agree that women and men should be paid the same amount of money for equal work. Nevertheless, not only do women still get paid less than men, but they are also segregated into lower-wage occupations.

TIMELINE FOR FEMINIZATION OF POVERTY AS A POLITICAL DILEMMA

1940s and 1950s: Poverty rates among men and women increase. At this time, women were only slightly more likely than men to be poor.

Early 1960s: Poverty in the United States becomes a major issue. Poverty for both men and women increases, but women's poverty in relation to men's is higher. Lyndon Johnson declares a War on Poverty.

1964: Mollie Orshansky, an economist with the Social Security Administration, develops a poverty line, an amount of money needed to support the basic needs of a household, to measure and establish a threshold for receipt of government assistance. (Over the years, the poverty line is criticized for only offering an arbitrary cutoff point, which denies poor people government assistance.)

1960s: Aid to Families with Dependent Children (AFDC) allows poor families to receive government assistance based on income below the poverty line.

Late 1960s: Head Start, a program to enhance the educational opportunities of poor children, is established and is a success.

1970s and 1980s: The poverty rate among young men and women starts to decline, but men's poverty rate declines faster than women's rates. The feminization of poverty peaks in 1970 among whites and in 1980 among blacks.

1980s: The feminization of poverty levels off.

1996: Young women have the highest poverty rate, and elderly men have the lowest, a reversal from 1950.

GROWTH OF FEMALE-HEADED HOUSEHOLDS

Divorce

One of the major contributors to women's poverty is the increase in divorce. White women may be more affected by divorce than minority women, who may have a higher chance to be poor even before marriage. The most obvious reason for a woman to experience poverty after divorce is due to the decline in income. Even if the woman is working and contributing income to household expenses, the loss of another income can be devastating. Also, if the divorce involves children, this will contribute even more to a woman's poverty if she maintains custody of them, which is true in the majority of cases. After a divorce, many men do not pay their ex-wives spousal support or child support to take care of the children. And if they do, the amounts for support are typically not very high. According to the U.S. Census Bureau, of all the men and women who are to receive child support payments, with the majority of them being women, only two-thirds receive any payment and 40 percent of the two-thirds who receive payment do not receive the full amount due.

Overall, then, the increase in the divorce rate means that a large proportion of women are living separately from men and have only themselves to rely on for economic support. Often, too, more women than men will stay divorced, whereas men are more likely to remarry. Women, on average, make less than men and they often have the sole responsibility for taking care of children.

Increase in Children Being Born Outside of Marriage

The number of children being born outside of marriage has increased over the decades. According to the U.S. Census Bureau, in 1960, about 6 percent of all births were to unmarried couples. In 1996, more than 33 percent of all births were to unmarried couples. The increase is even more pronounced for black families. In 1960, about 22 percent of all births were to unmarried couples; in 1996, the number increased to 70 percent. There are several reasons for these increases. First, there has been a decline in the rate of marriage. Fewer people are getting married and those who do are postponing marriage to a later age. The decline in marriage and the postponement of it increase the chances for couples to have an out-of-wedlock birth. Second, there has been a decline in the birth rate of married couples. Couples who are married are having fewer children than in the past or are remaining childless. Thus the number of births outside of wedlock seems higher in comparison. Third, there has been an increase in the birth rate of single women of various ages.

Many people point to the high rate of pregnancy among unmarried teenagers as a major social problem, but the rate of pregnancy among both white and black teenagers is actually lower today than it was in 1960. The proportion of teen births that occurs outside of marriage has, however, increased because women who become pregnant are less likely than in the past to get married to the father of the children, so the number of never married mothers is now higher. Also, with advances in fertilization technology, some women are choosing to have a child without the involvement of a father.

Teenage mothers are at high risk for poverty because of several factors including lower educational attainment, joblessness, and health problems. Also, many teenage mothers are more likely to be poor before getting pregnant. So the poverty they experience as single mothers is exacerbated by being poor in the first place. Many teenage mothers and fathers may drop out of high school to take care of their children. Especially teenage mothers may find that it is too difficult to care for an infant and attend school. Thus they may be lees likely to complete high school than those who delay childbearing until after graduating. Lower educational attainment means lower availability of job opportunities, and those jobs that are available do not pay well or include benefits.

Independent Living in Older Age

Elderly women are also at high risk for being poor. People are now living longer than ever before, and women are more likely to live longer than men, which means that they need more money to live on in their older years. Elderly women are more likely to be poor than men because of several reasons. First, more of the elderly population is living independently than they were years ago. The majority of this age group used to live with their adult children, but they now live in their own apartments or in retirement communities, or, if they are ill, in nursing homes. Second, as women are now living independently more often and outliving their male spouses, they have to rely more heavily on Social Security income. For women who are divorced, this can be problematic. These women have to rely on their own Social Security benefits, which they have been contributing to throughout their working lives. Women may receive lower Social Security payments as a result of their shorter work histories and lower earnings. So although these women may have some retirement income, it may not be as much as men, and it may not be enough to cover many of the medical and other expenses one has as one ages.

CONTROVERSIAL ASPECTS OF THE GROWTH OF FEMALE-HEADED HOUSEHOLDS

The more controversial aspects of the feminization of poverty involve the increase in the divorce rate and the number of children being born outside of marriage. Certainly the numbers point to these factors as significant reasons for women's poverty. Some would argue that these changes signify a decline in morals as people no longer value the sanctity of marriage. This may in part be true, but there are also other factors to consider when contemplating the reasons for a high divorce rate and rearing children outside of marriage.

Demographers note that the continuing rise in life expectancy has an effect on the length of marriages. In times when people did not live as long, marriages were shorter, and a marriage now that ends in a divorce may have ended instead with the death of a spouse. Another reason that the large number of female-headed households receives attention is the changes in women's roles. Many people argue that it was better for society when women did not have paid jobs and were full-time homemakers. This idea regarding women's lives, however, was not necessarily the norm for many families. Many poor or working class or minority women did indeed have jobs outside of the home, so women have always been participating in paid employment. What is apparent through this trend, however, is that more women are less financially dependent on their husbands than they were previously. Thus because women are more independent within a marriage, the interdependence of a married couple may be weaker than it was before.

ECONOMIC FACTORS

As noted previously, women who are married are less dependent on their husbands for income, mainly because they are working outside of the home and because of the decline in men working. Women's employment increased dramatically from 1950 until today, but rose the most rapidly during the 1970s and 1980s. These years also saw a decline in men's employment as a result of layoffs in manufacturing and other blue collar employment. What has changed significantly is the number of married women and women with children who are now part of the labor force. According to the U.S. Department of Labor, in 1990, more than 73 percent of married mothers with school-age children were in the labor force; 59 percent of married mothers with preschool-age children were in the labor force. It is important to remember, however, that despite these increases, wages and often the types of jobs for women are not comparable to those of men.

EXPLAINING THE PAY GAP

Women today still earn less than men. On average, women make about 75 percent of what men earn. Researchers cite various reasons for this discrepancy. One explanation is the human capital theory, which points to individual characteristics and skills that workers bring to their jobs. Thus age, marital status, prior work experience, education, and whether or not one has children are all human capital factors. Certainly, these factors can affect women and men differently, and although it can explain some of the reasons for the pay gap, it does not explain it well if many factors such as education, work experience, and age are the same.

The dual labor market theory is another explanation for the pay gap between men and women. The dual labor market is separated into two sectors: the primary market and the secondary market. The primary labor market is composed of jobs with good wages, benefits, and opportunities for advancement. Many women are employed in this sector, but many more women are concentrated in the secondary labor market as characterized by lower wages, short or nonexistent promotion ladders, and few, if any, benefits. Thus according to labor market theory, it is not necessarily the individual characteristics that affect job placement, but the structure of the labor market.

CONTROVERSIAL ASPECTS OF THE WAGE GAP

Some people believe in the human capital theory as a valid way to explain the wage gap between men and women, and, of course, the underlying principles of it make sense. When probing deeper regarding prior experience or marital status or existence of children, however, the picture becomes more complicated. Many women take time out of the labor force to have children; thus they are already losing years of experience Men who have children are not affected in the same way. Further, there are some who would argue that it is a woman's choice to have children; if she does, then she will have to deal with the limits it places on her job opportunities. Many women, however, want to be mothers, and society itself heavily emphasizes that women should want to fulfill this role.

CHANGES IN PUBLIC BENEFITS

From 1935 to 1996, a federal program called Aid to Families with Dependent Children (AFDC) assisted poor mothers and their children regardless of the circumstance of their poverty. For some women, poverty was due to widowhood or spousal desertion. With AFDC, women could receive government assistance to help pay for housing and other expenses related to raising a child. During the War on Poverty in the 1960s, the assistance AFDC provided was helpful in keeping poverty on a lower level. With the rise in women's employment, the divorce rate, and the number of children being born out of wedlock, however, the value of this assistance declined. Further, in the 1960s and later, when welfare became identified with black families, the government started to reevaluate its effectiveness in relieving poverty. In 1996, AFDC was changed to Temporary Assistance for Needy Families (TANF), which set more restrictions on the assistance that poor families could receive. TANF now stipulates a lifetime limit of benefits and requires that recipients find work within two years. Where AFDC was more flexible in terms of understanding the various factors that may contribute to poverty, TANF, with, its emphasis on work and responsibility, suggests that poverty is an individual deficiency of the poor. Many suggest that the changes in welfare have helped many people to decrease reliance on government assistance and move on to self-sufficiency. Others argue that because fewer people are receiving assistance today, one cannot conclude that these people and families are better off.

CONTROVERSIAL ASPECTS OF CHANGES IN PUBLIC BENEFITS

The changes in public benefits that occurred in 1996 have required poor women work in order to receive any benefits. Requiring women to work directly challenges those who believe that women should not work outside of the home. Further, when these women do find work, they usually find jobs in the secondary labor market. These jobs often do not pay enough for them to support themselves and their families, and they do not offer such benefits as sick leave for themselves or their children. The other difficulty lies in finding reliable, quality, and inexpensive childcare. Although not receiving assistance any longer, many women with children remain poor because they have to pay for childcare. Childcare is often expensive and not available to fit the various schedules working mothers in the secondary market may have.

CONCLUSION

The reasons for the feminization of poverty are manifold. Demographic and economic changes are part of the explanation for the rising rates of women's poverty. Changes in the family such as the delay of first marriage, the rise in divorce, and the number of children being born outside of marriage are the most controversial in terms of people thinking that the feminization of poverty could be avoided if society "just went back to the way it was." But certain changes are inevitable, such as the length of life expectancy that strains a marriage. Economic factors that cause women to be paid less than men or to be in jobs not as highly valued as men are also a factor in women's poverty.

Although the main focus of this discussion has been the feminization of poverty in the United States, the feminization of poverty is also problematic worldwide, particularly for women in developing countries. Women living in poverty are often denied basic human rights such as access to education and health services. And like women in the United States, women in developing countries also have the primary responsibility for childcare. Raising children alone is a main contributor to the feminization of poverty, but having and raising children is a job that should be rewarded, not punished.

See also Gender and International Development; Race and Racism: Social Stratification in the United States; Welfare Reform; Work: Paid versus Unpaid.

Further Reading: Feinberg, Renee, *The Feminization of Poverty in the United States: A Selected, Annotated Bibliography of the Issues, 1978–1989* (New York: Garland Publishers, 1990); Katz, Michael, *The Undeserving Poor: From the War on Poverty to the War on Welfare* (New York: Random House, 1989); Lord, Shirley, *Social Welfare and the Feminization of Poverty* (New York: Garland Publishers, 1993); Northrop, Emily, *The Diminished Anti-poverty Impact on Economic Growth, the Shift of Services, and the Feminization of Poverty* (New York: Garland Publications, 1994); O'Connor, Alice, *Poverty Knowledge: Social Science, Social Policy, and the Poor in Twentieth-Century U.S. History* (Princeton, NJ: Princeton University Press, 2001); Pearce, Diana, "The Feminization of Poverty: Women, Work, and Welfare," *Urban and Social Change Review,* February 30, 1978; Piven, Frances Fox, and Richard A. Cloward, *Regulating the Poor: The Functions of Public Welfare* (New York: Random House, 1971); Scott, Hilda, *Working Your Way to the Bottom: The Feminization of Poverty* (London: Pandora Press, 1985); U.S. Census Bureau, *Statistical Abstract of the United States* (Washington, DC: U.S. Government Printing Office, 2001); U.S. Department of Labor, *Employment and Earnings* (Washington, DC: U.S. Department of Labor, 2002).

Marcella Gemelli

FETAL RIGHTS

Recent advances in prenatal technology, fetal surgery, and fetal diagnostic techniques have foregrounded concern for the fetus as both a patient and a "person." Fetal rights are argued to emphasize the separateness of mother and fetus such that the increasing autonomy of the fetus potentially threatens the bodily integrity of the woman.

BACKGROUND

Visual access to the fetus through increasingly sophisticated ultrasound technology has resulted in the recognition of fetal personhood much earlier in development than ever before. This forges the fetus as less of a biological abstraction and more of a "person" before actually being born (Maynard-Moody 1995). Indeed, many pregnant women themselves suggest that seeing a fetus through ultrasound signals the beginning of a relationship with a "baby" or separate person. A woman's relationship to her pregnancy or her "baby" is similarly structured by her interactions with other people in public;

she must negotiate institutionalized moral and cultural assumptions about the nature of her relationship to the fetus (Markens, Browner, and Press 1997). Discourses of fetal rights arise from the notion that a mother and fetus are separate individuals. For proponents of fetal protection, the womb is the most dangerous place a fetus will ever inhabit; in the womb the fetus is vulnerable to potentially "irresponsible" maternal behavior such as drug or alcohol abuse. Abortion or the termination of a pregnancy is often considered to be the ultimate violation of fetal rights. Antiabortion or pro-life advocates, also known as *fetalists*, argue that the protection of the fetus should not remain the sole responsibility of the mother (Michaels 1999). Drawing on cases of "fetal abuse," they argue that fetuses as potential children should be protected by the government (Michaels 1999).

The most bitter and contested battleground surrounding the debate over fetal rights rests within the prosecution of pregnant women who are criminally charged for fetal abuse (often as a result of drug and alcohol use or smoking during pregnancy). In a few cases, most notably that of Angela Carder in 1987 who was simultaneously ill with cancer and pregnant, women have been required to undergo cesarean sections to save fetal life (Daniels 1993). Fetal protectionists contend that the creation of a "hostile environment" for the fetus during pregnancy indicates that a woman is unfit for motherhood (Daniels 1993). As the social recognition of the fetus as person comes increasingly earlier in pregnancy, feminists argue that this humanization negates the citizenship rights of the mother (Daniels 1993; Politt 1990). More specifically, feminists and women's advocates argue that prosecution of women in favor of fetal rights unfairly discriminates against pregnant women as citizens and compromises women's bodily integrity or the right to control one's own body, a hallmark of American liberal democracy (Daniels 1993; Casper 1997). In general, racially and economically privileged women (for example, white and middle class) are better able to defend their reproductive rights than poor and minority women, particularly with regard to refusing medical treatment or paying for drug or alcohol rehabilitation. Although pregnancy involves certain ethical obligations, it is legally and politically problematic to assume that a woman must sacrifice her self-sovereignty for public interest even if we do not condone her lifestyle choices during pregnancy. As a consequence of such protracted and divisive political feuds surrounding fetal rights, pregnant women are increasingly perceived as merely "uterine environments" and their bodies are policed as sites for "public inspection" (Duden 1999, 24). Scientists and medical researchers often try to distance themselves from discussions of the humanity of the fetus primarily as a means of continuing groundbreaking fetal tissue research and genetic engineering that uses "living" fetal cells. In this way, researchers purposely position the fetus as a "research tool" and not a human (Casper 1994, 317). In contrast, fetal surgeons construct the fetus as undeniably human in its status as a separate "patient," which potentially detracts from the status of the maternal patient (Casper 1994). With fetal surgery, medical focus shifts from the health of the mother to the health of the fetus.

PEOPLE

British filmmaker, Julia Black, presents a unique perspective on fetal rights in her documentary, *My Foetus,* airing for the first time in April 2004. Heavily pregnant, Black takes the viewer on a personal journey as she meets doctors and scientists from both sides of the abortion debate and questions whether she can still be pro-choice when confronted with the reality of the procedure. Black shows an abortion for the first time on British television at four weeks of pregnancy along with the remains of aborted fetuses at 7, 10, 11, and 12 weeks . This highly controversial and eye-opening look at the reality of abortion and the politics of fetal rights raises interesting questions for Black (who evidently underwent an abortion at the age of 21). In an article written for *The Guardian* before the release of the film, Black writes, "How could I, or anyone else, make a moral judgment about whether a late abortion is right or wrong without knowing the circumstances that led to that woman ending her pregnancy? The goal to isolate the foetus and make you see it as a baby is easily achieved with these images, but doing so makes us lose sight of the woman. I had easily been swept along by the emotive power of the images so no wonder the anti-abortion movement is keen for them to be shown."

THE EMERGENCE OF THE DEBATE

Whereas American reproductive rights discourse primarily focused on women's freedom of "choice" in the 1960s and 1970s, more recently the politics of pregnancy has centered on the social relationship between the mother and fetus or the mother's moral accountability to the fetus. Historically, mother and fetus have not been consistently perceived as separate beings; in general, the fetus was not granted "rights" distinct from the mother until the rise of the antiabortion movement after *Roe v. Wade,* the landmark 1973 court decision securing American women's right to abortion. *Roe v. Wade* established that a fetus is not considered a person under the Fourteenth Amendment and that women are not liable for fetal death before the third trimester (Blank 1992, 99). A powerful antiabortion movement coupled with court decisions granting the fetus legal rights renewed the state's interest in reproductive politics. By the 1980s, Massachusetts set the legal precedent in *Commonwealth v. Cass* by recognizing the fetus as a "person" and allowing for the prosecution of those who "murder" a fetus (Daniels 1993, 15). As a consequence, at least 10 states enacted fetal rights laws, giving the fetus status as a person.

The consecration of the fetus as person in law is intimately connected with the scientific and cultural imaging of the fetus. As technological innovations in fetal surgery and visualizing technology encourage the suggestion that it is possible for fetuses to exist outside of the mother's body, commonly known as fetal viability, the preservation of "life" is an overriding concern for many Americans, as well as the government. Fetal viability continues to be a key source of debate in determining the rights of the unborn. Medical professionals generally agree that 28 weeks is the pivotal point of viability, even though viability can come as early as 24 weeks (Blank 1992, 102). These markers are determined on the basis of the knowledge that at least 40 to 60 percent of fetuses born at 28 weeks could survive outside of the womb (Blank 1992, 102). Ultrasonography, however, establishes fetal viability as early as 15 weeks and the attribution of unmistakably "human" features, especially in the second trimester, affects this definition. As technology advances, the appropriateness of viability measurements is subject to change. For many supporters of fetal rights, fetal viability begins at conception, regardless of whether a fetus is able to survive outside of the womb. Paradoxically, now pregnant women can be charged for "abusing" a fetus but not necessarily for aborting the fetus (Blank 1992, 100).

CONSTRUCTING FETAL "PERSONS"

The baby/fetus dichotomy relies on emotional appeal and visual access to the fetus in order to create the sociocultural need for fetal protection. For many feminists, the visual portrayal of fetuses on an ultrasound screen undeniably provokes emotional responses from people that aids in the construction of fetal personhood (Raymond 1993).

Ultrasonography is no longer strictly a medical procedure; the images are used by women as a means to bond with the fetus for "entertainment" and also in the fetal rights movement to perpetuate the notion that fetuses are children. In particular, with the advent of three- and four-dimensional ultrasound technology, imaging of the fetus become increasingly sophisticated. It is no longer necessary to visit a hospital for an ultrasound; numerous three-dimensional ultrasound clinics operate out of local shopping malls across the United States. The imperative to define fetus as "baby" is mediated by the ultrasound photo; the photo blurs the distinction between fetus and baby

DID YOU KNOW?

The emotive fetal images of Swedish photographer, Lennart Nilsson, have significantly contributed to the personification of the fetus in American visual culture. Using fetuses from late abortions, Nilsson's 1965 photo essay in *Life* magazine juxtaposes bodily dismemberment and fetal tranquility in this spectacle of a "human being in the making" (Franklin 1991, 194). That the fetuses were photographed essentially in "death" (as they are actually dead fetuses from late-term abortions) is ironic considering the fetuses are meant to be representing "life" in the photo essay. Feminist scholar Karen Newman contends the *Life* article is a "tangle of contradictions" in which clever backlighting, surgical and chemical preparations, and photographic enlargement of the fetuses to almost twice their actual size contribute to the "aesthetic artifice" of this simulation of "life" (1996, 15). Although Nilsson's essay was intended as a glimpse into human development, the photographs and accompanying text portray the fetus as struggling through the travails of pregnancy. Sarah Franklin similarly suggests these images have been essential in creating "an iconography of fetal innocence" to suit the politics of fetal protectionism in the United States after the essay's publication (1991,195).

and also diminishes the importance of the mother's body in the picture. The mother's body (commonly represented by the placenta) is not exposed in the new forms of ultrasound primarily because its presence disavows the fetus as an independent subject. The placenta shows how the mother and fetus are different in that the mother provides the sustenance for the fetus to exist as a separate body, but it also unites them in a complex process of gestation, thus maintaining the dependence relationship. Photography, however, has recast the uterus as a public space with ultrasound such that this "socially embedded seeing" contains what it also produces—a fetus without a mother (Hartouni 1997, 25).

REPRESENTING THE FETUS

In popular media, the fetus is represented as unmistakably "human," with fingers, toes, and bulging eyes. In American antiabortion rhetoric, fetal images are used as rhetorical hyperbole appealing to emotion (Hunter 1994, 46). Feminists argue that it is the persuasive fetal images that motivate belief in the rights of the fetus, regardless of the accuracy of their visual claims. While still acknowledging the attachment that many Americans and particularly women have to images of fetuses, the American Civil Liberties Union (ACLU) argues that the laws supporting fetal rights potentially create an antagonistic relationship between mother and fetus and also may encourage doctors to compel women to undergo certain medical procedures (for example, cesarean sections) in favor of the protection of fetal life (ACLU 1996). In particular, the ACLU suggests that fetal protection bills should be carefully scrutinized legally and politically (1) to avoid the infringement of women's reproductive rights, and (2) to reflect why Americans both support and oppose fetal protection (ACLU 1996).

Feminists are concerned that increasing protection of fetal rights significantly undermines American women's access to abortion and effectively dismantles *Roe V. Wade*. For example, the signing of the Unborn Victims of Violence Act in 2004 by President George W. Bush makes injury to the fetus a federal crime (White House 2004). The public intention of the bill is to protect pregnant women from harm, but for feminists it is an underlying challenge to women's rights in favor of the fetus. Moreover, charging pregnant drug addicts with fetal abuse may discourage these women from seeking the appropriate care to manage their addiction and maintain their own health.

For many Americans it is hard to deny that pregnant women do have certain responsibilities to the unborn; however, the institutionalized social and medical management of pregnancy as an experience to be had in the public is extremely problematic. The privileging of fetal rights potentially encourages the subordination of women's reproductive rights in protecting the survival of the fetus at all costs. On the other hand, not recognizing fetal identity may alienate many Americans who do see fetuses as babies. Moreover, American women experience their relationship to the politics of fetal rights differently on the basis of class, race, sexuality, and religious or cultural background. For example, the rules of self-sacrifice in pregnancy are commonly seen as the inevitable path to motherhood for many middle-class women. In contrast, poor women are seen as being ill-equipped to make responsible choices simply because they do not have the financial means to defend themselves. Also, whether or not the pregnancy is planned can affect a woman's perception of the fetus as a "baby" or "parasite" (Oaks 2001). Despite the social meanings associated with the public fetus, not all women think of a fetus as a "baby"; women's understandings of fetal identity are contingent on historical, economic, cultural, and political contexts. The crux of the fetal rights debate rests in how women can be pregnant without sacrificing their rights as citizens.

See also Abortion; Birth Control; Birthing Practices; Family Values.

Further Reading: American Civil Liberties Union, "What's Wrong with Fetal Rights: A Look at Fetal Protection Statutes and Wrongful Death Actions on Behalf of Fetuses," 1996, available at: http://www.aclu.org/reproductiverights/fetalrights/16530res19960731.html; Black, J., "My Abortion and My Baby," *The Guardian*, 2004, available at: http://observer.guardian.co.uk/focus/story/0,6903,1185340,00.html; Blank, R. H., *Mother and Fetus: Changing Notions of Maternal Responsibility* (Westport, CT: Greenwood Press, 1992); Casper, M., "At the Margins of Humanity: Fetal Positions in Science and Medicine," *Science, Technology, and Human Values* 19, no. 3 (1994): 307–323; Casper, M., "Feminist Politics and Fetal Surgery: Adventures of a Research Cowgirl on the Reproductive Frontier," *Feminist Studies* 23, no. 2 (1997): 232–262; Daniels, C., *At Women's Expense: State Power and the Politics of Fetal Rights* (Cambridge, MA: Harvard University Press, 1993); Duden, B., "The Fetus on the 'Farther Shore': Toward a History of the Unborn," in *Fetal Subjects, Feminist Positions,* ed. Lynn Morgan and Meredith Michaels, 13–25 (Philadelphia: University of Pennsylvania Press, 1999); Franklin, S., "Fetal Fascinations: New Dimensions to the Medical-Scientific Construction of Fetal Personhood," in *Off-Centre: Feminism and Cultural Studies,* ed. Sarah Franklin, Celia Lury, and Jackie Stacey, 109–205 (London: Harper Collins, 1991); Hartouni, V., *Cultural Conceptions: On Reproductive Technologies and the Remaking of Life* (Minneapolis: University of Minnesota Press, 1997); Hunter, J. D., *Before the Shooting Begins: Searching for Democracy in America's Culture War* (New York: Free Press, 1994); Markens, S., C. H. Browner, and Nancy Press, "Feeding the Fetus: On Interrogating the Notion of Maternal-Fetal Conflict," *Feminist Studies* 23, no. 2 (1997): 351–372; Maynard-Moody, S., *The Dilemma of the Fetus: Fetal Research, Medical Progress, and Moral Politics* (New York: St. Martin's Press, 1995); Michaels, M. W., "Fetal Galaxies: Some Question About What We See," in *Fetal Subjects, Feminist Positions,* ed. Lynn Morgan and Meredith Michaels, 113–132 (Philadelphia: University of Pennsylvania Press, 1999); Newman, K., *Fetal Positions: Individualism, Science, Visuality* (Stanford, CA: Stanford University Press, 1996); Nilsson, L., "Drama of Life Before Birth," *Life,* April 30, 1965; Oaks, L., *Smoking and Pregnancy: The Politics of Fetal Protection* (New Brunswick, NJ: Rutgers University Press, 2001); Pollitt, K., "Fetal Rights: A New Assault on Feminism," *The Nation,* March 26, 1990; Raymond, J. G., *Women as Wombs: Reproductive Technologies and the Battle over Women's Freedom* (San Francisco: Harper Collins, 1993); The White House, "President Bush Signs Unborn Victims of Violence Act of 2004," Remarks by the President at Signing of the Unborn Victims of Violence Act of 2004, Office of the Press Secretary, April 1, 2004, available at: http://www.whitehouse.gov/news/releases/2004/04/20040401-3.html.

Meredith Nash

FIBROMYALGIA

Fibromyalgia, a disorder that predominantly affects women, is marked by painful tender points distributed throughout the body and often severe fatigue. The controversy concerning fibromyalgia stems from divergent medical and sociological views on its cause, cultural attitudes about women's mental and physical health, and debates about whether fibromyalgia really exists.

BACKGROUND

Fibromyalgia is controversial because it is so little understood and is often associated with traditional gendered notions of women's mental health. The symptoms of fibromyalgia include chronic widespread musculoskeletal pain, stiffness, areas of numbness, easy fatigability, and disturbed sleep. It spans all ethnicities and socioeconomic statuses, affecting women nine times more frequently than men. Some feminist social scientists contend that the disorder disproportionately affects women of working-class backgrounds (Barker 2005). Diagnosis occurs predominantly between the ages of 30 and 50, with prevalence increasing with age. Approximately 3.4 percent of women and 0.5 percent of men in the United States are diagnosed with fibromyalgia (Gilliland 2005).

The exact epidemiology of fibromyalgia is unknown and many theories have been postulated to understand this elusive disease. An emerging correlation between sleep patterns and symptoms of fibromyalgia demonstrate that stage four sleep is often disturbed in people with fibromyalgia. Stage four sleep is the deepest stage of nonrapid eye movement sleep, during which the body enters a restorative phase to repair damaged body tissue. In this stage of sleep, heart rate, blood pressure, and respiration rate decreases, whereas digestion and hormone secretion increases. Also, medical studies reveal that people with fibromyalgia have decreased levels of growth hormone, which could be a result of disturbed stage four sleep. Growth hormone is released from the brain during stage four sleep and is important for muscle repair and strength. This link between disturbed stage four sleep and low levels of growth hormone could explain why physical exertion often results in extended periods of pain and fatigue (Gilliland 2005).

People with fibromyalgia have also been found to have decreased serotonin levels (Gilliland 2005). Serotonin is a chemical in the brain that regulates mood, affect, pain sensitivity, and sleep cycle. Decreased serotonin levels have historically been associated with clinical depression, a relationship that contributes to the explanation of why 30 percent of people diagnosed with fibromyalgia also carry a psychiatric diagnosis, most often depression (Gilliland 2005). This contributes to the stereotype that women with this illness are "crazy," or clinically depressed, rather than experiencing "real" physical symptoms.

DIAGNOSIS

There is great disparity in how doctors view and diagnose fibromyalgia and how sufferers experience medical treatment. Although links to hormone and neurotransmitter deficiencies have been made, there is no definitive blood test to diagnose fibromyalgia, rendering it a purely clinical diagnosis. Because health professionals have difficulty measuring this invisible disease, and because it predominately afflicts women, the validity of fibromyalgia as a diagnosis is frequently questioned. Although the medical field has come to recognize it as a legitimate disease, reservations regarding its authenticity and verifiability continually arise (Bohr 1995). Doctors are seen as the societal and cultural authority on medical knowledge, the givers of information, whereas the patients are seen as the receivers (Greenhalgh 2001). A doctor's duty is "to see," but a patient's role is "to be seen," a relationship complicated when the patient presents complaints that cannot be seen (Barker 2005). Until recently, doctors were predominately male, adding a gendered power dynamic to the doctor-patient relationship. A woman with fibromyalgia is thus dependent on the doctor's legitimization of her pain experience, and she may feel compelled to maintain a submissive and warm doctor-patient relationship to achieve the goal of medicalized legitimization of her disease (Greenhalgh 2001).

Many who are eventually diagnosed with fibromyalgia first proceed through a series of psychosomatic diagnoses such as hysteria, nervous illnesses, and hypochondria. As a result, appropriate medical treatment is delayed and necessary accommodations and disability benefits are denied (Vickers 2001). After having pain and physical limitations discredited and disbelieved, the biomedical diagnosis of fibromyalgia is often a relief, even if it is effectively incurable and frequently disparaged by the medical and public communities (Barker 2005; Greenhalgh 2001).

SOCIAL SUPPORT

As scholars have pointed out, fibromyalgia is a disease that is not considered crippling, deforming, or degenerative and therefore is often minimized or doubted. Social service workers often assist persons with fibromyalgia to negotiate with the legal system for access to disability accommodations. Mutual-help forums have been created by and for people with fibromyalgia who seek peer support and empathy. Lists of "fibro-friendly" healthcare professionals—those who are not skeptical about whether fibromyalgia truly exists—are often created and distributed for fellow group members (Barker 2005). Joining with others provides the opportunity to change self-oppressive views, to value personal experiences, and to fight together against disability oppression, as advocates of fibromyalgia patients have argued.

CONCLUSION

The number of people diagnosed with fibromyalgia is rapidly increasing, and the label is becoming a common term in today's vocabulary. The different assumptions about fibromyalgia are inextricably related to the fact that the majority of people diagnosed are women. The combination of the biomedical analysis and the social construction of fibromyalgia result in conflicts that directly play out in doctor-patient relationships. Kristin Barker, a medical sociologist who has conducted extensive research on women's experiences with fibromyalgia, sums up these divergences: patients tend to define fibromyalgia as a disease, but physicians may not; patients assert that tender points are objective evidence of diagnosis, but physicians may not; patients tend to favor organic explanations, but physicians may hold to psychosomatic causes. The controversy about whether fibromyalgia is a valid medical disease results in very real consequences for its sufferers—minimization of symptoms; delay of essential medical treatment; and denial of accommodations, social services, and disability benefits. Those inflicted with fibromyalgia symptoms must contend not only with the physical pain but also with the cultural messages that often invalidate their experiences, a controversy reminiscent of earlier illnesses such as cancer before a proven diagnostic test was available. Until a medical test is developed and the symptoms are understood and legitimized by the medical establishment, it is likely that sufferers will continue to be faced with negative stereotypes about their conditions.

See also Disability and Gender; Medicine and Medicalization: Views on Women's Bodies.

Further Reading: Barker, Kristin K., *The Fibromyalgia Story: Medical Authority and Women's Worlds of Pain* (Philadelphia: Temple University Press, 2005); Bohr, Thomas W., "Fibromyalgia Syndrome and Myofascial Pain Syndrome. Do They Exist?" *Neurologic Clinics* 12, no. 2 (1995): 365–384; Foltz-Gray, Dorothy, *The Arthritis Foundation's Guide to Good Living with Fibromyalgia,* 2nd ed. (Atlanta: Arthritis Foundation, 2006); Gilliland, Bruce C., "Fibromyalgia, Arthritis Associated with Systemic Disease, and Other Arthritides," in *Harrison's Principles of Internal Medicine,* 16th ed. ed. Dennis L. Kasper, Eugene Braunwald, Anthony Fauci, Stephen Hauser, Dan Longo, and J. Larry Jameson, 2055–2057 (New York: McGraw-Hill, 2005); Greenhalgh, Carol, *Under the Medical Gaze: Facts and Fictions of Chronic Pain* (Berkeley: University of California Press, 2001); Hahn, Harlan, "An Agenda for Citizens with Disabilities: Pursuing Identity and Empowerment," *Journal of Vocational Rehabilitation* 9, no. 1 (1997): 31–37; Mactavish, Jennifer, and Iwasaki, Yoshitaka, "Exploring Perspectives of Individuals with Disabilities on Stress-Coping," *Journal of Rehabilitation* 71, no. 1 (2005): 20–31; Mollow, Anna, "Identity Politics and Disability Studies: A Critique of Recent Theory," *Michigan Quarterly Review* 43, no. 2 (2004): 269–296; Swain, John, Sally French, Collin Barnes, and Carol Thomas, *Disabling Barriers—Enabling Environments* (London: Sage Publications, 2004); Vickers, Margaret H., *Work and Unseen Chronic Illness: Silent Voices* (London: Routledge, 2001); Wendell, Susan, *The Rejected Body: Feminist Philosophical Reflections on Disability* (New York: Routledge, 1996).

Aimee Burke and Andrew S. Valeras

G

GENDER AND GLOBALIZATION: FREE TRADE ZONES

Free trade zones, which often employ women at low wages in developing countries, have been debated on economic, social, and political grounds. Supporters believe that their "trickle down" effects will help developing economies and the women they employ, even if women's wages and work conditions are poor; opponents argue that they serve to exacerbate global inequalities, exploit women workers, and crystallize the "drive to the bottom" in fair labor practices.

BACKGROUND

Free trade zones, also known as export processing zones (EPZs), employ predominantly female assembly line workers and are an important component of the global economy. From the start, factories located in EPZs have hired women on the basis that they are more "aptly suited" to assemble garments, computers parts, and other small items, and because their labor is cheaper. Located in designated areas of a country, sometimes on the borders of two countries, as in the case of Mexico's *maquiladoras* (assembly factories), these industrial zones have relaxed tax laws, labor laws, environmental laws and minimal health and safety codes. Ideally, these zones create industry and boost the economies of developing countries while increasing the profits of transnational corporations. Although EPZs have existed for several decades, international free trade agreements in the 1990s eliminated old trade barriers, including import and export taxes, making EPZs the optimal location to build factories that serve as the "global assembly line."

The assembly lines inside of the EPZs typically depend on importing parts of a whole product. The finished product is put together and exported out, ready for retail consumption. For example, a factory that assembles computers imports components or intermediate goods from all over the world tariff free, and once the computers are assembled, they are shipped to other countries to be sold. Approximately 75 percent of this workforce is female. Women's labor is desirable for several reasons: their labor is cheaper than men's; they are perceived as "more docile" and therefore less likely to place demands on their employers; they are more likely to accept part-time work with no benefits; and their "nimble fingers" are perceived to be better suited for assembly line work (Pearson 1998). Generally, women can be hired for about half the pay men demand.

SUPPORTERS OF EXPORT PROCESSING ZONES

Advocates of EPZs claim that this system is advantageous for everyone: the consumer, the corporations, and the workers. According to this view, consumers get cheaper prices and laborers are lifted out of abject poverty. Proponents believe that employment outside of the home allows women more autonomy, and having access to income creates the opportunity for women to afford better healthcare. Supporters believe that this process is a stepping-stone for greater economic opportunities for all developing nations. Not all supporters dispute the widely documented poor working conditions, but many believe that factory jobs are "better than" the alternative: prostitution, unemployment, or starvation.

Besides factory workers, consumers and investors benefit from EPZs as well, according to this view. Wal-Mart, the world's largest corporate employer, is a prime example. Wal-Mart products are often produced in EPZs and Wal-Mart jobs are directly dependent on the sale of its retail goods. The relationship between consumption in industrialized countries (the primary consumer beneficiaries of EPZ-produced goods) and EPZs is therefore reciprocal. For Wal-Mart to continue to create worldwide employment, EPZs are necessary; and for jobs to be created in EPZs, transnational corporations must demand labor at the lowest price.

OPPONENTS OF EXPORT PROCESSING ZONES

Opponents raise issues pertaining to the labor rights of EPZ workers, environmental health hazards, and the general lack of value attributed to poor and working class women in developing countries (Wright 2001). Free trade agreements have no clauses protecting workers, so factory owners can demand mandatory overtime, use child labor, have an unsafe working environment, and condone sexual harassment. These workers do not have the right to unionize. In fact, corporations consistently maintain that wages must remain low or factories must move to "stay competitive." EPZs and free trade agreements leave modern workers with almost no power for collective bargaining (Armbruster-Sandoval 2005).

To "stay competitive," many companies have shifted U.S.-based jobs "overseas" to Mexico, the Caribbean, or Asia. Mexico's *maquiladora* sector, which is one of the largest EPZs in the world, is now facing a similar fate, as factories relocate to Asia in search of a cheaper labor force. The PBS documentary, *Maquilapolis,* documents this phenomena as it has affected maquiladora workers in Tijuana, Mexico.

FEMINIST DEBATES ON EXPORT PROCESSING ZONES

Most feminist scholars agree that the lack of rights that female workers have in EPZ factories should be of concern, but some argue that because these workers are earning better wages than they would otherwise, they are actually benefiting from EPZs and from globalization in general (Lim 2001). Some scholars have shown how traditional gender roles are changing because of the EPZs. For example, in Mexico's *maquiladora* sector, many women workers have migrated from rural parts of the country to work in the factories. As they make the transition to the highly urbanized lifestyle on the border, their views on their gender roles have changed as well, creating tensions among men and women in the home, at work, and in local communities (Salzinger 2004). In this region, society is dealing simultaneously with men's unemployment and women's double responsibility for reproductive (e.g., childcare, housekeeping, cooking) and productive labor.

Ciudad Júarez, Mexico, located five miles from El Paso, Texas, is a good example of the geopolitical problems of EPZs worldwide. This particular geography is a literal line between the rich and the poor, "Americans" versus "Mexicans," men versus women, and the powerful versus the disempowered. After the signing of the North American Free Trade Agreement (NAFTA) in 1994, a series of murders began to take place in this border city. Since 1994, almost 400 women and girls have been murdered and almost that many remain missing in Ciudad Juárez and Chihuahua, Mexico (Amnesty International 2006). At least one-third of the victims are *maquiladora* workers.

The Mexican government has not recognized that these crimes have the common thread of gender-based violence. The police are accused of desecrating the memories of the women by questioning their sexual purity, linking them, among others, to prostitution and lesbianism and to living "double lives" (Fregoso 2003). Human rights activists argue that blaming the victims for deviant behavior has reinforced cultural stereotypes about these workers as valueless and contributes to poor women's ongoing sense of powerlessness (Wright 2001). Feminist and labor activists argue that the *maquiladora* management should be involved in finding the culprits, but supporters of these factories, including the managers themselves, argue that they should have nothing to do with the investigation, despite the fact that some of the murders have been directly linked to their bus lines and factories (Portillo 2001).

CONCLUSION

In the capitalist system, corporations are responsible to their stockholders to generate profits, not to the workers. Supporters of EPZs believe that the positive economic benefits of providing labor to poor countries will eventually "trickle down," making EPZs a win-win situation for poor countries and the female workers they employ. In contrast, opponents argue that until retail consumers in industrialized nations vote with their dollars, and unless more stringent international labor standards are adopted, the system is unlikely to change. Admittedly, feminists and labor activists face an uphill battle because multibillion dollar companies have more money and support. Whether women workers' lives will improve has yet to be seen and even feminist scholars continue to debate the pros and cons of this form of employment for female employees.

See also Colonialism and Imperialism; Gender and Globalization: Trends and Debates; Gender and International Development.

Further Reading: Amnesty International, "Mexico: Killings and Abductions of Women in Ciudad Juarez and the City of Chihuahua—The Struggle for Justice Goes On," Amnesty International, "Mexico: Killings and Abductions of Women in Ciudad Juarez and the City of Chihuahu—The Struggle for Justice Goes On," Amnesty International News Service No. 40, February 20, 2006, http://www.amnestyusa.org/document.php?id=engamr4101220065, accessed October 3, 2007, News Service No. 40, February 20, 2006, accessed May 5, 2007; Armbruster-Sandoval, Ralph, *Globalization and Cross-Border Labor Solidarity in the Americas: The Anti-Sweatshop Movement and the Struggle for Social Justice* (New York: Routledge, 2005); Fregoso, Rosa Linda, "The Complexities of 'Feminicide' on the Border," in *Color of Violence: The Incite! Anthology,* ed. Incite! Women of Color Against Violence, 130–137 (Boston: South End Press, 2006); Fregoso, Rosa Linda, *Mexicana Encounters: The Making of Social Identities on the Borderlands* (Berkeley: University of California Press, 2003); Funari, Vicki, and Sergio de la Torre, dir., *Maquilapolis* (PBS, 60 min, 2006); Lim, Linda, *The Globalization Debate: Issues and Challenges* (Geneva: International Labour Organization, 2001); Pearson, Ruth, "'Nimble Fingers' Revisited: Reflections on Women and Third World Industrialisation in the Late Twentieth Century," in *Feminist Visions of Development,* ed. Cecile Jackson and Ruth Pearson, 171–188 (New York: Routledge, 1998); Portillo, Lourdes, dir., *Señorita Extraviada (Missing Young Woman)* (Women Make Movies, 74 min, 2001); Ross, Robert J. S., *Slaves to Fashion: Poverty and Abuse in the New Sweatshops* (Ann Arbor: University of Michigan Press, 2004); Salzinger, Leslie, *Genders in Production: Making Workers in Mexico's Global Factories* (Berkeley: University of California Press, 2004); Wright, Melissa, "A Manifesto Against Femicide," *Antipode* 33, no. 3 (2001): 550–566.

Wonda Baugh

GENDER AND GLOBALIZATION: TRENDS AND DEBATES

Debates concerning the gendered effects of globalization include whether or not women in so-called third world countries are being exploited for their cheap labor, the degree to which globalization benefits or harms poor countries, and whether or not women's status has improved as a result of globalization and related processes of migration and economic restructuring.

BACKGROUND

Globalization is a multifaceted process and multidisciplinary topic, making it difficult to define. There are many elements of globalization: economic, political, social, and ideological. Even though the term *globalization* is widely used, both by lay people and experts in different fields, there is no one agreed upon definition of globalization. One popular perspective defines globalization as the "inexorable integration of markets, nation-states and technologies to a degree never witnessed before—in a way that is enabling individuals, corporations and nation-states to reach round the world farther, faster, deeper and cheaper than ever before" (Friedman 2003). On the other hand, there are scholars and activists who perceive globalization not as an inexorable process but as a deliberate economic liberalization that reduces the power of individuals and states, and increases that of market forces (Mittelman 2000).

Chen and Carr (2002, 1) succinctly summarize the meanings of globalization:

> Globalization means different things to different people. In its broadest sense, the term encompasses all types of economic and cultural transfers between nations—including domination of the media and the widespread use of the world wide web. In a narrower sense, it refers to the economic exchange of goods and services internationally and international financial flows.

The debate on the impacts of economic globalization often centers on these questions: Is economic globalization good or bad for people in developing countries? And, does globalization positively or negatively affect women's status, especially poor women? Critics contend that economic globalization is bad, because, according to this view, the process of global economic production is carried on the backs of poor people in developing countries through the extraction of their natural resources and cheap labor. In the case of factory production, poor women in particular have been targeted as the cheapest of all laborers, making them particularly vulnerable to globalization's negative effects (Salzinger 2003). Supporters argue that because globalization is a complex process, its effects on people in developing countries are more nuanced and can even offer positive benefits such as increased access to labor markets and consumer products for poor and middle class sectors (Lim 1997). Both sides address the fact that there is a host of factors that determine the benefits or the costs of economic globalization for different people. Those factors include social class, gender, racial/ethnic identity, and geographical location.

International institutions such as the World Bank and the International Monetary Fund (IMF) have played important roles in shaping the economies of poor nations, placing them at the center of debates on gender and globalization. Globalization and the rise of international political institutions arguably change the meaning of modern nation-states (Ohmae 1995). As global norms and institutions become more powerful, free trade may limit the ability of states to set policy and protect domestic companies. Observers across the ideological spectrum agree that the integrated world clearly needs new institutions to set framework of rules that govern the international economy. The World Bank and the IMF have been credited for creating a secure environment for the open market, but they have been criticized for not emphasizing human development and human rights (Rodrik 1997). The majority of members of both the World Bank and the IMF are industrial countries. Consequently, there has been an underrepresentation of poor countries' interests, including the centrality of poor people in development (Drakakis-Smith 1994). Critics contend, then, that poor countries are marginalized in the process of the creation of rules that govern global markets. Based on these contrasting views on globalization and new forms of global governance, who benefits from globalization? What happens when economic globalization deepens, rather than alleviates, poverty? Does economic globalization alter gender relations between men and women? If so, how?

THE FOREIGN DEBT CRISIS AND STRUCTURAL ADJUSTMENT POLICIES

One important way in which globalization has affected the lives of men and women in poor countries is through the foreign debt crises of the 1980s and subsequent structural adjustment policies (SAPs) put into place by international institutions to prevent poor nations from defaulting on their debt payments. SAPs, also known in some regions as economic reconstruction programs (ERP) or as new economic policy (NEP), were introduced first in Latin America, and later in Africa, the Caribbean, and Asia, as a way to enable poor countries to get concessional loans from the IMF and the World Bank to pay off their debt. Essentially it is an international lending program, and like all lending programs (for governments or for individual households), there are eligibility requirements. To begin with, debt-ridden countries can gain access to these loans only if they agree to the terms dictated by the World Bank and the IMF. The general emphasis of SAPs is on integrating poor economies into the global economy through a "free market" approach that emphasizes less state intervention in the economy, privatization, economic liberalization, and cuts in social spending to curb the costs of the debt. Ideologically speaking, SAPs are premised on the idea that the market, not the government, shall govern the economy. These policies have often led to increases in traditional economic indicators such as gross domestic product (GDP) and higher rates of economic growth; yet they tend to benefit large capitalist owners over small business people and wealthy over poor consumers. For poor people, SAPs have meant higher prices of basic necessities such as transportation, healthcare, education, and food. Increased unemployment often follows the privatization of state industries and agencies, leading to the increased displacement of workers in certain industries such as oil, gas, mining, and agriculture. Because SAPs and other free market policies encourage debtors to enter the global economy, these countries have to compete among each other and with industrialized countries in the increasingly globalized market. One result of this process is the spiraling "race to the bottom." In an attempt to entice investors from industrial countries, poor developing countries compete to offer the lowest wage, the cheapest raw materials, the most lenient labor, and/or the most lenient environmental regulations, often leading to further problems related to global social stratification and environmental hazards (World Bank 2000).

THE GENDER IMPACTS OF STRUCTURAL ADJUSTMENT POLICIES

The impacts of SAPs were initially perceived to be gender neutral. It was soon clear, however, that it was not the case. Women have often been at the forefront of antidebt protests, a phenomenon studied by critics and supporters of globalization alike (Lind 2005). Cutbacks in government services such as healthcare or childcare means that care work had to be rolled back to families. The elimination of government subsidies, coupled with the introduction of user fees in the healthcare sector (a result of the privatization of healthcare) often means that sick family members are cared for at home by their female relatives, rather than at a clinic or hospital. This new tendency leads to the increase of women's domestic work and it also squeezes their time for gainful employment.

The first sectors that tend to be cut back at the beginning of the implementation of the SAPs are education and healthcare. Because both sectors constitute heavy concentration of women workers, they suffer from either job loss, pay cuts, or salary stagnation. Most of these jobs are not well compensated to begin with, as a result of a widely held notion that because they are "feminine occupations," they are "less important" than "masculine occupations" such as engineering, for example.

Unemployment in the wake of SAPs is often exacerbated by price increases in basic food items. Women shoulder the lion share of economic and social burden, as they are more likely than men to manage and budget the household economy, a point observed by many scholars (Benería and Feldman 1992). In an attempt to make ends meet, women have greater propensity to put their extra income into the family's budget. In contrast, it has been widely documented that economic hardship doesn't seem to change men's tendency to spend any disposable income on personal items such as alcohol or cigarettes (Elson 1991).

Despite these negative effects, some scholars point out that economic globalization does not always affect women in developing countries in a negative manner. For example, the establishment of multinational corporations in many developing countries has opened new employment opportunities for women. Women have a greater chance to be hired by these employers as a result of their preferences for female employees, as mentioned earlier. They believe that women are more suitable than men to carry out work that requires patience and attention to detail such as in computer assembling or sewing. There are other perceptions of female workers that work in their favor, namely docility and submissiveness. They are less likely to demand changes in the workplace, which results in easier labor management, although even in Mexico's *maquila* sector, one of the largest of its kind in the world, some women have organized associations to address their work conditions in the factories (Salzinger 2003). Some studies document appalling working conditions, low wages, and human rights abuses in multinational corporations in many countries, leading to an active anti-multinational corporation, anti-sweatshop and anti-globalization movement (Ross 2004). Some, however, highlight rarely mentioned benefits that these foreign companies bring. Although from a Western perspective labor conditions and wages are far from ideal, such companies provide job opportunities that otherwise wouldn't exist. Rural women who have no job prospects in their place of residence migrate to urban areas to avail themselves of these new job opportunities, leading to an interesting and often contradictory set of issues for women's roles in these rapidly modernizing societies (Ong 1987, Lim 1997). Compared to local companies, some foreign companies offer higher wage and better working conditions. Better educated women also find jobs in more lucrative parts of multinational corporations, as well as in tourism industries, leading to new questions about the exploitative versus the liberatory nature of women's integration into these global production processes.

FEMALE LABOR FORCE PARTICIPATION AND WOMEN'S STATUS

Whether paid employment has resulted in an increase in status for women continues to be a matter of debate. Increased numbers of women in the labor force is not always the sign of progressive development, especially when it is based on a rise in the supply of labor rather than an increase in demand. Although economic globalization avails some women employment opportunities in the formal labor market, many more enter the informal sector out of necessity. The *informal sector* is a term used to describe the unregulated part of the economy, such as home-based industry, petty trading, and so forth. Increased poverty that follows economic crisis and/or SAPs often makes female participation in the labor market a necessity. As part of their survival strategies, poor households encourage more family members, sometimes including children, to enter the labor market. Given the complexity of the association between labor force participation and women's status, the impact of work on women's status is likely to vary depending on a host of factors such as level of education, nature of employment, ownership and control over resources, and cultural gender ideologies that determine women's place in a given society.

Gender ideologies that rigidly delineate men's and women's roles into the male breadwinner and the female homemaker usually do not provide ample room for demographic changes in gender roles. In this social context, economic globalization often poses predicaments for women. On the one hand, they provide income earning opportunities; on the other hand, these opportunities often clash with other expected roles such as mothering, dependence on men, and participation in public spheres of society (Singerman and Hoodfar 1996).

MALE DETERIORATING ECONOMIC DOMINANCE AND WOMEN'S STATUS

In some contexts of poverty and economic restructuring, men have lost their jobs, leading to increased gender conflict in their households. According to some accounts, in some Muslim countries, men's experience with economic difficulty has contributed to the collective increased control over women. According to these observers, some telling indicators include the growing popularity of

Islamic dress and *hijab* (head cover) and the more conservative personal status laws that govern marriage, divorce, and roles of husbands and wives (Goodwin 1994). Also, there has been an increase in formal speeches or publications that strongly encourage women's return to the home and their traditional roles (Abu-Lughod 1998). In some countries, so widespread is the backlash against working women that El-Mikawy (1999) calls this tendency the "conservative consensus."

The occurrence of the conservative consensus is somewhat ironic, for a substantial number of families across the Muslim world have to rely on two incomes to maintain a middle class existence or simply to get by. Several authors, however, point out that the increasingly conservative climate and the rise of male unemployment, as well as the reduction in male migration to oil-rich countries, are not a coincidence (Abu-Lughod 1998).

Another example of cultural clashes concerning gender and modernization concerns women workers in the factories of Mexico's *maquiladora,* or assembly factory, sector, a free trade zone on the northern border of the country. Since 1993, more than 500 women have been murdered in Ciudad Juarez, a large city that borders El Paso, Texas, and is home to hundreds of global factories. Most of the victims worked in *maquiladoras,* foreign-owned factories in this border city. These murders were shocking, not only because of their sheer numbers, but also because of their callousness. The victims were raped, mutilated, and murdered, their decaying bodies tossed in garbage-strewn desert in the outskirts of the city (Zebadúa-Yoñez 2005). These women fit a profile: they were young, poor women, many of whom came from other parts of the country to avail themselves for employment opportunities in *maquiladoras* (Monárrez Fragoso 2003). Although the killings caused panic among people of Ciudad Juarez, it was met with indifference by the police and the government (Lydersen 2003).

Of importance, some scholars and activists have pointed out that the ritualistic killing of these women workers is a result of men being uncomfortable with the progress women have made by entering the *maquiladora* labor force. Many researchers have documented how and why factor management preferred female over male employees, in part owing to their perceived "nimble fingers" (i.e., the perception that women could assemble small computer parts or garments better than men), as well as the perception of their greater docility and lesser need for a full-time job or livable wage. Because of these gender stereotypes, more women than men were hired during the initial years of Mexico's Border Industrialization Program, allowing women to make higher incomes than their male counterparts in many cases. This disjuncture between female wage earnings and traditional cultural conceptions of women as "secondary" breadwinners, as homemakers, and as secondary in status to men, let to increased intrahousehold and community conflicts between men and women, a process that continues today. The so-called feminization of the labor force, which free trade zone factories in particular have tended to propagate, has been seen by observers as a possible cause of the recent murders of women in Ciudad Juarez, in that they symbolize a kind of progress for women that has not been the same for men (Wright 2004).

In this sense, the murders of female workers in Ciudad Juarez arguably reveal the negative effects of indiscriminate economic globalization. Female labor force participation in Ciudad Juarez threatens the social order by highlighting women's gain and men's loss. Working women were able to assert control over their lives, however minimally, while at the same time men were often out of work and therefore unable to demonstrate their dominance. Consequently, the murders in Ciudad Juarez can be perceived as a result of the collision between machismo (or sexism) and economic globalization (Monárrez Fragoso 2003; Zebadúa-Yoñez 2005). The murderers could commit their acts with impunity because violence against women is not perceived as a social problem. Furthermore the *maquiladoras* that represent the global market echo the local opinion about women—that they are worthless, temporary, and disposable (Haddrill 1990).

As with any development issue, globalization has its positive aspects as well. It has been opening windows of opportunities previously unavailable for women. Economic globalization brings a wide array of consumer goods and forms of knowledge to people in developing countries. Many people from developing countries experience relative deprivation, a gap between what they expected to attain and what they actually could obtain. At the same time, the flow of information makes people from developing countries keenly aware of the economic gap between their countries and those more affluent ones. This knowledge, coupled with a demand for cheap labor in wealthy countries, serves as a catalyst for international migration.

ECONOMIC GLOBALIZATION, INTERNATIONAL MIGRATION, AND WOMEN'S CARE LABOR

Male migrants typically cross international borders to take jobs in construction and manufacturing. Female migrants leave their home countries to avail themselves as domestic and care workers. The shrinkage of industrial work and the development of informal jobs in service work and care work in many developed country present fewer job opportunities for male migrants and more for their female counterparts (Hondagneu-Sotelo 2001, 2005). In the early 2000s, about 95 million women left their home countries to live and work in a different country. They account for nearly half the world's immigrants (UNFPA 2006). Women's representation among all international migrants has risen from 46 percent in 1960 to 49 percent in 2000 (United Nations 2006).

Women have migrated for as long as men have, but the acknowledgment of their participation in international migration came only recently. One might wonder, why is this the case? Often, women are assumed to stay at home while men migrate for work, an assumption that reflects observers' own traditional gender ideologies. The main role of men in a lot of societies is that of breadwinner, whereas women are the homemakers, the nurturer of their children. From this perspective, it is logical to assume that many male immigrants will migrate alone, leaving behind wives who will take care of their family in the absence of their husbands. Alternately, when women do migrate, they do so to accompany or support their fathers or husbands (Hondagneu-Sotelo 2005). Statistics show a different picture. Women from developing countries have always formed a

DID YOU KNOW?

Many women from poor countries have migrated to wealthier countries to work as maids, nannies, or domestic servants. The high numbers of Latin American women, in particular, who have left their home countries in Central or South America in search of economic opportunities in the United States, have led to the phenomenon of what sociologist Pierrette Hondagneu-Sotelo (2000) refers to as "transnational motherhood." As these women leave some or all of their children at home, to be cared for by extended family members, they seek employment in the United States as nannies, taking care of the children of wealthy families in upscale urban neighborhoods. In fact, more professional women in the United States rely on paid caretakers for their children than ever before, a contradictory result of the forces of globalization: on one hand, globalization has brought with it new opportunities in rich countries for women to enter professional jobs in the service industries, offering them higher economic status than ever before. Yet because of this, the demand for poor (especially migrant) women to work as caretakers has significantly increased, leading to the rapid growth of private childcare companies, daycare centers, and nanny services (Ehrenreich and Hochschild 2002).

substantial proportion of migrants since 1960, although the proportion slightly increased in 2000. The gap between statistics and analysis is due to unchanging perception of women's passivity in the immigration process and their place in the home. In conclusion, feminization of international migration is not a new phenomenon at all, even if it is portrayed as such. Ehrenreich and Hochschild (2002) argue that lack of attention toward female migrants can be attributed to the intersections of their gender, race, class, citizenship, and occupational opportunities (or lack thereof). Research shows a wide range of diversity among foreign female migrants in terms of their socioeconomic status and racial/ethnic categories (Ehrenreich and Hochschild 2003; Hondagneu-Sotelo 2001, 2005). All female international migrants, however, tend to be lumped into one general category: as women, nonwhite, poor, originally from third world countries, and working in underpaid occupations. They are often seen by critics as serving the "underbelly" of globalization (Sassen 2002).

Although discrepancy of income between developed and developing nations is an important determinant of international migration, people often neglect to mention the wage gap between men and women in the home countries of the migrants. In fact the *2004 United Nations World Survey on the Role of Women in Development* (United Nations 2006) highlights the fact that gender inequality in sending countries is the strongest factor for women to migrate. Lack of decent employment in the home country, coupled with household financial stress and greater earning potential abroad, are strong incentives for crossing international borders.

Debates on female migration as a result of globalization revolve around the effects of migration on women's status and/or empowerment. On one side of the debate, observers perceive the feminization of international migration as an important, although largely unrecognized, vehicle for poverty reduction (UNFPA 2006). In this view, the feminization of international migration is positive for the migrants. On the other side of the debate, observers argue that the feminization of international migration breeds a triple marginalization based on race, gender, and class, the last defined in the context of global stratification. More specifically, many female immigrants experience subordination because of their status as nonwhite, female, and as coming from third world countries (Ehrenreich and Hochschild 2003; Hondagneu-Sotelo 2001, 2005). This is the predominant view expressed in the scholarship on the feminization of international migration. Yet other scholars such as Momsen (1999) argue that given the complexity of the process of international migration, classifying immigrant women as either "victim or victor" is oversimplification. Although female migrants experience varying degree of stress, difficulty, or even abuse, undoubtedly some of them return home unscathed, physically as well as psychologically. Additionally, some immigrants are able to obtain monetary gain from international migration and are able to alleviate their family from poverty (Oishi 2002; UNFPA 2006). Many migrant women seize the opportunity to buy land or real estate with their earnings; hence they experience a visible upward mobility (Oishi 2002). Consequently, some researchers prefer to place female international migration within the context of empowerment, however limited, and often with additional costs (Momsen 1999; Oishi 2002).

CURRENT ISSUES: GLOBALIZATION AND HUMAN TRAFFICKING

Additional issues concerning the effects of globalization on women include the increased trafficking of human beings that has resulted, in part, from increased global communication and transportation networks. Although the trafficking of human beings entails cross-border migration, it is often treated as a category on its own. The main international legal framework on trafficking, the *Palermo Protocol to Prevent, Suppress and Punish Trafficking in Persons, especially Women and Children* (UN 2000), defines trafficking as including the

> recruitment, transportation, transfer, harbouring or receipt of persons, by means of the threat or use of force or other forms of coercion, of abduction, of fraud, of deception, of the abuse of power or of a position of vulnerability or of the giving or receiving payments or benefits to achieve the consent of a person having control over another person, for the purpose of exploitation. Exploitation shall include, at a minimum, the exploitation of the prostitution of others and other forms of sexual exploitation, forced labour or services, slavery or practices similar to slavery, servitude or the removal of organs.

Many observers agree that the trafficking of human beings, like the flow of other commodities, is becoming an integral part of economic globalization. Gunde (2004) aptly calls trafficking as "the dark side of globalization... that brings opportunities of the weak, poor, and disposed, as well as for criminals." Trafficking of human beings includes those who are not at the bottom of the totem pole, but the poor form the majority of this commodification of human bodies (Enriquez 2006; Poulin 2004). To some degree, the trafficking of human beings intertwines with the effects of SAPs, for in some cases these market-oriented policies have encouraged the development of tourism and entertainment industries. In poor countries reliant on tourism, this industry increases rural to urban migration, as well as international migration from developing to developed countries, as a result of the disintegration of livelihood security. Many poor women enter prostitution and related sexual industries such as massage parlors, bars, and dancing clubs (Poulin 2004) as a result of increased state initiatives to develop their tourism industries, which cater primarily to first world male clients. Other women have been trafficked for the purposes of forced marriage, bonded labor, or organ trade.

The trafficking of human beings, particularly of women, is a symbol of economic inequality between developing and developed nations. Poulin (2004, para 6) argues: "we can see that, in every case, the 'goods' in this market move transcontinentally and transnationally from regions with weak concentrations of capital towards regions with stronger concentrations." Bertone (2000) writes that the trafficking of women will not continue without the Western patriarchal system that is hungry for "exotic" women from developing countries. Poulin (2004) and Sassen (2002) note that the trafficking of women will not abate in the near future because governments as well as entrepreneurs benefit from the commodification of women's bodies. It is difficult to find literature that defends sex tourism and trafficking, although it is important to point out that some supporters of globalization view these industries as natural outgrowths of national economies rather than as products of global inequalities, making them view the

THE ANTI-GLOBALIZATION PROTESTS IN SEATTLE, WASHINGTON

In late November and early December 1999, the United States witnessed widespread protests against the World Trade Organization's (WTO's) meetings being held in Seattle, marking the "birth" of the anti-globalization movement in the global North. Although critics of globalization have long organized in the global South to address the negative effects of globalization on their countries, the Seattle protests marked the first time that people in the global North became aware of their own roles in globalization and of globalization's negative effects on poor and migrant communities in the United States. Protestors broke the glass windows of several businesses including Starbuck's, McDonald's, and others located in downtown Seattle, as a way to protest the dominant model of global development being proposed by the WTO and other "free market" advocates. Although critics argued that violent protest does not lead to democratic political change, nobody could deny that the protests served as a "wake up call" for northerners' understandings of how their countries play complex roles in international economic and political relations.

local exploitation of women as sex workers or the trafficking of humans as issues that are separate from the debates on economic globalization.

CONCLUSION

It is difficult to consider the impact of globalization as merely "positive" or "negative." How people fare in this monumental global restructuring process depends on their gender, class, race, and geographic locations. Generally speaking, poor people, and especially poor women, have to contend with the negative impacts of globalization. Lack of skills and formal education often limit their ability to compete with their more privileged counterparts in taking advantage of the opportunities that globalization brings. Theoretically, cultural gender ideologies sometimes have restrictive effects on women, as in the case of Muslim societies where a conservative gender ideology is present. Yet at times, traditional gender ideologies sometimes translate into more job opportunities for women, as in the case of Mexico's global factories. Many foreign companies tend to hire women because of the pervasive belief that women are able to pay attention to details and work more aptly with small items than are men. Similarly, more women can participate in international migration, a pattern emanating from globalization, to fulfill first world demands for nannies, maids, and caretakers of elderly relatives. Some women are able to enjoy the liberatory aspects of economic globalization, primarily because of class-related privileges, and, to a lesser degree, a relaxed, less restrictive gender ideology in their society. Others continue to suffer from their status as cheap labor in a global economy that rests on their shoulders yet undervalues their worth as human beings. In short, the impact of globalization depends on the complex intersections of class, race, gender, geographic location, employment opportunities, and culturally ascribed gender ideologies.

See also Gender and Globalization: Free Trade Zones; Gender and International Development; Immigration: Laws and Policies Concerning Entry into the United States; Mexican Female Migrants; Sex Trafficking.

Further Reading: Abu-Lughod, L., "The Marriage of Feminism and Islamism in Egypt: Selective Repudiation as a Dynamic of Postcolonial Cultural Politics," in *Remaking Women,* ed. Lila Abu-Lughod, 243–269 (Princeton, NJ: Princeton University Press, 1998); Benería, Lourdes, and Shelley Feldman, eds., *Unequal Burden: Economic Crises, Persistent Poverty and Women's Work* (Boulder, CO: Westview Press, 1992); Bertone, A. M., "Sexual Trafficking in Women: International Political Economy and the Politics of Sex," *Gender Issues* 18, no. 1 (2000): 4–22; Chen, Martha Alter, and Marilyn Carr, "Globalization and the Informal Economy: How Global Trade and Investment Impact on the Working Poor," Working Paper on the Informal Economy No. 1 (Geneva: International Labor Organization, 2002), available at: http://www.wiego.org/publications/wiego.php, accessed May 8, 2007; Drakakis-Smith, David W., "Food Systems and the Poor in Harare Under Conditions of Structural Adjustment," Geografiska Annaler Series B, *Human Geography* 76, no. 1 (1994): 3–20; Ehrenreich, Barbara, and Arlie Russell Hochschild, eds., *Global Woman: Nannies, Maids, and Sex Workers in the New Economy* (New York: Henry Holt, 2002); El-Mikawy, Noha, "The Informal Sector and the Conservative Consensus: A Case of Fragmentation in Egypt," in *Women, Globalization and Fragmentation* *in the Developing World,* ed. Haleh Afshar and Stephanie Barrientos, 15–29 (New York: St. Martin's Press, 1999); Elson, Diane, ed., *Male Bias in the Development Process* (Manchester, UK: Manchester University Press, 1991); Enriquez, Jean, "Globalization, Militarism and Sex Trafficking," speech delivered at the International Meeting of the Women World March, Lima, Peru, July 4–9, 2006, available at: http://www.catw-ap.org/speeches_papers/20061118_gmst.htm, accessed May 8, 2007; Friedman, Thomas, *The Lexus and the Olive Tree* (New York: Anchor Books, 2003); Goodwin, Jan, *Price of Honor: Muslim Women Lift the Veil of Silence on Islamic World* (Boston: Little, Brown and Company, 1994); Gunde, Richard, "The Dark Side of Globalization: Trafficking and Transborder Crime to, through, and from Eastern Europe," Introductory remarks at a forum on trafficking of humans and human organs, Los Angeles, UCLA International Institute, May 14, 2004, available at: http://www.international.ucla.edu/article.asp?parentid=11513, accessed May 8, 2007; Haddrill, M., "Women Say Juarez Killings Show System's Bias," *Dallas Morning News,* October 11, 1999; Hondagneu-Sotelo, Pierrette, *Doméstica: Immigrant Workers Cleaning and Caring in the Shadows of Affluence* (Berkeley, CA: University of California Press, 2001); Hondagneu-Sotelo, Pierrette, "Gendering Migration: Not for 'Feminists Only'—And Not Only in the Household," Working Paper No. 05-02f, Princeton, New Jersey, Princeton University, The Center for Migration and Development, 2005; Lim, Linda, "Capitalism, Imperialism and Patriarchy: The Dilemma of Third World Women Workers in Multinational Factories," in *The Women, Gender and Development Reader,* ed. Nalini Visvanathan et al., 203–215 (London: Zed Books, 1997); Lind, Amy, *Gendered Paradoxes: Women's Movements, State Restructuring and Global Development in Ecuador* (University Park, PA: Penn State University Press, 2005); Lydersen, Kari, "The Disappeared: In Juarez's Maquiladoras, Murders of Women Continue," in *These Times,* May 19, 2003, available at: http://www.inthesetimes.com/article/321/, accessed May 8, 2007; Mayo, Yolanda Quiñones, and Rosa Perla Resnick, "The Impact of Machismo on Hispanic Women," *Affilia: Journal of Women and Social Work* 11, no. 3 (1996): 257–277; Mittelman, James H., *The Globalization Syndrome: Transformation and Resistance* (Princeton, NJ: Princeton University Press, 2000); Momsen, Janet Henshall, "Maids on the Move," in *Gender, Migration and Domestic Service,* ed. Janet Henshall Momsen, 1–20 (New York: Routledge, 1999); Monárrez Fragoso, Julia, "Serial Sexual Femicide in Ciudad Juarez, 1993–2001," *Atzlán: A Journal of Chicano Studies* 28, no. 2 (2003): 153–178; Ohmae, Kenichi, *The End of the Nation State: The Rise of Regional Economies* (Minneapolis: University of Minnesota Press, 1995); Oishi, Nana, *Gender and Migration: An Integrative Approach,* Working Paper 49, San Diego, University of California, The Center for Comparative Immigration Studies, 2002; Ong, Aihwa, *Spirits of Resistance and Capitalist Discipline: Factory Women in Malaysia* (Albany: State University of New York Press, 1987); Poulin, Richard, "Globalization and the Sex Trade: Trafficking and the Commodification of Women and Children," *Canadian Women Studies/Les cahiers de la femme* 22, nos. 3–4 (2004): 38–43, available at: http://sisyphe.org/article.php3?id_article=965, accessed May 8, 2007; Rodrik, Dani, *Has Globalization Gone Too Far?* (Washington, DC: Institute for International Economics, 1997); Ross, Andrew, *Low Pay, High Profile: The Global Push for Fair Labor* (New York: New Press, 2004); Salzinger, Leslie, *Genders in Production: Making Workers in Mexico's Global Factories* (Berkeley: University of California Press, 2003); Sassen, Saskia, "Counter-geographies of Globalization: Feminization of Survival," in *Feminist Post-Development Thought,* ed. Kriemild Saunders, 89–104 (London: Zed Books, 2002); Singerman, Diane, and Homa Hoodfar, eds., *Development, Change, and Gender in Cairo: A View from the Household* (Bloomington: Indiana University Press, 1996); United Nations (UN), "Palermo Protocol to Prevent, Suppress and Punish Trafficking in Persons, especially Women and

Children," 2000, available at: http://www.uncjin.org/Documents/Conventions/dcatoc/final_documents_2/convention_%20traff_eng.pdf, accessed May 8, 2007; United Nations (UN), *2004 World Survey on the Role of Women and Development: Women and International Migration* (New York: UN Department of Economic Affairs, Division for the Advancement of Women, 2006); United Nations Development Program (UNDP), *Human Development Report* (New York: Oxford University Press, 1999); United Nations Population Fund (UNFPA), *UNFPA State of World Population 2006: A Passage to Hope: Women and International Migration* (New York: UNFPA, 2006); Whirledbank, "Structural Adjustment Program," 2007, available at: http://www.whirledbank.org/development/sap.html, accessed May 8, 2007; World Bank, "Is Globalization Causing a 'Race to the Bottom' in Environmental Standards?" World Bank Briefing Papers, 2000; World Bank, *Global Economic Prospects 2006* (Washington, DC: World Bank, 2005); Wright, Melissa, "From Protests to Politics: Sex Work, Women's Worth, and Ciudad Juárez Modernity," *Annals of the Association of American Geographers* 94, no. 2 (2004): 369–386; Zebadúa-Yoñez, Verónica, "Killing as Performance: Violence and the Shaping of Community," *E-misférica: Performance and Politics in the Americas* 2, no. 2 (2005), available at: http://hemi.nyu.edu/journal/2_2/zebadua.html, accessed May 8, 2007.

Dewi Susilastuti

GENDER AND INTERNATIONAL DEVELOPMENT

Debates on integrating women into development address whether current economic development approaches, including globalization initiatives, are actually improving or deteriorating women's living conditions around the world.

BACKGROUND

Since the 1970s, international organizations such as the United Nations have become concerned with how to integrate poor women into national development processes as a way to address persistent gender inequalities and foster better living conditions for all citizens in poor nations. From the start, there has been lively debate concerning how women should be included in the development process and whether the current global development model of neoliberal, or market-led, development has positive or negative effects for poor women around the world. Three dominant approaches have emerged since the 1970s: women in development (WID), women and development (WAD), and gender and development (GAD). These approaches have sparked further debates about their effectiveness (or lack thereof) in truly eradicating the "global feminization of poverty," which refers to the fact that there are now more women living below the poverty line than there were three decades ago, despite the best attempts of economists and development planners to eradicate global poverty (Chen 1995).

Women in Development

The first scholar to address the issue of women in development (WID) was Danish economist, Ester Boserup, who published *Women's Role in Economic*

Development in 1970. Boserup, a United Nations researcher, focused her attention on the female farming system in Africa. In her work she showed not only that African women played active roles as producers, especially in the agricultural sector, but also that the transfer of new technologies to men via development policies was likely to have a negative impact on women's work. Moreover, she claimed that including women in the modern (i.e., export-oriented) sector would eventually have a positive effect on economic growth, in addition to improving women's lives. Her work was consistent with the dominant economic theory of those times, the so-called modernization approach. Modernization theory is based on the assumption that economic development proceeds through stages, and that modernization (i.e., the adoption of more advanced technologies and the increase in industrial production, which would ultimately lead to a wealthier, industrialized society) would be beneficial for all third world countries.

Boserup's research helped raise awareness about women's disadvantaged position in economic development processes, and motivated future researchers to address the fact that development may have different effects on women and men. UN agencies and donors started to target specific sectors of women, both in rural and urban areas, with projects aimed at improving their disadvantaged position in the economic system and integrating them into the development process. One effect of this attention to women as economic agents has been the promotion of various studies investigating what constitutes "women's work" and how it is estimated and evaluated (Benería 2003, 131–160). For example, before this research, the multiple tasks that women perform in their daily lives were not accounted for: tasks such as childrearing, subsistence farming, domestic labor, and community organizing were not considered "real" in global accounting models until feminist researchers began to address women's work as an additional aspect of the economy. Influences from Western feminism, which addressed women's "double burden" as housewives/mothers and as paid laborers, also contributed to this emergent consciousness about the multiple ways in which poor women contributed to the economy (Waring 1990).

In Mexico City in 1975, at the first World Conference on Women, conference attendees adopted a World Plan of Action that proposed some guidelines to the international community, with the aim of reaching the following goals: (1) full gender equality and the elimination of gender discrimination, (2) the integration and full participation of WID, and (3) an increased contribution by women in the strengthening of world peace. This conference also launched the United Nations Decade for the Advancement of Women (1975–1985), whose goals were to highlight the role of WID and to address the problems they encountered in participating in development processes. As a result of the UN commitment to the issue of gender and development, two new agencies were created within the UN system: the International Research and Training Institute for the Advancement of Women (INSTRAW) and the United Nations Development Fund for Women (UNIFEM), both of which were based on the WID framework.

Women and Development

During the 1980s, WID policies underwent major criticisms. Some scholars observed that WID led to the integration of women in development without questioning a notion of development solely based on economic growth and modernization. They considered this an "add women and stir" approach, reminiscent, in their view, of liberal feminist approaches that sought only to integrate women into the political and economic system without questioning the underlying systems themselves. This critique was raised in particular by third world feminists, who contended that the problem was not the fact that women were not integrated into development, but that they were integrated into development processes that exploited them (Sen and Grown 1987; Visvanathan, Duggan, Nisonoff, and Wiegersma 1997). These feminists contended that WID did not challenge the broader economic framework and that it focused mainly on the need to include women in the paradigm of development, treating them as untapped resources, which, when adequately integrated, would help make the market economy more "efficient," more so than help bring women out of poverty. Other scholars highlighted the fact that the WID approach tended to foster stereotyped images of third world women as "victims," "poor," and "backward," without acknowledging that women in the third world are differentiated in terms of race and class (Mohanty 1991). Finally, the WID approach was accused of not paying attention to the unequal relations between men and women.

As a result of the attempt to redress the faults of WID and to overcome its limitations, new approaches emerged: the women and development approach (WAD), and later, the gender and development approach (GAD). The WAD approach is a neo-Marxist approach that stems in part from dependency theory and world systems theory. In contrast to modernization theory, which presumes a linear path to development and expects all countries to be able to achieve prosperity so long as they take certain steps to modernize their economies, dependency theorists argue that the development of first world countries (the "core") is grounded on the exploitation of third world countries (the "periphery"), a relationship that stems from European colonization and continues today. According to this view, as long as first world countries rely on the cheap labor and raw resources of third world countries, and as long as third world countries cannot escape persistent poverty and foreign debt cycles, this unequal relationship of dependency will continue to exist. Drawing from and elaborating on dependency and world systems theory, WAD scholars believe that women (especially poor, working women) have always been active participants in the process of development and that their oppression stems primarily from their countries' historical dependency on industrialized capitalism. In this way, the WAD approach shifts the attention away from the disadvantaged position of women in society to a critique of the broader socioeconomic framework, especially women's marginalization in capitalist peripheral societies.

Examples of projects stemming from this framework include women's labor unions and projects designed to support female microenterprise owners, particularly in the form of microcredit. Two widely emulated projects include the

SELF-EMPLOYED WOMEN'S ASSOCIATION

SEWA, the Self-Employed Women's Association, is an Indian trade union founded in 1972. SEWA organizes women workers employed in the informal sector in India. Its activities are grounded in two principles: struggle and development. SEWA's strategy is to fight against the limitations imposed on women by society and to develop economic alternatives to achieve the goal of full employment and self-reliance. SEWA embraces gandhian principles of egalitarianism and inclusion. Accordingly, SEWA organizes its members without any distinction in terms of race, caste, or religion. The association offers to its members a wide range of services: a bank, a health plan and employment insurance, and a training institute (the SEWA Academy). In the 2000s, SEWA has more than 700,000 members who are mainly concentrated in rural areas of India. Its success in organizing self-employed women has led to the creation of sections of SEWA outside the country as well, including in South Africa and Yemen.

In the 1990s, SEWA came to the forefront, as it was able to successfully lobby the International Labor Organization to promote the adoption of the ILO Convention concerning Homework (1996). This convention was particularly important for self-employed women workers in India, as not only did it extend to home workers the protections guaranteed to standard workers, but it also pulled home-based work out of a state of "invisibility," which was making it an exploitative form of labor. In 2006, SEWA was a candidate for the Nobel Peace Prize, losing to the Grameen Bank and its founder, Muhammad Yunus.

Self-Employed Women's Association (SEWA) of India, which was established by a group of women workers (see Sidebar Self-Employed Women's Association) and the Bangladesh-based Grameen Bank, designed to provide poor women with small business loans. In 2006, the Grameen Bank and its founder, Muhammad Yunus, won the Nobel Peace Prize for their contributions to social and economic development.

Gender and Development

In many ways, the WAD approach was an important step toward developing the GAD approach, which continues to have great salience today among practitioners, policymakers, and activists. The GAD approach was "inaugurated" during the World Conference to Review and Appraise the Achievements of the UN Decade for Women, held in Nairobi, Kenya in 1985. It is the product of a much longer transnational dialogue among feminist activists and scholars in the South, and from an improved dialogue among activists and scholars from the North and South.

Most fundamentally, the GAD approach aims at addressing gender power relations between women and men by shifting the focus from "women" to "gender." As a consequence, women are not treated as a separate group; on the contrary, the attention is focused on the different needs of women and men and on the necessity of achieving true gender equality. In theory, the GAD approach aims to transform gender roles and challenge relations of power between women and men, thereby endowing it with transformative potential for broader socioeconomic frameworks that the WID approach was unable to achieve. By addressing gender roles and relations, GAD is targeting at the same time the "condition" of women (i.e., poverty) and their "position" (i.e., status, defined especially in legal terms) in society. Because of the shift from women to gender, GAD supporters hoped that there would be less likelihood of the "ghettoization" of women's issues or women-oriented projects in specific units and offices within international organizations and national governments, and more chance of a gender analysis being incorporated into all institutional divisions and policy frameworks. In sum, the adoption of the GAD approach marked a shift from the centrality of women's direct need to access resources to the necessity of redistributing power between men and women, particularly through a series of legal and political reforms that would lead to increases in women's rights according to the law. In conjunction with this, the GAD approach also held the promise to be more sensitive to issues of difference among women, including racial, ethnic, religious, sexual, and geographic differences. The WID approach did not address differences among women, except between women of the first versus third world, and the WAD approach only addressed class differences among women, typically viewing global capitalism as the primary cause for all other forms of oppression such as racism and religious intolerance, rather than applying a more intersectional analysis that came out of select GAD scholarship, particularly that produced by academic scholars (e.g., Mohanty 1991).

In 1995, the GAD approach was institutionalized and sanctioned at the Fourth UN Conference on Women held in Beijing, China, a conference designed to follow up on proposals made at the earlier UN conferences. The conference document, the Beijing Platform of Action, declared that gender should be "mainstreamed" in every policy at all levels of governance, meaning that the different needs of women and men need to be taken into account in the designing and implementation of all state policies.

CRITIQUES OF WID, WAD, AND GAD

Several critiques of GAD and earlier approaches have emerged since the 1980s. To begin, the GAD approach has been challenged on the grounds that the new focus on gender, including the notion of gender mainstreaming, bypasses earlier concerns about women's specific needs and about sexism. By focusing on gender and presumably "bringing men in," critics fear that the GAD focus on gender might lead to less, rather than more, attention to women's specific needs and disadvantages and to a dismissal of funding for women-oriented activities and projects. Moreover, another problem highlighted by GAD critics is that the insistence on differences among women may actually constitute an obstacle for the recognition of their commonalities.

In addition to these criticisms, new approaches have emerged that combine WID, WAD, and/or GAD frameworks with other variables such as the environment, racism, or sexuality. For example, the women, environment, and sustainable development (WED) approach was elaborated in the 1980s under the impulse of third world women activists and scholars observing the negative effects of economic growth on the environment, and noting that poor women are the most likely to be hit by environmental crisis. WED advocates problematized the traditional notion of economic development to foster "sustainable development." Sustainable development is a process of development that conciliates the fulfillment of human needs with the preservation of natural resources, without endangering the fulfillment of the needs of future generations. The WED approach also promotes the idea that an increased participation of poor women from the global South in the management of development would help in meeting the overall goal of sustainable development. One of the most famous groups of third world women promoting the direct participation of women in the management of natural resources is the green belt movement, a grassroots organization in Kenya that connects the fight for good governance and respect of human rights with the protection of the environment. The founder of the green belt movement, Wangari Maathai, received the Nobel Peace Prize in 2004. Development Alternatives with Women for a New Era, a network of feminists from the global South, has also addressed sustainable development since its inception in 1984.

Recent developments in feminist theory have expanded the issue of gender and development to include a broader notion of survival, from one focused on material needs to one focused on emotional and safety needs, and on sexuality. Although sexuality is a central element in the life of all individuals, it is a matter that tends either to be ignored by development practitioners, viewed only through a traditional lens of maternity and reproduction, or to be addressed mainly with regard to health crises such as the HIV/AIDS pandemic (Gosine 2005). Recent studies highlight the fact that development policies are often based on assumptions about the sexual identity and practices of the beneficiaries, many of which are rooted in Eurocentric understandings of sexuality. For instance, development policies targeting women in the third world address them mainly as mothers and caretakers, hence assuming that they are heterosexual and that they reproduce, rather than viewing them more broadly as having sexual autonomy and as active participants in the public domain (Lind and Share 2003).

ALTERNATIVES TO DEVELOPMENT: IMAGINING A POST-DEVELOPMENT ERA

The various problems related to economic development have led scholars and activists to explore the possibility of alternatives to the mainstream economic model and to develop the concept of "post-development" (Escobar 1995; Saunders 2002). Post-development is based on the idea that modernization and capitalism are not liberating either women or men; on the contrary, they are promoting exploitative conditions all over the world. There are different post-development approaches, but in general they promote alternative definitions of development that include a concern for the well-being of individuals beyond the satisfaction of economic (i.e., monetary) needs. Although post-development thought as a field is a recent phenomenon, earlier thinkers promoted similar ideas. For example, Mohandas (or "Mahatma") Gandhi, the leader of the Indian fight for independence (1916–1945), strongly criticized the Western paradigm of development and worked to create an alternative economic model based on local production and self-reliance. Other exponents of post-development include Colombian-born anthropologist Arturo Escobar, now a professor in the United States, who authored the ground-breaking publication, *Encountering Development: The Making and Unmaking of the Third World* (1995) and Indian physicist and activist, Vandana Shiva, who has helped lead the struggle for the protection of the environment in India (Shiva 1989).

CONCLUSION

The debate concerning the need to integrate women into development, and the best conditions for doing so, continues to take place among scholars and practitioners of the global South and North. WID, WAD, GAD, GED, alternative forms of development, and alternatives to development all highlight different aspects of the relationship between women and broad economic change such as that promoted in development policies. Whereas the WID approach stresses the necessity of integrating women into an otherwise benevolent process of capitalist development, the remaining approaches question the validity of development models centered on economic growth. The GAD approach, with its emphasis on the concept of gender, highlights the need to address relations of power between women and men. More fundamentally, perhaps, some scholars argue that to truly understand global gender inequalities, scholars and practitioners must first question the notion of development itself, with the goal of fostering a broader understanding of development that is linked to the overall well-being of individuals that goes beyond the economic sphere.

See also Colonialism and Imperialism; Environmental Justice; Gender and Globalization: Trends and Debates; Human Rights: International Laws and Policies.

Further Reading: Antrobus, Peggy, *The Global Women's Movement. Origins, Issues and Strategies* (New York: Zed Books, 2004); Benería, Lourdes, *Gender, Development and Globalization: Economics As if All People Mattered* (New York: Routledge, 2003); Boserup, Ester, *Woman's Role in Economic Development* (New York: St. Martin's Press, 1971); Chen, Martha Alter, "The Feminization of Poverty," in *A Commitment to the World's Women: Perspectives on Development for Beijing and Beyond,* ed. Noeleen Heyzer, 23–37 (New York: UNIFEM, 1995); Escobar, Arturo, *Encountering Development: The Making and Unmaking of the Third World* (Princeton, NJ: Princeton University Press, 1995); Gosine, Andil, "Sex for Pleasure, Rights to Participation, and Alternatives to AIDS: Placing Sexual Minorities and/or Dissidents in Development," IDS Working Paper 228, Institute for Development Studies, Brighton, England, February, 2005; Jaquette, Jane S., and Gale Summerfield, *Women and Gender Equity in Development Theory and Practice: Institutions, Resources, and Mobilization* (Durham, NC: Duke University Press, 2006); Jain, Devaki, *Women, Development and the UN: A Sixty-Year Quest for Equality and Justice* (Bloomington: Indiana University Press, 2005); Lind, Amy, and Jessica Share, "Queering Development: Institutionalized Heterosexuality in

Development Theory, Practice and Politics in Latin America," in *Feminist Futures: Re-imagining Women, Culture and Development,* ed. Kum-Kum Bhavnani, John Foran, and Priya Kurian, 55–73 (New York: Zed Books, 2003); Marchand, Marianne, and Jane L. Parpart, eds., *Feminism/Postmodernism/Development* (New York: Routledge, 1995); Mohanty, Chandra Talpade, "Under Western Eyes: Feminist Scholarship and Colonial Discourses," in *Third World Women and the Politics of Feminism,* ed. Chandra Talpade Mohanty, Ann Russo, and Lourdes Torres, 51–80 (Bloomington: Indiana University Press, 1991); Nalini, Visvanathan, Lynn Duggan, Laurie Nisonoff, and Nan Wiegersma, eds., *The Women, Gender and Development Reader* (New York: Zed Books, 1997); Saunders, Kriemild, ed., *Feminist Post Development Thought* (New York: Zed Books, 2002); Sen, Gita, and Caren Grown, *Development, Crises, and Alternative Visions: Third World Women's Perspectives* (New York: Monthly Review Press, 1987); Shiva, Vandana, *Staying Alive: Women, Ecology, and Development* (New York: Zed Books, 1989); Waring, Marilyn, *If Women Counted: A New Feminist Economics* (New York: Harper Collins, 1990).

Federica Gentile

GENDER IDENTITY DISORDER

Gender identity disorder (GID) is a hotly contested diagnostic category used by the American Psychiatric Association (APA) to label nonconforming gender identity expression as a mental illness. Activist groups are challenging the pathologizing of gender identity expression and claim that similar to the declassification of homosexuality as a mental illness in the 1970s, nonconforming gender identity expression, too, must be declassified and cease being labeled a mental illness. Supporters believe that gender is a biological fact and that lack of identification with the gender assigned at birth is a dysfunction.

BACKGROUND: GENDER IDENTITY DISORDER DIAGNOSIS

GID is one of the most controversial categories of mental disorders in the DSM. Those who believe it should be eliminated from the DSM contend there is little evidence to support its use and that gender roles and expectations are not binary categories as the DSM suggests. Gender identity is a social construction and its pathology has been created by the medical profession. Therefore the category should be dropped altogether from the next version of the DSM (DSM-V, which is now under discussion and targeted for a 2010 release date). Psychologist Daryl Hill argues that GID is not a mental disorder at all and that it is largely a diagnosis designed to alleviate the stress experienced by social institutions and parents who cannot accept a child's exploration of gender roles and expectations that do not fit prescribed categories (Hausman 2003).

Supporters of the diagnosis disagree with this analysis. They believe that gender is a biological fact and the diagnostic category is valid because gender-congruent roles and behaviors are an expectation of society. Thus if individuals do not identify with the gender they are "born into," it is a "dysfunction" and should be labeled and treated as such.

GENDER IDENTITY DISORDER DIAGNOSTIC CRITERIA

A. A strong and persistent cross-gender identification (not merely a desire for any perceived cultural advantages of being the other sex). In children, the disturbance is manifested by four (or more) of the following:

1. Repeatedly stated desire to be, or insistence that he or she is, the other sex.
2. In boys, preference for cross-dressing or simulating female attire; in girls, insistence on wearing only stereotypical masculine clothing.
3. Strong and persistent preferences for cross-sex roles in make-believe play or persistent fantasies of being the other sex.
4. Intense desire to participate in the stereotypical games and pastimes of the other sex.
5. Strong preference for playmates of the other sex.

B. Persistent discomfort with his or her sex or sense of inappropriateness in the gender role of that sex.
C. The disturbance is not concurrent with a physical intersex condition.
D. The disturbance causes clinically significant distress or impairment in social, occupational, or other important areas of functioning.

Source: American Psychiatric Association, DSM-IV-TR 302.85, 2000.

Others argue for GID reform instead of complete removal of the category from the DSM. GID Reform Advocates is one group dedicated to keeping the diagnosis of "gender dysphoria" as a serious medical condition that can be treated with medical intervention but declassifying gender nonconformity and "cross-gender" identities that are legitimate expressions of gender. They argue the criteria for a mental disorder should rise to the level of a "clear therapeutic purpose" for intervention that is based on distress or impairment for the individual. It should not be based on socially defined gender nonconformity constructs.

The World Health Organization's International Statistical Classification of Diseases and Related Health Problems (10th Revision 2003) classifies gender identity variance in a similar fashion as the Diagnostic and Statistical Manual of Mental Disorders (DSM IV-TR, 2000), published by the American Psychiatric Association. Gender identity variances are classified as diseases under the broader category of "gender identity disorders."

WHO NEEDS A GID DIAGNOSIS?

People who consider themselves gender variant encompass a wide range of perspectives on whether GID should be a disease and have a wide range of perspectives on body transformation from one sex to another. Some seek body modification surgeries; others do not. To pursue body transforming procedures in the United States, such as sex reassignment or hormone therapies, however, an individual usually enters the mental health system and obtains a diagnosis of GID after seeing a mental health therapist for a certain amount of time. Often without this designation, an individual cannot proceed with surgical interventions to modify the body. Activists groups continue to challenge essentialist assumptions of gender identity expression that pathologizes individuals who do not align themselves with traditional binary sex/gender categories; males must be men and females must be women, for example. In addition, activists see the pathologizing of gender identity expression as a form of social control that the DSM IV-TR legitimizes. Supporters of GID as a mental disorder argue that individuals who experience "gender distress" and "gender dysphoria" are in need of psychological and medical interventions to help them cope with their condition.

CONCLUSION

To date, the APA has supported the pathologizing of nonconforming, cross-gender, and gender-variant identities. Activists in and outside of the mental health profession continue to challenge this stance. Whether gender identity disorder will be declassified by the APA as a mental illness in the next revisions of the DSM will be one of the most hotly debated issues facing the association.

See also Gender Socialization; Sex Reassignment Surgery; Third Genders; Transgender and Transsexual Identities.

Further Reading: Bornstein, Kate, *Gender Outlaw: On Men, Women, and the Rest of Us* (New York: Vintage Books, 1994); GID Reform Advocates, "What Is GID," December 5, 2006, available at: http://www.gidreform.org; Hausman, Ken, "Controversy Continues to Grow Over DSM's GID Diagnosis," *Psychiatric News,* American Psychiatric Association, 38, no. 14, (2003): 25; Israel, Gianna, and Donald Traver, *Transgender Care: Recommended Guidelines, Practical Information and Personal Accounts* (Philadelphia: Temple University Press, 1997); Lev, Arelene Istar, *Transgender Emergence: Therapeutic Guidelines for Working with Gender-Variant People and Their Families* (New York: Haworth Press, 2004); Parker, James, and Philip Parker, *Gender Identity Disorder: A 3–1 Medical Reference* (San Diego: ICON Health Publications, 2004); Run, Henry, *Self-Made Men: Identity and Embodiment among Transsexual Men* (Nashville, TN: Vanderbilt University Press, 2003); Scholinski, Daphne, *The Last Time I Wore a Dress: A Memoir* (New York: Riverhead Books, 1997).

Stephanie Brzuzy

GENDER SOCIALIZATION

Gender socialization refers to the complex set of processes through which individuals behave in a particular set of ways according to their proscribed gender. Debates concerning gender socialization stem from religious versus secular views on gender, sexuality and family, culturally divergent perspectives on "appropriate" gendered behavior, and whether gender roles are derived from biology or are socially constructed.

BACKGROUND

Gender can be understood as a signifier of sex. Because sexual difference is a primary organizing principle of most societies, gender socialization, through which individuals are encouraged to consistently signify their sex, constitutes one of the most powerful aspects of socialization in any society (Kessler and McKenna 1985; Richardson 1988). Members of a society don't simply learn how to eat—they learn a complex set of rules for how they must, should, or may eat, given their sex; members of society don't simply learn to engage in religious ceremonies—they learn how they must, should, or may engage in religious practices, given their sex; members of society don't simply learn how to walk, run, or dance—they learn how they must, should, or may walk, run, and dance as members of a particular sex. Not everyone easily or readily accepts the gender socialization of a given society, but the process of attempting to shape behavior into masculine and feminine inflections impinges on almost every member of any particular society at most times.

Feminist scholars have noted that gender socialization begins in an individual's life even before the individual is born (Richardson 1988). With the advent of new technologies that allow prospective parents to know—or even select—the sex of their children long before their births, the process of gender socialization may begin even earlier than in previous generations (Rapp 2000). Anticipating the birth of a male or female child, parents are expected to begin the process of marking the child's sex in a variety of ways, including selecting a name that signifies the baby's gender, preparing a space for the child that will reflect his or her membership in one gender group or the other, and imagining the future

AS NATURE MADE HIM

Some of the most famous arguments for the power of gender socialization have been inspired by misfortune. In a number of reported instances, physicians circumcising male infants have destroyed the boys' penises, and have subsequently recommended raising these children as girls. In the best known case, psychologist John Money reported that a biologically male child was successfully being raised as a girl after such a tragic incident. Although Money reported that the child was "lost to follow-up" during adolescence, researcher John Colapinto wrote a book in the patient's adulthood chronicling his life, which was marked by difficulty around issues of sex, gender, and sexuality. Although the patient was treated as a girl in childhood, s/he chose to transition into masculinity as an adult. Biological essentialists see this case as evidence of the power of biology over society; social scientists who believe that socialization is more powerful than biology argue that the patient's transition into maleness reflects the facts that his initial sex reassignment didn't take place until he was nearly two years old, that he had been socialized as a boy until the accident, and that his family was deeply ambivalent about the sex reassignment and therefore inconsistent in its socialization practices.

of this child in ways that are no doubt shaped by gendered expectations. When the child is born, tradition compels those in attendance to first announce the child's sex—"Congratulations, you have a baby girl"?—and from the moment of that first pronouncement, those considered boys and those deemed girls face continual socialization into masculinity and femininity across the life course. Among Eurocentered white North Americans, "femininity" remains associated with fragility, delicacy, nurturing behaviors, and an emotional orientation toward the world, whereas "masculinity" remains associated with "toughness," assertiveness, and an "action orientation" toward the world.

Agents of Socialization

Sociologists call institutions and individuals acting in the service of imparting the norms, traditions, languages, and lifeways of a given society "agents of socialization." For most people, the first agent of gender socialization is the family. Within the contexts of families, children learn about gender in a variety of ways. Among psychologists, Alfred Bandura's social learning theory of behavioral modeling (1962) serves as a useful conceptualization of the ways children learn to behave by observing others' behaviors. Decades of research on modeling has demonstrated that children learn a variety of behaviors through observation, and are able to pick and choose from among behaviors they've seen in the conduct of others; boy and girl children are able to "act like" the "opposite" sex when asked to do so, even when their typical behavior is consistent with the norms for their own sex. Behaviorists argue that socialization is a function of punishment and reward; in terms of gendered behavior, this would mean that children learn to repeat the behaviors deemed appropriate for their gender because they receive positive reinforcement for these and receive negative reinforcement for cross-gendered behaviors. Sociologists speak in related terms of positive and negative sanctions for particular behaviors playing a significant role in socialization, and also offer social scientists a model of socialization based on Mead and Cooley's work on "the looking glass self." In this model, individuals develop a sense of themselves by observing others' reactions to them, as though the people around them are mirrors reflecting back an image of the individual as intelligent, attractive, interesting, and capable, or as missing these qualities. In terms of gender socialization, the Mead/Cooley model suggests that individuals are constantly receiving messages about how they measure up to the conventional standards for gender, and that, in response to these messages reflected back by observers, individuals develop a core sense of themselves—in the case of gender socialization that sense would be of oneself as masculine or feminine in varying degrees—or as a person who violates conventional norms of gender (see Jary and Jary 1991).

The degree to which an individual can comfortably violate gender norms during the process of socialization varies by sex, class, and culture, among other variables. Girls who violate gender norms by engaging in forms of play considered masculine, rejecting dolls and playing house, for example, are often accepted as tomboys until they enter adolescence, but boys who reject rough play and conventionally masculine pursuits are often goaded for their gender nonconformity (Richardson 1988). Sociologists interpret the difference in the ways gender nonconforming children are treated as reflecting the status differences between men and women in society; for girls to engage in masculine pastimes or presentation of self is for them to assume the traits of the dominant group, if only temporarily, and in this way girls are seen as paying homage to masculine power—and are understood not to be appropriating that power but simply briefly imitating it. On the other hand, boys who refuse to engage in traditional masculine pursuits and opt instead for interests considered feminine are stigmatized because they are relinquishing the symbols of masculine power. As a result, it is less possible for boys to comfortably wear "girls'" clothing or try out girls activities than it is for girls to dress in "boys'" apparel or to play sports considered squarely in boys' domain. Often, social class is related to the degree to which individuals may express gender nonconformity in adulthood, with greater access to financial resources allowing individuals to live outside of gender conventions with fewer negative sanctions, such as limited employment opportunities.

Certainly, family members as primary agents of socialization are in a position to comment on violations of the gender code, but by the time children reach school age, additional agents of socialization begin to exert influence on their sense of gendered identities. Peers provide powerful positive and negative sanctions through their ability to include and exclude others, depending on their assessment of an individual's status, and they have the capacity to teach friends and classmates how to "do gender" in ways considered desirable. More formally, schools provide a powerful socializing influence along the lines of gender. From early on, for example, students are often asked to line up in girls' and boys' lines, to go to girls' and boys' bathrooms (unlike at home), and to participate in sex-segregated play and learning. Educators are often predisposed toward seeing boys and girls as fundamentally different in their learning styles and social needs and may reinforce gender differences by expecting students to perform better in particular academic areas based on their sex. Research on gender nonconforming children indicates that their gender fluidity may be well accepted within their families, only to be the focus of negative attention and intervention when they enter elementary school. Of interest, some research indicates that boys perform better in coeducational environments, but girls perform better in single-sex learning environments. One interpretation of this finding is that in coeducational environments, even the boys who perform worst feel superior to girls in their classes, and girls removed from these environments feel the liberty to perform better when not faced with negative comparisons to boys.

GENDER SOCIALIZATION AND SEXUALITY

In Western societies, there exists a strong connection between assumptions about normative gender presentation and normative heterosexuality. In her famous conceptualization of "compulsory heterosexuality," Adrienne Rich (1980, 1994) explicates the concept that heterosexuality is not simply a set of sexual

ARE MEN AND WOMEN BETTER SUITED FOR PARTICULAR KINDS OF WORK?

Are men and women better suited for particular kinds of work? If so, is this a function of nature or of nurture? In the West, middle class white women in the twentieth century were discouraged by male physicians, educators, fathers, and husbands from engaging in hard physical labor, earning incomes in factories, and engaging in vigorous athletic activity, as a result of ideologies that positioned women as weak and delicate, the "fairer sex." Concurrently, however, working class and poor white and black women routinely undertook challenging physical labor in sweat shops and as domestic servants for the white women who were seen as constitutionally weak because of their femininity. In most other societies across the globe, women have routinely engaged in challenging physical labor—in fields, on farms, in childrearing—and their attractiveness has, in other societies, been associated with physical strength and endurance, as well as intellectual competence and beauty (Matthaei and Amott 1996).

practices but a set of social practices that depend on and continually reproduce the subordination of women. Rich argues that if heterosexuality were the only possibility for human beings, the complex web of laws, institutions, and traditions that compel members of society into heterosexual arrangements would be unnecessary. That is, heterosexuality would not be compulsory through the pressure of juridical structures but simply universal.

Suzanne Pharr (1988) elaborated on the relationship between sexism and heterosexuality in *Homophobia: A Weapon of Sexism*, by arguing that homophobia, the fear and hatred of gays and lesbians, as well as heterosexism, the privileging of heterosexual relationships and people in them, are undergirded by forms of sexism that are directly related to gender. For example, in instances of antigay hate crimes against men, perpetrators often choose victims not because of any express knowledge of their sexual practices or identities, but because their behaviors are somehow in violation of norms for masculinity. The fear of being identified as gay or lesbian, as a result, often inhibits both heterosexual and gay, lesbian, and bisexual people from pushing the limits of normative gender roles. In childhood, boys are at risk of being identified as either "sissies" or "fags" for gender-nonconforming behavior, even before they or their antagonists have a conscious awareness of sexual identities. In adulthood, being perceived as gay or lesbian puts both men and women at risk of harassment and violence, and those perceptions are often based not on sexual information but on gender presentation. Robert Connell (2005) and Michael Kimmel (2005) have both explored this connection as it shapes men's experience in contemporary Western societies. Connell introduced into the literature the concept of "hegemonic masculinity," a way that dominant systems of masculinity establish requirements for male participation in the white, heterosexual, dominant class. Kimmel (2005) has explored the impact of being a sexual outsider on the lives of gay men, even those who are white and wealthy, because they fail to meet the standards of hegemonic masculinity. The process of gender socialization, therefore, is not as simple as compelling individuals to learn the rules for "acting like a girl" or "acting like a boy." Gender socialization is always tied inextricably to socialization around issues of sexual identity and sexual behavior, as well as to class, race, religion, and a host of other factors shaping the social environment that is the social context for any particular individual.

Gender Socialization across the Life Course

Because childhood gender socialization plays such a significant role in our development as children, it can be tempting to assume that gender socialization occurs only in the context of the family and only in the early years of human development. Although the family, an individual's first frame of reference, plays a significant role in gender socialization, it does not completely control the socialization of its members, as nearly every parent eventually discovers. Both formal institutions and informal groups become significant players in the gender socialization of individuals. Schools and classmates exert various forms of influence on individuals' developing sense of gender. Schools that require uniforms, for example, often opt for gender-specific uniforms that allow boys the liberty of wearing pants but require girls to wear skirts and to have more modesty as a result. Peer groups both reinforce gender norms and challenge them; peer groups may pressure individuals into adopting the codes of normative masculinity, femininity, and heterosexuality, or they may offer individuals models of masculinities and femininities that differ from the hegemonic model; for example, "gangsta masculinity" differs from the model of masculinity proffered by the dominant group, as does "baby dyke" femininity.

Gender socialization in adolescence continues to be tied to notions of normative gender, with "good girls" being defined as girls who do not engage in sexual activity and "real boys" being defined as those who do. In her book *Slut! Growing Up Female with a Bad Reputation,* Leora Tannenbaum carefully documents that obvious sexual double standard underwriting these expectations of young men and young women. She also documents how easily a young woman's reputation can be spoiled by rumor and gossip related to her sexuality, no matter the relationship between the woman's actual behavior. In this sense, young women are subject to being controlled by possible definitions of their sexuality. Knowing that a disgruntled date can spread rumors about her behavior, a young woman is put in a no-win situation in which her reputation as a "good girl" or as a slut or "used goods" is dependent not on her sexual behavior but on her management of complex social situations in which she may be expected to trade sexual favors to protect her reputation as a good girl.

The process of gender socialization continues through adolescence, and into the phases of adult life, many experience status as a student, a spouse, a parent, a worker, and a professional. In each of these life experiences, expectations for men and women differ significantly (Richardson 1988). To be a "good husband" carries with it a different set of expectations, pressures, and restrictions than does being "a good wife." Along the lines of professions and occupations, men and women either gravitate into or are pressured toward divergent roles in a largely sex-segregated work force. Although women have entered traditionally male occupations in greater numbers in the last two decades, and some men have taken up occupations that were associated with women in the last half of the twentieth century, it remains the case that the U.S. Congress is strongly male dominated, that men still hold most of the CEO seats of Fortune 500 companies, and that nursing remains a woman-dominated occupation. In earlier generations of feminist theorizing, writers took up the question of whether women were overrepresented in some fields and underrepresented in others as a result of preference or as a result of discrimination. Ultimately, we can see this pattern as a function of both. Women may be attracted to occupations that emphasize skill sets and personality traits cultivated during the process of early gender socialization, which can be seen as a process of discrimination itself, and as being disadvantaged by our society's assignment of less value to those occupations precisely because they emphasize the skills and traits associated with femininity. In most municipalities, for example, childcare workers (mostly women) earn less than sanitation workers (mostly men), even though these occupations require similar levels of education and training.

See also Femininities and Masculinities; Nature versus Nurture; Sex versus Gender.

Further Reading: Bandura, A., *Social Learning through Imitation* (Lincoln: University of Nebraska Press, 1962); Connell, Robert W., *Masculinities: Knowledge, Power, and Social Change* (Berkeley: University of California Press, 2005); Jary, David, and Julia Jary, *The Harper Collins Dictionary of Sociology* (New York: Harper Collins, 1991); Kessler, Suzanne J., and Wendy McKenna, *Gender* (Chicago: University of Chicago Press, 1985); Kimmel, Michael, *Manhood in America: A Cultural History* (Oxford: Oxford University Press, 2005); Matthaei, Julie, and Teresa Amott, *Race, Gender, and Work: A Multicultural Economic History of Women in the United States,* rev. ed. (Boston: South End Press, 1996); Pharr, Suzanne, *Homophobia: A Weapon of Sexism* (Little Rock, AR: Women's Project Publishing, 1988); Rapp, Rayna, "Constructing Amniocentesis: Maternal and Medical Discourses," in *Perspectives on Race and Ethnicity*, ed. Amber Ault, 166–174 (Madison, WI: Coursewise Publishing, 2000,); Rich, Adrienne, "Compulsory Heterosexuality and Lesbian Existence," *Signs* 5, no. 4 (1980): 631–660; Rich, Adrienne, "Compulsory Heterosexuality and Lesbian Existence," in *Blood, Bread, and Poetry* (New York: Norton Paperback, 1994); Richardson, Laurel, *Dynamics of Sex and Gender* (New York: Harper Collins, 1988); Tannenbaum, Leora, *Slut! Growing Up Female With a Bad Reputation* (New York: Harper, 2000).

Amber Ault

GLASS CEILING

Although women have made strides in achieving greater equality with men, one on-going issue is the continuing scarcity of women in leadership roles. The reasons for this imbalance remain contested, but it has been suggested that a "glass ceiling" exists that prevents or reduces the promotions of women beyond a certain point. Critics argue that these gender discrepancies are based on individual preferences and cohort effects rather than on gender biases.

THE PROBLEM

During the past three decades inequality between men and women has declined. The number of women who receive undergraduate degrees now exceeds that of men, and an increasing number of women have advanced degrees. Women's labor force participation has also grown steadily and women's work patterns are now increasingly similar to those of men. Nevertheless, even with these changes, vertical segregation between men and women has not disappeared. The term *vertical segregation*, or *authority gap*, refers to the fact that men are still more likely than women to be in positions of power and authority.

THE METAPHOR OF THE GLASS CEILING

Scholars argue that a glass ceiling exists that prevents or reduces the promotions of women, especially in male-dominated fields where women are in the statistical minority. According to the Federal Glass Ceiling Commission, the glass ceiling is the "unseen, yet unbreachable barrier that keeps minorities and women from rising to the upper rungs of the corporate ladder, regardless of their qualifications or achievements" (1995, 4). The glass ceiling is conceptualized in various ways. Some see it as a literal barrier beyond which women do not advance; others see it as women encountering progressively greater barriers as they move up the hierarchy. The scarcity of female CEOs of major companies is an example of the effect of the glass ceiling.

EXPLAINING THE GLASS CEILING

Although direct discrimination against women is partly responsible for the glass ceiling, discrimination is just one contributing factor. Research has shown that a lack of informal mentoring, sexual harassment, and a failure to comply with equal employment opportunity rules also contribute to the glass ceiling.

THE GLASS ESCALATOR

Although a "glass ceiling" seems to exist that prevents women from obtaining top positions, especially in male-dominated fields, the opposite seems to be true of men in female-dominated fields. Research has found that in fields such as nursing and social work, men may experience a "glass escalator" that pushes them toward positions of greater authority (Williams 1992). This finding undermines the idea that any individual who is a "token," or member of a group in the statistical minority, will experience discrimination.

Mentoring is important to one's chances of reaching the highest positions, yet the majority of successful male workers are reluctant to mentor women. This may be due to worry about gossiping or sexual harassment charges, or possibly because women are often stereotyped as being weak and therefore not good candidates for top positions. Studies have also documented how negative treatment and sexual harassment of women in male-dominated fields may lead them to perform less effectively and discourages their promotion (Kanter 1977; Woodzicki and LaFrance 2005). Furthermore, although there are indications that equal opportunity policies have made direct gender discrimination less acceptable in general, they seem to fail women in higher corporate positions because of their inconsistent enforcement (Charles and Grusky 2004).

CONTROVERSIES SURROUNDING THE GLASS CEILING

Several scholars have argued that labor market discrimination against women exists equally across all levels of employment and therefore conclude that the concept of the glass ceiling is irrelevant. Some proponents of the glass ceiling, however, hypothesis point out that as a result of cumulative effects, this would also logically lead to the smallest percentage of women at the highest levels of the hierarchy. This theoretical position may be part of a broader move in glass ceiling research from focusing only on movement into top positions to now examining upward job mobility in a more general sense (Baxter and Wright 2000).

It also has been argued that gender differences in authority are not the result of a glass ceiling but result from other factors, including cohort effects or differences in job preferences. Although researchers acknowledge that a portion of the difference in authority may be due to cohort effect (where the differences in the levels of skills and experience in previous generations explain the gap), most research has found that vertical discrimination exists at a much greater level than it would if based solely on a cohort effect (Jacobs 1989). The idea that men and women may have different job preferences has received some empirical support, as people's employment aspirations do appear to be partly shaped by what is socially appropriate and feasible given their gender. The idea that differences in job preferences play a significant role in vertical segregation, however, has not been adequately tested, and establishing a clear-cut causal order between preferences and outcomes remains difficult.

CONCLUSION

The glass ceiling hypothesis attempts to describe and explain one form of vertical discrimination. Although there is strong evidence for a gender gap in authority, there has also been research that did not find evidence of a systematic glass ceiling effect (Hultin 2003). Some conflicting results may be due to the variety of ways that researchers conceptualize the glass ceiling. The continuing existence of an authority gap between men and women is a problem for those who are concerned with achieving gender equality, in part because vertical segregation contributes to general power imbalances and the gender wage gap.

See also Comparable Worth; Equal Rights Amendment; Work: Paid versus Unpaid.

Further Reading: Baxter, Janeen, and Erik Olin Wright, "The Glass Ceiling Hypothesis: A Comparative Study of the United States, Sweden, and Australia," *Gender and Society* 14 (2000): 275–294; Charles, Maria, and David Grusky, *Occupational Ghettos: The Worldwide Segregation of Women and Men* (Stanford, CA: Stanford University Press, 2004); Federal Glass Ceiling Commission, *Good for Business: Making Full Use of the Nation's Human Capital* (Washington, DC: U.S. Department of Labor, 1995); Hultin, Mia, "Some Take the Glass Escalator, Some Hit the Glass Ceiling?: Career Consequences of Occupational Sex Segregation," *Work and Occupations* 30, no. 1 (2003): 30–61; Jacobs, Jerry, *Revolving Doors: Sex Segregation and Women's Careers* (Stanford, CA: Stanford University Press, 1989); Kanter, Rosebeth, *Men and Women of the Corporation* (New York: Basic Books, 1977); Williams, Christine, "The Glass Escalator: Hidden Advantages for Men in the 'Female' Professions," *Social Problems* 39 (1992): 253–267; Woodzicka, Julie, and Marianne LaFrance, "The Effects of Subtle Sexual Harassment on Women's Performance in a Job Interview," *Sex Roles: A Journal of Research* 53, nos. 1–2 (2005): 67–78.

Medora Barnes

H

HETEROSEXISM AND HOMOPHOBIA

Heterosexism and homophobia comprise beliefs and actions that negatively influence the lives of gay, lesbian, bisexual, and non-normative heterosexual people. Defenders of the heterosexual norm argue that homosexuality is unnatural and that laws and policies should not be created to protect homosexuals from discrimination. Those who work to eliminate heterosexism argue that privileging heterosexuality as the only sexuality that is normal and right serves to oppress nonheterosexual people.

BACKGROUND

Homophobia is defined as the irrational fear and hatred of gay men and lesbians. It combines the words homosexual and phobia, hence the definition related to panic or fear of people who are sexually attracted to a person of the same biological sex. Many people contend that the word heterosexism is a more accurate concept, as fear or panic is not the defining issue as much as the power and privileging of heterosexual people over gay men, lesbians, and bisexual people. Heterosexism assumes that all people are and should be heterosexual and asserts that heterosexuality is normal, natural, and right. Heterosexism operates similarly to other dimensions of oppression in that one category (heterosexuality) is accorded more power and privilege in society than others (homosexuality, bisexuality, asexuality) and that prejudice is targeted at nonheterosexuals. Heterosexism is accepted by most people because the privilege itself is invisible. Viewed as "the way it is" or "the way it's supposed to be" learning heterosexism seems natural and right.

NORMATIVE HETEROSEXUALITY

Adrienne Rich claims that if heterosexuality were not compulsory, most women would not choose it because of the inequality and subordination of women. Heterosexuality, in her view, is a political institution. This is difficult to dismiss because heterosexist prejudice is seen throughout the institutions of society. Male power and control can be seen in limitations on female freedom and choice; sexual assault, battering, incest, and pimping; male privilege in law; and denial of a full range of female sexuality.

On the cultural level, traditional gender roles of masculinity and femininity, definition of the family, religious views condemning same-sex sexuality as a sin, lesbian-baiting, name calling, and antigay jokes all enforce heterosexism and antigay prejudice. Lack of civil rights protections in employment and housing, in access to the rights of marriage, and in the military policy of "Don't Ask, Don't Tell" (wherein people in the military can be gay but they cannot act on it or talk about it) are institutional level discriminations.

These and other limitations form a constant message that the gay or lesbian person does not deserve the same rights, protections, or access to resources that heterosexuals have available to them. Validation from the culture is absent and key mechanisms for job enhancement, adoption or foster parenting children, or relationship benefits such as joint insurance or access to your partner in a medical emergency are lacking. These messages reinforce that the gay or lesbian person is a second-class citizen. To defenders of the heterosexual norm gaining these rights is seen as "special rights" or rights that are not deserved or warranted because nonheterosexuals should not be viewed on equal footing. Any move in the direction of equal rights or treatment would be endorsing the "gay lifestyle."

HOMOPHOBIA AND SEXISM

Homophobia is intimately related to sexism in that the denigration of the feminine is central to both. According to Suzanne Pharr in her work on homophobia as a weapon of sexism, homophobia works in hand with heterosexism to enforce compulsory heterosexuality and the nuclear family. Political conservatives and religious fundamentalists criticize feminists and homosexuality for undermining the traditional family.

Misogyny, the cultural hatred of women, is expressed through the disempowering and belittling of girls and women and the encouragement of dependence on men. Lesbians are perceived as man-haters and as females who can do without men; therefore they are outside of the natural order. Gay men are viewed as traitors to male privilege and also a threat to male dominance and the natural order. In fact, men who are even slightly effeminate and not necessarily gay are suspect. Heterosexuality and female subordination are usually part of the same belief system for people who believe in the rightness of male dominance.

MATTHEW SHEPARD (1976–1998)

Matthew Shepard, a student at the University of Wyoming, died from his injuries sustained in a beating and robbery after he was tied to a fence in a remote area and left. Aaron McKinney and Russell Henderson targeted Shepard as a gay man for the attack in what became a highly publicized murder and trial. The attackers changed their story three times, including trying the "gay panic defense." Henderson pled guilty and testified against McKinney to avoid the death penalty. He was sentenced to two consecutive life sentences without the possibility of parole in 1999. McKinney went to trial and was convicted of two counts of felony murder. Shepard's parents spoke out against the death penalty so that he had "life in memory of one who no longer lives." McKinney is serving two consecutive life sentences without the possibility of parole.

This murder energized debate about hate crimes and how to respond to them. Candlelight vigils were held all over the country in Shepard's honor. Reverend Fred Phelps picketed Shepard's funeral and trial with antigay signs such as "God Hates Fags" and "Matt Shepard rots in Hell." In 1999, President Clinton tried to have sexual orientation added to federal hate crimes legislation, but the effort failed. The Local Law Enforcement Enhancement Act (LLEEA) to expand federal protection to sexual orientation, gender, gender identity, and disability was introduced into Congress in 2005 but has yet to pass. Matthew Shepard's parents founded the nonprofit Matthew Shepard Foundation and work to increase public visibility around issues of respect and dignity for gay men and lesbians.

LESBIAN-BAITING

An outspoken woman or a woman who does not accept subordinate status may be "lesbian-baited"—called a lesbian whether or not she is one. The purpose of this name calling is to silence her or encourage her to change her behavior. As a result of political backlash to gains won by the Women's Liberation Movement, the label *feminist* in many circles is mistakenly equated with lesbian, and as a consequence many women resist the feminist description. To avoid being called a lesbian some women choose to be reformist and not radical—in other words, to tone down their lives and views. The only reason lesbian-baiting has the power to control women's actions is because it carries a negative connotation. The contemporary phrase, "That's so gay," is another example of a denigrating phrase that is based on homophobia.

BISEXUALITY AND BIPHOBIA

Bisexuality connotes attraction to both women and men. One of the results of heterosexism is a binary sexuality framework of gay/lesbian and straight. There is only a dichotomy, leaving no way to think about a third or in-between category. Therefore people who do not fit into the two categories are excluded from consideration. In this case, people who are bisexual are invisible.

Not only are bisexual people invisible but they are stigmatized. Heterosexuals may stigmatize them because of their same-sex attraction. Gay/lesbian people may stigmatize them because they are not gay in the "right" way, as in not solely gay. To come out as bisexual may mean a loss of gay/lesbian community. Although the community is called lesbian, gay, bisexual, and transgender (LGBT), bisexual is not equally mentioned or validated at events, in legislation, in publications, or in educational outreach efforts.

Internalized heterosexism/homophobia contributes to biphobia because of the pain of oppression as LGB people. Lesbians and gays who negatively stereotype bisexuals or fail to acknowledge them are acting out horizontal hostility. Bisexuals become the "other," which is a common dynamic of oppression, and allows for myths such as bisexuals are not to be trusted, are going through a phase, or are promiscuous. The idea that there is only one way to be gay or lesbian, and hence belong to the gay community, leads to the questioning of bisexual identity.

From a strictly heterosexual perspective, bisexuality is wrong. It may be viewed as sinful, sick, or perverted to be attracted to someone of the same biological sex, even if one is also open to heterosexual relations.

HOMOSEXUALITY, BISEXUALITY, AND PEOPLE OF COLOR COMMUNITIES

For a person of color to come out as LGB is a major risk of loss of community. Many people of color may have to choose between being true to themselves or their family and community. Religious institutions, which are often antigay and heterosexist, play a major role in the social life of communities of color. Bisexual people of color may find themselves estranged from both their communities and the lesbian and gay community. There have always been LGB people of color, although this reality is not publicly embraced. Furthermore, the labels used may not have been *lesbian* and *gay*, but expressions such as womanist or men who have sex with men.

SEXUAL ORIENTATION CONFUSED WITH GENDER IDENTITY

Heterosexism uses homophobia to blame gay men and lesbians for many societal ills. This victim blaming is an essential component of every form of oppression. Not only does power and control apply to the personal categories of sexual orientation where heterosexuality is privileged, but sexual orientation is often confused with gender identity. Sexual orientation refers to the object of a person's romantic or intimate desire. Gender identity is an individual's internal sense of whether that person is male-identified, female-identified, neither, or both. A common mistake is to assume that every transgender person is gay and to confuse a gender issue (related to sense of self) with a sexual orientation (related to desire).

Gender normativity assumes a gender binary of men and women. Like heterosexism, if a person does not fit into the norm, it is seen as unnatural and wrong.

People who are androgynous, masculine women, effeminate men, transgender, or intersex are judged as abnormal. They are outside of societal expectations and may be subject to harm. In fact, many hate crimes that are seen as homophobic are really about gender transgression—people are attacked because they violated a gender norm that the attacker(s) found unacceptable rather than a sexuality norm. For example, an effeminate man may not be gay, but his femininity may anger other men who harm him because they feel his femininity is not manly. In this case, the heterosexual standard incorporates elements of traditional notions of manhood and womanhood that should be adhered to without deviation.

INTERNALIZED HOMOPHOBIA

Young children in elementary schools are exposed to societal homophobia on the playground when the words "faggot," "gay," and "dyke" are used in a derogatory way to tease and humiliate other kids. Boys are especially vulnerable to this form of social control. The antigay climate in schools is well documented in annual reports by the Gay, Lesbian, and Straight Educators Network (GLSEN). Hence, individuals grow up surrounded by homophobia in schools, in the media, in families, in peer groups, in religious sermons, and in legislation throughout the life course. Simultaneously, young people grow up being taught that the only acceptable way to be is heterosexual, and they are surrounded mostly by heterosexual role models. One of the consequences of this pervasive exposure to negative messages for someone who is, in fact, LGB is internalized homophobia—the entrenched belief that it is wrong, perverted, and "less than" to be gay, lesbian, or bisexual.

Many gay and lesbian young people miss school days or quit school entirely before graduation because the classrooms, hallways, and bathrooms are physically and psychologically unsafe places. The suicide rate for young gay people is three times the national rate for teens in general. Low self-esteem, higher rates of alcohol and drug use, and mental health problems are serious problems in the gay and lesbian communities as a result of individuals feeling that they need to be secretive about being gay or lesbian or that they are immoral or sick.

RELIGION AND HOMOSEXUALITY

Much of the opposition to homosexuality comes from religious institutions that interpret their sacred texts as condemning same-sex feelings and behaviors. Some interpretations of the Koran and the Bible are seen as forbidding same-sex acts and label them as sinful. Many religions take political stands against homosexual rights because they feel legal approval would be incompatible with their teachings.

There are, however, welcoming religious and spiritual groups both within and separate from the dominant religions. The Web site of Parents and Friends of Lesbians and Gays lists 24 such accepting groups. Affirmation, the gay and lesbian Mormon group, "believes in the worth of every soul regardless of their sexual or gender orientation," and they try to meet the needs of people who "experience frustration or alienation" as a result of their sexual orientation. DignityUSA supports LGBT people in the Catholic Church and holds the view that any sexuality can be compatible with the teaching of Jesus Christ.

Most of the affirming groups are within mainline religions (Baptist, Jewish, Evangelical, Lutheran, etc.), but a few are specifically LGBT-oriented. The Metropolitan Community Church is specifically a LGBT-affirming church, and Soulforce advocates for freedom from religious and political oppression through nonviolent means.

Some religious groups will perform same-sex commitment ceremonies and some have lesbian and gay clergy. Both of these issues are highly controversial, however, and organized religion stands as one of the most homophobic and heterosexist institutions in U.S. culture.

COMING OUT

Because of the repression and secrecy of being gay or lesbian, many individuals are "closeted"; that is, they do not tell others in their life that they are gay or lesbian. This means they cannot live full and free lives and need to pick and choose to whom and when they reveal their sexual orientation. To come out as gay or lesbian entails taking risks of safety and losing friends, family, and jobs. Coming out is a personal decision with political consequences. It is political because it brings the person into opposition with a power structure that has placed him or her in a subordinate position. Gay or lesbian individuals are saying that they are who they are and should be fully accepted as such.

One strategy of the political movement for gay and lesbian rights is advocating that all gay and lesbian people come out—for one reason, for others to realize how many gay and lesbian people there really are, and for another, to break down stereotypes and myths as others realize gays and lesbians are in every type of group, class, and occupation. Until the risks are diminished, however, this is an understandably difficult act for many to take. For those who believe heterosexuality is the only acceptable sexual orientation and that homosexuality is a choice, coming out is problematic. Sometimes this alters their views and they accept the homosexual person; other times rejection is their option.

PSYCHOLOGICAL TREATMENT

Homosexuality as a mental illness was removed from the American Psychiatric Association's DSM-II in 1973; however, some renegade people are still trying to treat homosexuality as a mental illness. Generally referred to as "reparative therapy" or "conversion therapy," these therapists believe homosexuality is wrong, is a choice, and is caused by environmental factors. These practitioners tend to come out of a religious perspective and usually incorporate prayer and religious worship in the treatment. Scripture reading, group and individual counseling, aversion therapy, and sometimes electroconvulsive shock therapy are other treatments. The majority of critics view this approach as a discredited therapeutic model, most often based on a religious objection to homosexuality, that it can cause serious psychological harm, and that there is no empirical evidence that these treatments work. The American Psychiatric Association opposes reparative therapy.

LEGAL PROTECTIONS AND HATE CRIMES

As of 2003, 24 states had no antidiscrimination laws that included sexual orientation. Eleven states had some protection for public employees. Ten states include sexual orientation in their antidiscrimination legislation. There is no federal level antidiscrimination protection.

Hate crimes, which are on the increase against gay and gender-variant people, are message crimes in that they go beyond the crime against the person who is targeted to send a message to the group that the individual is a member of. For this reason, taking a stand against hate crimes is important to say that it is not acceptable to target this group and that it is a serious offense. Of 46 states with hate crime legislation, only 27 states and the District of Columbia include sexual orientation.

The Local Law Enforcement Enhancement Act (LLEEA), introduced into the House of Representatives and the Senate in May 2005, would add sexual orientation and gender identity to existing hate crimes legislation. The last federal hate crime act was passed in 1968 and does not include sexual orientation, gender, gender identity, or disability. So far, only the House has passed the LLEEA (in September 2005). Opponents of legal protections usually view these as steps to legitimize a sexual orientation they disapprove of. Consequently, although not endorsing discrimination or hate, they do not want to endorse homosexuality by protecting it through legal measures.

ADVANCES IN GAY AND LESBIAN RIGHTS

The gay rights movement for equality, full legal rights, and social acceptance formally dates back to June 27, 1969, when lesbian, gay men, and gender-variant people stood up to police during a raid at the Stonewall Bar in New York City. There has been a flurry of activism since then from gay pride parades and events to countless educational forums and trainings, national coming out days, marches on Washington, the formation of national organization such as the Human Rights Campaign, lobbying for legislation, efforts toward full acceptance of gays serving in the military, advocacy for full marriage rights and benefits, and more. *Lawrence v. Texas* was a milestone for gay and lesbian people when in June, 2003, the Supreme Court struck down existing sodomy laws, reversed its own 1968 *Bowers v. Hardwick,* and affirmed the Constitutional right to privacy.

TIMELINE: NOTEWORTHY EVENTS IN 2005

January: Antigay Christian leader James Dobson denounces Sponge-Bob SquarePants as promoting a prohomosexual agenda.

January: First ruling upholding the Defense of Marriage Act dismisses a lawsuit by two women from Massachusetts trying to have their marriage recognized in Florida.

March: Voters in Topeka, Kansas (home of Fred Phelps) uphold an antidiscrimination ordinance against gays and lesbians in municipal hiring.

April: The Oregon Supreme Court nullifies nearly 3,000 marriage licenses issued in 2004 to same-sex couples.

May: A study published in the *Proceedings of the National Academy of Sciences* adds to biological evidence of sexuality differences based on brain responses to sexual smells.

June: Spain becomes the third country to legalize same-sex marriage, after the Netherlands and Belgium.

July: Canada becomes the fourth country to legalize same-sex marriage.

August: The California Supreme Court says gay couples who raise children are lawful parents and must provide for their children in case of relationship dissolution.

September: Michael Magidson and Jose Merel are found guilty of second-degree murder of transgender teen Gwen Araujo in 2002.

September: Governor Schwarzenegger vetoes the same-sex marriage bill passed by the California state legislature.

October: Connecticut's civil union law goes into effect.

December: *Brokeback Mountain* is released and stirs national discussion about gay relationships.

CONCLUSION

Homophobia and heterosexism hurt everyone by locking people into rigid gender roles and expectations with only one acceptable sexual orientation. People are unable to be their authentic selves and contribute their full potentials to society. Homophobia silences and stigmatizes people because they are different, including nonconforming heterosexuals. Homophobia may never be completely eliminated in society, but the pressure toward a more equal and accepting society continues.

Every step that moves in favor of gay and lesbian rights is seen as part of a "gay agenda" to those who see homosexuality as an unnatural choice. Each legal protection or access, whether an antidiscrimination law or access to two-parent adoption, means a message of societal approval to people who are gay or lesbian. This tension between different views of natural and perverted, inborn and choice, and right and wrong, is closely linked to people's views of morality and of civil rights. Unfortunately, there is no compromise position. As long as there are distinct positions in religion, politics, and ideas of human nature around the issue of sexual orientation, there will be some who apply their perspectives to others about who they can be and how they can behave.

See also Bisexuality; Lesbians and Gays in the Military; Same-Sex Marriage; Sexual Identity and Orientation; Sexual Orientation and the Law.

Further Reading: Blasingame, B. M., "The Roots of Biphobia: Racism and Internalized Homophobia," in *Closer to Home: Bisexuality and Feminism,* ed. E. R. Weise, 47–53 (Seattle: The Seal Press, 1992); Blumenfeld, W., ed., *Homophobia: How We All Pay the Price* (Boston: Beacon Press, 1992); Gay, Lesbian and Straight Educators Network, available at: www.glsen.org; Lorde, A., *Sister Outsider* (Trumansburg, NY: The Crossing Press, 1984); Neisen, J. H., "Heterosexism: Redefining Homophobia for the 1990s," *Journal of Gay and Lesbian Psychotherapy* 1, no. 3 (1990): 21–35; Parents and Friends of Lesbians and Gays, available at: www.pflag.org; Pharr, S., *Homophobia: A Weapon of Sexism* (Inverness, CA: Chardon Press, 1988); Rich, A., "Compulsory Heterosexuality and Lesbian Existence," *Journal of Women in Culture and Society* 5, no. 4 (1980): 631–660; Sears, J. T., and W. L. Williams, *Overcoming Heterosexism and Homophobia: Strategies That Work* (New York: Columbia University Press, 1997).

Lori Girshick

HIV/AIDS

Women are becoming infected with HIV/AIDS at increasing rates, mostly as a result of unprotected heterosexual sex. The risk factors leading to transmission of HIV/AIDS for women are biological, behavioral, social, and economic in nature.

BACKGROUND

HIV/AIDS is a fast-growing epidemic in the United States that has traditionally been associated with certain segments of the population, mostly homosexuals and intravenous drug users, and thus evokes much public debate around the responsibility of society to treat its sufferers. HIV/AIDS lacks boundaries, it

FAST FACTS ON HIV/AIDS

- 78 percent of all HIV/AIDS infections were acquired through heterosexual sex.
- Women account for 64 percent of all heterosexually transmitted infections.
- HIV/AIDS is the fifth leading cause of death for all women, surpassed only by cancer and heart disease.
- HIV/AIDS is the leading cause of death among African American women ages 25–34 years.
- 50 percent of women do not know they are being exposed to HIV/AIDS when engaging in sexual activities.
- 14 percent of men who engage in homosexual sex have unprotected sex with women as well.

Source: CDC 2004, 2006.

impacts I.V. drug users, men who have sex with men, women, adolescents, and older adults. There are two fundamental viewpoints regarding why women are at increased risk of being infected with HIV/AIDS. The social inequality viewpoint contends that women are at increased risk of the disease as a result of their devalued position in society. Conversely, the biological viewpoint believes that the gynecological design of women, coupled with poor behavioral decision making, has substantially contributed to the growing rates of infection among women.

SOCIAL INEQUALITY VIEWPOINT

The social inequality viewpoint contends that the patriarchal system is a leading cause of the increased HIV/AIDS infection rates among women. Economic inequality, gendered violence, racism, ageism, and sexism are regarded as the foundational causes of women's increasing infection rates. Such structural barriers reduce the ability of women to navigate their social and sexual environments. Women of color are especially disadvantaged in terms of infection rates. African American and Hispanic women represent 25 percent of the United States female population, yet account for 81 percent of all female AIDS cases (Prather, Fuller, King, Brown, Moering, Little, and Phillips 2006). Women of color are statistically poorer than white women, and thus have limited access to quality medical care, nutrition, and information about HIV/AIDS prevention.

In addition, the media control women's sexuality by promoting unrealistic expectations in terms of sexual behavior, physical appearance, and sex role expectations. The influences of the media are acted out in intrapersonal relationships between men and women, as evidenced by domestic violence, infidelity, and sexual violence. For African Americans, the media and the hip hop culture greatly influence sex roles and decisions regarding sexual behavior (Thompson-Robinson, Richter, Shegog, Weaver, Trahan, Sellers, and Brown 2005).

Women are more likely to acquire HIV/AIDS through heterosexual sex than injection drug use, blood products, transfusions, and other undetermined modes of exposure combined (CDC 2004). Many women believe that monogamy protects against HIV/AIDS, even when neither partner has been tested before engaging in sexual activity (Thorburn, Harvey, and Ryan 2005). Once in a relationship, whether monogamous or not, women often believe they can trust their partner not to infect them and therefore do not use safer sex practices. All of these factors are combined with a previous history of alcohol abuse, childhood sexual abuse, current domestic abuse, and the use of illicit drugs to increase women's likelihood of infection.

BIOLOGICAL VIEWPOINT

From a biological point of view, there are fundamentally three reasons why women are at increased risk of contracting HIV/AIDS. These include biological factors, behavioral factors, and a revised definition of AIDS by the Centers for Disease Control (CDC).

RISK FACTORS FOR HIV/AIDS UNIQUE TO WOMEN

- Social (e.g., gender inequality)
- Economic (e.g., unequal pay resulting in an inability to afford medical treatment)
- Structural (e.g., racism, ageism)
- Interpersonal (e.g., domestic violence)
- Biological (e.g., gynecology)
- History of sexually transmitted infections

Biologically, HIV/AIDS presents itself differently in women than in men and is mostly presented in terms of gynecological issues, such as recurrent vaginal yeast infections. The disease may also go undetected as a result of concurrent medical conditions in which the symptoms mirror those of HIV/AIDS. Young and older women are especially vulnerable to transmission as the vaginal lining is much thinner than for women of reproductive age, which increases the risk of vaginal tearing during intercourse (Spearman and Bolden 2005). Women also respond to treatment differently than do men. As most of the current treatments have been developed and tested by men, the impact of drug therapy on women is only beginning to come to fruition.

Several behavioral factors contribute to women's increased risk of infection. Women are engaging in nonmonogamous relationships in which safer sex is not practiced and are basing this decision on their partner's physical appearance and attractiveness (Hong, Goldstein, Rotheram-Borus, Wong, Gore-Felton, and the NIMH Healthy Living Trial Group 2006). Women are also more likely to perceive their partners as being HIV-negative than other at-risk populations. Among older women there is a misperception that safer sex practices are not required because there is no risk of contracting sexually transmitted infections (Spearman and Bolden 2005).

In 1993, the Centers for Disease Control (CDC) expanded the definition of AIDS to include gynecological diseases. The impact of this decision was a 250 percent increase in the number of women diagnosed with HIV/AIDS from 1992 to 1993 (Dworkin 2005). Women were now eligible for inclusion in drug trials and studies of disease progression that they were previously excluded from, and gender-specific manifestations of the disease are now designated symptoms. Women, however, are still less likely than men to receive the most effective treatments for the disease as a result of misdiagnosis, lack of adequate medical care, and poverty.

CONCLUSION

The HIV/AIDS infection rates of women will likely continue to increase into the foreseeable future as current prevention methods and treatment options fail to address the underlying issues of the disease. The power imbalance between women and men contributes to the poor access women have to medical care, disease testing, and treatment. Despite these structural barriers, what responsibilities do women have to protect themselves from HIV/AIDS? HIV/AIDS is a largely preventable disease, and although biologically women are at increased risk of infection, that disadvantage can be mitigated by behavioral change. Women must shift from passive sexual receivers to active sexual participants to decrease their risk of disease.

See also Medicine and Medicalization: Views on Women's Bodies; Sexual Identity and Orientation.

Further Reading: Aidala, Angela A., Gunjeong Lee, and Samantha Garbers, "Sexual Behaviors and Sexual Risk in a Prospective Cohort of HIV-Positive Men and Women in New York City, 1994–2002: Implications for Prevention," *AIDS Education and Prevention* 18, no. 1 (2006): 12–32; Centers for Disease Control, 2004, available at: www.cdc.gov/hiv/topics/women/index.htm; Dworkin, Shari L., "Who Is Epidemiologically Fathomable in the HIV/AIDS Epidemic? Gender, Sexuality, and Inter-Sectionality in Public Health," *Culture, History and Sexuality* 7, no. 6 (2005): 615–623; Hong, Daniel S., Rise B. Goldstein, Mary Jane Rotheram-Borus, F. Lennie Wong, Cheryl Gore-Felton, and the NIMH Healthy Living Trial Group, "Perceived Partner Serostatus, Attribution of Responsibility for Prevention of HIV Transmission, and Sexual Risk Behavior with 'Main' Partner among Adults Living with HIV," *AIDS Education and Prevention* 18, no. 2 (2006): 150–162; Prather, Cynthia, Taleria R. Fuller, Winifred King, Mari Brown, Marilyn Moering, Stacey Little, and Keydra Phillips, "Diffusing an HIV Prevention Intervention for African American Women: Integrating Afrocentric Components into the SISTA Diffusion Strategy," *AIDS Education and Prevention* 18, Suppl. A (2006): 149–160; Spearman, Marilyn S., and Jacquelyn A. Bolden, "Identification of Factors That Reduce Rates of Detection of HIV/AIDS among Women 50 Years and Older," *Journal of African American Studies* 9, no. 2 (2005): 51–59; Thompson-Robinson, Melva V., Donna L. Richter, Marya L. Shegog, Mike Weaver, Leah Trahan, Denethia B. Sellers, and Vanisha L. Brown, "Perceptions of Partner Risk and Influence on Sexual Decision-Making for HIV Prevention among Students at Historically Black Colleges," *Journal of African American Studies* 9, no. 2 (2005): 16–28; Thorburn, S., S. M. Harvey, and E. A. Ryan, "HIV Prevention Heuristics and Condom Use among African-Americans at Risk for HIV," *AIDS Care* 17, no. 3 (2005): 335–344.

Laura J. Zilney

HOMOSEXUAL REPARATIVE THERAPY

As part of the belief that homosexuality is caused by environmental factors, some mental health professionals and Christian leaders have attempted to cure homosexuality and/or homosexual behaviors through reparative therapy, but the success and ethics of such procedures are highly controversial.

BACKGROUND

Homosexual reparative therapies are a group of experimental techniques that attempt to change a person's sexual orientation or sexual behaviors from homosexual to heterosexual. Such therapies range from electroshock therapy and orgasmic reconditioning to self-talk and reframing thoughts (Christianson 2005). Professional organizations such as the American Psychological Association, American Psychiatric Association, National Association of Social Workers, U.S. Office of the Surgeon General, and American Psychoanalytic Association condemn such procedures as ineffective and/or unsafe. Throughout the 1970s and 1980s, these major health associations each took the formal position that homosexuality is not an illness or pathology. Some health professionals and conservative Christian organizations, however, advocate for reparative therapies as safe and effective cures for homosexual orientation and/or behavior. Reparative therapy thus emerges as both a mental health and religious issue.

MENTAL HEALTH

Beginning in the early 1990s, some mental health professionals countered the official positions of the major professional organizations and insisted that homosexuality was a mental disorder that could and should be changed. One of the most famous of these thinkers is Joseph Nicolosi, who, along with Charles Socarides and Benjamin Kaufman, founded the National Association for Research and Therapy of Homosexuality (NARTH) in 1992. NARTH offers a variety of services that are designed to offer an alternative perspective to that of the other professional organizations, but despite the commitment to scientific inquiry, Nicolosi is closely affiliated with religious organizations including Dr. James Dobson's Focus on the Family. Nicolosi and his colleagues at NARTH believe that homosexuality is largely linked with improper gender identification (www.narth.com). Nicolosi has written several books about his treatments that are primarily targeted toward homosexual men, and he argues that homosexuality is primarily caused by psychological factors including childhood sexual abuse. Nicolosi is also responsible for making the distinction between "homosexuals," or those who are "same-sex attracted," and "gays," or those who accept and act on their attractions.

Another famous thinker in the reparative therapies debate is Robert Spitzer, a psychiatric researcher from Columbia University. His controversial 2001 study argued that at least 200 people had changed their orientation from homosexual to heterosexual. Spitzer sought to challenge the generally held position that there is no evidence that homosexuals can change their orientation. His hypothesis was that reparative therapy could lead those with "predominately homosexual" orientation to change to "predominately heterosexual" orientation. His study, which involved interviews of 143 males and 57 females who had indicated change for five or more years, revealed that some people do in fact change their sexual orientation. Most of Spitzer's participants were Christian and 93 percent of them indicated that religion was extremely important in their lives (Spitzer 2003). This fact and methodological and sampling issues have led to scathing criticisms of Spitzer's study by other professionals. Jack Drescher and Kenneth Zuckerman's 2006 edited book, *Ex-Gay Research* critiques the Spitzer study by locating it in a series of political and cultural dynamics that challenge the veracity of the research. Nonetheless, Spitzer's study is a significant event for both proponents and opponents of reparative therapies.

DID YOU KNOW?

Gary Cooper and Michael Bussee were among the many founders of "ex-gay" organization, Exodus International in 1976. While working for an organization called "EXIT" (Ex-gay Intervention Team), they helped organize a weekend meeting of several ex-gay groups that would soon become Exodus. However, the two fell in love, left their wives, and were united in a commitment ceremony at a Metropolitan Community Church in 1982. In the 1992 documentary *One Nation Under God*, Bussee and Cooper critique ex-gay movements, particularly Exodus as fraudulent, arguing that ex-gay movements lead to self-hatred. Sadly, Cooper died in 1989 of AIDS-related complications.

EX-GAY MINISTRIES

Although many of the mental health practitioners who advocate reparative therapy are affiliated with religious organizations, ex-gay ministries function without turning to science to support their claims. Rather, ex-gay ministries premise their work on the idea that homosexuality is a sin and people need to leave the "lifestyle" to be right with God. The first ex-gay ministry, "Love in Action," started in San Francisco in 1973 (Christianson 2005). Exodus International, the largest network of ex-gay organizations, began in 1976. In 2004, the name changed to the Exodus Global Alliance. Although this outreach ministry still seeks to provide "freedom from homosexuality" through the power of Jesus Christ, the name change indicates its desire to focus on locations other than the United States and Europe (www.exodusglobalalliance.org). Like many ex-gay organizations, Exodus claims a high success rate, although the methods for collecting the data are often subject to criticism by professional organizations. Adding to the critique, Exodus and many other ex-gay organizations are often plagued with accusations that their members and leaders engage in homosexual behavior. This was made most famous with the case of John and Anne Paulk, two ex-gays who married and were the poster children for the ex-gay movement. In 2000, photographs were released of John Paulk at a gay bar in Washington D.C., causing rifts throughout the Christian right, particularly Exodus, where Paulk was chair of the board of directors. Controversial or not, ex-gay ministries continue to thrive, and prominent public religious leaders such as D. James Kennedy, the late Jerry Falwell, Pat Robertson, and James Dobson all advocate against homosexuality and for reparative therapy. It is interesting that only the Roman Catholic organization, Courage, recommends celibacy for homosexuals as opposed to changing their orientation.

CONCLUSION

Despite the controversy over the validity of reparative therapies, because of conservative religious positions on homosexuality, these practices are not going anywhere. Adding to the mix are a growing number of ex-ex-gays that have come out to tell their stories of journeying from gay to straight to gay again. These individuals who now denounce reparative therapy were once among its biggest advocates. One only wonders when the ex-ex-ex-gay movements will begin to emerge.

See also Female Sexuality and Dysfunction; Heterosexism and Homophobia; Sexual Identity and Orientation.

Further Reading: Bright, Chuck, "Deconstructing Reparative Therapy: An Examination of the Processes Involved When Attempting to Change Sexual Orientation," *Clinical Social Work Journal* 32, no. 4 (2004): 471–481; Christianson, Alice, "A Re-emergence of Reparative Therapy," *Contemporary Sexuality* 39, no. 10 (2005): 8–17; Drescher, Jack, and Kenneth Zuckerman, eds., *Ex-gay Research: Analyzing the Spitzer Study and its Relation to Religion, Politics, and Culture* (Binghampton, NY: Harrington Park Press, 2006); Erzen, Tanya, *Straight to Jesus: Sexual and Christian Conversions in the Ex-gay Movement* (Berkeley: University of California Press, 2006); Exodus Global Alliance, 2006, available at: http://www.exodusglobalalliance.org/; Malony, H. Newton, "Pastoral Counseling and Sexual Identity," *Journal of Psychology and Christianity* 24, no. 4 (2005): 361–367; National Association for Research and Therapy of Homosexuality, 2006, available at: http://www.narth.com/; Nicolosi, Joseph, "A Developmental Model for Effective Treatment of Male Homosexuality: Implications for Pastoral Counseling," *American Journal of Pastoral Counseling* 3, nos. 3–4 (2001): 87; Nicolosi, Joseph, *Reparative Therapy of Male Homosexuality: A New Clinical Approach* (Lanham, MD: J. Aronson Press, 1991); Robinson, B. A., "Reparative and Similar Therapies: Studies of their Effectiveness and Safety," Ontario Consultants on Religious Tolerance, May 2006, available at: http://www.religioustolerance.org/hom_exst.htm; Spitzer, Robert L., "Can Some Gay Men and Lesbians Change their Sexual Orientation? 200 Participants Reporting a Change from Homosexual to Heterosexual Orientation," *Archives of Sexual Behavior* 32, no. 5 (2003): 403–417; Sullivan, Andrew, "They've Changed, So They Say," *New York Times*, July 26, 1998, 15.

Karma R. Chávez

HUMAN RIGHTS: INTERNATIONAL LAWS AND POLICIES

International women's human rights law demands that the unequal status of women be addressed as a violation of their rights and as a breach of the obligations of governments to guarantee equal rights to all. Controversies surrounding women's human rights stem from divergent views on the role of tradition and culture in shaping gender relations, debates concerning what constitutes a human rights violation, and tensions concerning whether rights frameworks should be defined in universal or culturally relative terms.

BACKGROUND

International human rights standards and procedures have historically been perceived as gender neutral. This neutrality has often amounted in practice to the disregard of women's specific oppression and lack of rights. What women have learned through time is that their needs, interests, and rights are neither automatically recognized nor ensured unless they speak out and fight for them. This struggle has not come without a price, however. The international women's human rights movement has achieved a great many successes for women locally and globally, but there are still a wide-ranging number of debates within the movement, as well as from outside it. Women still face explicitly discriminatory laws and practices. Opportunities to enjoy their rights and freedoms are often also hindered by implicit societal, cultural, and religious norms that discriminate against women. Debates on how to define and best achieve international women's human rights are also fraught with complexity. The liberal nature of human rights and its inability to conceive of private domain issues as violations of these rights, the universality of all women's oppression, and the differences of various cultures' relationship to women dominate the current arguments about women's human rights. Although international women's human rights provide a framework for women's struggle against oppression, women still face wide-ranging challenges.

HISTORY OF INTERNATIONAL WOMEN'S HUMAN RIGHTS

The history of international women's human rights goes back long before the creation of the United Nations (UN). Recent feminist scholarship credits the beginning of international women's human rights to fifteenth-century *Le Livre de la Cite des Dames* (*The Book of the City of Ladies*) by Christine de Pizan who argued for women to be educated, to be able to live and work independently, to participate in public life, and to be masters of their own fate (Fraser 2006, 7–8). Mary Wollstonecraft's *Vindication of the Rights of Women*, published in 1792 in response to the promulgation of the natural rights of man theory, is also considered a key text in the movement. Networks of women activists also organized across borders in the antislavery struggle and women's suffrage movement long before the term *women's human rights* gained usage. The creation of global institutions such as the UN, however, certainly strengthened the international women's human rights movement.

After the horrors of World War II, the victors of the war, the Allied Powers, set out to create a system to prevent war and intervene in conflict. The UN Charter was signed in San Francisco in 1945, which created a system for global governance. During the Charter's creation, civic and religious groups in many countries were prompted to call for the inclusion of an international bill of rights. The United Nations Declaration of Human Rights adopted in 1948 and its two covenants, the International Covenant on Civil and Political Rights (ICCPR) and International Covenant on Economic, Social, and Cultural Rights (ECOSOC), are collectively called the international bill of rights.

In many ways, the work of international women's organizations came to fruition with the establishment of the UN. Led by South American delegates, most notably women from Brazil, Mexico, and Dominican Republic, and with support from Indian and North American nongovernmental organizations (NGOs), the linkage between women's rights and human rights was effectively made in the UN Charter in its introduction and four separate articles (Fraser 2006, 36). Women also fought for a separate commission to deal specifically with women's issues, the Commission on the Status of Women (CSW). Established in 1946, the CSW is still in existence today.

Human rights in general and women's human rights more specifically has gained momentum in the twentieth century. The 1975 International Women's Year Conference brought 5,000 representatives to Mexico City. Developing country representatives suggested that development would bring equality, but women from industrialized countries cited numerous areas of discrimination in their countries. Despite many of the groups' differences, in the end, contentious women came together around similar interests and showed the power of the international women's human rights movement. Women's international human rights conferences have provided a unifying forum for women around the world. They have also been places where debates in the movement have been voiced the loudest. From varying ways to improve the lives of women, to the debate on the liberal nature of human rights and its inability to include private sphere issues into human rights frameworks, to cultural relativist arguments, these issues have played center stage at the numerous women's human rights conferences over the years.

During the World Conference on Human Rights in Vienna in 1993, every government at the conference discussed the issue of violence against women and added support to international women's human rights. The 1995 UN World Conference on Women affirmed the conclusion of the Vienna Conference and continued to strengthen women's human rights. A list of celebrated successes in women's human rights include the 1994 Cairo Conference on Population and Development, with its prioritization of women's autonomy and health; the drafting of the Convention on the Declaration on the Elimination of Violence Against Women (CEDAW) and the international recognition of violence against women as a serious human rights issue; the negotiation of the protocol to the Women's

TIMELINE OF INTERNATIONAL HUMAN RIGHTS AND WOMEN'S RIGHTS

1945: United Nations Charter

1946: Commission on the Status of Women

1948: United Nations Declaration of Human Rights

1966: International Covenant on Civil and Political Rights (ICCPR)

1966: International Covenant on Economic, Social, and Cultural Rights (ECOSOC)

1975: First World Conference on Women, Mexico

1979: Convention on the Elimination of All Forms of Discrimination Against Women (CEDAW)

1993: Vienna Conference on Human Rights/Vienna Declaration and Program of Action

1994: United Nations International Conference on Population and Development (ICPD), Cairo Conference

1995: Fourth World Conference on Women, Beijing/ Beijing Declaration and Platform for Action

2000: Beijing + 5: Gender, Equality, Development, and Peace for the Twenty-first Century

Convention to allow individual complaints; the recognition of the need for gender analyses throughout the UN; the prosecution of rape as a war crime at the ad hoc tribunals in Rwanda and Yugoslavia; the inclusion of gender analyses and women's human rights frameworks within multiple international agreements; the increased participation of feminist and women's NGOs at all levels of UN activity; and the increased representation of women in senior positions at the UN (Buss and Manji 2005, 3–4).

INTERNATIONAL WOMEN'S HUMAN RIGHTS TOOLS

Even though the international system lacks a central law-making body to enact legislation, treaties are the primary way in which international law is made. These treaties create rights and obligations for the signed parties. The most powerful treaty related to women was drafted by the CSW and obligates states to eradicate discrimination against women. This text adopted by the General Assembly of the UN in 1979 was called the Convention on the Elimination of All Forms of Discrimination Against Women (CEDAW). The convention entered into force in 1981, faster than any other general human rights treaty. As of March 2006, 182 states were party to it (Dunoff, Ratner, and Wippman 2006, 505). In 1999, an additional protocol was added to CEDAW that allows individual women, or groups of women to bring claims of violations of rights protected under the Convention to the Committee and includes an inquiry procedure enabling the committee to initiate inquiries into situations of grave or systematic violations of women's rights.

Even though the international system is superseded by the autonomy of individual countries, reporting measures used under CEDAW can be strongly critical of a state or express the view that the state has not discharged its obligations under the treaty. Further reporting can put pressure on a government, particularly if the proceedings receive international or national publicity (Cook 1994, 23).

The UN system also has several agencies dedicated exclusively to issues related to international women's human rights. Besides the CSW, there are also six treaty-monitoring bodies within the UN, one of which is the Committee on the Elimination on the Discrimination Against Women. At its meetings held twice annually, the committee reviews national reports submitted by the country's parties within one year of ratification or accession to CEDAW, and every four years thereafter. They also provide recommendations to countries on the treatment of women. The International Research and Training Institute for the Advancement of Women (INSTRAW), which writes research and reports on the state of women in the world, is one of the five research and training institutes in the UN. Under the United Nations Development Program, the UN Development Fund for Women (UNIFEM) provides financial and technical assistance to innovative programs and strategies to foster women's empowerment and gender equality.

Several NGOs work at both the local and global level advocating for women's human rights. Some of the more well-known and highly funded organizations that have separate international women's human rights divisions include Human Rights Watch and Amnesty International. There are also international NGOs that work exclusively for international women's human rights including Sisterhood is Global and MADRE.

International mechanisms to promote international women's human rights are secondary to the sovereign law of individual countries. A general rule in international law is that domestic relief has to be exhausted before international law or regional tribunals will engage an issue of international concern, and therefore national protection of women's human rights is usually the first line of defense for women. Unfortunately, woman often do not seek remedies because they are unaware of their entitlements under domestic or international law. Making such information accessible is a major project in the empowerment of women to advance and assert their rights and freedoms as human beings. There are also major controversies on how best to provide this information and what exactly this information entails. The usefulness of liberal rights to women facing issues within the domestic sphere, where the human rights framework does not exist, is seen as useless. To the point that it can be deployed, information on human rights needs to be contextualized in relation to specific women's needs. This contextualization leads to another controversy related to the universalism of women's human rights and the cultural relativist argument that not only all women are different but that culture must be taken into account.

Regardless of whether appropriate information is available to women, equal rights for women are still denied. Women may be discriminated against simply for being female. The most pervasive violations of females are manifestations of violence against women in all their forms, from wife battery, incest, and rape, to dowry deaths and female sexual slavery (Bunch 2006, 57). Sometimes such rights are recognized by law but ignored in practices, and sometimes they are not recognized at all. Often women's rights are openly denied and despite the value of CEDAW, it is still marginalized by the international community through lack of support, country-specific reservations to specific parts of the text, and underfunding.

SUPPORTERS AND OPPONENTS OF A WOMEN'S HUMAN RIGHTS FRAMEWORK

Despite the problems associated with international women's rights, the movement has achieved many successes. Because women in most societies are starting from such an unequal position, even conducting discourse in the language of rights provides an invaluable tool to develop political and social grievances that are recognized by countries; however, there are several critiques of the system by feminists themselves. Many feminists wonder if legal rights can really offer anything to women. Women's disadvantages are often based on structural injustice and winning a case in court will not change this (Cook 1994, 4).

A common feminist critique of law is often associated with "liberal" feminism. It makes synonymous sexual equality and equal treatment. Disregarding any belief that the law should tolerate or recognize differences between women and men, liberalism seeks a solution in blindness toward difference. The strategy of liberal feminists is to require the law to fulfill liberal claims for its objectivity and principled basis. Liberal feminists have worked for reform of law, dismantling legal barriers to women being treated like men in the public sphere (Charlesworth 1994, 63). The assumption is that the disadvantages suffered by women can be compartmentalized and redressed by a simple requirement of equal treatment (Charlesworth 1994, 63).

This liberal "version" of law relies on the public/private dichotomy. The private sector is outside the realm of legal and political order and therefore regulation is seen as inappropriate. For example, domestic violence is invisible and unregulated. According to some feminists, women lead different lives than men; thus nondiscrimination on the basis of sex does not eradicate gender inequalities. This is based on the way in which this liberal international human rights law is interpreted and implemented. Forms of oppression that do not fit comfortably within the law are rarely recognized in international understandings. Oppression includes issues related directly to women such as the right to marriage, procreation, labor, property ownership, sexuality, and other manifestations of unequal citizenship that are routinely viewed as private, nongovernmental, and reflective of cultural differences (Lockwood 2006, viii). There has been historical resistance to viewing human rights as gendered. Women's rights such as the right to safety from domestic violence and rape have not been seen as human rights because a liberal framework only perceives of one type of human and one type of accountable actor. This leads to another problem associated with the liberal nature of international law: it requires governments to respect, ensure, and protect women's international human rights. International law makes a country accountable for violations of international treaty obligations that are attributable solely to the state. This means that countries are the only ones that can commit a human rights violation. Nonstate actors or private individuals are not held accountable under human rights law. Many violations to women's freedom are perpetrated in the private sphere by nonstate actors; thus liberal women's human rights frameworks are ineffective in dealing with these problems.

Feminists also question the legitimacy of a common oppression of women around the world. Accepting that men and women are different, some feminist also wonder if women around the world really have anything in common. A conceptual problem for all feminist analysis is that of essentialism, which assumes that all women have similar attributes and experiences and ignores the impact of other variables such as race, class, wealth, and sexuality on the position of women (Charlesworth 1994, 62). International law is by definition concerned with transnational standards, applicable in a vast range of circumstances, and therefore the notion of a common oppression is quite problematic for international women's rights. The potential for even discussing women's lives in an international system is questioned when issues of essentialism are raised. Women's lives vary depending on time, place, and context, and the possibility of common oppression for women worldwide becomes questionable.

CULTURAL RELATIVISM VERSUS UNIVERSALISM

Another debate in the international women's human rights system is that of universalism versus cultural relativism. Universalists see human rights as sprouting from a common system of values and humanity; therefore these rights can apply equally to all. According to supporters of universalism, human rights have not really been part of any region's history, but human rights are still valuable and globally applicable. There is a similarity in many values around the world that societies strive to protect. These values strongly resemble those of human rights, and this fundamental unity suggests an assumed universality that should not be broached.

Relativists instead argue that human rights are in no way universal, and these norms must be adapted to reflect wide variations in culture, beliefs, and economic and political circumstances. In 1947, the Executive Board of the American Anthropological Association sent a long memorandum to the UN Human Rights Commission stating that "standards are relative to the culture from which they derive." The memorandum noted further that "what is held to be a human right in one society may be regarded as anti-social by another people, or by the same people in different periods of their history" (Dunoff, Ratner, and Wippman 2006, 515).

Cultural relativists argue that Western affirmation of the universality of international human rights norms seriously debases other cultures. Female genital mutilation is one common example of the universal versus cultural relativist debate. Cultural relativists argue that women perform the surgery on other women as a right of passage associated with a culturally acceptable practice. Universalists see this as a form of women's oppression through controlling her sexuality and harming her bodily integrity. Cultural relativists also see human rights as a way to justify war and expand Western neoliberal economic policies. The insincere claim that Operation Enduring Freedom was landed, in part, to free Afghani women is one of many examples cultural relativists use in their argument against expanding women's human rights. Relativists desire an alternative system of human rights to achieve social justice and protection of humanity that is apart from current understandings of international human rights. Counter to cultural relativist claims, feminists highlight the use of cultural claims, particularly when they regard the freedom of women.

CONCLUSION

International women's human rights have changed many people's lives for the better. Women's legal, economic, and social status around the globe, however, is still inferior to that of men. The women's international human rights agenda ranging from standard law setting to policy and including actions at all levels from global to local, tends to fall between the cracks because of the lack of precedence given it by those in positions of power. Feminist continue to debate among themselves the best ways to improve the lives of women around the world, as well as how to face challenges from outright rejection of women's equality and the desire for women around the world to be treated differently depending on culture and context. These debates range from the ineffectiveness of liberal rights to the differences of women around the world and the need for culturally relevant context. International women's human rights are nothing new, but the challenges facing women are constant. Activists in international women's human rights will continue the struggle by seeking new and innovative ways to address the issue of women's freedom and equality.

See also Gender and Globalization: Trends and Debates; Gender and International Development; Terrorism and National Security; Third World and Women of Color Feminisms.

Further Reading: Bunch, Charlotte, "Women's Rights as Human Rights: Toward a Revision of Human Rights," in *Women's Rights: A Human Rights Quarterly Reader,* ed. Bert Lockwood (Baltimore: Johns Hopkins University Press, 2006); Buss, Doris, and Ambreena Manji, eds., *International Law: Modern Feminist Approaches* (Portland, OR: Hart Publishing, 2005); Charlesworth, Hilary, "What Are Women's International Human Rights?" in *Human Rights of Women: National and International Perspectives,* ed. Rebecca Cook (Philadelphia: University of Pennsylvania Press, 1994); Cook, Rebecca J., ed., *Human Rights of Women: National and International Perspectives* (Philadelphia: University of Pennsylvania Press, 1994); Dunoff, Jeffrey L., Steven R. Ratner, and David Wippman, *International Law: Norms, Actors, Process* (New York: Aspen Publishers, 2006); Fraser, Arvonne J., "Becoming Human: The Origins and Development of Women's Human Rights," in *Women's Rights: A Human Rights Quarterly Reader,* ed. Bert Lockwood (Baltimore: Johns Hopkins University Press, 2006); *Harvard Human Rights Journal,* available at: http://www.law.harvard.edu/students/orgs/hrj/; Hessford, Wendy S., and Wendy Kozol, eds., *Just Advocacy? Women's Human Rights, Transnational Feminism, and the Politics of Representation* (New Brunswick, NJ: Rutgers University Press, 2005); *Human Rights Quarterly,* available at: http://muse.jhu.edu/journals/human_rights_quarterly/; Kerr, Joanna, ed., *Ours by Right Women's Rights As Human Rights* (London: Zed Books, 1993); Lauren, Paul Gordon, *The Evolution of International Human Rights: Visions Seen*, 2nd ed. (Philadelphia: The University of Pennsylvania Press, 2003); Lockwood, Bert B., ed., *Women's Rights: A Human Rights Quarterly Reader* (Baltimore: The Johns Hopkins University Press, 2006); Merry, Sally Engle, *Human Rights and Gender Violence: Translating International Law into Local Justice* (Chicago: University of Chicago Press, 2006); Peters, Julie Stone, and Andrea Wolper, ed., *Women's Rights Human Rights: International Feminist Perspectives* (New York: Routledge, 1995); Seager, Joni, *The Penguin Atlas of Women in the World* (New York: Penguin Books, 2003).

Marjon Kamrani

I

IMMIGRATION: LAWS AND POLICIES CONCERNING ENTRY INTO THE UNITED STATES

Historically, immigration laws and policies concerning entry into the United States for both men and women often have resulted in adverse consequences for female immigrants. Controversies surrounding women's immigration concern historical biases about women's work and sexuality, the cultural emphasis on men as breadwinners, and racial biases toward specific groups seeking U.S. citizenship.

BACKGROUND

To understand how immigration laws and policy affect women, it is vital to question how these policies serve state interests. Broadly put, immigration laws place regulations on who can and cannot be a citizen of any nation-state. Citizenship refers to a legal and political position as active participant in a state. As Dobrowolsky and Tastsoglou write, "Migrants are prospective citizens in the legal as well as broader socio-economic and cultural sense. How a country deals with (im)migrant incorporation (and citizenship) has a great deal to do with the country's institutional and organizational arrangements for membership in its polity" (2006, 22–23). Immigration laws and policy then serve as a way of understanding how certain groups and people are accepted and fit within that country. Although U.S. borders remained relatively open well into the late 1800s, a series of legislation began to be passed toward the end of that decade to determining who could participate in the nation. In the 1920s, the legislation shifted to use racial categories and quotas as the primary mode of regulating who could participate. The goal here was to maintain a European white heritage within the citizenry. In the 1960s, legislation was revamped again in favor an economic logic, where immigrants seen as giving the most back to society were favored. Throughout these shifts, immigration laws have primarily privileged male immigration because men are most likely to have documentation of citizenship elsewhere, as well as because men throughout the world have been recognized as economically independent. As will be clear from the following brief historical review, female immigrants are disenfranchised in this system because of historical constructions of women's work and sexuality.

From the 1800s through the 1950s, foreign-born men gained entrance to the United States in greater numbers than foreign-born women. Although there are perhaps social and cultural explanations for this phenomenon, many scholars point to laws and policies of the day to explain the disparity. The 1875 Page Laws established the first formal regulation of the U.S. population through controlling the entrance of women into the United States. This law limited the immigration of unmarried Chinese women, deeming them likely prostitutes because of their marriage status (Moloney 2006). A few years later in 1882, Congress passed the Chinese Exclusion Act and the Immigration Act. The Chinese Exclusion Act formally recognized Chinese people as ineligible for naturalization on the grounds of race. This is perhaps the first legal mention of race as an evaluative standard in the U.S. immigration system.

More important, the Immigration Act enforced the deportation of immigrants who were seen as possible future dependents on the state, formally known as the likely to become a public charge (LPC). The impact of the LPC provisions unfairly affected women, in particular women who did not immigrate within a formally recognized family structure. This meant that unmarried women, throughout this period were highly targeted for deportation, not because they were practicing unlawful acts, but rather because they were marked as possible public dependents. Women who immigrated within a recognized family structure (meaning with a father or husband) were seen as having access to economic productivity via their male kin, whereas women immigrating outside of this structure were recognized as having less access themselves to economic productivity.

In 1885, derivative citizenship was introduced into law. This meant that foreign women (if racially eligible) took the nationality of their U.S. American husbands, instead of being able to naturalize on their own as men could. The breadth of this law expanded in 1907 under the Expatriation Act. Under this act, not only did all non-U.S–born women take the citizenship of their husbands, but U.S.-born women were included in the derivative citizenship laws. After 1907, a U.S.-born woman could lose her U.S. citizenship if she married a non-U.S. citizen (Nicolosi 2001). This law formally instituted citizenship as a masculine institution, as women could be politically recognized only through their father's or husband's citizenship. Moreover, it redefined women as members of their husband's race. The effect of this law was to deter women from marrying non-U.S. men. Because the majority of immigrants at this time were

MAID IN AMERICA

In 2005, the production company *Women Make Movies* released a compelling film about migration, women, and labor titled *Maid in America*. The film focuses on the lives of three Latina women who are domestic workers in the Los Angeles metropolitan area. In focusing on these three women's lives, audiences see the often harsh realities of domestic work in the United States, including the devaluation and abuse that women doing this work often experience. To combat this treatment, we see women in the documentary create grassroots labor collectives to ensure the protection of their rights as workers in the United States. In the words of the production company, "These women's stories vividly reveal how immigrants are redefining their roles, and underscores the vital role they play in many American households" (http://www.wmm.com/filmcatalog/pages/c664.shtml). For more interesting films concerning women and immigration, please see Women Make Movies productions (www.wmm.com).

men, the law also served as a deterrent to immigration, for immigrant men could no longer marry U.S. women and become U.S. citizens. Women who did marry non-U.S. citizens could regain citizenship only if their husbands were from Europe or Africa and (1) naturalized themselves, (2) died, or (3) divorced. These derivative laws would remain intact until the 1922 Cable Act, although the racial distinctions set forth in these laws remained long after the dismantling (Nicolosi 2001).

A few years later, the Johnson-Reed Immigration Act of 1924 set forth the first restrictive immigration laws in the United States. This act established numerical limits on who could immigrate to the United States and consequently created a global and national racial hierarchy for immigrants. Thus women married to those racially ineligible individuals became themselves ineligible for immigration, not even able to return to the United States if they left (Nicolosi 2001). Finally in 1934, women's citizenship was disconnected from the institution of marriage, allowing for the possibility of women's independent citizenship.

This history reveals the longstanding and contested connections between immigration and citizenship laws, gender, race, and economics in the United States. Although U.S. women gained suffrage in 1920, their citizenship was still derivatively determined though the marriage institution. This set in place a contested relation between marriage and citizenship that is still present in the logics of who can/should be a U.S. political subject. Moreover, these early laws established a relationship between nonmarried women and economic dependency that is present in the ways immigrant women are recognized today.

CONTROLLING THE BORDER

The preceding historical review illuminates that immigration law and policy are used as a mode of control to "*literally* construct the nation and the people in particular ways" (Luibhéid 2002, xviii). For instance, the shortage of nurses in the United States has led to the allotment of employment-based immigration for Filipino nurses, primarily women. Moreover, the national need for domestic work has resulted in the migration of skilled women to the United States to fill these positions (Dobrowolsky and Tastsoglou 2006). And today, women outnumber men in legally migrating to the United States. Although some theorists have attributed this phenomenon to legal emphasis of family reunification policy popular since the 1960s, currently women are active in migration flows including employment-based immigration, refugee resettlement, asylum, and undocumented migration. And there are certainly potential benefits for women migrants to the United States. First, for those women in sought-after occupations such as nursing, migration often means better financial security and greater resources in supporting kin relations. In general, women migrate to the United States for opportunities that they might not have in their home state. These opportunities include the ability to support one's family, social services, education, and the possibility to change one's social status. Changes in law and policy have drastically impacted women's ability to access these resources through migration.

Most contemporary immigration laws have not directly focused on women, but there are multiple current laws that can be understood as dramatically affecting the lives of immigrant women, both for the better and to their detriment. The Immigration Reform and Control Act (IRCA) or Simpson-Rodino Act of 1986 was the first formal legislation to combat illegal migration with increased spending for border security along the U.S.-Mexico border allotted in the two years after this act. IRCA allowed many migrants identified as either legal authorized workers or special agricultural workers eligibility for legalization while setting forth penalties for U.S. employees who hired undocumented workers. Unfortunately, women, who were also long-term workers in the United States were often not eligible the legalization programs offered to male migrants. Also, post-IRCA, the number of women apprehended at the border increased, which scholars attribute to a desire to reunite with the male family members who had gained legal status.

Furthermore, in 1996 the Illegal Immigration Reform and Immigration Responsibility Act passed restricting public benefits that immigrants could receive before citizenship. Although they were paying taxes that funded the programs, these reforms barred them from receiving food stamps, Temporary Assistance for Needy Families (TANF), Medicaid, and other such services. Proponents of these changes were working to better meet the needs of U.S. citizens in need of welfare programs in a diminishing welfare state. But in 2002, the Senate Finance Committee reformed these bills, installing provisions for states to be able to provide aid to legal immigrants, including English as a second language courses, cash assistance, and children's health insurance for pregnant women. Also under the 1996 Welfare Reform Act, immigrant women have been able to claim legal resident status as "qualified aliens" in conjunction with the 2002 Violence Against Women Act. This provides a means for immigrant women who have experienced gendered violence to gain immigration relief.

The Enhanced Border Security and Visa Reform Act passed in 2001, however, has made it much more difficult to even enter the United States, demanding stricter surveillance of border regions of the United States, as well as women living in the United States with a student visa.

EFFECTS OF IMMIGRATION POLICY

Although proponents of border security and anti-immigration laws note that the increased spending at the border has made border regions safer for both women and men, many human rights organizations critique the laws for making the border much more dangerous for those seeking entrance to the United States, legally or otherwise. First, the anti-immigration laws have made it more difficult for undocumented women to work in abuse-free environments because there are diminishing ways to report abuse. Second, with increased border surveillance, crossing the southern U.S. border has become increasingly dangerous. The number of deaths on the border has risen significantly with the increased surveillance and patrol of the U.S.-Mexico border, and many of these deaths are women. Migrant women report being sexually assaulted in the process of crossing, and in some cases by the Immigration and Nationalization Service (INS) officers patrolling the border. Moreover, the Women's Commission on Refugee Women and Children conducted a study of women held in immigration detention centers in the United States and found that women held in detention were regularly strip-searched, shackled during transportation, harassed, sexually and emotionally abused, and denied food. This abuse has led many women in detention to choose deportation rather than waiting for their immigration and asylum cases to be heard in the courts. This detention is most troublesome because the Refugee Convention states that individuals who enter the United States illegally should not be held in detention unless there is a question of their identity or whether they are dangerous to the public. Yet the practice of detention continues to women's physical and psychological detriment.

VIOLENCE AGAINST WOMEN AND ASYLUM

Seeking asylum is another way women have sought residency or citizenship in the United States. Most recently, women seeking asylum for gender-based persecution has become a central issue to understanding women's relation to the U.S. immigration system because gender isn't formally recognized as grounds for persecution. Asylum seekers are individuals who enter the United States or another nation and claim that they need asylum on the basis of some past or perceived future political persecution. To claim basis for asylum women must (1) show "both a subjective and objective basis for her fear" through testimonies or the reasonable man test, (2) prove a history of persecution or well-founded fear in the future, and (3) account for the persecutor's motive based on one of the five enumerated grounds of race, religion, nationality, membership in a particular social group, or political opinion (Franke 2000). Race and religion are established causes of political persecution, but gender is left to the elusive category of a "social group." Moreover, gendered forms of violence such as rape, domestic violence, forced sterilization, forced killings, female genital mutilation, and sex trafficking are less recognized forms of political persecution. This means that women both have to prove that the forms of violence they have encountered are political, but also they must prove that they are members of a certain social group that is persecution (Akibo-Betts 2005). Although the INS issued guidelines for workers in understanding gender and gendered forms of violence in 1995, women asylum seekers still struggle in getting their claims recognized as political persecution by immigration authorities. Advocates for these women point out that all women have the right to live in safety; opponents argue that allowing these forms of violence to be recognized as persecution would open up the "floodgates" of women making these claims. The advocates rebut with the fact that Canada has seen an increase of only 2 percent since recognizing domestic violence as a form of persecution.

One of the first cases to be successfully recognized as gender persecution in the United States is *Kasinga v. BIA*. This case drew national attention in 1996 and then again in 1999 because it brought questions of female genital mutilation (FGM) as a cultural practice into public discourse. Kasinga, citizen of Togo and member of the Tchamba-Kunsuntu ethnic group, fled Togo and requested asylum. Kasinga's father was opposed to the practice of FGM and polygamous marriages and as a rich, successful businessman he had enough power to prevent his daughter from enduring the procedure. At age 16 Kasinga's father died, and her relatives then took control of her life. Her father's sister forced her to marry a man 30 years her senior who already had three wives. Furthermore,

OLIMPIA LAZO-MAJANO'S ASYLUM CASE

In 1981, Olimpia Lazo-Majano's husband fled El Salvador because he was a member of a rightist-parliamentary group and no longer wanted to participate. He quit and was subsequently wanted by guerrilla forces throughout the nation. Lazo-Majano stayed in El Salvador to work as a domestic and through this work she began washing the clothes of childhood acquaintance Rene Zuniga, sergeant in the armed forces of the Salvadoran military. Not long after, Zuniga began to threaten Lazo-Majano as well as physically and sexually violate her, telling her that if her husband returned to El Salvador, he would "cut both of them into pieces" for being subversives. In 1982, Lazo-Majano entered the United States. From there she applied for asylum based on the grounds of political gender-based persecution. The Board of Immigration Appeals denied her case, citing that "the evidence attests to mistreatment of an individual, not persecution." On appeal, Lazo-Majano claimed persecution on the basis of her political opinion, imputed by Zuniga as being "subversive," and the judges agreed that although this political opinion was in "camouflage," "when Zuniga manipulatively chooses to regard Olimpia as a subversive, he attributes to her the political opinion of a subversive, and she is being persecuted on account of political opinion"; thus she was granted asylum.

both her new husband and her guardian aunt required Kasinga to undergo the FGM procedure for the marriage. Under these circumstances, Kasinga fled Togo for asylum in the United States.

The case was brought to the courts and the defendants argued for gender-based asylum because there was extensive documentation of discrimination against women in Togo. The first immigration judge denied her claims, arguing that FGM "was not persecution, and it was not linked to one of the five 'enumerated grounds.'" The Board of Immigration Appeals reversed the decision, however, noting that FGM was indeed persecution and that Kasinga's ethnic identity plus her gendered identity made her case count as gender-persecution. This case was a positive move toward the greater public recognition of women as political subjects.

SEXUALITY AND ASYLUM

Dynamics of gender also began to enter case law through asylum seekers claiming persecution based on sexual orientation and/or sexual identity. Precedence for sexual orientation and sexual identity as a social group category was established in 1994 with *Toboso-Alfonso v. BIA* when Janet Reno, then attorney general, designated gays and lesbians as particular "social groups." Since then, hundreds of asylum seekers have sought and gained asylum in the United States on these grounds. Moreover, there is increasing precedence for transsexual asylum seekers and gay asylum seekers living with HIV/AIDS since the 1994 ruling. Yet the distinction between making asylum claims on the basis of sexual orientation and sexual identity is important to note: Whereas asylum on the grounds of sexual orientation refers to one's "sexual conduct," sexual identity refers to the visible manifestation of non-normative gender. Of importance, for women making gender-related claims, the terms *gender* and *gendered identity*, are absent from the case law. The distinction is clear in the following case.

Giovanni Hernandez-Montiel, Mexican citizen, who knew he was gay from age eight when he realized he was attracted to other men. At age 12, Hernandez-Montiel began dressing as a woman. This began a string of incidents including being kicked out of school because of his sexual orientation, threats by parents of other children warning him not to "pervert" their sons, and being arrested and raped by police officers because "it was illegal for homosexuals to walk down the street and for men to dress like women." The case for asylum went through several appeals, but it set precedence for a distinction between *sexual orientation* and *sexual identity* as immutable "social group categories." What is interesting about Hernandez-Montiel is the distinction between these two terms. The courts came to understand that "sexual orientation and sexual identity are immutable; they are so fundamental to one's identity that a person should not be required to abandon them.... Sexual identity goes beyond sexual conduct and manifests itself outwardly, often through dress and appearance." For Hernandez-Montiel, this distinction shifted the grounds for his membership. Instead of his membership being "Mexican gay men," his persecution was more valid and recognizable when he was named as "a member of the 'particular social group' of gay men in Mexico with female sexual identities."

What is important about asylum seekers claiming persecution on the basis of sexual orientation and/or sexual identity is that the system predominantly recognizes male subjects that have been persecuted. Not only are women claiming sexual orientation and/or sexual identity as the basis of persecution less likely to file these claims, their cases are most often denied on the grounds that the fear of future persecution is questionable. Although there is clearly a relationship between the expressions of identity and manifestations of persecution in both sets of cases, the omission of gender is a clear indicator that women who speak up about the violence they experience are not the kind of immigrant women the United States desires.

CONCLUSION

Women have a contentious relationship with the U.S. immigration system. Historically, this has meant only being recognized through patriarchal familial relations. This legacy most certainly continues and, thus, women who are recognized as immigrating outside of the traditional family—crossing the border instead of applying for family reunification, asking for asylum on the basis of domestic violence, lesbian asylum seekers who claim persecution—rupture this legacy and are highly disadvantaged within the immigration system.

See also Gender and International Development; Human Rights: International Laws and Policies; Mexican Female Migrants.

Further Reading: Akibo-Betts, Sonia, "The Canada-U.S. Safe Third Country Agreement: Why the U.S. Is not a Safe Haven for Refugee Women Asserting Gender-Based Asylum Claims," *Windsor Review of Legal and Social Issues* 19 (2005): 105–129; Bernstein, Elizabeth, and Schaffner, Laurie, *Regulating Sex: The Politics of Intimacy and Identity* (New York: Routledge, 2004); Bhabha, Jacqueline, "Embodied Rights: Gender Persecution, State Sovereignty, and Refugees," *Public Culture* 9, no. 1 (1996): 3–32; Crawley, Heaven, *Refugees and Gender: Law and Process* (Bristol, UK: Jordan Publications, 2001); Franke, Lindsay, "Not Meeting the Standard: U.S. Asylum Law and Gender-Related Claims," *Arizona Journal of International and Comparative Law* 17 (2000): 605–627; Gardner, Martha, *The Qualities of a Citizen: Women, Immigration, and Citizenship, 1870–1965* (Princeton, NJ: Princeton University Press, 2005); Hondagneu-Sotelo, Pierrette, *Gender and U.S. Immigration: Contemporary Trends* (Berkeley: University of California Press, 2003); Luibhéid, Eithne, *Entry Denied: Controlling Sexuality at the Border* (Minneapolis: University of Minnesota Press, 2002); Moloney, Deirdre M., "Women, Sexual Morality and Economic Dependency in Early U.S. Deportation Policy," *Journal of Women's History* 18, no. 2 (2006): 95–122; Musalo, Karen, "Symposium: Beyond Belonging: Challenging the Boundaries of Nationality: Revisiting Social Group and Nexus in Gender Asylum Claims: A Unifying Rationale for Evolving Jurisprudence," *Depaul Law Review* 52 (2003): 777–808; Nicolosi, Ann Marie, "We Do Not Want Our Girls to Marry Foreigners: Gender, Race, and American Citizenship," *NWSA Journal* 13, no. 3 (2001): 1–21; Tastsoglou, E., and A. Dobrowolsky, eds., *Women Immigration and Citizenship: Making Local, National, and Transnational Connections* (Burlington, VT: Ashgate Publishing, 2006); Women's Commission for Refugee Women and Children, *Liberty*

Denied: Women Seeking Asylum Imprisoned in the United States (New York: Women's Commission for Refugee Women and Children, 1997).

Sara McKinnon

INTERSEXUALITY

Born with nonstandard genitals, chromosomes, or internal reproductive organs, intersex people have been historically viewed by doctors as gender aberrations. Those who hold this view typically defend standard medical treatment for intersex individuals based on their belief that it enhances the individual's quality of life. Advocates for intersex rights, on the other hand, reject the medical protocol of surgery without patient consent and advocate for intersex conditions to be viewed as acceptable biological variance.

BACKGROUND

Intersexuality is a broad term that encompasses a variety of conditions revolving around nonstandard genitals, chromosomes, and internal reproductive organs. How these biological standards are defined varies widely according to the medical or social views on intersexuality. An obvious variation, such as the presence of both a penis and a vaginal opening, contrasts with a decision about whether a clitoris is "too large" or a penis "too small." Medical authorities tend to support surgery and related forms of body modification on infants as a way to make their lives better in the long run. Much controversy surrounds the fact that intersex infants are assigned a gender by doctors that may or may not correspond to how the individual identifies as he or she matures. In addition, doctors may perform life-altering surgeries on infants and adolescents without their consent, based on their interpretation of these variations.

An intersex person may have standard-looking genitals at birth. Variances such as chromosomal arrangements other than XX and XY remain unknown unless DNA testing is conducted. Individuals may not know that they have an intersex condition until puberty, when they go through unexpected secondary sex changes, or later, when they learn upon trying to get pregnant that they are infertile. Many others may never know that they have an intersex condition.

According to the Intersex Society of North America (ISNA), the leading advocacy organization for intersex individuals, 1 to 2 in 2,000 infants are born with genital variance for which a specialist is called in for consultation. More dramatic is the estimate that one in 100 births is born with nonstandard conditions that lead to the diagnosis of intersexuality. Of this amount, approximately 1 to 2 per 1,000 births undergo "normalizing" surgeries.

Historically, the term *hermaphrodite* was commonly used to describe this condition, both among humans and among other species. Since the 1990s, advocates have argued for the usage of the term *intersex* over hermaphrodite. Historically, the term *hermaphrodite*, derived from the Greek mythological figure who was both male and female, is based on a biological definition of sex. The condition was determined specifically by the presence of male and female gonads or gonadal tissue in the individual. In recent years, critics have argued that the term *hermaphrodite* addresses only one aspect or condition related to genital variance and therefore is a misleading term. Furthermore, they argue, the term does not address the spectrum of issues faced by intersex people, including the variety of medical conditions that contribute to genital variance as well as the social implications of the medicalization of intersexed bodies, including forced surgeries, secrecy, and shaming.

Researchers have shown that historically many species are in fact intersexed, meaning they may share both male and female traits, either at the same time or at different times in their lives. Biologist Joan Roughgarden suggests that *hermaphrodism*, the term she uses to describe the condition, is more common in the world, all species considered, than having separate sexes in separate corresponding bodies. Although humans do not have the ability to switch gonads (ovaries and testes) and internal reproductive organs, some humans are born with variations of genital and/or reproductive anatomy. Other scientists believe that hermaphrodism or intersexuality is a deviation of the normal range of female and male bodies and continue to support the modification of intersexed infants on this basis.

INTERSEX CONDITIONS

Intersex conditions include a wide range of physical organ variations, unique chromosomal arrangements, hormonal blocks or adrenal gland malfunctions, underdeveloped reproductive organs, or other biological differences that blur the culturally defined male/female distinctions. Some of these conditions involve pain for the individual and require medical attention to avert further discomfort; other conditions do not cause pain yet are viewed as abnormal in cultural terms. Debates on intersex surgery often vary according to the type of condition one has.

For example, congenital adrenal hyperplasia (CAH) is a common cause of intersexuality among XX children who undergo masculinization at birth or at puberty as a result of adrenal gland malfunction. People with CAH have problems making cortisone (which helps to handle stress) and also may experience a life-threatening condition caused by a disruption of salt metabolism (they require medication to correct the body's salt level). This condition requires medical attention regardless of the doctors', parents', or patients' views on their gender identity. Likewise, androgen insensitivity syndrome (or AIS) can potentially lead to medical problems, although not always. In this case, XY children are highly feminized as a result of a block of testosterone to properly masculinize their bodies. They usually have undescended testicles but female secondary sex characteristics. The vagina may be absent or have no cervix. The females do not menstruate and are not fertile. This is a genetic inheritance and runs in families. Turner's syndrome is characterized by the underdevelopment of female ovaries, breasts, uteruses, and vaginas. These females are missing a second

X chromosome and typically are short, have a broad chest and widely spaced nipples, lymphedema, low hairline, low-set ears, and are infertile.

Other conditions do not necessarily cause pain or discomfort for the patient and are therefore more controversial, as surgery is not necessarily medically necessary but merely a response to cultural norms. Again, there is great variation in people's experiences with these conditions, but generally they tend to be physically nonharmful to the individual. Conditions that fall into this category include hypospadias, where the urethral opening is somewhere along the shaft (or on the base) of the penis rather than the tip of the penis; and Klinefelter's syndrome, which is found in males with 47 XXY patterns and who tend to have male genitals, small testes, little body hair, and often some breast development. After puberty, the ejaculate contains no sperm, leading to sterility. Other medical standards used for diagnosing an individual as intersex include men with *micropenises* and women with an enlarged clitoris. In addition, there is a great deal of chromosomal variation among individuals: males are not always XY and females are not always XX. About 1 in 20,000 men are XX, with a similar number of women XY. Other genes on the chromosomes have been found to influence sex development as well, and often these conditions go undetected because they do not cause any problems for the individual.

INTERSEXUALITY AND GENDER IDENTITY

Gender identity refers to the internal sense an individual has of his/her maleness or femaleness. Many studies show that hormones have an impact on the brain, specifically the hypothalamus, affecting gender identity and sexual orientation. Perhaps ironically, doctors who perform intersex surgery have primarily acted under the belief that an individual's gender identity is largely the result of social conditioning. They believe that it is possible to make a boy a girl or vice versa by manipulating their bodies, introducing hormones, and raising them in that gender role. This has not proven to be strictly true. One of the unfortunate consequences of infant "normalizing" surgeries is that an individual may lose genitals or tissue that they want later to be in line physically with their gender identity. Furthermore, many types of surgery that involve altering the vagina or penis often lead to lack of sensation in the genital area, lack of ability to experience sexual pleasure, and additional complications related to the procedures themselves.

Psychologist Dr. John Money, founder of the Gender Identity Disorder Clinic at Johns Hopkins Medical Center, believed that growing up with one physical sex is psychologically healthier and advocated for sex reassignment surgery of infants. If the intersex child had surgery by age 18 months and the parents brought the child up in the assigned gender identity, the child would become a normal boy or girl. Much of the proof of the perceived success of sex reassignment surgeries rested on one case, that of John/Joan, a highly publicized case of a boy raised as a girl after a botched circumcision (see Sidebar The Story of John/Joan (David Reimer)). For decades, no follow-up studies were done on intersex babies and proof of success rested on this one case, which later proved to be unsuccessful.

THE STORY OF JOHN/JOAN (DAVID REIMER)

David Reimer, an identical twin boy, was born in 1965. At circumcision his penis was accidentally burned off and doctors recommended he be seen by psychologist Dr. John Money, founder of the Gender Identity Disorder Clinic at Johns Hopkins Medical Center. Dr. Money advised David's parents to change his sex through the construction of a vagina and the introduction of hormones and to raise him as a girl. He had his testicles removed at age 22 months. Because this was not a case of intersex or gender questioning, and there was a twin brother who made an ideal control to study, their experiences could provide data for theories about gender socialization and identification. This story, written about as the "John/Joan case," purported successful gender socialization—Brenda (as she was renamed) was living the life of a normal, happy girl.

However, this was not true. Brenda never fully felt like a girl. She was given estrogen to develop secondary sex characteristics and there were yearly visits to the Hopkins clinic. Brenda, in fact, had difficulty with her peers and hated the visits to Dr. Money. At 13 she became depressed and refused to go back to Johns Hopkins. Her family finally told her about her gender reassignment, and at age 15 Brenda began living as a boy and took the name David. David later chose genital surgery, double mastectomy, and testosterone. He married and was a stepfather to three children. He went public with his story in a *Rolling Stone* interview in 1997, and journalist John Colapinto reported his experience in the bestselling book, *As Nature Made Him: The Boy Who Was Raised As A Girl*. Sadly, David Reimer committed suicide in 2004.

In Western science, one of the faulty assumptions in labeling people as boys or girls concerns the fact that many people have both masculine and feminine biological traits. There are numerous aspects, including hormones, chromosomes, and physical external and internal organs, that contribute to people's genetic make-ups. Where intersexuality begins or ends is up for debate. For many observers, the idea that someone is "all male" or "all female" is difficult to assess, for there is great variability in hormonal levels and influence; in the size, shape, and length of genitals; and in specific medical conditions that help shape one's experience of gender identity. As critics argue, assigning a gender identity based on biological traits is not as accurate as waiting for the individual to say what his/her gender identity feels like internally.

MEDICAL VIEWS ON INTERSEX SURGERY

Standard medical protocol when an infant is born with ambiguous genitals is to call in pediatric specialists who can do chromosomal and genetic testing to determine what is going on with the baby. Variations in external sex and internal reproductive organs are treated as birth defects to be corrected. This represents a bias in medicine that the variations are not "normal."

Of primary concern is whether the parents will bond appropriately with an infant who looks "different." Most doctors believe they are acting in the best interests of the child and the parents by performing surgeries that create genitals that parents expect. Surgeries on infants occur by 18 months, but some surgeries are done at puberty—all times when the child cannot give consent.

Prevailing thinking also dictates that children not be told about their surgeries and treatments. The belief is that if the children don't know they will simply accept the doctor visits or the hormone therapies and they won't get upset. Intersex activists are speaking out against this today, but many children are still not told what was done to them or why. Numerous doctor visits and multiples surgeries, however, are confusing to children and adolescents

Many studies, including Dr. John Money's Ph.D. dissertation research, showed that intersex people who did not have "normalizing" surgeries have lower rates of psychological problems than the general population. Except for a few major life-threatening illnesses or conditions, such as gonadal cancer, lack of a urinary opening, or a metabolic crisis, intersex people advocate postponing any surgical intervention until the individual can be fully informed and make his/her own decision about his/her body.

The recommended protocol advocated by intersex people who have experienced the shame, secrecy, and trauma of the "optimal gender of rearing model" requires a paradigm shift in thinking. The previous model, based on the idea that you can raise a child to be the gender doctors and parents assign, assumes socialization overrides biological influences. Advocates argue this is not the case and children should be assigned a gender, their genitals left intact, and only when they are old enough to determine their own gender identity, consent to any surgical or hormonal therapies. The previous approach also advocated keeping the truth from children about their bodies, leaving them with feelings of shame, confusion, and feeling like freaks. Children should be given age-appropriate information about their conditions. They should have access to their medical records, and they should not be lied to.

INTERSEX TREATMENT AS A HUMAN RIGHTS ISSUE

On May 27, 2004, the Human Rights Commission of the City and County of San Francisco held a historic public hearing on the medical "normalization" of intersex people. Framed from a human rights perspective, their comprehensive report issued in 2005 urged the end to so-called normalizing surgeries on intersex individuals without their consent. The report specifically says the social discomfort of others (parents, medical personnel) is not valid ethical grounds to perform surgeries on intersex people. It is also wrong to perform life-altering surgeries on individuals without their consent. Informed consent is a key aspect of "best practices" policy for every medical organization, including the American Academy of Pediatrics. This is especially sensitive when the intervention is not medically necessary yet has a substantial impact on quality of life. Surgical decisions can be delayed without risk until the patient can make his/her own decisions, maintaining his/her autonomy and integrity.

Testimony from intersex people, family members, doctors, and researchers affirmed that the public needs to be better informed on a range of issues; for example, intersex conditions are not rare, genital variability is not the same as abnormality, gender identity is not tied to genitals, and surgeries often have severe life impacts. Testimony from intersex people addressed their view that only they can determine their gender identity and that gender identity cannot be created through socialization or surgical intervention. This directly contradicts the long-held medical protocol that one can be made into a boy or a girl. Most intersex people prefer that their bodies remain intact.

INTERSEX ACTIVIST RESPONSES TO MEDICAL PROTOCOL

Standard medical practice to operate on intersex infants was first challenged in an organized effort in 1995. Cheryl Chase, intersex herself, founded the Intersex Society of North America (ISNA) that year, originally as a support group, but quickly transformed into an advocacy organization. Since then, ISNA has worked to educate medical personnel, parents, and the public, bringing together intersex people, addressing medical conferences, and advocating for the end of surgery without consent, secrecy, and shaming. Bodies Like Ours, an intersex peer support group, was started in 2002 by Betsy Driver, born with CAH. Other groups such as Intersex Initiative, UCSF Center for Gender Equity, and other online groups, provide information, public speakers, and advocacy for the rights to self-determination for intersex people.

CONCLUSION

When intersex conditions are viewed as abnormalities or birth defects, the medical response is to normalize the body. Doctors and some parents believe that this is in the best interest of the child, as it decreases the likelihood of the intersex individual feeling different or abnormal. Critics argue that medical interventions serve to comfort the parents and doctors more than helping the intersex individual. When intersex conditions are seen as human variations (especially those conditions that do not cause pain for the individual), medical practitioners may choose to wait to see how the child develops. In this scenario, proposed by advocated for the intersexed, the protocol becomes one of educating the public, monitoring the condition, and listening to the child as he/she matures.

Intersex activists have formed a powerful support movement to address the secrecy, shame, and physical damage to their bodies caused by unnecessary surgeries. They are educating each other, the public, and, most important, doctors and the American Pediatric Association to understand the consequences of surgeries before consent, shaming examinations, and the pathological treatment of bodies that are different from the norm. The issue of medical intervention into intersex conditions goes beyond understanding the conditions of individual bodies; it also concerns reframing deeply held, divergent biological and cultural views on what is natural and normal.

See also Femininities and Masculinities; Gender Identity Disorder; Nature versus Nurture; Sex versus Gender.

Further Reading: Arana, Marcus, "A Human Rights Investigation into the Medical 'Normalization' of Intersex People," in *A Report of A Public Hearing by the Human Rights Commission of the City and County of San Francisco* (San Francisco: Human Rights Commission, 2005); Bodies Like Ours, available at: http://www.bodieslikeours.org; Chase, Cheryl, "Hermaphrodites with Attitude: Mapping the Emergence of Intersex Political Activism," in *The Transgender Studies Reader,* ed. Susan Stryker and Stephen Whittle, 300–314 (New York: Routledge, 2006); Colapinto, John, *As Nature Made Him: The Boy Who Was Raised As A Girl* (New York: HarperCollins, 2000); Fausto-Sterling, Ann, "The Five Sexes, Revisited," *The Sciences* 40, no. 4 (2000): 18–26; Intersex Society of North America (ISNA), available at: http://www.isna.org; Kerlin, Scott, and Dana Beyer, "'The DES Sons' Online Discussion Network," *Transgender Tapestry* 100 (2002): 18–23; Kessler, Suzanne J., *Lessons from the Intersexed* (New Brunswick, NJ: Rutgers University Press, 2000); Preves, Sharon E., "Sexing the Intersexed: An Analysis of Sociocultural Responses to Intersexuality," *Signs* 27, no. 2 (2002): 523–556.

Lori Girshick

INTIMATE PARTNER VIOLENCE

Targets of intimate partner violence, including domestic violence, are disproportionately women. Violence against intimate partners is universally considered unacceptable, but debates continue concerning whether it should be legally regulated and how, and what the appropriate community responses should be to the problem.

BACKGROUND: A WOMEN'S ISSUE

Intimate partner violence, which includes domestic violence, crosses racial, ethnic, age, and socioeconomic boundaries and is the leading cause of injuries for U.S. women ages 15–44. Each year in the United States, approximately 1.5 million women are targets of violence by an intimate partner, roughly the same number of people who have heart attacks annually (Bureau of Justice Statistics 2003). In addition, women are five to eight times more likely than men to be abused by an intimate partner, and up to 14 times more likely to experience serious injury from a physical assault by a partner. There are cases that involve a woman as perpetrator and a man as target, and physical violence occurs in about 25 to 33 percent of same-gender relationships, approximately the same rate as heterosexual couples (Peterman and Dixon 2003). The dynamics of relationship violence, however, overwhelmingly involve men as perpetrators and women as targets. *Target* is the term used in the social justice movement to refer to oppressed groups who are "targets" of prejudice and discrimination from oppressors (Adams, Bell, and Griffin 1997). Therefore its use in the context of intimate partner violence holds meaning when considered in the context of patriarchy, sexism, and gender discrimination. Traditionally, violence between spouses has been referred to as domestic violence. The term *intimate partner violence*, however, has emerged recently to broaden the focus to include nonmarried partners and to bring a more contemporary discussion to the many types of intimate partnerships that exist in U.S. society.

Intimate partner violence involves three components: (1) a pattern of behavior that starts small and grows worse over time; (2) abusive behaviors that include isolation, coercion, control, and emotional abuse and can, but does not have to, include physical and/or sexual abuse; and (3) a behavior that is perpetrated by a current or former spouse or relationship partner. Susan Schechter, considered one of the founders of the Battered Women's Movement, explains: "Brutality is not necessarily confined to hitting, pushing, and pulling out hair. Its extreme, yet not infrequent, forms often leave women severely scarred, physically and emotionally. Terror and intimidation, experienced by all battered women, reach unbearable proportions for some." (Schechter 1982, 14).

The sociopolitical movement around intimate partner violence has made great strides in the past 100 years. Although cases have been documented throughout history and literature, it is only recently that spousal violence has been considered a crime. In fact, the common phrase "rule of thumb" originated

AND THEY LIVED HAPPILY EVER AFTER . . . MESSAGES IN CHILDREN'S FAIRY TALES

Children's fairy tales, games, toys and literature are filled with messages about how girls and boys, women, and men should look, behave, think, and feel. In taking a closer look at these messages, there exists a set of core ideas that explains what relationships should be like. For example, in the Walt Disney children's story "Snow White and the Seven Dwarves," a witch poisons Snow White with an evil spell, only to be broken by the kiss of a handsome prince. When the prince kisses Snow White, she awakes and they ride off on his white horse to be married in his castle. This story is filled with messages about beauty, relationships, marriage, and the roles of men and women. Of particular note is that the prince kisses the sleeping Snow White, an act of nonconsensual sexual activity that is illegal in many states (owing to the fact she is asleep and unable to consent). Also, the act of marrying and "living happily ever after" occurs almost immediately after the prince's kiss. The story's ending requires no relationship building, and Snow White is not consulted about the outcome. In fact, after the prince enters the story, Snow White never speaks again. Similar messages exist in more contemporary fairy tales as well. In the 1989 Walt Disney movie, *The Little Mermaid*, Ariel goes to the witch under the sea to learn how she might capture the affection of a handsome prince. The witch tells Ariel she must give up her voice, singing, "You'll have your looks! Your pretty face! And don't underestimate the importance of body language! . . . Come on, they're not all that impressed with conversation. True gentlemen avoid it when they can. But they dote and swoon and fawn on a lady who's withdrawn. It's she who holds her tongue who gets her man." Being bombarded by these messages day in and day out socializes girls and boys into gendered roles that create unrealistic expectations about love, marriage, and relationships.

from a rule in English common law that allowed a husband to beat his wife with a stick no thicker than his thumb (Sigler 1989). In the late 1800s in the United States, feminists began making strides in raising public awareness of then what was referred to as "wife abuse," as a significant social problem. During that period several states began to grant divorce for cruelty, and Alabama and Massachusetts initiated spouse abuse laws, making it illegal to "beat a wife with a stick, pull her hair, choke her, spit in her face, or kick her to the floor" (Pagelow 1984, 284). Nonetheless, spousal abuse was not seen as a widespread social problem until the 1970s.

THE BATTERED WOMEN'S MOVEMENT

The battered women's movement largely came out of the feminist movement and was launched through several pivotal events. The first largely publicized domestic violence shelter, Chiswick Women's Aid, opened in England in 1971. The first shelter in the United States was Haven House in Pasadena, California, which opened quietly in 1964. In 1976, the National Organization for Women focused on "wife beating" as a national priority and the National Coalition for Domestic Violence was formed in 1978. Susan Schechter's (1982) pivotal book, *Women and Male Violence: The Visions and Struggles of the Battered Women's Movement,* framed intimate partner violence in the context of sexism, gender inequality, and the oppression of women. All of these events and the voices of women activists have brought these issues to the forefront of public discussion and laid the foundation for the current laws of all 50 states making spouse abuse illegal.

SYSTEMIC RESISTANCE: MAINTAINING THE STATUS QUO

There was significant resistance to the emergence of intimate partner violence as a social problem rather than a private family matter. Traditional ideas of family and gender roles fueled the idea that men had the right to use physical aggression against their wives, and many held the viewpoint that spousal abuse was a private matter and should remain out of the public light. Messages from societal institutions reinforced the idea that divorce was unacceptable and that the best way to stop domestic violence was for the woman to be a better wife and not anger her husband. Even as laws developed making spouse abuse illegal, strong messages remained in communities that domestic violence did not warrant intervention from the larger community.

Additional resistance came from the social and policy movements throughout the nineteenth and twentieth centuries. Typically in the United States, social issues cycle through public focus, with particular focus on one or two issues at a time. Domestic violence gained public focus for brief periods, but fell to the background as other issues took focus. For example, in the late 1800s, momentum was gaining around the issue of protecting "battered wives" in the courts, but it was then overshadowed by the child protection movement for 25 years. In the early 1900s, the founding of the Protective Agency for Women and Children of Chicago brought a focus on stranger rape. When the agency attempted to enact policies helping battered wives to secure divorces, the political retribution resulted in their voice being silenced on the public stage.

Lack of public focus on domestic violence was further reinforced by popular explanations about reasons for domestic violence. In the 1940s and 1950s, the psychological theories of Sigmund Freud placed blame on battered wives, labeling them as masochistic, untrustworthy, and not to be believed. In the same era, alcoholism began to be recognized as a medical disease, and medical professionals suggested that men who were violent toward their wives while using alcohol were acting as a result of a disease and not at fault for their behavior. It was not until the feminist movement in the 1970s that domestic violence began to command consistent attention and condemnation in the public arena.

WHO ABUSES

Issues of Power and Control

What causes one person to abuse the partner while another does not? Why do men abuse significantly more often than women? Although there are many different explanations for why this happens, one has moved to the forefront of the discussion: the abusive partner holds the idea that he/she has the right to have control over his/her partner. This mostly has to do with a batterer's internal beliefs and attitudes and is generally supported by messages from a patriarchal society that condones aggressive behavior. Abusers use tactics such as intimidation; coercion and threats; economic and emotional abuse; and minimizing, denying, and blaming to control their targets. For example, if a woman says to her partner she is planning to leave, the batterer may use a tactic such as, "You're so crazy and such a bad wife, no one else would have you." After continually hearing only these messages with minimal alterative input because of the batterer's systematic isolation from support systems, a target may come to believe her abuser and believe she has no choice but to remain in the relationship.

Societal Messages and Gender Role Socialization

Men should be providers, and women should make a good home. Men don't cry, and women are too emotional. Fathers roughhouse and play sports with their sons, but raising the children and parenting are the responsibility of the mother. If something is going wrong, it is the man's job to fix it. These messages overshadow every aspect of life in U.S. society. The messages come from many places including movies, television, faith institutions, the courts, laws and legislative bodies, schools, and children's stories, and they create a society where interpersonal violence is acceptable. If it is a man's job to fix everything, and men are supposed to be in control, it is an easy leap to the idea that men must keep their wives and girlfriends "in line." Men are often encouraged and supported by their friends, family, and acquaintances in this idea. A high school-age young man may be recounting a disagreement with his girlfriend to his friends in the locker room before gym class. A common response from one of the young men might be, "Did you show her who's the boss?" This remark conveys the idea that men are supposed to be in charge. Even young people whose families make a concerted effort to communicate ideas of gender equality and respect are still bombarded with these messages from larger society. An additional consequence of these messages is the belief that "family problems" should stay "in the family." Although intimate partner violence is illegal in all 50 states, many batterers are not arrested by law enforcement or are given minimal consequences by the courts (National Opinion Research Center 2004). Also, the lingering viewpoint that men are in charge of the behavior of their wives and families further causes bystanders to look the other way.

Follow the Leader: Do What I Do

Another idea that attempts to explain why batterers abuse is called social learning theory (Bandura 1977). It argues that people behave in certain ways by observing these behaviors in others. For example, a man may abuse his wife because he saw his own father abuse his mother throughout his childhood. Research conducted with human subjects draws these conclusions: (1) aggression can be learned by observing aggressive role models (e.g., Bandura and Ross 1961), and (2) violence occurs across generations in families (e.g., Widom and Maxfield 2001). In about half of domestic violence cases where men abuse their wives, they abuse their children as well (Ver Steegh 2000). A total of 85 percent of children living in homes where domestic violence occurs are either eye witnesses, hear the violence, or attempt to intervene. Some of these explanations are controversial because some people believe they excuse abusive behavior. For others, social learning theory provides an important explanation for why some batterers abuse. If batterers learned to be abusive by observing role models, perhaps they can learn to behave differently by observing positive role models. Recent advertisements that show cultural heroes, such as sports figures and well-known television and movie heroes giving positive messages about their beliefs about relationships and how they should treat their partners, may be an attempt to influence these learned attitudes and behaviors.

WHY DO WOMEN STAY? THE PERSPECTIVES OF BATTERED WOMEN

"I don't understand. I would have left the first time he hit me." Advocates frequently hear this question as people in the United States struggle to understand the dynamics of interpersonal violence. Operating in the context of the same societal messages that targets receive, many people believe interpersonal violence starts with physical violence and leaving is a single, uncomplicated event. In reality, leaving is a process that can be frightening, overwhelming, and dangerous. The following is a discussion of barriers to leaving a violent partner.

Til Death Do Us Part

A 13-year-old girl is talking with her mother about marriage and love. The mother says, "Now, relationships are hard work. There will be rough times. You have to compromise and sometimes you have to put your husband's needs before your own." This mother may have good intentions, but this message rarely comes with a clarification of where to draw the line. Where does compromise stop? In which situations might I put my own needs aside? And what behavior should I and should I not be willing to accept from my partner? Many people can identify similar messages they received about relationships as they grew up, and most could say physical violence would cross a line. But interpersonal violence does not start with physical violence; it is an escalation of behaviors over time. If a target is constantly told she is a horrible person and no one else would have her, and then one day her partner smashes a vase on the wall next to her head, it does not seem like such a large step if next time her partner hits her. And despite the fact a large number of marriages currently end in divorce, there still remains a cultural expectation that marriages should last forever.

Risks of Leaving

The most dangerous time for violence to occur is immediately after a partner leaves the relationship. In fact, "women who are separated from their husbands have a risk of violence about . . . 25 times more than that of married women. Up to 75 percent of domestic assaults reported to law enforcement agencies occur after the separation of the couple, with women most likely to be murdered when reporting abuse or attempting to leave an abusive relationship" (Barnett, Miller-Perrin, and Perrin, 2005, 5).

Systemic Barriers and Lack of Resources

Systemic barriers create further difficulties for leaving. For example, a woman may wish to go to a domestic violence shelter, but she may find that all of the beds are full. Also, women often lack the financial resources to start a life on their own and may have minimal education and/or employment history to sustain life independently. This is further exacerbated by the societal message that men work and support the family. It is not uncommon for women who are targets of interpersonal violence to have never worked outside the home or been on their own.

The situation becomes more complicated if children are involved. Experts agree that witnessing domestic violence is abusive and psychologically damaging to children, putting them at higher risk for long-term physical problems, using substances, experiencing mental health issues, and being a target or perpetrator of abuse (Felitti, Anda, Nordenberg 1998). Nonetheless, most custody hearings occur separately from and may involve no reference to domestic violence legal proceedings occurring previously or simultaneously in criminal courts. In approximately 70 percent of cases involving domestic violence, fathers who contest custody are awarded sole or joint custody (Zorza 2001). This phenomenon is rooted in the batterer's ability to control his behavior; most batterers are able to present as charming and in control, and often use legal proceedings to convince the court the target is "crazy" and an "unfit mother." Many abusive husbands use court-mandated visitation or child-exchange times as opportunities to verbally or physically harass the target and children. It is estimated that during visitation, 5 percent of fathers threaten to kill the mother, 25 percent threaten to hurt their children and 34 percent threaten to kidnap their children (National Coalition Against Domestic Violence 2003). And as with many other social problems, those with financial, transportation, and educational barriers experience further difficulty in leaving, as they have fewer resources to draw upon in times of crisis.

CONCLUSION

The movement to end intimate relationship violence still faces an uphill battle in gaining full support in the legal system. For example, until 2006, Arizona's laws still made spousal rape a significantly less serious category of felony than stranger or acquaintance rape, and many states do not protect nonmarried domestic partners, either same or other gender, under their domestic violence laws. And although U.S law now clearly indicates that intimate partner violence is a crime, the general acceptance of it remains entrenched in cultural icons and norms, evidenced by referring to men's sleeveless undershirts as "wife beaters" and using violent expressions as commonplace in U.S. slang ("If my friend is late to the movie I am going to kill him!"). Yet, although further social reform is still needed, the battered women's movement in the 1970s created the foundation on which today's activists stand.

See also Child Sexual Abuse; Sexual Assault and Sexual Harassment.

Further Reading: Adams, Maurianne, Lee Anne Bell, and Pat Griffin, eds., *Teaching for Diversity and Social Justice: A Sourcebook* (New York: Routledge, 1997); Bandura, A., *Social Learning Theory* (Englewood Cliffs, NJ: Prentice Hall, 1977); Bandura, A., D. Ross., and S. A. Ross, "Transmission of Aggression Through Imitation of Aggressive Models," *Journal of Abnormal and Social Psychology* 67 (1961): 575–582; Barnett, Ola, Cindy L. Miller-Perrin, and Robin D. Perrin, *Family Violence Across the Lifespan* (Thousand Oaks, CA: Sage Publications, 2005); Bureau of Justice Statistics, "Intimate Partner Violence," *Crime Data Brief, 1993–2001* (Washington, DC: U.S. Department of Justice, Bureau of Justice Statistics, 2003); Felitti V. J., R. F. Anda, and D. Nordenberg, "The Relationship of Adult Health Status to Childhood Abuse and Household Dysfunction," *American Journal of Preventive Medicine* 144 (1998): 245–258; Gondolf, Edward W., *Final Report: An Extended Follow-Up of Batterers and Their Partners* (Indiana, PA: Mid-Atlantic Addiction Training Institute, Indiana University of Pennsylvania, 2001); National Coalition Against Domestic Violence, "Child Visitation Offers Opportunities for Domestic Violence," *Womensnews,* February 2003; National Opinion Research Center, *General Social Survey: 1972–2004 Cumulative Data File* (Storrs, CT: Roper Center for Public Opinion Research, University of Connecticut, 2004); Pagelow, M., *Family Violence* (Westport, CT: Praeger, 1984); Pence, Ellen, and Michael Paymar, "The Power and Control Wheel,"

(Figure 1.1), *Domestic Violence Information Manual: The Duluth Domestic Abuse Intervention Project* (New York: Springer Publishing Company, 1993); Peterman, Linda M., and Charlotte G. Dixon, "Domestic Violence Between Same-Sex Partners: Implications for Counseling," *Journal of Counseling and Development* 81 (2003): 40–47; Schechter, Susan, *Women and Male Violence: The Visions and Struggles of the Battered Women's Movement* (Boston, MA: South End Press, 1982); Sigler, R. T., *Domestic Violence in Context: An Assessment of Community Attitudes* (New York: Lexington Books, 1989); Ver Steegh, Nancy, "The Silent Victims: Children and Domestic Violence," *William Mitchell Law Review* 775 no. 26 (2000); Widom, C. S., and M. G. Maxfield, "An Update on the "Cycle of Violence," NCJ Publication #184894 (Washington, DC: U.S. Department of Justice, 2001); Zorza, Joan, "Batterer Manipulation and Retaliation: Denial and Complicity in the Family Courts," *Feminista* 4 (2001), http://www.feminista.com/archives/v4n7/zorza.html, accessed October 3, 2007.

Kathryn Woods

K

KINSEY SCALE OF SEXUAL BEHAVIOR

Alfred Kinsey's comprehensive, scientifically based research on human sexuality has been controversial because of the subject matter, participant selection, and research methodology. His Heterosexual-Homosexual Rating Scale (HHRS), which revealed that many people who identify as "heterosexual" actually partake in "homosexual" sexual practices or have same-sex erotic feelings, challenged the acceptable social norms of the time and continues to do so today.

BACKGROUND

Alfred Kinsey was a pioneer in the scientific examination of human sexuality. He was the first scholar to comprehensively document what people do sexually and how they feel about their behavior. Kinsey overcame many obstacles and challenged numerous critics in the development and subsequent publication of his two wide-ranging volumes on human sexuality. The trailblazing nature of Kinsey's research cannot be comprehended without understanding the historical context in which he was raised. Understanding who Kinsey was as a person assists in examining how and why the controversies developed over his research in reference to subject matter, research participants, and methodology. The most well-known and controversial elements of Kinsey's research, the Heterosexual-Homosexual Rating Scale, which places sexuality on a continuum and delinks sexual behavior from identity, continues to be hotly debated even now. Undoubtedly, Kinsey's influence on the public and public perceptions of sexuality have changed since he developed his scale.

HISTORY OF THE STUDY OF HUMAN SEXUALITY

To understand the significance of Alfred Kinsey to the study of human sexuality, it is necessary to understand the social environment that preceded him and shaped his ideas. Historically, the study of human sexuality began in earnest in the early nineteenth century (Table K.1). During this period, religion and its moralists were the leading authorities in defining what was appropriate behavior and what sexual knowledge was to be shared with the public. The lives of citizens were centered on the doctrines and religious laws created by the Church, which shaped how people interacted with one another, including sexually. The approach of religion was based on a Judeo-Christian perspective, which focused on the moral necessity of heterosexual sex to ensure procreation. Activities outside of sex for reproduction, including sex for pleasure or personal enrichment, were considered immoral and punishable by God. Slowly, the control over sexuality and its study shifted to the law, with its focus on the rights of property owners. This change was a result of the increasing power of the wealthy and the declining importance of the Church as a moral authority. As such, the law tended to focus on crimes against the wealthy, for instance a laborer having sexual relations with his employer's daughter or his employer's farm animals, and these acts were severely punished. The punishments were not as a result of the sexual element of the act, but reflected the desire to preserve the socioeconomic class structure. By the mid- to late-nineteenth century, the authority over sexuality shifted again, this time to the medical establishment with its focus on the disease and deviance aspects of human sexual functioning. The concentration on deviance allowed society and lawmakers to better define the types of behavior that were considered socially and culturally acceptable. Recently, a hybrid model has been used whereby authority over sexuality is found in the medical establishment, law, and the social organization of society.

Table K.1

Judeo-Christian Religion		***Law***		***Medical***		***Hybrid*** - Medical, social and legal
(Focus on so-called right and wrong sexual activities)	→	(Focus on rights of the wealthy and property owners)	→	(Focus on disease and deviance)	→	(Focus on defining and punishing deviance and treating the diseased)

KINSEY'S OWN HISTORY AND ITS INFLUENCE ON HIS RESEARCH

Alfred Kinsey was born in Hoboken, New Jersey, in 1894 to a traditional Victorian-era family. He had very little experience sexually during his formative years and held traditional values about appropriate sexual behavior—all of which changed dramatically over the course of his lifetime. He attended Harvard University where he received his doctorate in biology in 1919, and he moved to Indiana to teach zoology at the state university in 1920. Kinsey was originally best known for his research in taxonomy and evolution, and his meticulous attention to detail in his research studies. When asked to assume responsibility for the marriage course at Indiana University in 1938, he applied the same attention to detail in structuring the course content. Kinsey soon learned that very little accurate research existed about human sexuality and set out to gather his own research through the collection of sex histories. A renown workaholic, Kinsey and his staff collected more than 18,000 sex histories in the course of his career and published two volumes on the research, *Sexual Behavior in the Human Male and Sexual Behavior in the Human Female*, which are still relevant today. Kinsey died in 1956 at the age of 62. His legacy remains alongside all of his research materials at The Kinsey Institute (formerly the Institute for Sex Research) at Indiana University.

It has only been in recent history that sexuality has been associated with shame and indignation, and it is during this time period, referred to as the Victorian era, in which Alfred Kinsey was raised. Despite his conservative upbringing, Kinsey decided to approach the study of sexuality as an objective scientist with a goal of documenting the full variety of sexual behavior in minute detail. The purpose of Kinsey's research was to provide a basis in which to study human sexuality scientifically without placing value judgments on the activities or the participants. Kinsey gathered his research through personal interviews that covered topics such as masturbatory experience, premarital petting, nocturnal emissions ("wet dreams"), premarital intercourse, homosexual contacts, and animal contacts. His findings for males were released in 1948 and his findings for females in 1953.

CONTROVERSIES IN KINSEY'S RESEARCH

Kinsey's research challenged the most basic assumptions the public had regarding human sexuality and demonstrated that supposedly "normal," law-abiding citizens engaged in a wide array of sexual activities. The subject matter was extremely controversial because it dealt with matters the public regarded as private. Moreover, controversy surrounded whom Kinsey selected for his research subjects and the methodology he used. Kinsey was the first to learn that sexual responsiveness and participation in sexual activities are different across socioeconomic classes and education levels. Previously, members of society assumed that everyone complied with the Victorian social values and norms of abstinence until marriage and having sexual relations only to produce children. Moreover, Kinsey was the first to discover that orgasm is unrelated to ejaculation in men, and that orgasm is experienced differently by each individual (Kinsey, Pomeroy, and Martin 1948, 159, 160).

There was controversy over the subjects Kinsey interviewed for his studies. Critics contended that Kinsey was using data obtained from children, and that children were being asked about their sexual practices and observed engaging in sexual behaviors. Critics argued that Kinsey sexualized children by seeking to understand the types of sexual activities in which they partake. The view that children are not sexual and do not express themselves in sexual ways is a holdover from the Victorian era. Kinsey's critics claimed that publicizing that children masturbate and engage in sexual play encourages the activities of pedophiles and child molesters. In fact, several of the critics actually considered Kinsey and his team pedophiles. In actuality, Kinsey's research subjects were all adults and mostly Caucasian, Protestant or Catholic, and from the upper socioeconomic classes. Those subjects from rural communities and lower socioeconomic classes were often found in prisons, as more than 17 prisons contributed inmates to Kinsey's research (Kinsey et al. 1948). Moreover, Kinsey did not interview children regarding their sexual habits, but instead gathered his data on childhood sexuality from interviews with adults who were asked to recall the sexual things they did as youngsters. What was discovered is that sexuality and sexual expression exist from birth and are expressed in a variety of ways throughout the developmental cycle. Kinsey was instrumental in illustrating that at least 70 percent of preadolescent children have genital play with other youngsters, and that most of that play is homosexual (Kinsey et al. 1948, 167).

KINSEY'S RESEARCH METHODOLOGY

Alfred Kinsey conducted his sexological research using face-to-face interviews with participants. Although some of the elements listed here may seem commonsensical, in the 1940s and 1950s they represented significant departures from standard research methodologies. Kinsey contended that for research to be scientifically valid, it must contain the following elements:

- A minimum of 300 interviews for each group of people studied (e.g., men, women, Catholic, homosexual).
- Shortcomings must be identified at the outset. For Kinsey this was a lack of older participants, the exclusion of children, lack of religious representation, too few participants from the lower socioeconomic classes, and few minorities.
- Data must be recorded in real time, using a rapid-fire question system. Kinsey and his staff covered more than 300 questions in less than 45 minutes.
- Questions must be asked using the language the participant comprehends, and subjects must be forced to prove their answers to the interviewer by reiterating responses throughout.
- Disclosure of personal information or controversial issues, such as religion or politics, must be avoided, as it may taint the research findings.

The methodology used by Kinsey to conduct his research was controversial. Many considered suspect the use of in-depth interviews to gather data on such a sensitive topic. Critics contended that subjects would be less inclined to give truthful answers in a face-to-face setting and were likely to provide the answers they thought the interviewer wanted. Kinsey went to great lengths to ensure that the subjects were comfortable with the interviewer and that their privacy was ensured. Kinsey detailed how effective interviews should be conducted and outlined when and how the interviewer should probe the subject if they suspected the subject was holding back information or not being completely honest (Kinsey et al. 1948, 44–74). The techniques developed by Kinsey continue to be a model used by academics and researchers in how to conduct interviews.

The most controversial finding in Kinsey's research was his discovery that sexuality is not constant and that most people engage in both heterosexual and homosexual activities throughout their lives. Kinsey's research was published at a time when homosexuality was illegal, and prisons were filled with men who were convicted of having consensual sex with other men. What made this finding contentious was Kinsey's inclusion of the heterosexual-homosexual rating scale. This scale visually demonstrated a range of possible sexual orientations from exclusively heterosexual, with no homosexual contact ever (a 0 on the scale), to exclusively homosexual, with no heterosexual contact ever (a 6 on the scale). What Kinsey learned was that very few individuals rated a zero or a six, and most fell within the remaining five categories (see The Kinsey Institute Web site for more information www.kinseyinstitute.org/resources/ak-hhscale.html).

THE HETEROSEXUAL-HOMOSEXUAL RATING SCALE

The intent of Kinsey's scale and its actual use by academics and therapists varied considerably. Kinsey intended his HHRS to illustrate the fluidity of sexuality; however, the scale has been used to assign labels to people's sexual orientation and to characterize homosexuality as medically and/or psychologically abnormal. For Kinsey, the development of the HHRS as a classification system based on relative amounts of experience with heterosexuality and homosexuality did not equate with how an individual self-identified their sexual orientation. In reference to the HHRS scale, Kinsey claimed, "The world is not divided into sheep and goats. It is a fundamental of taxonomy that nature rarely deals with discrete categories" (Kinsey et al. 1948, 639). Moreover, Kinsey believed, "While emphasizing the continuity of the gradations between exclusively heterosexual and exclusively homosexual histories.... An individual may be assigned a position on this scale, for each period in his life.... A seven-point scale comes nearer to showing the many gradations that actually exist" (Kinsey et al. 1948, 639, 656). As such, a person may be exclusively homosexual at age 10, and by age 30 that person may be exclusively heterosexual in their behavior. This would result in the individual being placed in different categories for the different age periods.

One of the critiques of the HHRS is that it focuses solely on behavior and does not account for feelings and fantasies. Critics suggest that by categorizing someone on the HHRS, it attaches a label to their sexuality, which often has significant political implications. Labels limit the possibilities of behavior and thought and are fundamentally irrelevant to what an individual thinks and feels sexually. Labels attached to sexuality developed in the nineteenth century as a way to reinforce Victorian mores (Foucault 1978). It may be difficult in our society to have a label removed; if someone is labeled homosexual, bisexual, or a sexual deviant, that label is likely to remain with them indefinitely. For this reason critics of Kinsey have identified the HHRS as problematic. In our society, people label others according to their behavior (or suspected behavior) and there are often consequences attached. For instance, until recently people who had sexual relations with members of the same sex were considered to be mentally ill and subject to incarceration and civil commitment into mental institutions. Although society's attitudes have become more tolerant concerning homosexual behavior, there are many other sexual labels that exist resulting in discrimination and intolerance (e.g., bisexuality, frigidity, promiscuity).

According to critics, self-identification is the most relevant "label" people can attach to themselves (Klein 1978, 9, 12, 20; Diamond 2005, 125). For instance, if a man is in prison and engages in homosexual activity simply because that is what opportunity exists, but regards himself as strictly heterosexual, according to critics of Kinsey, he should be labeled as exclusively heterosexual as he self-identifies as such. Kinsey, however, studied only behavior and was not concerned with how people labeled themselves or their attitudes about sex and sexuality. Consequently, Kinsey would categorize this individual as homosexual during the time period he spent in prison. Although the argument made by critics regarding divorcing behavior from emotion is valid politically and socially, it misinterprets the intent of the HHRS. Kinsey never attached a label of heterosexual, homosexual, or bisexual to any of his subjects and strongly believed in separating individuals from their behavior (Young-Bruehl 2001, 187). Kinsey regarded his subjects as more than what they do sexually and believed it was more appropriate to describe the nature of sexual activities or sexual stimuli that individuals respond to erotically (Young-Bruehl 2001, 187). Kinsey believed that such sexual activity and stimuli are a product of cultural mores and values.

INFLUENCE OF KINSEY'S RESEARCH ON THE PUBLIC

The publication of Kinsey's research was highly anticipated and received significant media attention. This represented the first time that the public had access to such candid and far-reaching information on sexuality. The media highlighted and sensationalized the sections on masturbation, homosexuality, animal contacts, and prostitution. The research findings on women, published five years after the male volume, were much anticipated by the public. Alongside the media hype, several negative consequences resulted from the public release of Kinsey's research. The public was now confronted with scientific statistics as to what people actually did sexually. This ultimately led to the creation of expectations for both women and men. The number of partners one had sex with, how many orgasms one had, the types of positions that should be used during

THE KINSEY INSTITUTE (FORMERLY THE INSTITUTE FOR SEX RESEARCH)

The Kinsey Institute has its origins in the first course on marriage that Kinsey taught at Indiana University. Students approached Professor Kinsey with a variety of questions he was unable to answer. This led him to search for scientific research on human sexuality; however, he quickly discovered that few studies existed and those that did were heavily value-laden and relied on very small samples. As a result, Kinsey assembled a team of researchers and began to take the sex histories of students, faculty, and friends. Soon, Kinsey and his staff had accumulated a great deal of sexological information, and, to guarantee the confidentiality of the records, he established the Institute for Sex Research as a nonprofit organization in 1947. The first trustees of the Institute were Kinsey, Paul Gebhard, Clyde Martin, and Wardell Pomeroy. The purpose of the Institute was to continue research related to human sexuality and administer research materials, a library, case histories, and other related items. The Kinsey Institute, as it is now called, has broadened its mandate to include the promotion of research and scholarship in the areas of human sexuality, gender, and reproduction. It now provides education to the community and professionals, clinical and research training, and public tours and presentations.

sex, and how often one should masturbate all seemed to be dictated by Kinsey's findings. Without an adequate understanding of statistics, the public could not separate averages and incidences from normality. Slowly, women and men began to question their sexuality if their behavior did not coincide with Kinsey's findings. Such expectations still exist today and have been reinforced by the public release of other highly regarded sexological research such as Masters and Johnson's sexual response cycle findings. Similar to Kinsey, Masters and Johnson conducted laboratory tests to ascertain what physical and physiological changes occur when individuals are sexually excited. The result of their research was the development of the sexual response cycle. Although the intent of the cycle is to explain generally what changes occur in the body during sexual arousal and activity, the media and the public regard the cycle as an absolute. Consequently, individuals who do not respond sexually in the same manner as represented in the cycle are considered sexually dysfunctional. The end result has been a perpetual curiosity and near obsession with all things sexual.

CONCLUSION

Alfred Kinsey's research had a profound impact on the study of human sexuality. His findings challenged society's conservative, Victorian outlook. Kinsey learned that sexual expression is extremely varied, and that people who appear "normal" and moral are engaging in activities considered inappropriate by much of society, such as masturbation. Kinsey demonstrated that socioeconomic factors, such as level of education and income, are the greatest predictors of sexual behavior. Behavior, and not attitudes, was considered to be the most important element to be studied. As such, Kinsey developed the Heterosexual-Homosexual Rating Scale to categorize his subjects' behavior at particular times in their lives. Although the main intent of the scale was to demonstrate the fluidity of sexuality over the course of a lifetime, it is now used to assign labels to individuals and to pathologize certain forms of behavior. Despite the shortcomings of his research, which Kinsey clearly articulated in his 1948 volume, his research methods and interview format continue to be in use in academic institutions around the world. Kinsey was a pioneer in the field of sexology and has laid the foundation on which all present sexological research is based. It is likely his influence will continue for many more years.

See also Bisexuality; Female Sexuality and Dysfunction; Sexual Identity and Orientation.

Further Reading: Condon, Bill, *Kinsey* (film, Qwerty Films, 2004); Diamond, Lisa M., "A New View of Lesbian Subtypes: Stable Versus Fluid Identify Trajectories over an 8-Year Period," *Psychology of Women Quarterly* 29 (2005): 119–128; Foucault, Michele, *The History of Sexuality Volume 1* (New York: Vintage Books, 1978); Haeberle, Erwin J., *The Sex Atlas New Popular Reference Edition* (New York: The Continuum Publishing Company, 1982); Kinsey, Alfred C., Wardell B. Pomeroy, and Clyde E. Martin, *Sexual Behavior in the Human Male* (Philadelphia: W. B. Saunders Company, 1948 [1998]); Kinsey, Alfred C., Wardell B. Pomeroy, and Clyde E. Martin, *Sexual Behavior in the Human Female* (Philadelphia: W. B. Saunders Company, 1953 [1998]); The Kinsey Institute for Research in Sex, Gender, and Reproduction, "Publications," available at: http://kinseyinstitute.org/publications/index.html; Klein, Fred M. D., *The Bisexual Option* (New York: Arbor House Publishing Company, 1978); Young-Bruehl, Elisabeth, "Are Human Beings 'By Nature' Bisexual?" *Studies in Gender and Sexuality* 2, no. 3 (2001): 179–213.

Laura J. Zilney

L

LEFTIST ARMED STRUGGLE

Women's participation in leftist armed struggle and revolutions involves the contradictory deployment of their traditional gender roles, tensions between motherhood and political activism, and the paradox of actively engaging in violent combat, which often ends life, to defend life as they understand it.

BACKGROUND

Scholars have long been fascinated by the nature of women's participation in leftist armed struggle and revolutionary movements. In contexts as diverse as Mozambique, Cuba, Nicaragua, Ireland, Chechnya, South Africa, Palestine, and the United States, some women have chosen to take up arms as a way to defend their beliefs and fight for what they see as a more equitable society. Feminist scholars disagree as to whether women's participation in armed struggle leads to changes in gender relations, or whether they are simply fighting alongside their male counterparts for reasons that are fundamentally the same as those that motivate men. Often, women join armed struggles to "live in freer countries and to have more options in life" (Kampwirth 2002, 6); to struggle for independence, as in the case of the Palestinian struggle for statehood; to combat serious inequalities, as in the case of apartheid South Africa, where women played a key role in its dismantling; and to combat military authoritarian rule, as in the case of Central American countries long controlled by right-wing military regimes. Rather than fighting for "gender justice," as is the case for many self-defined feminist movements around the world, these women have joined struggles based on their ethnic, racial, religious, or imagined national community. Yet through their participation, many have also changed their views on gender and in some cases, they have developed new movements that reflect their newly formed gender consciousness. This has been true in the New Left in the United States, where women who had participated in male-based social movements during the 1960s, including the antiwar, peace, free speech, civil rights, and socialist democratic movements, later formed their own movements, which became the basis of what we now consider second-wave feminism.

WHY WOMEN PICK UP ARMS

Women who participate in armed struggle are seen as heroes by some and brainwashed, naïve, or co-opted by others. In the Palestinian Occupied Territories, women have long been recruited to join the Palestinian Liberation Organization (PLO) and more recently, Hamas. Although Palestinians have been divided on how to acquire official statehood, either through violence or non-nonviolence, women have often been recruited to join the armed struggle as a result of the ongoing lack of male soldiers and to the perceived desperation of their living situation.

Research on female suicide bombers points out that there are both "supply" and "demand" reasons for the increased presence of women in the ranks of suicide bombers, which has led some to argue that "the face of terror is increasingly female" (Handwerk 2004, 1). It is true that women have been recruited in higher numbers since the 1980s, but there are also structural and ideological reasons why women are opting to join in higher numbers than before. Although important debates continue as to what constitutes revolutionary activism versus terrorism (Kampwirth 2002; Neuberger and Valentini 2004), what these acts of martyrdom demonstrate are women's forms of commitment to defending their imagined community—whether on the basis of ethnicity, religion, or the pursuit of statehood—through violence.

WHY WOMEN DISARM

Just as women have joined leftist armed struggles, so too have many later made the transition to other forms of activism that do not involve violence, some even adopting an alternative nonviolent or pacifist strategy. Scholars have asked, how or to what extent is this transition linked to their understandings of their gender roles? Sometimes, women disarm alongside their male counterparts as their revolutionary movements successfully achieve control of the state, as in the case of the Cuban revolution, or acquire independent statehood, as in the case of anticolonial movements in Africa, Asia, Latin America, and the Caribbean (Yuval-Davis 1997). As revolutionary movements take on state power, women have sometimes been recruited to be part of the new state vanguard, as in the case of the Sandinista revolution in Nicaragua, which incorporated women into the governmental leadership, whereas other women have been asked to "return to their homes," the idea being that they return to their traditional gender roles as mothers and caretakers, leaving the official domain of politics to men, as in the case of many independence movements fighting against European colonization, where women's rights were seen as secondary to the larger anticolonial struggle and placed on the back burner once independence was acquired (Yuval-Davis 1997). Yet women who become actively involved in politics, whether violent or nonviolent, have difficulty balancing their newly created public roles with their traditionally expected roles in the private realm of family life. As a result, many women in revolutionary movements throughout the world, including in the United States, have gone on to create their own forms of women's rights movements that directly address "gender justice," a theme that many women fighters did not see as necessary at the beginning of their participation, yet later came to identify as important.

CONCLUSION

Many observers agree that women often joined leftist armed struggle, including Marxian-influenced revolutions, nationalist, and anti-imperialist movements, as a way to struggle for a "freer society or country" rather than as a way to seek "gender justice." Through their participation, they face a series of paradoxes concerning their gender roles in armed struggle, including the tension between serving in active combat versus performing their traditional gender roles, and additional tensions concerning whether they should partake in forms of violence to achieve equity and combat discrimination in their communities or nations, or seek alternative, nonviolent channels to protest what they view as a lack of rights or freedom.

See also Politics and Political Ideologies: Leftist Women; Political Parties; Terrorism and National Security.

Further Reading: Handwerk, Brian, "Female Suicide Bombers: Dying to Kill," *National Geographic,* December 13, 2004, available at: http://news.nationalgeographic.com/news/2004/12/1213_041213_tv_suicide_bombers.html, accessed May 25, 2007; Holt, Maria, "Palestinian Women and the Intifada: An Exploration of Images and Realities," in *Women and Politics in the Third World,* ed. Haleh Afshar, 186–203 (New York: Routledge, 1996); Kampwirth, Karen, *Women and Guerilla Movements: Nicaragua, El Salvador, Chiapas and Cuba* (University Park, PA: Pennsylvania State Press, 2002); Neuberger, Luisella de Cataldo, and Tiziana Valentini, *Women and Terrorism* (New York: Palgrave MacMillan, 2004); Yuval-Davis, Nira, *Gender and Nation* (Thousand Oaks, CA: Sage Publications, 1997).

Amy Lind

LESBIAN, GAY, BISEXUAL, TRANSGENDER, AND QUEER MOVEMENTS

Social movements working to secure lesbian, gay, bisexual, transgender, and queer (LGBTQ) rights face opposition from both conservative and radical sectors, placing them in conflict with both external and internal actors about how to achieve equality for sexual and gender minorities.

BACKGROUND

A social movement is loosely defined as a group of people with a common objective who collectively organize their efforts for the purposes of social change. In the twentieth century, LGBTQ social movements have worked individually and collectively, with multiple objectives, including decriminalizing same-sex sexual activity, garnering public visibility, securing equal rights, achieving mainstream acceptance, and AIDS activism. Although the objectives shifted in different periods and within various movements, the obstacles facing LGBTQ social movements continue to take fairly consistent forms: homophobia, social conservatism, religious beliefs that condemn same-sex relations, the assumed correctness of heterosexuality, lack of LGBTQ representation in media and politics, the protection of rigid definitions of gender, and internal divisions. The organizations, key individuals, and events that have shaped LGBTQ movements are slowly working their way into the heterodominant narratives of U.S. history. This entry offers one history of U.S. LGBTQ social movements, emphasizing key organizations and events that shaped these complex histories.

HOMOPHILE MOVEMENT

The homophile movements marked the earliest stages of LGBTQ organization. In a time when same-sex attraction was not only taboo, but criminalized as "obscene," homophile organizations were geared toward creating safe spaces where gay men and women could meet, build relationships, and find support systems. In 1897, German physician Magnus Hirschfeld founded the Scientific-Humanitarian Committee, thought to be the first advocacy for homosexual and transgender rights. In 1926 in Chicago, Harry Gerber founded the first known U.S. homophile organization, The Society for Human Rights. The organization was short-lived, as a member's wife reported its existence to the police and Gerber was arrested for obscenity. The appearance of homosexuality in early Hollywood was curbed by the 1935 motion picture code's ban of any and all references to homosexuality. In 1937, the homosexual prisoners of Nazi concentration camps were first marked with pink triangles, which later became a prominent symbol for gay oppression. Bohemian collectives continued to offer a gay underground in larger American cities in the first half of the twentieth century, but the mere accusation of homosexuality could lead to loss of employment, loss of parental custody, arrest, institutionalization, and public humiliation in local papers.

The 1948 publication of Kinsey's *Sexual Behavior in the Human Male* challenged the popular misconception that homosexuals comprised a fractional percentage of the population. The Los Angeles-born Mattachine Society had its first meeting in 1950, with five men in attendance, including Radical Faeries founder Harry Hay, who is claimed to have written the first gay rights manifesto in the United States. The Mattachine Society splintered in 1952, leading to the creation of One Inc., a group containing the Mattachine Society as well as female members. Their publication, *One Magazine,* became the first pro-gay periodical in the United States. The group eventually published the *One Institute Quarterly,* which is now known as *The Journal of Homosexuality.* In 1952, the "sex-change" operation of Christine Jorgenson became an international story and brought immense visibility to transgender issues.

In 1955 in San Francisco, the meeting of four lesbian couples led to the first national lesbian rights organization in the United States. Founders Del Martin and Phyllis Lyon of the Daughters of Bilitis began a nonprofit organization exclusively for lesbians, opening an office in 1957. Their publication, *The Ladder,* sought to explore the differences between gay men and lesbians, educate membership and the general public on lesbian issues, endorse women's movement solidarity, and promote lesbian poetry and literature.

1960s TO STONEWALL

Extending on the work of homophile groups of the 1950s, the 1960s introduced a period in which gay and lesbian organizations further pushed objectives of visibility, media representation, and legal protection. The *New Left,* a term used to distinguish itself from the politics of the 1950s *Old Left,* sought to extend past labor issues and adopt a broader agenda for social justice and equality. Heterosexism and misogyny, however, were ever-present in the political organizing that often characterizes the 1960s-era activism of the New Left. The radical movements that united to end racism, poverty, and the Vietnam War reportedly engaged in gay-baiting activities, outward antigay sentiment, and the perpetuation of misogyny. This forced many homosexual men and women who were active in social justice efforts, such as the civil rights movement and the National Organization for Women (NOW), to downplay or disguise their homosexuality, whereas others opted to remove themselves completely.

In 1961, San Francisco drag queen Jose Sarria ran for city supervisor, becoming the first openly gay person to run for public office. In 1962, Illinois became the first state to legalize same-sex acts between consenting adults. "Gay Lib" was emerging throughout the latter 1960s, pushing for media visibility and government recognition. In June 1964, *Life* magazine ran the cover story "Homosexuality in America," offering increased visibility for the growing gay subculture. In 1965, the "Gay is Good" movement and the creation of ECHO (East Coast Homophile Organization), led by longtime activist and D.C. Mattachine president Frank Kameny, held the first of many protests at The White House and government agencies. The movement actively worked to alter the negative image of homosexuality as sick, perverted, and sinful, enforcing a strict dress code for protests—men in suits and women in dresses. The strategy of presenting "safe" representations of gays and lesbians by adhering to traditional gender roles alienated transgender communities. In January 1967, the Los Angeles homophile group Pride led a several hundred-person protest in response to police raids of gay bars.

The Stonewall Riots of June 1969 marked a historic event and a radical shift in the social and political advancement of LGBT movements. On June 28, 1969, plainclothes officers raided the Stonewall Inn, a Greenwich Village bar commonly frequented by drag queens; however, the events escalated from a routine raid to an impromptu demonstration. There is no concrete reason why this raid, a common practice at the time, was met with resistance. Some argue it was because queer icon Judy Garland had just passed away. Others argue it was just time to fight back; they were simply fed up with the harassment. Outside the bar, an assembled crowd of bar patrons and local pedestrians taunted the police, throwing various objects, until the police were forced to retreat into the bar. The police reported "riot" lasted approximately 40 minutes; however, news of the events spread throughout the community, and larger crowds assembled the next evening. On this night, and on the third night of rioting on July 2 (there were two days of rain), the demonstration grew more violent, but also more organized. The police tried to clear the streets, but the protesters refused to hide, insisting on standing their ground, claiming their rights, no longer willing to run away in fear. These three nights are now referred to as the historic Stonewall Riots. The riots made international news, creating a surge of LGBT visibility, which showed gays and lesbians resisting shame, harassment, and persecution.

IS STONEWALL THE BIRTH OF GAY PRIDE?

One year after the Stonewall Riots, in June 1970, approximately 15,000 gays, lesbians, and drag queens came together for a series of Pride events, celebrating the one-year birthday of gay liberation. Approximately 1,000 marched in Los Angeles, and others gathered in Chicago and San Francisco. Internationally, commemorative celebrations were reported in Buenos Aires, Argentina; Lima, Peru; and Nicaragua.

This annual celebration, now referred to commonly as "gay pride," is celebrated internationally. The efforts and organizations that existed decades before Stonewall should not be overlooked in their important contribution to the movement, and the designation of "birth" is contested, but the Stonewall Riots marked a major turning point in LGBT liberation. As much as Stonewall is recognized globally as a major moment in gay history, however, it is problematic to locate the birth of all LGBTQ rights in the United States. For example, many countries have their own "Stonewall," such as in Australia. At the first Sydney Mardi Gras in 1978, police officers arrested lesbian and gay partygoers. Numerous marches and protests took place across the country and led to the release of the arrested individuals. This effective response built strong momentum to the Australian lesbian and gay movement and is likened to the Stonewall Riots in the United States. Similar parallels are drawn in countries such as Canada and Ireland, who honor Stonewall, along with their own unique histories and accomplishments. Many countries, such as Norway, Sweden, Canada, South Africa, and many Eastern European nations, have achieved far greater equality for LGBTQ populations than the United States. Furthermore, the notion of a LGBTQ rights is arguably a Western concept, as sexuality and sexual identity take on different meanings within different cultures. Although LGBTQ movements throughout the world differ greatly, many do honor the Stonewall Riots in their pride celebrations and marches. The rainbow flag, designed by San Francisco artist Gilbert Baker, has become an international symbol for LGBTQ pride.

THE POST-STONEWALL 1970S: THE CONSOLIDATION OF A GAY RIGHTS MOVEMENT

After Stonewall, the goals of gay and lesbian visibility, legal protection, and social acceptance gained national momentum, introducing a strong awareness of diversity within LGBT communities. Several organizations emerged in the late 1960s and early 1970s, including the Gay Liberation Front (GLF), the Gay Activist Alliance (GAA), the Radicalesbians, and smaller organizations like The Latin American Homosexual Committee, the Gay Latino Alliance, and the Street Transvestite Action Revolutionaries (STAR). Led by the motto, "Out of the closets, into the streets," the GLF sprang up in multiple U.S. cities. Although short-lived, the GLF introduced a radical alternative to the homophile organizations that came before it, rejecting assimiliationist tactics and pushing for radical reform. The tension of assimilationist politics, or the strategy of trying to fit into dominant ideas of "normal," and anti-assimilation perspectives anticipates the queer politics of the early 1990s. Although bisexuals were active in early homophile organizations, the anti-assimilation politics of groups such as GLF allowed bisexuals freedom from rigid gay/straight definitions. As the GLF adopted a broad agenda, supporting the women's movement, the Black Panthers, and protesting the Vietnam War, some members of the GLF split off to the form the Gay Activist Alliance. The GAA sought an agenda more immediately focused on the advancement of gay rights. A second division resulted from female members who felt the GLF privileged the concerns of gay men over lesbians. The Radicalesbians originally formed in 1970 under the name Lavender Menace, a response to Betty Freidan's comment that lesbians were a "lavender menace" to the advancement of women's issues. The Radicalesbians sought to claim their rightful place in the women's movement, arguing that gender oppression and homophobia were inextricably linked, both tied to the project of patriarchy. The group attempted a nonhierarchal structure and insisted on female separatism, completely distancing themselves from all men, as well as from women who accepted traditional heterosexual values. Although the group was short-lived, its work in the early 1970s had a profound impact. In 1971, the National Organization of Women officially declared lesbian rights as a feminist issue.

In 1970, Black Panther leader Huey Newton openly declared support for the gay liberation movement. In 1971, Dr. Frank Kameny ran for U.S. Congress as the first openly gay candidate. In 1974 Kathy Kozachenko became the first openly gay or lesbian to hold U.S. public office, soon followed by Elaine Noble. In 1972, the United Church of Christ ordained William Johnson, the first openly gay ordination in a mainstream U.S. church. That same year, lesbian and gay rights were advocated at the Democratic National Convention. Lesbian and gay activists began appearing on television, popular magazines, and newspapers and lesbian and gay representations appeared in several films. In 1975 the first ever gay Native American organization was formed, Gay American Indians, soon organizing in more than 20 different tribes. Male cross-dressing support groups proliferated throughout the 1970s and1980s. The first trans-inclusive civil rights protection legislation was passed in Minneapolis in 1975.

The National Bisexual Liberation Group (1972) and Bisexual Forum (1975) were formed. In 1977, The National Coalition of Black Gays was founded in New York. On December 15, 1973, all homosexuals across the nation were "instantly cured," as homosexuality was declassified as a psychiatric disorder by the American Psychiatric Association.

MID-1970s: THE BIRTH OF MODERN ANTIGAY ACTIVISM

The price of political and social gain in the post-Stonewall era was soon met with conservative backlash. In 1975–1976, Robert Grant founded The American Christian Cause to counter the "gay agenda." The most visible figure of this backlash was Anita Bryant, a former Miss America contestant and orange juice spokesperson, who launched a nationwide crusade accusing "militant homosexuals" of corrupting the nation's children through recruitment. Her "Save the Children" campaign began in response to an ordinance in Dade County, Florida, preventing housing and employment discrimination against homosexuals. Marking the first of a series of setbacks, Arkansas recriminalized same-sex acts between consenting adults only two years after repealing its antisodomy laws. The Dade Country ordinance was repealed, and Florida signed legislation to prevent gays and lesbians from adopting children. Openly gay San Francisco supervisor Harvey Milk, however, fought and successfully led a defeat to the Briggs Initiative, which would make it illegal for openly gay, lesbian, or gay/lesbian advocates to teach in California public schools. On November 27, 1978, former supervisor Dan White assassinated Harvey Milk and Mayor George Moscone. Upon White's conviction of manslaughter, rather than murder, thousands of outraged protesters demonstrated outside city hall, leading to a violent night of rioting in the streets. The 1970s began with the fueled momentum of Stonewall and concluded with the growing backlash of the Religious Right. In September 1979, however, the first openly gay judge, Stephen M. Lachs, was appointed to the Los Angeles Supreme Court. In October of that year, the first National Lesbian and Gay Rights March on Washington D.C. was held, with approximately 100,000 participants in attendance.

THE 1980s: GAY RIGHTS ENTER NATIONAL POLITICS

In 1980, The Democratic National Convention became the first major political party to take on a gay rights platform. In 1981, Mary Morgan became the first openly lesbian judge. In 1982, approximately 50,000 people attended the first-ever Gay Games. Although slowed by the backlash of the Moral Majority's antigay crusade, LGBT visibility and social advancements continued to move forward. This took a dramatic shift, however, beginning with the report of a "Rare Cancer Seen in Homosexuals" in the *New York Times* on July 2, 1981. Within a year, the "gay cancer" was officially termed AIDS (acquired immune deficiency syndrome), and rapidly spread to epidemic proportions in the gay male community. LGBT objectives radically shifted to community support and political outcry. Gay Men's Health Crisis, founded by a group of gay New York males including Larry Kramer, organized support for the escalating numbers of sick and dying within the community and fought for government and media recognition of the growing epidemic. As the majority of the early AIDS cases in the United States afflicted gay men, the fear of spreading AIDS and an ignorance surrounding transmission ushered in a wave of homophobia.

The media's construction of the AIDS epidemic, although shamefully slow to respond, began with the representation of primarily anonymous white gay men. Gay men of color and trans-communities were highly underrepresented, but greatly affected. AIDS awareness was subject to the cult of personality, as the death of Rock Hudson, the horrific AIDS-phobic stand-up routines of comedians like Eddie Murphy, and later figures such as Ryan White and Magic Johnson shaped the popular conceptions of HIV and AIDS. While President Reagan remained silent and Reverend Jerry Falwell declared AIDS as God's wrath on the homosexual, two organizations mobilized to demand attention for the thousands of lives being lost in silence. In 1987, Larry Kramer and more than 300 activists founded the AIDS Coalition to Unleash Power (ACT-UP), launching a series of public demonstrations and public disturbances. Highly controversial in its tactics, ACT-UP was successful in forcing attention to a multitude of injustices surrounding AIDS prevention, education, and awareness. A second response to the nation's refusal to address the AIDS epidemic was the Names Project AIDS Memorial Quilt. Since 1987, this public memorial has brought together more than 40,000 individual sections, which travel around the country, testifying to the enormity and humanity of the lives that continue to be lost.

Increasing visibility in the political sphere, Massachusetts Representative Gerry Studds announced he was gay on the House floor in 1983, becoming the first openly gay member of Congress. Congressman Barney Frank came out in 1987, the same year as the second lesbian and gay march on Washington, which reported approximately 500,000 participants. Two days later, the largest protest in the history of LGBT politics took place on the steps of the Supreme Court, resulting in more than 600 arrests. The Human Rights Campaign (HRC) was founded in 1980 and grew into the largest LGBTQ organization in the United States. The HRC claims a mission to work to secure rights for LGBT populations, support LGBT political candidates, and create a strong LGBT presence in the political system, although it has been heavily criticized since the early millennium by many gay activists for lack of results and for primarily serving the needs of white, middle class gay men. The National Gay and Lesbian Task Force, founded in 1973, differs in its outspoken claim to support coalitional systems between issues of race, class, gender, and sexuality, but lacks the size or funding of the HRC.

1990s–2000s: GAY VERSUS QUEER MOVEMENTS

Still battling the devastating effects of AIDS on the gay community, LGBTQ social movements splintered even further, adopting a broad range of agendas. The 1990s brought in a revitalized militancy in certain factions of the LGBT movement, most visibly by Queer Nation. Adopting a radical and combative agenda, Queer Nation used short-term, attention-grabbing demonstrations to increase LGBTQ visibility and combat homophobia. Slogans such as "We're Here, We're Queer, Get Used to It" and "Dykes and Fags Bash Back" exemplify their no-apologies politics. Sometimes working directly with ACT-UP, the loosely organized Queer Nation gained attention for demonstrations, such as same-sex kiss-ins in malls and infiltrating straight bars for "Queer's Night Out." The reappropriation of the term *queer* and queer politics was more welcoming to the bisexual and transgender populations, who had commonly been marginalized by more reform-based organizations.

A multitude of additional movements within the LGBTQ movement umbrella continued to organize. In 1991, the first Black Lesbian and Gay Pride event took place in Washington D.C. The Lesbian Avengers assembled their first meeting in 1992, and by April 1993 took part in, what is argued to be, the largest lesbian demonstration to date. The third march on Washington in 1993 grew to more than a million participants. Media representation in film, television, and a handful of LGBTQ celebrities pushed mainstream visibility. In 1995, the UN integrated sexuality and gender identity into the agenda for human rights. LGBTQ visibility was at an unprecedented high, but with this visibility there came several setbacks. Clinton's signing of the Defense of Marriage Act denied same-sex partners access to spousal benefits offered by the federal government to married couples. The military "Don't Ask, Don't Tell" policy was instituted in 1993, forbidding lesbian and gay members of the military to come out of the closet. In 1998, the murder of Matthew Shepard, a young gay male from Wyoming, made international news. The Shepard murder brought the discussion of homophobia and hate crimes to the forefront of media discussion, as well as garnering attention for the man who protested Matthew Shepard at his own funeral, Reverend Fred Phelps.

CONCLUSION

As the LGBTQ movements continue to grow and change, the agendas, tactics, inclusions, and exclusions will continue to shift as well. From GenderPAC, an organization dedicated to creating safe social spaces for all gender identities, and the prominence of female-to-male (FTM) activist Jamison Green to the existence of bisexual organizations that refuse to cloak bisexuality within strictly gay, lesbian, or heterosexual categories, the movements are extending away from the once white, gay, male center of gay liberation. From radical queer politics that seek to abandon the institution of marriage entirely, all the way to Log Cabin Republicans who continue to fight for gay assimilation, marriage rights, and normative inclusion, the multiple identities and politics under the umbrella of LGBTQ movements in the United States remain both for and about the diversity of sexual and gender experiences.

See also Bisexuality; Female Sexuality and Dysfunction; Homosexual Reparative Therapy; Kinsey Scale of Sexual Behavior; Lesbians and Gays in the Military; Queer; Same-Sex Marriage; Sexual Identity and Orientation; Sexual Orientation and the Law; Transgender and Transexual Identities.

Further Reading: Adam, Barry D., *The Rise of the Lesbian and Gay Movement* (Boston: Twayne, 1997); Carter, David, *Stonewall: The Riots that Started a Gay Revolution* (New York: St. Martin's Press, 2004); Cruikshank, Margaret, *The Lesbian and Gay Liberation Movement* (New York: Routledge, 1992); Engel, Steven M., Jeffrey C. Alexander, and Steven Seidman, *The Unfinished Revolution: Social Movement Theory and the Lesbian and Gay Movement* (New York: Cambridge University Press, 2001); Feinberg, Leslie, *Trans-Liberation: Beyond Pink and Blue* (Boston: Beacon Press, 1998); Marcus, Eric, *Making Gay History: The Half Century Fight for Lesbian and Gay Equal Rights* (New York: HarperCollins, 2002); Rimmerman, Craig, *From Identity to Politics: The Lesbian and Gay Movements in the United States* (Philadelphia: Temple University Press, 2001).

Dustin Goltz

LESBIANS AND GAYS IN THE MILITARY

From the time of the Revolutionary War to the era of "Don't Ask, Don't Tell," evidence of homosexuality has been grounds for exclusion or discharge from the U.S. military. The continued presence of lesbians and gays in the military has prompted heated debate over military necessity, personal rights, and the culture of the armed forces. The outcome of this controversy will likely affect other contemporary conflicts between lesbian and gay rights movements and traditional values.

BACKGROUND

In June 2006, the Department of Defense found itself back in the middle of the controversy over lesbians and gays in the military. Researchers from the Center for the Study of Sexual Minorities in the Military had recently uncovered an official Pentagon document that classified homosexuality as a mental illness. Members of Congress and medical experts were quick to criticize the document, pointing out that the American Psychiatric Association had stopped classifying homosexuality as a mental disorder in 1973. This debate triggered a much larger dispute over how lesbian and gay service members should be classified by the military. Since the Department of Defense declared that "homosexuality is incompatible with military service" in 1982, lesbian and service members have become a topic of heated debate. Should sexual identity be a standard for inclusion or exclusion from the U.S. military? Does sexual identity have any impact on military performance? Should lesbian and gay individuals be allowed to enlist and serve as long as they do not reveal their sexual orientation? Should they be able to serve openly? What consequences do these military regulations have for the broader social debate over lesbian and gay rights in the United States? Politicians, military leaders, legislators, judges, activists, and service members have all struggled with these questions.

The introduction of "Don't Ask, Don't Tell, Don't Pursue, Don't Harass" in 1993 addressed some of these concerns, but not all. "Don't Ask, Don't Tell," as the policy came to be known, officially prohibits the military from asking recruits or current service members about their sexual orientation. Lesbian, gay, or bisexual service members, however, are still prohibited from revealing their sexual orientation or engaging in "homosexual conduct" (Belkin and Bateman 2003). Supporters of this policy argue that allowing lesbians and gays to serve openly would be bad for troop morale and damaging to unit cohesion, which could significantly diminish military performance and put other soldiers at risk. They also point out that the military operates under its own rules and regulations, making it immune to state and federal antidiscrimination laws. Opponents of this policy argue that the military's current bias against lesbians and gays is equivalent to its previous opposition to racial integration. They contend that the stigmatization and harassment of lesbian and gay service members are violations of basic rights, and they view the numerous military investigations into the sexual lives of service members as governmental interference into private life. Finally, they argue that any benefits generated by "Don't Ask, Don't Tell" are outweighed by the high costs of investigations and discharge proceedings.

HISTORY BEHIND THE MILITARY'S REGULATION OF SEXUALITY

U.S. military regulation of sexuality goes back as far as the Revolutionary War, when Lieutenant Gotthold Frederick Enslin became the first American soldier to be dismissed for homosexual conduct. In March 1778, Enslin was court-martialed and dishonorably discharged from the Continental Army for his actions. Contemporary conversations about lesbians and gays in the military often reference this incident, but it is important to note that Lieutenant Enslin's removal from the army was not based on his sexual orientation. He was removed for engaging in sexual acts that were prohibited by military law. Until World War II, the military had no specific laws or policies regarding homosexuals. The Articles of War of 1920 classified "sodomy" as a punishable offense, but were applicable to both straight and gay service members (Burrelli 1994).

The lack of specific regulations did not prevent the U.S. military from policing sexual conduct. The Newport Sex Scandal of 1919–1921 was one of the military's first systematic attempts to purge gay service members from the ranks. Afraid that sailors stationed at the Navy base in Newport, Rhode Island, were in danger of being morally corrupted by the local gay community, the Navy set out to investigate. They recruited several enlisted sailors to entrap and then testify against suspected "perverts" in court (Brenkert 2003). During the course of this investigation, a number of sailors were caught, court-martialed, and sent to prison. Prominent civilians, such as the Reverend Samuel Neal Kent, were also caught up in the dragnet, bringing the investigation—and Assistant Secretary of the Navy Franklin Delano Roosevelt—to national attention. Significantly, the scandal did not result from the navy's findings, but rather from the graphic accounts given by the young sailors who had volunteered for the investigation.

Lesbians and gays were not officially excluded from military service until World War II, when the introduction of standardized psychological screening shifted the military's focus from homosexual conduct to homosexual status. In 1942, the army revised its draft regulations to include criteria for differentiating

KEY DATES

1778: Lieutenant Gotthold Frederick Enslin becomes the first American soldier dismissed from the American military for homosexual conduct.

1919: Navy orders first systematic investigation into allegations of homosexual conduct at Newport naval base. Numerous sailors are entrapped, court-martialed, and sent to prison.

1942: United States Army begins to mandate screening of sexual orientation for all who enlist.

1950: Uniform Code of Military Justice standardizes exclusion of lesbians and gays from all branches of the armed services.

1982: Pentagon declares that "homosexuality is incompatible with military service."

1994: "Don't Ask, Don't Tell" policy is enacted by the 1994 Defense Authorization Act.

2005 and 2007: Representative Martin Meehan introduces and reintroduces Military Readiness Enhancement Act, which seeks to overturn "Don't Ask, Don't Tell."

between homosexual and "normal" draftees, and added procedures for rejecting those who were not deemed "normal" by the screening protocol. Women who wished to enlist in the Women's Army Corps (WAC) were screened using the same criteria, although homosexuality did not become an official reason for disqualification until most of the WAC recruiting had been completed (Berube 1990). During this time, the high demand for service members meant that many of the regulations were loosened or ignored to allow gays and lesbians to enlist and serve. After the war was over, however, Congress enacted the Uniform Code of Military Justice, which standardized the military's restrictive approach to homosexuality across all branches of the armed services.

As the lesbian and gay rights movement emerged in the United States in the 1970s, military policy on homosexuality became the subject of both protest and legal challenge. Although this movement was unsuccessful in overturning the ban against gays and lesbians serving in the military, it did uncover enough inconsistencies in enforcement to prompt the military to review and revise its regulations in the early 1980s. The new policy sought to establish more uniform procedures for discharging lesbian and gay service members and to identify the extenuating circumstances under which those who had engaged in homosexual conduct might be retained. But the basic approach to lesbians and gays in the military remained—the first sentence of Department of Defense Directive 1332.14 reads: "Homosexuality is incompatible with military service."

"DON'T ASK, DON'T TELL"

The development and enactment of "Don't Ask, Don't Tell" in the early 1990s remains one of the most significant—and most contested—revisions of military policy on homosexuality. In 1993, shortly after taking office, President Bill

WHAT IS "DON'T ASK, DON'T TELL"?

"Don't Ask, Don't Tell" refers to the current policy on lesbians and gays serving in the U.S. armed forces. According to this policy, the military is prohibited from asking recruits or current service members questions about their sexual orientation; and lesbians, gays, and bisexuals currently serving in the military are prohibited from revealing their sexual orientation or engaging in homosexual conduct. This policy was the product of a compromise reached between President Clinton, the Pentagon, and Congressional leaders, and was enacted in 1994.

Clinton announced that he planned to fulfill his campaign promise by lifting the ban on lesbians and gays in the military. He gave Secretary of Defense Les Aspin six months to draft a new policy, one that would end discrimination based on sexual orientation in the U.S. military. While waiting for this policy, President Clinton ordered the Department of Defense to stop asking military recruits about their sexual orientation, and asked that those who were being discharged under the current policy be placed on stand-by.

Clinton's proposals were strongly opposed by the Joint Chiefs of Staff, high-ranking Pentagon officials, Senate Armed Services Committee (SASC) chair Sam Nunn (D-GA), and many conservative members of Congress. While Secretary of Defense Aspin commissioned studies on the current policy, both the SASC and the House Armed Services Committee held numerous hearings on the topic, during which Pentagon officials, military commanders, service members, and various experts testified on the potential impact of allowing lesbians and gays to serve openly in the U.S. military. The majority of the testimony offered was in opposition to lifting the ban (Herek 1996).

The final outcome of this controversy was "Don't Ask, Don't Tell, Don't Pursue, Don't Harass," a title that reflects the compromise reached in the new policy. Before "Don't Ask, Don't Tell," military officials were permitted to ask potential recruits or current service members about their sexual orientation to prevent the enlistment or initiate the removal of lesbians and gays from the military. "Don't Ask, Don't Tell" prohibits military officials from asking direct questions about sexual orientation, but it also prevents lesbians and gays wishing to enlist and serve from saying or doing anything that would reveal their sexual orientation to others. They are also prohibited from engaging in any type of homosexual conduct, whether on duty or off duty. Also, if a commander believes that a service member has demonstrated a "propensity" for homosexual conduct, discharge proceedings can be initiated (Halley 1999). That lesbians and gays are now allowed to serve as long as they don't serve openly has done little to dampen the debate over gays and lesbians in the armed forces.

ARGUMENTS FOR UPHOLDING THE BAN

Individuals and organizations opposed to lesbians and gays serving openly in the U.S. military offer various arguments in support of their position. Moral values certainly play a role in this debate, but the most common arguments involve issues of military necessity and key distinctions between military and civilian law. During the Congressional hearings held in 1993, for instance, Pentagon officials testified that lesbians and gays must be banned from military service to maintain necessary levels of troop morale, unit cohesion, and discipline.

These arguments have less to do with the actual performance in the military, and more to do with the responses of heterosexual service members to lesbians and gays in their own units (Halley 1999). During basic training and deployment, military personnel live in close proximity to one another. Service members also have little to no privacy when they dress or shower. Proponents of banning lesbians and gays from military service argue that allowing homosexuals to train and reside with heterosexuals would be like giving male service members the opportunity to observe female service members in various states of undress. Service members would feel awkward or uncomfortable and troop morale would decrease significantly.

Openly lesbian or gay service members are also viewed as a threat to unit cohesion. Unit cohesion is generally defined as the fostering of mutual trust and commitment to one's fellow soldiers, and is necessary for both overcoming hardship and achieving military objectives. Proponents of the ban contend that even if military officers are instructed to exhibit tolerance, the homophobic culture of the military will lead to tension and additional violence between gay and straight service members (Herek 1996). They also argue that the inclusion of lesbians and gays in sex-segregated units will increase the possibility of sexual harassment and precipitate breakdowns in the chain of command.

Finally, those who support the military's right to exclude or discharge service members based on sexual orientation point out that the military acts under its own laws, rules, and regulations; that service members are faced with a number of restrictions on their personal behavior that would not be acceptable for civilians; and that the U.S. military is immune to both federal and state laws prohibiting discrimination (Ray 1993). Important distinctions between civilian and military law help to account for the failure of numerous legal challenges to "Don't Ask, Don't Tell."

ARGUMENTS FOR ALLOWING LESBIANS AND GAYS TO SERVE OPENLY

Because they are arguing against the status quo, gay-rights advocates and others who favor overturning the current ban have to both refute the arguments of their opponents and offer their own arguments for allowing lesbians and gays to serve openly in the military. They have uncovered studies commissioned by the Department of Defense and conducted independent research to dispute the claim that lesbian and gay service members are bad for troop morale or disruptive to unit cohesion. According to these advocates, recent surveys of enlisted military personnel show a marked increase in the number of service members who say they would be comfortable serving alongside lesbian and gay service members (Kuhr 2007).

WHY CAN'T LESBIANS AND GAYS SERVE OPENLY IN THE U.S. MILITARY?

Department of Defense Directive 1332.14, formalized in 1982, contains many of the military's main arguments against lesbians and gays serving in the armed forces: "Homosexuality is incompatible with military service. The presence in the military environment of persons who engage in homosexual conduct or who, by their statements, demonstrate a propensity to engage in homosexual conduct, seriously impairs the accomplishment of the military mission. The presence of such members adversely affects the ability of the Military Services to maintain discipline, good order, and morale; to foster mutual trust and confidence among service members; to ensure the integrity of the system of rank and command; to facilitate assignment and worldwide deployment of service members who frequently must live and work under close conditions affording minimal privacy; to recruit and retain members of the Military Services; to maintain public acceptability of military service; and to prevent breaches of security."

From the perspective of advocates on this side of the debate, the military ban is symbolic of a more general refusal to grant full citizenship rights to lesbian, gay, and bisexual individuals. Like the right to vote or the right to enter into legal contracts, military service is a key "marker" of citizenship in the United States (Belkin and Bateman 2003). The controversy that surrounded the integration of African Americans into the U.S. armed forces in 1948 contained the same tension between military inclusion and social progress. Opponents of the current ban point out that the military advanced similar arguments in this debate, stating that the integration of racial minorities would jeopardize military performance by dampening morale and damaging unit cohesion. Pursuing this analogy, they contend that the general success of racial integration in the U.S. military—and the number of foreign militaries who now allow lesbians and gay men to serve openly—suggests that overturning the ban would not adversely affect military performance.

Moving from principles to procedural issues, opponents of "Don't Ask, Don't Tell" argue that the policy costs too much, and that the money and time it takes to investigate and discharge could be better spent elsewhere. According to a California blue ribbon commission report released in 2006, the policy cost American taxpayers $364 million and resulted in the loss of almost 10,000 service members in its first decade (White 2006).

CONCLUSION

More than 25 years after the U.S. military said that "homosexuality is incompatible with military service," the country finds itself facing a combination of historical and cultural factors that are likely to have a significant impact on the debate over lesbians and gays in the military. In the face of an extended war in Iraq, the military has been forced to step up recruiting efforts and prolong tours of duty, but a troop shortage remains. It is clear that the discharge or exclusion of particular service members has come into conflict with military necessity.

At the same time, "Don't Ask, Don't Tell" has been denounced by dozens of former senior military officers and service members. John Shalikashvili, an army general who was head of the Joint Chiefs of Staff when the Pentagon adopted the policy, changed his mind and came out against it in early 2007. In 2005, Representative Martin Meehan (D-MA) introduced the Military Readiness Enhancement Act, which would allow lesbians and gays to serve openly in the military. The bill had 122 co-sponsors, but failed to pass the Republican-controlled House. Meehan, a senior member of the House Armed Services Committee, reintroduced the measure in February 2007, reinvigorating the debate over gays and lesbians in the U.S. military.

See also Lesbian, Gay, Bisexual, Transgender, and Queer Movements; Military History; Sexual Identity and Orientation; Sexual Orientation and the Law.

Further Reading: Belkin, Aaron, and Geoffrey Bateman, eds., *Don't Ask, Don't Tell: Debating the Gay Ban in the Military* (Boulder, CO: Lynne Rienner Publishers, 2003); Berube, Allan, *Coming Out Under Fire: The History of Gay Men and Women in World War Two* (New York: Free Press, 1990); Brenkert, Benjamin, "The Newport Sex Scandal, 1919–1921," *Gay and Lesbian Review Worldwide* 10, no. 2 (2003): 13–15; Burrelli, David F., "An Overview of the Debate on Homosexuals in the U.S. Military," in *Gays and Lesbians in the Military: Issues, Concerns, and Contrasts,* ed. Wilbur J. Scott and Sandra Carson Stanley, 17–32 (New York: Walter de Gruyter, 1994); Halley, Janet E., *Don't: A Reader's Guide to the Military's Anti-Gay Policy* (Durham, NC: Duke University Press, 1999); Herbert, Melissa S., "Guarding the Nation, Guarding Ourselves: The Management of Hetero/Homo/Sexuality among Women in the Military," *Minerva: Quarterly Report on Women and the Military* 15, no. 2 (1997): 60–76; Herek, Gregory M., "Social Science, Sexual Orientation, and Military Personnel Policy," in *Out in Force: Sexual Orientation and the Military,* ed. Gregory M. Herek, Jared B. Jobe, and Ralph M. Carney, 3–14 (Chicago: University of Chicago Press, 1996); Kuhr, Fred, "Gays in the Ranks: Who Cares?" *The Advocate,* February 31–33, 2007; Ray, Ronald D., *Gays: In or Out? The U.S. Military and Homosexuals: A Sourcebook* (Washington, DC: Brassey's, 1993); Rimmerman, Craig A., ed., *Gay Rights, Military Wrongs: Political Perspectives on Lesbians and Gays in the Military* (New York: Garland Publishing, 1996); Shilts, Randy, *Conduct Unbecoming: Lesbians and Gays in the U.S. Military, Vietnam to the Persian Gulf* (New York: St. Martin's Press, 1993); White, Josh, "Don't Ask Costs More Than Expected: Military's Gay Ban Seen in Budget Terms," *Washington Post,* February 14, 2006, sec. A.

Carrie Anne Platt